NEIGHBOR

A Christian Introduction
to World Religions

ING FAITHS

Winfried Corduan

InterVarsity Press
Downers Grove Illinois

InterVarsity Press
P.O. Box 1400, Downers Grove, IL 60515
World Wide Web: www.ivpress.com
E-mail: mail@ivpress.com

InterVarsity Press® is the book-publishing division of InterVarsity Christian Fellowship/USA®, a student movement active on campus at hundreds of universities, colleges and schools of nursing in the United States of America, and a member movement of the International Fellowship of Evangelical Students. For information about local and regional activities, write Public Relations Dept., InterVarsity Christian Fellowship/USA, 6400 Schroeder Rd., P.O. Box 7895, Madison, WI 53707-7895.

Cover photographs: Tony Stone Images

ISBN 0-8308-1524-4

Printed in the United States of America ♾

Library of Congress Cataloging-in-Publication Data

Corduan, Winfried.
    Neighboring faiths: a Christian introduction to world religions/
Winfried Corduan.
        p.   cm.
    Includes bibliographical references.
    ISBN 0-8308-1524-4 (alk. paper)
    1. Religions.   2. Christianity and other religions.   I. Title.
BL85.C74   1998   97-36552
261.2—dc21   CIP

26	25	24	23	22	21	20	19	18	17	16	15	14	13	12	11	10	9	8	7	6	5	4	3	2	1
20	19	18	17	16	15	14	13	12	11	10	09	08	07	06	05	04	03	02	01	00	99	98			

To the Lighthouse to Singapore
teams of 1992, 1994 and 1997

Figures

Maps

Tables

Acknowledgments

It would be impossible for me to thank everyone who had some part in this book. Many people, perhaps a priest who explained a particular ritual to me or a layperson who shared some of her most cherished possessions with me—her religious beliefs—never even told me their names. A list of all the people who have been my hosts and my teachers, both formally and informally, at home and abroad, would run into the thousands.

Yet I must name specifically all my friends at Singapore Youth for Christ (Albert Lee, Christopher Tan, Loh Tze Khoong, Michael and Soo Li Yong, Albert Ang and many others) for their self-giving friendship. I need to thank Wandering Wheels and my old friends and new acquaintances at Rift Valley Academy in Kijabe, Kenya, for making the adventures of a lifetime possible. Taylor University has enabled me to travel and pursue learning experiences over the years. Mere words can never express my thanks to June, Nick and Seth for letting me go off for weeks at a time, year after year, to live in the world of Karl May.

I need to thank Jim Hoover of InterVarsity Press for being so receptive to this project. Professors David Clark, Irving Hexham and Terry Muck provided invaluable criticism and encouragement. Dean Dwight Jessup made a sabbatical available in which to write most of this text. My departmental secretaries, Mrs. Joanne Giger and Mrs. Kari Manganello, participated cheerfully in the final preparation of the manuscript. My wife, June, this time together with sons Nick and Seth, did her usual thorough job of proofreading the manuscript as well as encouraging me to write it.

Introduction

The world has not really shrunk—it just feels like it. International travel is more accessible to more people than ever before. Increasingly, people of different backgrounds and different cultures live side by side, sometimes adapting their ways to each other, many times trying to maintain their ancient heritages despite strong pressure to give them up. Over the last few decades the United States and Western Europe have experienced an unprecedented influx of people from remote reaches of the globe. In contrast to earlier immigrants, these people are not ready to jettison their own cultures and jump into a melting pot. They want to eat their customary foods, wear their customary clothes and observe their own traditions and festivals. At the same time, Americans and Europeans are obliged more than ever to do business in parts of the world that are geographically and culturally remote from their homelands. Being successful depends on being able to make their way through cultures with different expectations.

Crosscultural Religious Encounters

The crosscultural encounters occurring at the turn of this millennium inevitably include religion. Of course, different religions have always met, competed with and shaped each other to some extent. Different religions have even made themselves at home in the daily lives of individuals in various times and places. Almost everyone living on this planet today must cope with the presence of differing beliefs and forms of worship right in their own backyards. Some of these encounters are adversarial, some even violent.

As Terry Muck has observed, there are new and different religions right in our neighborhoods.[1] Christians must learn to live in a world of religious plurality. Christians desiring contact with neighbors who belong to a different religion need information regarding their food preferences, holidays, religious customs and symbols, and—above all—beliefs about the central reason for human existence.

Many of these non-Christian folk appear to be happy with their religions and are not searching for a better way. They hold on to their beliefs and seem to find as much satisfaction in them as Christians do in theirs. Thus, for Christians, the encounter with non-Christian believers more than ever appears to be a meeting between "neighboring faiths."

Far from being the private religion of desert nomads, Islam is a strong political force in the world today. Many contemporary global conflicts wear religious labels. Businesspersons need to be conscious of their clients' religious boundaries. Schools in most metropolitan areas must figure out how to accommodate the religious needs of all pupils, including immigrants and long-time residents. Religion is at the heart of many people's lives, and getting to know them means getting to know their religion.

The Christian and the Study of World Religions

Consequently, Christians who seek to be relevant to the world in which they live must understand the beliefs of the people with whom they share the globe. My own introduction to world religions came relatively late in my academic preparation. I had already begun graduate study at Rice University when my department chair, Niels C. Nielsen, thrust a copy of John B. Noss's *Man's Religions* into my hand and said, "Corduan, get educated!" I must have said something embarrassingly ignorant about an Asian religion, although I do not remember what it was. I remain grateful to Professor Nielsen for this forthright exhortation.

As I prepared myself for a career in Christian philosophical theology, I continued my study of world religions. At Rice I took several seminars in the subject and taught some courses that included various non-Christian religious components. When I came to Taylor University, my job description included teaching a course in world religions as well as courses in philosophy and theology.

There is an old dictum that no one ever learns a subject as well as someone who is forced to teach it. While not neglecting my calling in the areas of philosophy and theology, I have availed myself of numerous opportunities to build competence in world religions. Reading books was an important aspect of my study, but I also found occasion to learn a little Sanskrit and a little Arabic to make my credentials more credible. Most important, Taylor University has encouraged its faculty to pursue international travel, and I have been a beneficiary of this policy. I have been allowed to participate regularly in study/teaching trips with groups of students, and I have received grants to go to Asia and Africa simply to study. As I encountered people's religious worlds in their home environments, I honed the theoretical and historical descriptions of those religions that I had learned previously.

The idea for this book occurred to me in January 1992, while I was riding on the upper level of a bus making its way through the streets of Singapore. I was there with a group of students for a month-long study of world religions. We also assisted Singapore Youth for Christ. At that time my students encouraged me to write down what I knew, and I began to think seriously about writing this book. It is only fitting that this book be dedicated to my three (so far) Lighthouse to Singapore groups for all the encouragement they have given me.

Interreligious Encounters as Opportunities for Evangelism

The discussion in this book proceeds from an evangelical Christian perspective,[2] which sees interreligious encounters as opportunities for sharing the gospel of redemption. Consequently, this book goes beyond descriptions and summaries and identifies points of contact and cultural opportunities for gaining a hearing for the Christian gospel. Such an evangelical purpose requires an understanding of how a religion is lived out in real life, not just the "official" version of the religion as presented in authorized books. History, scriptures and theology are all indispensable for gaining an understanding of a religion, but the actual practice of a religion may differ from what has been written about it. I once heard a long-time missionary to Islamic countries bemoan the fact that many missionaries arrived in the country well schooled in the Five Pillars of Islam but woefully unaware of how Islam works in the everyday lives of its adherents. In this book I try to do justice not only to the theoretical-historical side of the religion but also to practical issues such as worship practices, festivals and home rituals.

Each chapter concludes with a section that begins "So You Meet a . . ." In it I discuss what to expect from encounters with adherents of the religion and how to proceed with attempts at evangelism. I make no claims for comprehensiveness. My remarks should not be seen as recipes or simple methods for winning souls. They do explain how to avoid making blunders, some of them based on my own mistakes.

I have chosen not to include a chapter on Christianity. I do not wish to imply that Christianity is not a religion or that it does not function as such. Of course, it is and it does. But this survey assumes a Christian starting point and a basically Christian audience. A chapter on Christianity would inevitably be patronizing—excessive for those who know it, insufficient for those who do not. So it seemed best to me to forgo the undertaking. Nevertheless, a few words need to be said about Christianity in order to clarify allusions that occur repeatedly in this book.

As I have already indicated, my own theological orientation is unabashedly evangelical. This orientation carries some important implications. First, Christianity is based on a revelation from God—the Bible—which consequently must be treated as truthful and authoritative. Rightly understood, the Bible declares the will of God on matters of religion (as well as on any other matters concerning which it may make affirmations). Christian theology is an accurate representation of God's will exactly insofar as it conforms to the biblical revelation.

Second, Jesus Christ is the Son of God. God entered history personally in Christ, who combines in himself a fully divine nature as well as a genuinely human nature. His life began with his birth to a virgin in Bethlehem, ended temporarily with his crucifixion and culminated with his bodily resurrection and ascension to heaven.

Third, human beings in their present nature are alienated from God and need redemption. God made provision for this need in the atoning death of Christ. A human person needs to trust in Christ by personal faith in order to experience salvation. This faith is the only means of salvation that God has disclosed.

Fourth, Christians should relate to other religions on the basis of sacrificial love. Evangelical Christianity does not recognize any other world religion as a valid way to God. Presenting the gospel to the world is a part of Christians' total calling to lead overtly redeemed lives. Divine revelation forbids the use of political or physical coercion in promoting Christianity, but it demands that Christians love the world selflessly and sacrificially. This love expresses itself in an empathic understanding of other people, humanitarian projects and a consistent witness to God's redemptive plan. All references to Christianity assume this viewpoint.

Original Monotheism
The discussion in this book is oriented toward original monotheism, the idea that all religion began with God—the Creator and the Revealer. I describe this theory further in chapter one. This orientation may seem natural for an evangelical Christian, but I believe that it is also a premise founded on solid evidence. It is worth noting that many books dismiss the best-known scholarly proponent of this theory, Wilhelm Schmidt, in an offhand manner for his religious convictions while dogmatically propagating developmental assumptions that have long been disproven.[3]

This theoretical starting point has also influenced how the religions treated in this book have been selected and arranged. The clearly monotheistic traditions, Judaism and Islam, lead the way. Baha'i, appearing later in the book for reasons of space, is monotheistic as well. Zoroastrianism represents an attempt to recapture the monotheistic maxim, which took hold only after several false starts. I discuss two broad, traditional religions, the African and the Native American. Of the two, the African religion has retained a more overt reference to God. Both religions are immersed in a world of spirits and rituals. Focusing on the religions of Asia, we see that the precursor of Hinduism, the religion of the prehistoric Aryans, may have had some monotheistic roots. Hinduism provides an ongoing demonstration of how much variety a religion can accommodate. Even belief systems that are now considered religions in their own right, Buddhism, Sikhism and Jainism, are direct outgrowths of the Hindu heritage. Finally, we look at the two major Asian syntheses, Chinese popular religion and Japanese religious culture, which combine elements of the Indic tradition (particularly schools of Buddhism) with local concerns. What we know of the Chinese heritage begins with the worship of a single god in the sky. There is virtually no memory of a monotheistic legacy in the Japanese synthesis, with which we conclude.

Some features in this book come from my many years of teaching a course on world religions (which has now become a two-course sequence). Each chapter concludes with study questions that students can use to test their understanding of the discussion. Years of suggesting term-paper topics have led me to add a list of such ideas to each chapter. Finally, I have provided a small "core bibliography" for each religion. This listing is obviously not intended to be comprehensive (how could it be?) or necessarily up to date (but then, few libraries are); instead, these are some of the more useful sources a student might find in his or her library that provide an entryway into further study of the subject.

Chapter 1

Religion
Study & Practice

World Population: 5,716,525,000[1]	
Professing Christians: 1,927,953,000	
Non-Christians: 3,788,472,000	
Religious Non-Christians: 2,727,089,000[2]	

What comes to mind when you think of the word *religion?* Many people would probably respond that religion is about the worship of a god or gods, and rightly so, since the worship of deities is at the heart of most religions.

We can picture a Friday prayer service in a mosque—the house of worship of Islam. The men of the community have assembled and are sitting in loose rows on the rug-covered floor in front of a pulpit from which an imam preaches instructions on how to live a life that is pleasing to God. At the end of the sermon the believers stand up, forming exact rows that face the niche at the front of the hall that points in the direction of Mecca. In unison they go through the prescribed postures of standing, bowing and prostrating themselves as they recite their prayer of devotion. This picture confirms the common notion that religion focuses on the worship of a god.

Now let us picture a Japanese Zen master addressing a group of American college students. "Look beyond words and ideas," he tells them. "Lay aside what you think you know about God; it can only mislead you. Just accept life as it is. When I am hungry, I eat." Is this religion?

Mary, an American college student, is not particularly interested in God and does not attend church services. But she is full of high ideals and has committed her life to the service of humanity. After graduation she plans to spend a few years in the Peace Corps and then reside in a poverty-stricken area of America where she can assist disadvantaged people in learning to lead a better life. In order to carry out this task to its fullest, Mary is already limiting her own personal belongings and is not planning to get married or raise a family. Is this religion?

Once as I was jogging through my neighborhood, I came upon the ultimate Elvis fan van. Elvis's picture was emblazoned on both sides. It sported ELVIS license plates and several Elvis bumper stickers. The seat covers featured life-sized pictures of Elvis, so that the van's passengers would essentially be riding down the road seated in Elvis's lap. I speculated about the van's owner. Was her house decorated in basic Elvis also? Was her entire life oriented around Elvis? Did she believe Elvis Presley to be alive? Can such devotion to an entertainer who died years ago be considered religion?

An Imperfect Definition

There are many commonly used words in the English language that elude a single definition. Take the word *ball*. You can have one and play soccer with it; you can go to one to see Cinderella dance; you can also have one in a more figurative sense exchanging funny stories with a friend. You may say that in basketball the center of attention is a ball because it is round and you can play with it. You may hear people refer to the sun in the sky as a great big ball, meaning that it is round, but you cannot play with it. Conversely, the object used in American football can be played with, but it is not round; nevertheless, we refer to it as a ball. In short, the word does not have one single definition that covers all aspects of its use. However, we rarely have trouble identifying what someone means when he or she uses the word *ball*.

The word *religion* functions in the same way. It conjures up definite images when someone utters it. We may think about Buddhism, Christianity or Islam; images of worship, gods, rituals or ethics. It is extremely unlikely that anyone would associate religion with baseball, roast beef or the classification of insects. However, it is quite difficult to come up with a definition of religion that includes everything we normally associate with religion and excludes everything we do not consider religion.

For example, a definition focusing on gods, spirits and the supernatural may be too narrow. There are forms of Buddhism (for example, Zen) that consider any such beliefs to be a hindrance to enlightenment at best. Yet are we prepared to deny that Buddhism is a religion? I think not.

This difficulty may lead us to define religion more broadly as the center of life that gives life meaning. This definition captures an important aspect of religion—the undergirding of values for life. Thus Mary, the woman who is devoting her life to the service of others, may be considered an example of a humanistic religion. Her entire life is structured around this commitment. What about the Elvis enthusiast? Do we want to include the Super Bowl, the alcoholic's struggle against addiction or the materialist's pursuit of wealth? There is no clear-cut criterion here; our answers may vary. The point, however, is our intuitive realization that there should be some meaningful distinction between what we call "religion" and other endeavors, no matter how absorbing. There is something wrong with asserting that Pablo is very religious because he works hard at playing the cello.

Religion (1) unifies our existence by providing the core values from which we derive meaning and goals and (2) directs us beyond the mundane routine of everyday existence. Many religions invoke gods, spirits or an afterlife to accomplish this. Other traditions take a more subtle approach. Zen Buddhism, as already noted, recognizes no positive role for supernatural entities. Its goal is the acceptance of life, and the road to such acceptance leads through an intuitive flash of awareness that is not a part of everyday life.

The feature of religion that directs us beyond the mundane is called "transcendence." Transcendence can come to us in many different ways, through supernatural agencies or through metaphysical principles (for example, the greatest good or the first cause), an ideal, a place or an awareness, to mention just some of the possibilities. Thus devotion to Elvis Presley—even the resurrected Elvis of the supermarket tabloids—lacks transcendence, and so it is probably not a genuine religion.

The following basic definition of religion can get us started:

A religion is a system of beliefs and practices that provides values to give life meaning and coherence by directing a person toward transcendence.

This definition surmounts the difficulties pointed out above, but it is extremely vague. Words such as *transcendence, values* and *meaning* would have to be defined to include an absolute listing of what is or is not a religion. But that is not the intent of this discussion. It is to establish a general perimeter that will allow us to identify the subject matter sufficiently for further treatment. It has already been noted that religion has to do with transcendence; it encompasses all of a person's life. How it does this varies from religion to religion. A survey of the various religions is needed to assess this function in detail, and that is precisely what this book sets out to do.

The Origin of Religion

How did religion originate? Half a century ago this question was in vogue. Today it is less fashionable. Scholars now prefer a subjective or psychological approach that is based on an analysis of symbolism. We will briefly describe this approach, and then we will look at two theories of historical origin: an evolutionary view and a theory of original monotheism.

The subjective approach views religion as the outcome of addressing human psychological needs and overlooks altogether the matter of historical origins. The evolutionary approach claims that religion is part of the overall development of human culture. Finally, original monotheism recognizes that religion began with a God who revealed himself at the very beginning of human history.

The Subjective Approach

Most contemporary scholars of religion do not occupy themselves with the question of the historical origin of religion (in contrast to scholars of the first part of the twentieth century). They simply accept the existence of religion as a given part of our humanity. Thus the origin of religion lies within us; the attempt to specify a possible time in nebulous prehistory when it all started is irrelevant. What matters is that we find religion wherever we find humanity. Humankind's instinctive interest in religion seems to be just as much a part of human disposition as its many other traits.

The subjective approach reasons that the seat of this religious disposition must lie below conscious beliefs. Our conscious belief systems, which deal with the content of our actual experience, are subject to change from moment to moment, but the religious impulse seems to be a constant of human experience. Therefore, it must be situated in our subconscious, nonrational faculties. It emerges in symbols and attitudes, not necessarily in well-formed beliefs. These factors are eventually expressed in the more concrete terms of the various religions with their specific beliefs and practices. Thus specific beliefs and practices are the outward expression of subconscious symbols and attitudes.

This approach understands religion as an intrinsically human phenomenon rather than the product of an encounter with an external reality. The gods live in our psyches, not on Mount Olympus or in their heavenly courts. What is considered divine revelation only discloses the terms in which we express the symbols that are inherent in our psyches, not the will of any divine being(s). Religious practices function to appease the unrelenting drives of our subconscious, not the demands of the supernatural. In short, all talk about God is really talk about what lies within us as human beings.

Certain individuals were instrumental in formulating this human-centered theory of religion. The nineteenth-century theologian Friedrich Schleiermacher contended that religion begins with a feeling, specifically the feeling of absolute dependence, not a set of beliefs. All human beings have this feeling, and since a feeling of dependence demands that there is something to depend on, the feeling is expressed in terms of depending on an Absolute, which is God. Note that this sequence proceeds from the feeling of dependence to the idea that there must be an object of dependence, not from the idea that there is a God to the idea that we depend on God.[3]

Somewhat later, philosopher Ludwig Feuerbach promoted the theory that the concept of God is actually a combination of idealized human traits. Human beings have the characteristics of love, power and knowledge (among others). An idealized picture of the human species would turn these traits into unlimited characteristics, producing a being with unconditional love, unrestricted power and all-exhaustive knowledge. This contrivance of the idealized human being is then called "God." Thus, in the final analysis, a person who worships God is really worshiping an ideal self-image.[4]

The psychological dimension of the human-centered approach to religion was broached by Sigmund Freud. In his explorations of the human subconscious, he believed that he discovered the basic human need for a father image. Since human fathers are imperfect, even at their best, people substitute an idealized father image that they refer to as "God." This notion is enhanced by the presence of an "oceanic feeling." Just as we may be awestruck by the size, depth and impenetrability of the sea as we view it from the shore, so our contemplations of the ideal father image leave us with a feeling of impenetrable vastness. At root, the religious vision is a symptom of psychological immaturity.[5]

In 1917 the religion scholar Rudolf Otto published an important study entitled *The Idea of the Holy*. In this work Otto traced the basic religious impulse back to an encounter with the consciousness of holiness, which is deeper than consciously held religious beliefs. Picture yourself thinking about God as you are kneeling in a majestic cathedral or gazing at an imposing mountain vista. Suddenly you are overwhelmed by a feeling of God's greatness and majesty; for a moment you have encountered holy reality. You sense that you have touched the untouchable. This feeling, according to Otto, has two components. A consciousness of fear and awe leads you to an awareness of your own microscopic significance in light of God's greatness, and you shrink away. But simultaneously you experience a feeling of attraction; you are mesmerized by and attracted to the holy reality. Otto referred to these two components as *mysterium tremens* and *mysterium fascinosum* respectively. For our purposes, the crucial point is that Otto places this psychological experience of the holy at the heart of religion. He, as well as Freud, understands the core of religion as residing in our subconscious, nonrational faculties.[6]

Other scholars have expanded on Otto's insights. Most prominent among them is the Romanian scholar Mircea Eliade. In numerous works Eliade has explored subconscious symbolism as it cuts across many different religious traditions. Wherever such a symbol appears, Eliade calls it a hierophany—a manifestation of the holy. Such hierophanies include water (as symbolizing spiritual purification), sacred buildings (as providing links to a spiritual dimension), and festivals (as representing reenactments of divine history).[7]

Such a symbolic approach to religion was also advanced by the analytical psychologist C. G. Jung. He correlated images that recur in human dreams with images expressed in religion and came to believe that the same manifestations of the human subconscious are present in both. His "symbolic archetypes" are pictures that seem to occur throughout human history and culture. Among the many archetypes, Jung included images such as the dragon (powerful forces of nature that sometimes must be slain) and the white-haired old man (the source of wisdom, sometimes representing God). According to Jung, these images have a life of their own, but they take on additional life in the context of a particular religion.[8] Jung's approach has been expanded and popularized by Joseph Campbell.[9]

In summary, these scholars' contributions differ in their specifics, but they all identify certain basic religious elements that constitute an important aspect of what it means to be human, such as feelings, thoughts or symbols. These elements reside primarily below the level of conscious awareness. When they are brought to consciousness, they are expressed in terms of religious beliefs.

These scholars and their followers have used this conclusion to advocate subjectivity as an exhaustive explanation for all religion. They claim that since these elements exist and since religion can be explained on the basis of their existing, we have all that we need to understand religion. Thus they conclude that religion is rooted in subjectivity.

But even if these elements did exist and even if they could be used to explain the nature of religion, it would not logically follow that this pattern is the true and complete explanation of all of religion. I may carry in my subconscious mind an abstract representation of God, but I cannot on that basis conclude that there is no independently existing, objective being that is God. God may have created me with that idea so that I can relate to God. Having a natural feeling of absolute dependence does not justify my inferring that religion is nothing but a feeling; there may very well be an independently existing God who has instilled that feeling in me.

Thus we see that the subjective approach to religion has only limited value. It can help us understand human nature and the human side of religion, but it does not help explain the origin of religion. First, it brackets the question of the historical origin of religion. Second, it does not help identify a psychological origin of religion, since everything that it points to as cause (for example, feelings, subconscious symbols) may in fact be the effect of religious reality (for example, a god or an actual experience).

It is good to study the symbolism of religion and the psychological side of the human religious experience as we seek an understanding of religion and religious people. It can also help us understand ourselves, regardless of where we may be on the spectrum of religious commitment.

Nevertheless, we are more than ever confronted with the question, Did religion begin with humans or with God? Thus we will proceed to look at two further approaches to the origin of religion, one that seeks to place religion in the context of human cultural evolution and one that places the origin with God, who created us and revealed himself to us.

The Evolutionary Approach

Many scholarly investigators of religion over the last two hundred years have promoted an evolutionary approach to the origins of religion. Even though few today still defend this approach, many scholars assume it. Many writers still assume that religion has an essentially human origin. The majority of books still present a picture of human beings coming to an increasing awareness of religious truths. Thus implicitly, if not explicitly, a loosely evolutionary approach still reigns. This approach rests on two assumptions.

The first assumption is a general commitment to an evolutionary view of life and culture. It must be remembered that Charles Darwin did not invent the idea of evolution—far from it! By the time Darwin published his conclusions, many scientists were already committed to the notion of an evolutionary development of life; they just did not know how it was supposed to have happened. Darwin's contribution was to devise a scientific model of what many people had expected to be true all along. From the late 1700s on—corresponding to the rise of romanticism—the notion that the present state of the world is the result of an evolutionary process proceeding from more primitive forms to more complex ones was accepted in many European intellectual circles. Not only physical nature but also society, knowledge and the human person were seen as part of a grand scheme of development that had attained a high level in the present and was undoubtedly destined to culminate in even greater heights.

Not surprisingly, this scheme understood religion as another ever evolving facet of human culture. Just as scholars arranged other aspects of human culture along an evolutionary line, even so they searched for a pattern of religious evolution. The point is that the evolutionary approach to religion, just like the evolutionary approach to biology, began with a philosophical commitment to the idea, which was then filled out with observations, not the other way around.

The second assumption has to do with anthropological method. The rising scholarly discipline of cultural anthropology served to provide the content for the expected evolutionary pattern. Western European scholars encountered numerous cultures that they considered "primitive." The evolutionary interpretation led them to believe that these "lower" forms of culture were indicative of humanity in its earlier evolutionary stages. Consequently, the developmental state of religion in these cultures was supposed to be representative of the religion of humanity in its infancy. All that was left to be determined was which culture represented the earliest form of religion. Thus the anthropological method set the agenda for research into the origin of religion.

Given these presuppositions, the following sequence of stages emerged in the writings of the religious evolutionists.[10] Although few scholars today would explicitly defend such a schematic picture of the evolution of religion, the evolutionary model is simply assumed to a large extent, and it certainly animates popularized presentations on the origin of religion.

Keep in mind that the forms of religion that these stages represent indisputably exist in various cultures around the world and have existed throughout history. The evolutionary approach sequences these stages according to a developmental pattern. Even if the evolutionary approach turns out to be unacceptable, however, the types of religion that these stages describe do exist. Figure 1.1 outlines the stages.

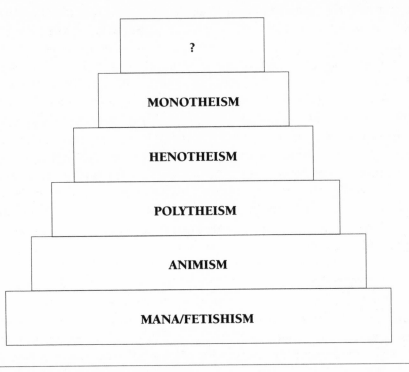

Figure 1.1. Stages in the evolutionary theory of religion

General awareness: mana and magic. What is the most "primitive" form of religion? Presumably a religion that is characterized by very little complexity and that reduces all spiritual reality to some fairly simple ideas. According to an evolutionary understanding, the first stage of religion begins with a basic feeling—a general awareness of a spiritual force in the world. This force is not personal and does not reveal itself. It pervades reality in the way that physical forces pervade the world. However, the distribution of the force may be uneven. Some people or natural phenomena, such as rocks, trees, and animals, may contain a greater amount of it. In some objects the force may be more accessible than in others, and in some places contact with the force may backfire because it is so concentrated.

Scholars of religion call this force *mana,* the name given to it by the inhabitants of Melanesia. It was first described by anthropologists studying religion in the Melanesian islands. We now know that a similar idea is recognized by many different tribes around the world.

In cultures that recognize mana, positive contact with this force is thought to provide power to achieve success in life in areas such as health, agriculture, and so forth. Negative contact with the force can spoil life. Thus it is desirable to achieve as positive a relationship as possible with mana. A great amount of mana may be localized in a special object such as a stick, a doll or a bone. Such an object, called a *fetish,* is then preserved and venerated. (Thus this stage may also be referred to as fetishism.)

It is crucial to recognize that in the mana stage all responsibility rests with the human being, who must harness the force in order to have a successful life. Someone whose life is characterized by difficulties may have abused the force and may need to refine his or her techniques of achieving contact with mana.

We call this form of religion "magic." Some scholars, such as Sir George Frazer, considered magic the initial phase of religion.[11] Magic may be defined as *the manipulation of spiritual forces in order to bring about a desired result.*

Note the components of this definition. Magic involves some form of manipulation, namely, some action by the human being. Furthermore, magic is goal oriented. The goal may be as specific as a child's recovering from illness or as general as assurance of a prosperous existence. Correct technique is paramount. Success or failure depends on only one thing—doing it right (although that may be tremendously complicated).

Magic is also found in higher forms of religion when people try to manipulate spiritual powers for their benefit. When they envision spiritual realities as personal spirits or even gods, they try to use them for their own ends. As we shall see shortly, this desire to manipulate the divinity leads the highest religions right back to ritual.

Animism. The next step in the evolutionary development of religion visualizes spiritual forces in terms of personal spirits. This stage is sometimes called "animism" (from the Latin word *anima,* which means "soul"). Animism recognizes many forces, which are pictured as personal beings (like souls) with distinct identities and even names. There are thought to be two basic types of spirits: nature spirits and ancestor spirits.

Nature spirits tend to have human form and personality, but usually they are not directly related to the human race. They inhabit objects such as animals, plants, rocks, streams and fields. They may speak a language and may even have some social order. To destroy their abode may be to destroy them as well. In some cultures, there may also be an analogous set of household spirits that inhabit human dwellings but generally function as nature spirits.

Ancestor spirits are departed family members but not necessarily direct ancestors. A departed relative who dies childless for reasons of age or social status may be considered an ancestor. These spirits retain their identity within the family; those who had high status in a clan or tribe may retain their status. Generally they are treated with the respect appropriate to honored senior members of the social group. Most animistic cultures have an automatic mechanism by which a deceased's term as venerated ancestor expires after a customary number of generations (sometimes when no more living persons have direct memory of the departed person), and the ancestor is then considered to be permanently gone.

Nature and ancestor spirits are finite. They have some powers that people do not have, but these powers tend to stem mostly from their disembodied state. They can come and go unseen, doing good or harm while nobody notices. But they are not "superior" beings; their powers are clearly limited. For one thing, their knowledge is limited, and they insist on being informed. They detest being surprised. For example, if you intend to get married, you had better consult your ancestors because this is a matter affecting the whole family. If you intend to plow a field, you must first notify the spirits living in the field so that they will not be caught unawares. Otherwise, the spirits may get angry and harm you.

There are limits on what the various spirits can do. They have specific domains of influence (for example, a family or a forest), and their actions are analogous to human actions, without the limitations of a body. Thus a particular spirit may on the one hand be able to cause sickness or on the hand heal a specific person. Another spirit may supply or withhold rain. Yet another may live in a deer, tied entirely to the deer's life. In short, these spirits may be able to do more than people can do, but they are not omnipotent.

Many spirits are good at discerning the interconnectedness of all the forces in the world because of their refined existence, and consequently they may have a better grasp of the direction of future events. Human beings can benefit from this insight by consulting the spirits through divination (fortunetelling, soothsaying). Divination does not usually predict specific events, which, as I mentioned, can also be startling to a spirit. However, it may indicate whether conditions are favorable or unfavorable for certain events to occur. A human being making plans may consult the spirits in order to discern whether the prognosis for success is favorable or not.

Consequently, the aim of this phase of religion is to maintain proper relationships with the spirits. They want to be treated with respect and deference. Life difficulties may be the result of inattention to the spirits. An acceptable outcome in regard to any endeavor depends on achieving a state of harmony with the spirits. Such harmony depends on the enactment of whatever ritual that culture uses to placate the spirits, frequently offerings and prayers.

Because the spirits are not all-powerful, it is possible to control them. In many cultures there may be an expert (a medicine man, witch doctor, or shaman) who is adept at getting the spirits to cooperate. Thus animism makes use of magic to deal with religious powers. If the spirits do not act as people want them to, they have only themselves to blame. No harm befalls those who are punctilious in their observances toward the spirits. Conversely, people who put themselves in harmony with the spirits find all kinds of good things coming their way.

Polytheism. At some point in the history of human culture, a transition was made from venerating finite spirits to worshiping gods. The distinction is primarily a quantitative one. Whereas spirits are at best only somewhat more capable than human beings, gods are vastly superior. They have vastly more power and knowledge than any human being. Since this stage recognizes many gods, it is referred to as *poly* (many) *theism* (gods).

The transition from animism to polytheism may occur in three different ways: (1) promoting an exalted ancestor spirit to divine status, (2) promoting nature and household spirits to divine status and (3) personifying abstract principles.

As already mentioned, ancestors who had a particularly high social status may retain that status after death. For example, a departed chieftain may be venerated, not only by his family but by the whole tribe. A person who possessed superior spiritual powers in life may be venerated after death by people who want to tap into those spiritual resources. For example, Ma-zu, a Chinese fisherman's daughter, manifested great miraculous deeds of virtue when she was alive. After her death, people recognized her as a goddess in her own right, not just a spiritually endowed human being. Thus a religious culture may produce gods by exalting distinguished ancestors.

Animists see various natural phenomena as harboring spirits. Greater objects are inhabited by more powerful spirits. For example, an imposing mountain may be the home of a fearsome god, or weather may be controlled by particularly powerful deities. Since fertility is crucial to survival in agricultural cultures, a goddess of fertility is frequently held responsible for agricultural successes or failures. Similarly, the spirit inhabiting a kitchen may be so important to the life of a family that it becomes transformed into a kitchen god. Thus the personal spirits of the animistic phase grow into the personal gods of polytheism.

As societies grow more complex, people pay increasing attention to abstract principles like justice and love, which may become identified with a particular god or goddess. For example, a culture might delight in the principle of liberty to such an extent that people made a statue personifying Liberty as a goddess and then held regular celebrations honoring the goddess. In a crisis, the people of that culture might appeal to the divine personage that is represented by the statue to preserve liberty for them. Other principles could also be personified as divine beings, with or without physical representations.

The sum total of gods and goddesses within a particular religion is referred to as its "pantheon"—for example, the ancient Greek pantheon or the contemporary Hindu pantheon. Relationships within a pantheon are characterized by a degree of order, frequently described in terms of tasks and family relationships. However, it would be a mistake ever to expect a pantheon to be completely consistent. In many instances, the relationships between the various deities are pretty fluid. Several gods may have similar offices, and there may be conflicting versions of the relationships of the gods to each other. For instance, in Hinduism the family of the god Shiva may be described as consisting of Shiva's wife, Parvati, and his two sons, Skandar and Ganesha. But a closer look at the actual stories involving these gods shows that Skandar is described either as Shiva's son by another goddess or Parvati's son by another god, but never as the son of both. Considering the many different ways in which a polytheistic pantheon can arise, such confusion comes as no surprise. It is consistent with the evolutionary hypothesis (though evolution does not represent the only explanation for it).

Since gods are more powerful and more knowledgeable than spirits, human beings need to acknowledge their superiority and submit to them. These gods are not as easily manipulated as mana or nature spirits. People may petition them for their favor, but the outcome rests with the will of the gods as well as the technique of the petitioner. Thus belief in gods ideally replaces magic with "worship," which can be defined as *recognizing divine beings as superior, submitting to them and entreating their favor.*

There is, however, plenty of room for magic. Apparent acts of worship take on magical significance when the worshiper believes that following the correct worship practices releases the god's favor. Yet the gods have their own agendas, and in the end all that the people may be able to do is to submit to them.

Henotheism. In this stage people recognize many different gods but worship only one. They do not deny the existence of many gods, but they worship only one of them. Henotheistic worship may have a social basis. For instance, a particular tribe, family or profession may be specifically attached to one god, whereas a similar group may be devoted to a different god. Henotheistic worship may also have a geographical basis: one god is thought to have exclusive domain over one specific region, whereas a different one is thought to rule over another area. Finally, an individual may choose to devote himself or herself to the worship of one god exclusively.

One example of henotheism appears in the Bible in the speech of an Assyrian commander who is referred to as the Rabshakeh (Isaiah 37 KJV; "field commander" NIV). He claims that the god of the Assyrians is stronger than the gods of the other nations, and he taunts the inhabitants of Jerusalem for relying on their God. (Of course, the Bible's own viewpoint is different; the conclusion of the story leaves no doubt that the biblical view is monotheistic.)

Monotheism. The evolutionary model views monotheism as the highest step of development. People finally come to realize that there is only one God. According to the hypothesis, monotheism was first accepted by the Jews (under Moses, though some claim under Amos). Then it was taken up by other religions, such as Christianity and Islam. The core of monotheism is the notion that there is only one God, usually described as the creator of the world and as vastly superior in all respects to any creature. The God of monotheism is the author of moral directives for creation. God alone is God, and God alone is worthy of worship.

However, there is an ambiguity in the historical development of monotheism in regard to the existence of lesser spiritual beings. Asserting that there is only one being who is magnificent enough to be called "God" does not rule out the existence of other supernatural beings, such as spirits, angels or saints. The question arises as to what extent human beings in a monotheistic system can have dealings with such beings without compromising their monotheism. Historically, all monotheistic systems have included people who carry on an active relationship with such nondivine (but supernatural) beings as well as other people who severely reprimand all such practices as compromising the true worship of the true God.

Beyond gods? Does the evolution of religion culminate with monotheism? Earlier Western scholars, carrying a Christian cultural baggage, tended to think yes, but subsequently others have disagreed. They have proposed that perhaps religion needs to advance one more step—beyond the need for a god altogether. Zen Buddhism, for example, relies on personal insights that are achieved apart from any supernatural help. Or perhaps a secular humanism is the highest stage that the human spirit can attain. This is in effect the proposal of the American philosopher John Dewey, who advocated a faith that dispenses with all supernatural elements.[12] The point is that the evolutionary model recognizes no given end point. We may be suspicious of any supposed "highest level," for it may be very likely nothing more than a reflection of the scholar's personal bias or preference.

Critique of the Evolutionary Model

The biggest problem with the evolutionary model of religion is that the kind of development it describes has never been observed. Certainly there is a lot of change in the religious life of many cultures. But the change occurs everywhere on the scale and proceeds in either direction. We have no record of any culture moving from a mana-like beginning to a monotheistic culmination, incorporating all stages in proper sequence. There seems to be no true pattern of upward development in any culture. The best that can be claimed is that the evolutionary model is an ideal that religious development should follow—but never has.

German scholar R. M. Meyer advocated an evolutionary pattern of religion similar to the one presented here.[13] He illustrated the early stage of fetishism (mana) with the story of a Norwegian peasant family that preserved and venerated the reproductive organ of their deceased horse, which they believed to have been imbued with a great amount of spiritual power for fertility. This episode represents an excellent example of religion within the context of mana. However, the story ends with the pious King Olaf (who lived around A.D. 1000) coming to this house on one of his trips promoting Christianity and throwing the object to the dog. Olaf's visit shows that the episode actually took place long after the culture had supposedly passed through animism and polytheism and was about to embrace Christian monotheism. As startled as the peasant woman in the story was that anyone would treat a sacred object so blasphemously, we can be just as startled that anyone would use a drastically out of sequence episode to illustrate the beginnings of religion. Although it may be interpreted as a "regression" to an earlier, more primitive stage, such a claim is arbitrary and can produce no evidence that there ever really was any such earlier stage to begin with. Is it not peculiar that someone would use an episode clearly out of sequence as evidence for the supposed sequence? To sum up, there is no historical validation of a grand evolutionary pattern in religion.

The anthropological method is ambiguous in a couple of ways. To begin with, we can challenge the assumption that contemporary "primitive" cultures reflect ancient cultures. Cultures are composed of many components, including social arrangement, level of technology and religion. But the fact that a particular culture is technologically undeveloped does not show that its religion demonstrates an early stage on a path of evolutionary development. The argument seems circular: a traditional culture is considered reflective of early human culture because of its supposed primitiveness, but it is called "primitive" only because someone has decided that it must be reflective of early human history (the two concepts are used virtually synonymously). For instance, a culture that uses stone tools is considered more ancient than some others, but it may have regressed to that stage from a more sophisticated one. Thus to equate "primitive" cultures or religions with the "early" stages of human development may simply be to announce a methodological *assumption*. To call it an "assumption" is not to invalidate the concept; in fact, there may even be good reason to accept it. In some cases good scholarly inquiry has supported certain assumptions (as we shall see shortly). But then along comes evidence suggesting that changes in religion have actually proceeded in a direction that is opposite from what the evolutionary model expects.

Furthermore, the anthropological method does not yield results in keeping with the evolutionary pattern. The evolutionary model expects the first two stages (mana and animism) to be free of any notion of gods. In point of fact, however, this is not found. Even strongly animistic cultures usually have gods, and most cultures have a vestigial belief in one supreme Creator God. And with this observation we have come to the competing model of the origin of religion—the idea of an original monotheism.

Original Monotheism
The subjective theory of religion and the evolutionary model both locate the beginnings of religion in the human person. Original monotheism locates the beginnings of religion in God. This approach finds a home within the religious context itself. Someone who believes in the Bible or the Qur'an, for example, would hold that the reality of God preceded human awareness of God. People responded to God's self-disclosure, and religion came into existence. Any changes in religion consist of either a closer approach to or a deviation from the divine disclosure.

What did such an original monotheism look like? Genesis 4:26 refers to the origins of religion when it says, "Then men began to call upon the name of the LORD" (NASB). This verse occurs right after it is mentioned that Adam and Eve had another son, Seth, and that Seth had a son of his own, called Enosh. What can we piece together about this first form of religion? (1) There is one God who has personhood (as opposed to being an impersonal force); (2) God is referred to with masculine grammar and has masculine qualities; (3) God apparently lives in the sky (heaven); (4) God has great knowledge and power; (5) God created the world; (6) God is the author of standards of good and evil; (7) human beings are God's creatures and are expected to abide by God's standards; (8) human beings have become alienated from God by disobeying God's standards; (9) God has provided a method of overcoming the alienation. Originally this reconciliation involved sacrificing animals on an altar of uncut stone.

Is there evidence, other than religious scriptures, that religion may have originated in this way? What could even count as evidence? As Robert Brow has pointed out,[14] archeology has been of virtually no help here. The altars would have been made of uncut stones, and once an altar was no longer in use, the stones would no longer be discernible as an altar. Presumably, some charcoal would remain, but that would not necessarily indicate the stones' use in worship.

Virtually every religious culture carries a vestige of monotheism that can be identified as a variation of the nine-point description. And cultures that are very primitive in terms of overall development provide some of the strongest support for original monotheism.

It is customary in scholarly circles to credit Catholic anthropologist Wilhelm Schmidt with the theory of original monotheism.[15] Of course, Schmidt was not the first person to believe that religion originated with God. Many people held that belief long before Schmidt, just as people knew about falling objects long before Isaac Newton. Wilhelm Schmidt's contribution lies in the scholarly documentation he provided concerning an original monotheism. In twelve lengthy volumes he brought together reports from traditional religions and cultures all around the world and collected their references to original monotheism.

To summarize his thousands of pages, in almost all traditional contexts—in Africa, America, Australia, Asia or Europe—we find belief in a God located in the sky (or on a high mountain) and almost always referred to with masculine language. This God creates the world (usually directly, although in a few stories through an agent such as a son). He provides standards of behavior, which he may enforce with lightning bolts. Particularly in later cultures, he stands apart from the routine worship of gods and spirits. There is a memory of a time when this God was worshiped regularly, but something intervened. Many (but not all) cultures that refer to this interruption explain that it happened because this God did not receive the obedience due him. Depending on the specific culture, this God now receives varying amounts of recognition. In some cultures he is called on only in times of calamity; in some he is worshiped by a special group of people only; in a number of cultures he continues to be recognized. If the description of God in a particular culture appears to lack one of these typical characteristics (as certainly does happen), it probably has all of the others.

Most tellingly, Schmidt asserted that the religion of cultures that seemed to be the most ancient featured exclusive worship of God and almost no magic. Without getting involved in a circular argument, he was able to identify some of the most primitive cultures by using a method he called "historical ethnology." These groups include African and Filipino Pygmies, Australian aborigines and a few native tribes of California. Each tribe strongly believes in a Creator God and practices little or no animism or magic. Thus Schmidt concluded that there is solid evidence for an original monotheism.[16]

Was Schmidt influenced by his Christian presuppositions? Of course he was—just as any other scholar would be influenced by his or her presuppositions. Presuppositionless scholarship is impossible. Whether or not Schmidt's presuppositions caused him to distort his data is hard to ascertain. In any event, Schmidt did not fabricate the data that show universal and ancient remnants of belief in an original God.

Consequently, we can conclude that there is good anthropological reason to believe in the thesis of original monotheism. Needless to say, if religion did originate with monotheism, it moved away from it. The fact of change is a given. To repeat: all of the phases described by the evolutionary model are found in reality, and there is constant change in all directions. Under the model of original monotheism we can draw three basic inferences.

First, there is one decisive change—the move away from monotheism. This change has to be seen as a falling away, perhaps best understood as decay or corruption. The human being turns away from God to something else: other gods, spirits, nature, even himself or herself.[17] Apparently the God of the sky seemed too remote. In times of personal crisis—a sick child, crop failure, marital problems—more immediate help was needed. Invoking the aid of fetishes or spirits seemed more potent. Thus God receded behind other spiritual powers. In biblical terms, people worshiped the creation instead of the Creator.

Second, there is no clear pattern in which this departure typically takes place. Monotheism could turn into henotheism, polytheism or animism. But one thing is certain: as monotheism is left behind, ritual and magic increase. This is not to say these elements do not occur within a fairly stable monotheistic context (of course they do!). However, once people abandon faith in one almighty, all-knowing God, the role that they play in attempting to find their way in a world dominated by spiritual forces becomes far more central, leading to an increase in spiritual manipulation techniques such as magic and ritual.

Third, once monotheism is abandoned, change usually continues to occur. Again, there is no single sequence in which things rearrange themselves, but an increase in ritual and magic persists. On the other hand, a "reform" movement that calls the culture back to a renewed awareness of God may spring up. This phenomenon may give rise to a serious tension between the ideal version of the religion and how its adherents actually practice it (they usually cling to rituals). In many cases this tension is a function of the distinction between the "standardized" version of a religion and its popular counterpart, the "folk religion." In contrast to the neat pyramid associated with the evolutionary view (fig. 1.1), original monotheism suggests a tendency toward magic and ritual (fig. 1.2).

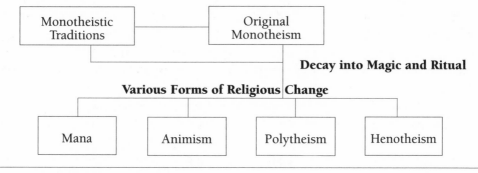

Figure 1.2. Decay into magic and ritual

This tendency toward magic and ritual is almost prevalent enough to be elevated to the level of a law analogous to the second law of thermodynamics, according to which randomness increases within any closed physical system: *A religious culture, left without strong guidance, will tend toward increased ritual and magic.*[18]

The Nature of Ritual

Ritual and magic are very similar. Both attempt to manipulate the spiritual world and thereby the physical world as well. Ritual may be defined as *a series of repeated actions that are performed in order to bring about a desired result.*

Rituals and anxiety. Most actions performed in a religious context involve some sort of ritual. These rituals may hold different meanings for each person participating in them, as well as for each religion that employs them. My own observation is that anxiety never seems to be too far away. Someone may object that the people who participate in a ritual (such as a Sunday-morning worship service or a funeral service) do not admit to any anxiety at all. But such an assurance belies the feelings that may have gone into the construction of the ritual to begin with. How would these people feel if suddenly they could no longer attend the ritual?

Rituals are performed in order to achieve some result, which may be as nebulous as "a blessing from God" or as specific as "a successful business deal." Receiving the desired result depends on executing the ritual properly. If the result does not come about, something about the ritual must be incorrect. An improperly performed ritual may even backfire, causing harm instead of benefit.

Let me illustrate this point with an example that is so oversimplified you may find it funny. But keep in mind that the basic human tendency is to increase ritual. Bear in mind also that even the theory of original monotheism recognizes that religions change and develop. There must be a reason for such development.

Say that you live in a hunting economy, and you set out to hunt. You ask your god to give you success, and then you make a suitable kill. A few days later you set out to hunt again but get nothing. What do you do? Obviously, you compare the two days. Suddenly you remember that you had not prayed to your god the second day! Are you ever going to set out on a hunt without praying again? Not likely! The risks of failure are too great for you to leave out anything that may promote success.

Now imagine that on the third day you pray to your god but still come up with nothing. One option would be for you to conclude that apparently praying to the god and a successful hunt were coincidental. Therefore prayer was useless. But people do not usually react in this way. They are far more likely to look for the reason for their lack of success in themselves—they must not have prayed correctly or they must have violated some other condition in dealing with the god. So you bring your actions in line with what you now think the expectations are. Maybe you will kneel when you pray instead of standing.

You will continue to refine your technique—and your life—as you experience failure or success. The crucial motivation lies in your anxiety over the hunt and the sustenance it provides. Eventually you have laid an extremely complex set of requirements on yourself in your attempt to cope with the vicissitudes of hunting. For example, before any hunt you may light a sacred fire, sacrifice a bit of meat left over from the last hunt, perform a lengthy chant or prayer to the god, hold your weapon to the sky or ask your ancestors to go with you. And you always perform the ritual in exactly the same way.

The development of a priesthood. Of course, all this accumulation of ritual plays itself out in a community context. Individuals consult with other members of the community in an attempt to help each other refine their techniques. Successes and failures, as well as the methods that lead to them, are shared.

Eventually a group of experts on ritual emerges. Their role may be to consult and assist, working cooperatively with their clients. This is the role traditionally played by a "medicine man," or ritual expert in a traditional context. He or she advises the client and directs the ritual, but it remains a joint effort.

In many cultures, though, the pattern goes one step further. The experts become the sole proprietors of the ritual. They constitute a priesthood that performs the ritual on behalf of the other members of the community (for a price). A priest is usually a professional who derives a livelihood from facilitating the spiritual observances of the common people. Joining this elite group often requires extensive training, by virtue of which the ritual domain becomes the prerogative of the priest. No one who has not completed the training can possibly perform the ritual properly, and any attempt to do so is strictly forbidden.

And the laity may be quite content to leave all rituals in the priesthood's hands. The priests are supposed to be the experts; they alone need to know what to do, why to do it and how to do it. As long as they are in charge, there is no need for the laity to get involved unnecessarily. This attitude is like the one that comes into play when my air conditioner breaks down. I call in the experts to fix it and generally trust their skill and judgment even if I do not understand what they are doing (but I will have to pay the bill). In the same way, the laypersons in our hypothetical community abandon themselves to the expertise of the priesthood, trusting their skill and judgment in religious matters.

The emergence of folk religion. At the same time further developments take place. Although the laity has consigned the performance of major rituals to the priesthood, it has not given up all of its religious consciousness. People continue to relate to the supernatural in ways that are still open to them and continue to create new ones. Thus the growth of ritual is a never-ending process. A religious culture may split as the religion develops. On the one hand, there is the religion of the experts with its inside knowledge of the culture's mythology and ritual, which may codify itself into a set of sacred writings that can only be read and understood by people with expert training. On the other hand, the religion of the common people tries to find its way apart from intensive training in practice and scripture. This is how a "folk religion" develops.

Folk religion consists of the lived, everyday practice of religion by common laypersons. Keep in mind, of course, that this distinction is imposed on people's religious practices by outside scholars. The participants may not be conscious that what they are practicing is folk religion. The dividing line cannot always be drawn with certainty. Nevertheless, it is crucial to recognize that there can be a vast difference between the theoretical-historical side of a religion and its counterpart in the lives of its common adherents.

Take the case of Christianity, for example. In the introduction to this book Christianity is summarized in terms of a belief system—a set of doctrines having to do primarily with sin and salvation. However, many people who consider themselves Christians would be unable to give such a summary and would not, even if they could, define their Christianity in such a way. There is a folk Christianity that defines the nature of Christianity in cultural terms that are far removed from the systematic theologies and histories of the church taught in seminaries.

There are many versions of folk Christianity. At the risk of stereotyping, let me describe the folk Christianity practiced in rural Indiana, where I live. The core practice is attending church on Sunday morning. To be considered valid, the Sunday service must be conducted in a building reserved for such a purpose, preferably one that has at least a small spire. The service should include hymns sung to organ or piano accompaniment, an offering and a sermon delivered by an ordained clergyman who basically repeats moral exhortations. From the point of view of the believer, it is *attendance* that constitutes the crucial requirement. Further participation in the life and function of the church is not nearly as crucial as simply being there. When greater involvement is encouraged, service to the building (maintenance or improvement) and participation in social occasions (especially carry-in dinners) are considered of equal value with teaching a Sunday school class or working on a committee. The requirement for attendance is especially crucial on one of the three highest holy days—Christmas, Easter and Mother's Day.

This folk Christianity has developed a belief system all its own. At the heart of it is the belief that God wants us to be "good" people. When asked, a believer may loosely define goodness in terms of keeping the Ten Commandments, without being able to name more than three or four of them. More practically, this goodness actually looks like the prevailing standards of decency and respectability of rural Indiana; a "good" Christian is essentially a pleasant friend and neighbor. The reward for at least occasional goodness is going to heaven. Those who achieve admission to the pearly gates become angels, complete with white gowns, wings and harps.

This caricature of folk religion points up the evident discrepancy between a "theologically correct" understanding of Christianity and the understanding of it that is held by many laypersons who consider themselves Christians. As a Christian myself, I believe that many Christians need to be taught more accurately what biblical Christianity is. But how does an outsider to the faith decide which of the many presentations of Christianity is the correct one? A non-Christian can only describe the various versions of Christianity and say that they are all somehow part of the diverse group of people who call themselves Christians. Non-Christians can only leave questions of Christian "truth" to Christian theologians.[19]

Readers of this book need to bear in mind that they are outsiders in terms of the religions it discusses. They also need to be aware of the various levels of development within the religions. In addition to the classical divisions that exist within religions— schools, branches, denominations and so on—there may be a huge gap between the "official" description of a religion and what some of the common adherents actually believe and practice. For example, the content of Islam is usually described in terms of the five pillars (chapter three). Your Muslim neighbor, however, may not be able to remember what they are. Instead, he or she may be preoccupied with warding off evil spirits. Similarly, a description of Buddhism in terms of the search for nirvana by means of the eightfold path (chapter eight) will at best be half the story. For many Buddhists, the heart of Buddhism is securing the blessings of Buddha for a successful life.

Someone who has formally studied a religion's history and scripture may have a better grasp of those aspects of the religion than many adherents. However, the perceptive scholar does not jump to the conclusion that, therefore, the adherent is "wrong" about his or her faith. Instead, the scholar must always be aware that a religion is composed of both the "expert" side and the folk side. For this reason it is extremely difficult to condense a religion into a set core of belief and practice.

It is impossible to predict what any given religious adherent believes and practices in relation to that religion. Be prepared for some ambiguity when you encounter someone who calls a particular religion his or her own. You may see or hear precisely what is described in this book. You may also see or hear something very different, since ultimately the experience of a living religion cannot be confined to authoritative sentences. People change, cultures change and religions change. And the life of the person within the religion changes—sometimes following the pattern, sometimes working against it.

Rites of Passage

Most religions celebrate the stages of life as people pass through them. These ceremonies have become so ingrained in human social life that their vestiges persist even into the most secularized cultures. A transition into a new stage of life calls for a ceremony to celebrate it. The ceremony may even come to be seen as bringing about the change to the extent that if the ceremony does not take place, the new stage of life is not attained. Rites of passage attend four life events—birth, puberty, marriage and death—in virtually all human cultures.

Birth. The beginning of life is usually marked by a celebration. Often the ceremony includes a recognition of the earth as mother—very diverse cultures place the baby on the ground for a moment. The infant receives a name (at least a childhood name) at the ceremony. Birth rites have continued into contemporary society. Modern religious people observe birth with circumcision, christening or dedication. Secular patterns of celebration include baby showers and distributing cigars.

Puberty. Almost all cultures mark the transition from childhood to young adulthood with a ceremony. (Interestingly, Chinese culture by and large, with some possible local exceptions, does not.) For girls the ceremony centers on the onset of menstruation; for boys the first nocturnal emission may serve to pinpoint the time. Many cultures schedule a ceremony for young people who have arrived at an age when all of them will have made the transition, and then all the young men and women of the same age undergo the ritual together.

Typical aspects of puberty rites include a physical ordeal that proves manhood or womanhood, circumcision for boys or clitoridectomy for girls, secret lore or a new name (which signals the beginning of a new life). In Judaism, bar mitzvah and bat mitzvah are religious rites of passage into adulthood, and in Christianity, confirmation. Secular American society marks the passage into adulthood also, for example with obtaining one's driver's license or with coming-out parties for debutantes in the South. In small-town America to this day, each person's high-school graduation class becomes a permanently fixed part of his or her identity.

Marriage. There is no such thing as a private marriage.[20] A marriage is initiated only with some publicly recognized ceremony. Different societies handle marriage differently. Marriage may be (1) freely chosen or arranged (or a combination of the two); (2) matriarchal or patriarchal, depending on whether the woman or the man possesses the leadership position; (3) matrilocal or patrilocal, depending on whether the man comes to live with the woman (hut, clan, village) or vice versa; (4) matrilineal or patrilineal, depending on whether the joint identity of the marriage or the offspring (frequently expressed with some modification of names) is reckoned through the woman's family or the man's, or (5) exogamous or endogamous, depending on whether marriage partners are expected to come from different clans or from the same clans.

These arrangements do not occur in any set patterns. For example, a culture can be matrilineal and patriarchal, or patrilineal and matrilocal. But the marriage itself is a part of that society, and no one can be properly married apart from the appropriate social sanctions. The wedding ceremony may or may not be religious. Although a civil ceremony before a public official is sufficient legally, couples who are not religious and may not attend another church service until it is time to christen their child frequently insist on adding a church ceremony to their wedding, sometimes days after the civil ceremony. In the United States, a religious minister functions as a representative of the state for purposes of weddings. Ministers are a routine choice—even when a civil ceremony might be more convenient and the couple has no further religious interest.

Death. The last of the four nearly universal rites of passage marks the end of life. Obviously, this rite of passage continues into our secularized society. It was asserted earlier that ritual has its roots in anxiety, and nothing elicits more anxiety than death and dead people. This anxiety is clearly demonstrated in the conventions and superstitions that surround death. For instance, why should the minister always walk at the head of the casket? Why should one never speak ill of the dead? The answer seems to lie in deeply rooted anxieties that the rite of passage is meant to assuage. Many religions teach that a departed person who has not been given the proper burial ritual will have a very unhappy afterlife and may return to earth as a ghost. In all societies funeral rituals are important ways of closing out the life of the deceased.

■ *So You Meet a Religious Person . . .*

What Can You Expect?

Who knows? The possibilities are endless. There are many religions, and religions themselves go through changes. Many religions have developed a distinctive "folk" version over the years, and any particular believer can have his or her own slant on the religion. So, when meeting a person who claims a particular religion, expect the unexpected. Too many evangelicals try to understand other religions on the basis of quick formulas. This is a mistake. Avoid imposing simple schemes on the basis of what the person is *supposed to* believe. For example, many Hindus are not pantheists, many Buddhists do not want to escape into nirvana and many Jews are not looking for a messiah. Sadly, many Christians do not believe that they are saved by grace through faith!

Relating the Gospel

Most conversations that Christians have with non-Christians are not evangelistic. But when the opportunity arises, a Christian may wish to share the gospel with someone who has not yet come to faith in Christ. This book is not a study of evangelism per se.[21] However, a study of non-Christian religions can suggest obstacles as well as points of contact in regard to sharing the gospel with the adherents of those religions. Needless to say, the details will vary from religion to religion as well as from person to person.

The Christian who wishes to share the gospel, particularly with someone who comes from a different culture, needs to be aware of the cultural package in which the encounter takes place. This is referred to as *contextualization*. Let us call the Christian who wishes to relate the gospel an "evangelist," without implying some kind of status as professional preacher or missionary. The non-Christian is the "receptor," the one who receives the gospel message. Finally, let us assume that the evangelist and the receptor are at home in different cultures. Theoretically, the evangelist should convey the gospel message to the receptor without attaching her own culture. Practically, this is impossible. The strident voices insisting that missionaries entirely strip away their culture from the gospel message obviously belong to people who have never been missionaries. An evangelist understands the gospel message best as it is embodied in her own culture. And for that matter, the gospel message in its original form is intertwined with a third culture, namely, the biblical one. Thus any evangelistic activity involves the interplay of three cultures: the biblical culture, the evangelist's home culture and the receptor's culture.

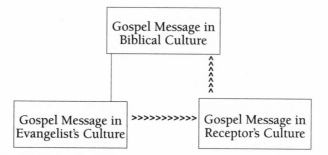

Figure 1.3. Interplay of cultures in evangelism

First of all, the evangelist must discern the gospel message in its biblical setting. Second, as far as is humanly possible, she must make sure that nothing in her culture obscures or supplants the gospel message. Third, the evangelist has to convey the message in such a way that the gospel is intelligible to the receptor in his culture and in such a way that the receptor can also trace his understanding of the gospel back to the biblical message itself. This is a difficult enterprise. Finding fault with those who attempt it imperfectly is far easier than carrying it out successfully.

Contextualization is the process by which the evangelist tries to situate her message in the receptor's culture. If the receptor is going to reject the message, it should at least not be for irrelevant reasons. In order to gain a hearing from the receptor, the evangelist tries to adopt as much of the culture of the receptor as is possible without compromising the message itself. Contextualization can involve outward cultural forms such as dress, food, language and manners. It can also include the concepts and images the evangelist uses to communicate the message. The apostle Paul epitomized contextualization when he reported, "I have become all things to all men so that by all possible means I might save some" (1 Cor 9:22).

In short, evangelism necessitates some contextualization. The message that Christ provides salvation through faith in him must remain clear; the cultural setting for the message must be such that the receptor can hear the message and respond to it.

Mastering the Material

When you have finished studying this chapter, you should be able to

1. provide a working definition of religion and show the difficulties with such a definition;

2. describe the subjective theory of religion in its various versions; show how the theory begs the question of the origin of religion;

3. identify the basis for an evolutionary theory of the origin of religion;

4. summarize the various phases of religion: mana, animism, polytheism, henotheism, monotheism;

5. distinguish between magic and worship;

6. point out the flaws in the evolutionary theory of religion;

7. describe the theory of original monotheism and the evidence adduced for it;

8. summarize the nature of ritual;

9. show how a priesthood develops out of the nature of ritual;

10. identify the difference between "expert" and "folk" religion;

11. enumerate the four nearly universal rites of passage and their general meaning;

12. identify the following persons and explain the contribution of each, as described in this chapter: Joseph Campbell, Mircea Eliade, Ludwig Feuerbach, J. C. Frazer, Sigmund Freud, C. G. Jung, Rudolf Otto, Friedrich Schleiermacher, Wilhelm Schmidt.

Term Paper Ideas

1. Trace the definitions of religion provided by various authors in comparative religion and philosophy.

2. Describe various types of magic as they have been classified by scholars from Frazer on.

3. Make an in-depth study of one type of spiritual being in the animistic phase (for example, ancestors in African religion or nature spirits in Australian aboriginal religion).

4. Compare and contrast the differing ways in which polytheism has come about in various cultures.

5. Chase down examples of henotheism in different cultures. You may want to explore the question of whether henotheism ever existed as an independent form.

6. Pull together and address various theories of the origin of monotheism with a critical eye.

7. Summarize descriptions of sky gods from many cultures, and compare and contrast some of the myths associated with them.

8. Do an in-depth study of Wilhelm Schmidt's contribution and the reception his work has received in the scholarly world.

9. Explore the notion of decay in the history of religion from the point of view of religion, philosophy, psychology or sociology.

10. Describe various theories on the nature of ritual. Defend the one that you find most suitable.

11. Write up a case study on the nature of folk religion.

12. Undertake a detailed description of the rites of passage in a specific culture. Identify components of the rites that are of clearly religious origin, those that are more likely derived from the culture per se and those that could be either.

Core Bibliography

General textbooks in religion. These also make good reference works, and they have served me well as sources.

Hopfe, Lewis M. *Religions of the World.* 6th ed. New York: Macmillan, 1994.

Lewis, James F., and William G. Travis. *Religious Traditions of the World.* Grand Rapids, Mich.: Zondervan, 1991.

Nielsen, Niels C., Jr. *Religions of the World.* 3rd ed. New York: St. Martin's, 1993.

Nigosian, S. A. *World Faiths.* 2nd ed. New York: St. Martin's, 1994.

Noss, David S., and John B. Noss. *A History of the World's Religions.* 9th ed. New York: Macmillan, 1994.

Matthews, Warren. *World Religions.* 2nd ed. Minneapolis: West, 1994.

Spiegelberg, Frederic. *Living Religions of the World.* Englewood Cliffs, N.J.: Prentice-Hall, 1956.

General Reference Works

Crim, Keith, ed. *The Perennial Dictionary of World Religions.* San Francisco: Harper & Row, 1981.

Eliade, Mircea, ed. *The Encyclopedia of Religion.* 16 vols. New York: Macmillan, 1987.

Hastings, James, ed. *Encyclopedia of Religion and Ethics.* 13 vols. New York: Scribner's, 1908-1926.

Hexham, Irving. *Concise Dictionary of Religion.* Downers Grove, Ill.: InterVarsity Press, 1993.

Chapter 2

Judaism

Estimated Membership
Worldwide: 14,117,000
United States: 4,300,000

We begin our survey of world religions with traditions that have maintained monotheism, starting with Judaism.

Three Questions

Since you don't offer animal sacrifices anymore, how do you think you can be saved and go to heaven? This question is one that evangelical Christians commonly ask Jews, and it reveals a gap between Christians' understanding of Old Testament Judaism and their understanding of modern Judaism. This gap involves three main misconceptions.

First, the question assumes a need for and a desire to be "saved." Personal redemption—salvation from sin and its consequences—is the crucial concern in Christianity, and Christians are taught that it is also an important aspect of the Hebrew Scriptures (the Christian Old Testament). However, this issue is not a major concern of modern Judaism.

Second, the question assumes that the purpose of religion is to provide some means of getting to heaven. Even though the concept of heaven is a part of the Jewish tradition, the sole purpose of Jewish religion is not to see who will and who will not get to heaven.

Third, the question seems to invoke an almost nostalgic, don't-you-wish-you-still-had-sacrifices attitude. Except for a few fringe groups, however, today's Jews are no more interested in reviving animal sacrifices than most Christians would be. Many Orthodox Jews believe that when the Messiah comes, the temple will be rebuilt and sacrifices will be reinstated. Until that day they are content to leave matters in the hands of the Messiah.

In the meantime they have more important things to worry about.

The concept of Judaism as a temporary provision between the end of the sacrificial system and the coming of the Messiah is not accepted by Jews. Modern Judaism considers itself as just as appropriate and mature in its present form as any other religion.

Then what is Judaism? It is very difficult to summarize the nature of Judaism in a brief explanation, but I can try. Judaism is a religion based on relationships: God's relationship with the human person, a person's relationship with God, people's individual relationships with each other, and the Chosen People's relationship with other nations. All these relationships are based on rules and traditions that are said to have originated with God.

But why keep God's laws if keeping them won't get you into heaven? This question implies that a desire for rewards and a fear of punishment are the only acceptable motives for obeying rules. This attitude, however, is quite immature. For example, college students should have developed morally to the place where (in the absence of overriding moral concerns) they comply with their parents' wishes out of love and respect, not out of fear of punishment or craving for reward. Similarly, Judaism asserts that it should not take a promise of reward or a threat of punishment to motivate people to obey God's laws. They should be obeyed out of love and respect for God.

Judaism does not revolve around a set of doctrines or a plan of salvation. Instead, it is a prescription for living life. The crucial question in Judaism is, What do you practice? or What are you doing with your life? not What do you believe? Different branches of contemporary Judaism provide somewhat differing styles of answers. The common denominator is the need to make a difference in the world through a life of righteousness. Doctrines, particularly beliefs about personal salvation, take a backseat to this concern.

In contrast to Christianity, which became a crosscultural religion within its first generation of existence, Judaism has retained a general ethnic identification. Although it has always recognized the "righteous Gentile," and some branches allow conversions,[1] on the whole "being Jewish" has included an ethnic and cultural heritage as well as a religious one. Nonreligious and nonobservant Jews are still Jews. This fact has at times led some Jews to mistakenly refer to all Western Gentiles as "Christians." Being an evangelical Christian always includes personal commitment to a set of religious beliefs. Being a Christian is never an ethnic or a cultural matter.

In order to understand contemporary Judaism, we need to go back to the destruction of the temple in A.D. 70 and consider the Jewish nation's response to this catastrophe. But to appreciate the full import of this event, we need to review the history of Israel.

The First Jewish Commonwealth

The early history of Judaism is frequently discussed in terms of two commonwealths. These are the major eras of Judaism with their particular characteristics. The First Jewish Commonwealth is reckoned from the time Moses received the law on Mount

Sinai (around 1450 B.C.) until the destruction of Judah by the Babylonians (587 B.C.). The Second Jewish Commonwealth begins with the destruction of Judah by the Babylonians and extends through the destruction of the temple by the Romans (A.D. 70). Some scholars say that the Holocaust and the creation of the modern state of Israel have initiated a third commonwealth.

The first commonwealth is the subject of much of the Hebrew Bible. Conservative dating methods[2] produce the following rough chronology. (The purpose here is to arrange events sequentially, not to affix authoritative dates.)

Date	Period or event
c. 2100 B.C.	Abraham
c. 1900 B.C.	Joseph in Egypt
c. 1450-1400 B.C.	Exodus and conquest; law given at Sinai
c. 1400-1050 B.C.	Period of the Judges
c. 1050-931 B.C.	United kingdom under Saul, David and Solomon (David at 1000)
931 B.C.	Divided kingdoms of Israel and Judah
722 B.C.	Fall of Samaria, end of kingdom of Israel
587 B.C.	Fall of Jerusalem, end of kingdom of Judah, exile to Babylonia
537 B.C.	End of exile, restoration of Judah, Persian overlordship
c. 440 B.C.	Last biblical prophet (Malachi)
332 B.C.	Conquest by Alexander the Great; Greek rulers
166 B.C.	Maccabean revolt, Hasmonean kingdom, Herod the Great installed by Romans (37 B.C.)
A.D. 70	Destruction of Jerusalem and the temple

The early period. The Hebrew Scriptures begin with God's creating the universe. His last direct act is to create a pair of human beings, Adam and Eve. Living at first in an idyllic state in a place described as a garden, the pair violated God's commandment and broke their direct relationship with God. Adam and Eve were expelled from the garden and went on to make their living through agriculture and animal husbandry. They had two sons, Cain and Abel, but Cain killed Abel in a fit of jealousy involving sacrifices offered to God; Cain had sacrificed fruit, Abel, an animal. Abel was replaced by a third son, Seth, and both Cain and Seth produced lines of progeny. Regular worship was initiated a few generations after Adam and Eve. "At that time men began to call on the name of the LORD" (Gen 4:26).

The early account continues with a global flood and the tower of Babel. Adam's descendants became contaminated morally (and possibly genetically, Gen 6:2). As a result, God punished them with a flood. Only Noah and his immediate family survived. After the flood God issued more specific moral obligations. But as the population grew, people attempted to build a tower that would reach all the way to heaven. Clearly they were challenging God, not submitting to him in worship. God frustrated their project by causing the people to speak different languages, thus disrupting their communication with each other, and they scattered all over the world. Thus the biblical story accounts for the fact of different cultures and the different religions associated with them.

The religion of this early period is not described with much detail beyond a recognition of God, sacrifices and ethical obligations. However, as religion becomes increasingly complex, it manifests the sinful human impulse away from God.

The patriarchs. By around 2100 B.C., religions in the fertile crescent had committed themselves to various elaborate polytheistic pantheons, but knowledge of the original God persisted. For example, even though Canaanite religion centered around various fertility goddesses, we also encounter the priest-king of Salem (Jerusalem), Melchizedek, who worshiped the high God (El). Similarly, Abram of the Sumerian city of Ur lived in a culture and family that worshiped a moon god, but he himself worshiped God. Abram and his wife, Sarai, migrated to Canaan, where (under the new names of Abraham and Sarah) they founded a clan that worshiped God alone. Abraham's son Isaac, born miraculously to him in his old age, and his grandson Jacob, along with Jacob's twelve sons, continued this tradition. The clan migrated to Egypt because of a famine in Canaan. There, over the next four hundred years, it grew into a nation of twelve tribes.

During the patriarchal period, religious worship consisted of animal sacrifices that the head of the clan made on behalf of his clan. The religious practices described in the book of Job fit this pattern, so some scholars believe the events described in Job belong to the patriarchal period.

Egypt and Sinai. During the four hundred years the Hebrews spent in Egypt, much of it as slaves, most of them forgot about God and adopted pagan religious practices (Josh 24:14). Moses reintroduced them to the worship of God. Around 1450 B.C. he led them out of Egypt in the name of God and then reestablished them in the monotheistic faith. Several events crucial to the later history of Judaism occurred in connection with the exodus: (1) the ten plagues on Egypt, (2) the Israelites' crossing the Red Sea, (3) the giving of the law at Mount Sinai and (4) the golden calf incident.

The ten plagues that God sent on Egypt culminated in the death of all Egyptian firstborn. The fact that these plagues did not touch the Hebrews led to the institution of the first Passover feast. As the Israelites left Egypt, God miraculously opened the waters of the Red Sea so that the Israelites crossed over on dry land. When the pursuing Egyptian army followed them into the sea, they drowned. This event became the Hebrews' defining moment in their self-recognition as God's redeemed people. Following the exodus, the entire nation camped in the vicinity of Mount Sinai, where Moses gave them the law that God had communicated to him. This law included

☐ the Ten Commandments, which served as the foundation for God's relationships with people and for people's relationships with each other;

☐ a complex legal code for social relationships that covered criminal and civil matters;
☐ instructions for building a portable sanctuary (the tabernacle), which was to be the central place of worship; the tabernacle's furnishings included the ark of the covenant (a chest containing the tablets of the law), an incense altar, a table for the bread of the Presence and a lampstand;
☐ a professional priesthood drawn from the tribe of Levi;
☐ a complex system of sacrifices of animals and agricultural products, to be administered exclusively by the priests;
☐ a code of ritual purity that included medical and hygienic precautions, dietary rules and prohibitions of Canaanite religious practices.

Even as Moses was receiving the law from God, the people, under the leadership of the first high priest, Moses' brother, Aaron, began to worship a golden calf. It served as a fertility symbol for the cattle-raising Hebrews. This event foreshadowed the nine-hundred-year tension that would exist between monotheistic religion and paganism in Israelite culture.

Conquest and judges. Under Joshua's leadership the Israelites entered the land of Canaan, parceled out land to the twelve tribes and lived for about three hundred years with very little central political or religious control. Worship of God focused on sacrifices performed by the priests at the tabernacle and at numerous local altars. Decay into pagan forms was a constant temptation to which the people succumbed numerous times. This period was marked by recurring cycles that consisted of (1) apostasy, (2) bondage to a foreign power sent by God as judgment, (3) crying out to God for deliverance and (4) deliverance by a heroic figure who then ruled over them as judge for a time.

The unified kingdom. The last judge was Samuel, who was also a priest (1 Chron 6:27). In addition to his duties at the tabernacle, Samuel performed sacrifices in various towns. When Samuel became old, the people demanded a monarchy. Samuel reluctantly granted it to them. The first king was Saul from the tribe of Benjamin, who ruled from Gibeon. The next king, David, governed from the newly conquered city of Jerusalem and made preparations for a permanent central worship facility to be constructed there. He moved the ark of the covenant to Jerusalem, purchased a future building site, amassed building materials and established regulations covering the priests' tours of duty by family and clan membership. The temple was actually built by his son Solomon. He erected a magnificent structure where sacrifices of various types were offered daily. The temple building included the main room, where the temple furnishings were located, and the inner sanctuary, the most holy place, into which the high priest entered once a year on the Day of Atonement to make an offering of incense. After the temple was established in 950 B.C., the Hebrews were not allowed to perform sacrifices at any other sites (Deut 12:1-14).

The divided kingdom. Under Solomon's son Rehoboam, the kingdom split into a northern kingdom, Israel, and a southern kingdom, Judah. The northern kingdom began with the political disadvantage of not having the central worship structure, which was in Jerusalem. For this reason its first king, Jeroboam, created two sanctuaries for golden calves and designated a new priesthood. A few generations later, under Ahab and his successors, the Canaanite worship of Baal became the official state religion.

Worship of God persisted, but never without serious opposition. Prophets such as Elijah and Elisha early on, followed by Hosea, Jonah and Amos, issued warnings from God. Their warnings went largely unheeded, and Assyria destroyed the kingdom of Israel in 722 B.C.

The southern kingdom alternately worshiped and rejected God. Some kings, such as Asa, Joash, Hezekiah and Josiah, were strict worshipers of God who opposed idolatrous practices. Others, most notably Manasseh, took the worship of idols to new heights. Religious abuses included worshiping various pagan deities, worshiping the bronze snake made by Moses (Num 21:8-9), worshiping God at unauthorized sites (the "high places") and eventually syncretistic worship practices in the temple (Ezek 8:14-18). The kingdom of Judah fell to the Babylonians in 587 B.C., and most of its people were deported to Babylon.

Two menorahs in Temple Sholom, Chicago—one traditional and one representing the burning bush.

The Second Commonwealth

Exile and restoration. The period of exile purged the nation of idolatry. The Persians under Cyrus conquered the Babylonians and allowed the Jews to return to their land, where they rebuilt the temple. The biblical record ends in the time of Ezra, Nehemiah and Malachi. Problems occurring at this time included a lack of obedience to the law, intermarriage with surrounding Gentiles and empty ritualism. However, it is crucial to realize that from this time on, monotheistic faith, along with a foundational commitment to the law, was no longer at risk in Jewish society.

Greek occupation and the Hasmonean kingdom. The benign overlordship of the Persians gave way to the tyranny of Alexander the Great's successors, the Seleucids, who attempted to Hellenize the Jewish nation culturally and religiously. The last of these rulers, Antiochus IV (who called himself Epiphanes, the "Appearing One"), committed the ultimate blasphemy of sacrificing a pig to Zeus on the altar of the temple in Jerusalem. The Jews had been fairly compliant up to this point, but that act went too far. The high priest Hyrcanus and his sons, led by the eldest, Judas Maccabee ("Judas the Hammer") instigated a successful revolt against Antiochus. They purified the temple and established a newly unified kingdom that lasted approximately a hundred years. This kingdom, known as the Hasmonean kingdom after Hyrcanus's clan, was nearly as large as the kingdom of David had been. It is significant that during this dynasty political power was held by the priestly family. This pattern continued throughout the rest of the second commonwealth.

The Roman occupation. When the Romans extended their empire into the Middle East, they installed a series of rulers over the Jews, the most notable of whom was Herod the Great. Herod was Idumean (from Edomite, a descendant of Esau), not Jewish. Herod worked hard to please the Jews by undertaking an extensive renewal project of the temple. This renovation amounted to a complete rebuilding. It was not actually finished until many decades after Herod's death, just a few years before it was demolished by the Romans. When Herod died, the Romans carved his kingdom into several tetrarchies. They also ruled some of the land directly through a procurator, for example, Pontius Pilate (Lk 3:1-2). Relations between Romans and Jews deteriorated until they came to full-blown war in A.D. 70. Jewish life during the Roman occupation, the time when Jesus of Nazareth lived, was characterized by (1) devotion to God, (2) messianic expectation and (3) party divisions.

First, it was a time of devotion to God. The nation as a whole was committed to keeping God's law and practicing the required temple sacrifices. As is always the case with human beings, there was a good deal of superficiality in some of this devotion.

Second, it was a time of messianic expectation. Several people appeared in Palestine claiming to be the Messiah, for example, a man named Judah in A.D. 6 who gathered a following in Galilee (Acts 5:37). These messiah figures tended to have a political orientation, their main purpose being to throw off Roman overlordship.

Third, it was a time of party divisions. There were a number of parties, political and religious, that made their presence felt in all areas of life. Most common people did not belong to a specific party but did identify or sympathize to varying degrees with one or the other. The main parties included the Sadducees, the Pharisees, the Herodians, the Essenes and the Zealots.

A priest did not have to be a Sadducee, but most of them were. As the party of priests, the Sadducees exercised important political power as part of their heritage from the Hasmonean era. The high priest, who was a Sadducee, was the leader of the Sanhedrin, the Jews' highest judicial and ecclesiastical council. Because the Romans supported their leadership, the Sadducees in return cooperated with the Romans to a considerable extent. The Sadducees' religious focus was on the temple sacrifices. They did not believe in angels or predestination, and they did not preoccupy themselves with messianic expectations (not surprising in a party holding the political reins). Recent excavations of priestly living quarters in Jerusalem have reinforced the idea that the Sadducees constituted a wealthy aristocracy.

A scribe did not have to be a Pharisee, but most of them were. Apparently the party of the Pharisees began with the scribes who copied the Scriptures. Consequently, Pharisees became experts on the content and the interpretation of the law. By the time of the Roman occupation, the Pharisees had become teachers (rabbis). They belonged to various schools, for example, the conservative school of Shammai and the popular, more liberal school of Hillel. In the fourteen hundred years since the Israelites first settled in the land, much of the law needed to be reinterpreted to fit changing conditions. The Pharisees took the lead in applying the law to these new situations.

On the whole, the rabbis followed the principle that it is always safer to take the most rigorous interpretation of the law. That way, someone who broke the law accidentally would be breaking a human interpretation of the law instead of God's actual command. Thus God's law would be protected from human trespass, a practice called "building a fence around the law." Laws about sacrifices were the domain of the Sadducees. The Pharisees emphasized meticulous observance of the law in all areas of life. In contrast to the Sadducees, they promoted belief in angels, predestination and messianic expectations. The Pharisees were more popular among the common people than the Sadducees.

The Herodians are mentioned in the New Testament without explanation. They were either a political party favoring the monarchy of the Herodian family or, possibly, a religious group that had been favored particularly by the Herodian dynasty. In that case they may have been identical with the Essenes.[3]

The Essenes left mainstream Judaism, possibly over the priest-kingship of the Hasmoneans. They are not mentioned in the New Testament, but they are described by Josephus (who does not mention the Herodians). They were particularly favored by Herod, who obviously had a vested interest in not reviving the Hasmonean dynasty. The Essenes lived communally and observed the law even more punctiliously than the Pharisees did. They believed they were the only remaining true Israelites and that God would eventually vindicate them. It is commonly accepted that the community living at Qumran, which bequeathed us the celebrated Dead Sea Scrolls, was a group of Essenes.

More nationalistic than religious, the Zealots promoted the independence of the Jews from the Romans. In the years before the final war, they carried out terrorist activities against the Romans and at times against Jews who cooperated with the

Romans. These attacks eventually led to full-blown war and the destruction of Jerusalem.

The Jewish state ended with the destruction of the temple in A.D. 70. Josephus tells us that the Roman general Titus had instructed his army not to burn the temple. The building was topped by rows of narrow, pointed strips of gold (presumably to keep pigeons from desecrating the sacred building), giving the effect of flames of gold arising out of the roof. Titus wanted to harvest this gold, but a soldier disobeyed and set fire to the wooden parts of the structure. In the conflagration all of the gold melted and flowed into the cracks between the building blocks. In order to retrieve the gold, Titus had a horde of slaves break down every wall, block by block, so that the entire building was reduced to rubble.[4] The temple was obliterated except for the western retaining wall of the mount (not a wall of the actual buildings), which became known as the Wailing Wall. With that event, the religion that had focused on temple sacrifices for a thousand years became dysfunctional.

The Rise of Rabbinic Judaism

The world of Judaism changed drastically with the destruction of the temple in A.D. 70. The Sadducees, the party of the priests, went out of business permanently. The Zealots made a last stand at Herod's old fortress, Masada, in A.D. 73, which ended with the mass suicide of 956 people on the eve of being captured by the Romans. The Herodians and Essenes never enjoyed much popular support and disappeared after the war.

The Pharisees, as the only remaining party, were in an ideal position to assume the leadership of Judaism. The Pharisees had never been strongly identified with politics and were not tied exclusively to the temple sacrificial system. As experts in the whole law, they were able to direct the continuation of a new Judaism without sacrifices. From this point on, Pharisaic Judaism was mainline Judaism. From the destruction of the temple into the present time, the agenda for Jewish life and practice has been set by the rabbis, who are the spiritual descendants of the Pharisees.

The newly emerging rabbinic Judaism emphasized obedience to the law. To this day, the main focus in Judaism is on observing the law, not on personal belief. In Christianity the fundamental issue is what a person believes. As a result, there are many Christian denominations that are divided over points of doctrine with very little discernible distinction in practice. On the other hand, in Judaism the extent to which a person obeys the law is seen as most crucial. Obviously, what a person believes is not irrelevant, since it will play an important part in determining personal practice. The major Jewish denominations differ for the most part on observance, not doctrine. For example, Orthodox Judaism contains a mystical as well as a rational strain, and the Reform movement, which is very open in its practice, can include conservative theology and liberal beliefs.

Fundamental Writings

Biblical writings. The first step in establishing rabbinic Judaism was to form a clear consensus of what constituted holy scripture. This matter was taken up by a conclave of rabbis in the Mediterranean town of Yavneh (Jamnia). Rabbi Yochanan ben Zakkai received permission from the Romans to meet there in the years following A.D. 90. We do not have exact transcripts of the proceedings at Yavneh. Consequently, some scholars dispute the traditional account of what was accomplished there. But according to ancient tradition, all the books that had been in use as inspired writings were considered with an eye toward settling once and for all whether they should be accepted into the canon of Scripture. After a long debate, they certified the writings that had been treated as Scripture in Palestinian Judaism all along; none of the other competing books (the so-called Apocrypha) made the list.

The emerging Christian community also accepted the books recognized at Yavneh. Thus the books recognized as Jewish Scripture are identical to the Protestant Christian Old Testament, the only difference being in their arrangement. The Hebrew canon was arranged into three major divisions: Torah, Prophets and Writings. The Torah consists of the "teachings," or the "law." It includes the five books revealed by God to Moses: Genesis, Exodus, Leviticus, Numbers and Deuteronomy. The Prophets are divided into the early prophets: Joshua, Judges, 1-2 Samuel, 1-2 Kings, and the later prophets: Isaiah, Jeremiah, Ezekiel, the "Twelve" (the minor prophets from Hosea to Malachi). The Writings include all other books, some of which are classified with the prophets in Christian Bibles: Psalms, Job, Proverbs, Ruth, Song of Songs, Ecclesiastes, Lamentations, Esther, Daniel, Ezra, Nehemiah, 1-2 Chronicles.

The Mishnah. Once the canon had been agreed on, the time had come to collect in writing the many interpretations of the law that had accrued over the centuries. This had never been done before, in order to avoid suggesting that the written interpretation rivaled God's written law in authority. But now it became a necessity. To this end, for several decades groups of rabbis met in Tiberius by the Sea of Galilee and hammered out many of the fine points of interpretation and application. Two rabbis who took the leadership in this process were Rabbi Meier and Rabbi Akiba. Their final result was a sizable tome called the Mishnah.

The Mishnah is divided into six categories: (1) *Seeds,* containing laws on agriculture and prayer; (2) *Feasts,* laws concerning holy days and the writing of scrolls; (3) *Women,* laws concerning marriage and other vows; (4) *Damages,* civil and criminal laws as well as prohibitions concerning idolatry; (6) *Holy Matters,* sacrifices and laws for the temple, and (6) *Purities,* ritual cleanliness and purification. Each division wrestles with seemingly innumerable questions and subquestions concerning obedience to the law. The law of Moses specifies that all leaven (yeast) is to be removed from a house prior to Passover (Ex 12:15). The Mishnah[5] addresses questions such as, When can we be sure that all leaven is gone? What about leavened dough that may have become stuck in a crack in the kneading trough? What do we do with cosmetics that may contain minuscule amounts of leaven? What do you do if you are not certain whether or not something contains leaven? In detail that appears not to leave the least little contingency untouched, the Mishnah addresses these issues. The rabbis applied the same thoroughness to all other interpretations of laws. This part of Judaism, which deals with the application of laws, is called Halakah. We can also speak of the "Halakic" tradition. It is a major component of Jewish orthodoxy.

The style of the Mishnah is not to give a simple exposition of the interpretations involved. Instead, each section may state a consensus where it has been attained, but it may also play off opposing viewpoints against each other where there is no unanimity. In a typical discussion we might read that whereas Rabbi Gamaliel stated one opinion, Rabbi Judah's view is slightly different. In fact, the bulk of the Mishnah consists of balancing different authorities, and frequently no final determination is reached.[6]

The Mishnah project ended temporarily when a second conflict with the Romans erupted in A.D. 136. A leader of a revived Zealot group, Bar Kochba, instigated a new rebellion that ended with

This ark, containing some Torah scrolls in the side chapel of Indianapolis Hebrew Congregation, bears the motif of the wanderings in the wilderness.

another crushing defeat by the Romans. Rabbi Akiba supported Bar Kochba because he thought he might be the Messiah; both were executed. Jerusalem was razed once again; this time the emperor Hadrian rebuilt Jerusalem as a pagan city and named it Aeolia Capitolina, dedicated to the god Jupiter. This second defeat exacerbated all the tragedies of A.D. 70. This time the Jews lost their homeland, not just their temple. For the next eighteen hundred years, the history of Jewish religion and culture is a history of a people in exile. A small remnant remained in the land as Judaism continued its development in other parts of the world. The land itself was occupied by the Romans, followed by the Byzantines, the Persians (briefly), the Arabs, the European crusaders, the Turks and the British before it once again became the Jewish homeland. The Mishnah was completed by Rabbi Judah the Prince, a scholar of distant royal descent, about A.D. 200. He finished it and gave it the form in which we have it today.

The Talmud. After the Romans destroyed Jerusalem, the Jewish people spread into many parts of the world. The first great center of Jewish life and religion in the dispersion was Babylon under the aegis of the revived Persian kingdom (the Sassanids). The Persians occasionally persecuted the Jews, but perhaps partially because the Persian religion (Zoroastrianism) was similar to the Jewish religion in many beliefs, the Persians were willing to let the Jews live and at times even thrive in their midst.

During this time more writings were composed and collected. In addition to further Halakic (legal) literature, less formal traditions, including stories illustrating the application of the law, were also committed to writing. This narrative strain was called Haggadah and became part of a second major collection, called the Gemara. Thus there now were two large works, the Mishnah and the Gemara. Eventually Mishnah (Halakah) and Gemara (Haggadah) were joined together into one massive tome called the Talmud.

Mishna (Halakah)	+	Gemara (Haggadah)	=	Talmud

There were actually two versions of the Talmud. The Palestinian (or Jerusalem) Talmud was finished in the fourth century. The larger Babylonian Talmud was finished in the fifth century. The magnitude of this work can be seen by the fact that an English translation spans seventeen dense volumes (plus an index volume).[7]

The Talmud is organized into fifty-five tractates of uneven length. A tractate contains many subsections. A typical subsection begins with a passage from the Torah. Then comes the discussion from the Mishnah, which takes up a only small space in relation to the whole. Then comes the Gemara, which is the larger part. Anyone reading the Mishnah who may have thought that all possible concerns had been raised and addressed will be overwhelmed by the Gemara. Many fine points are brought up, are split into even finer points and are analyzed at length. The Haggadah portions also provide illustrations from the lives of famous rabbis. For example, the discussion on removing leaven at Passover is based on only two or three verses from the Bible. In the English translation of the Mishnah it takes up five pages. In the English Talmud the discussion covers 298 pages.

In Hebrew the pages of the Talmud are arranged concentrically: Torah, which surrounded by Mishnah, which is surrounded by Gemara. Space is left on the outside for further development. The most conservative groups place the Talmud virtually on a par with inspired Scripture. Others consider it to be authoritative but not inspired. More liberal Jews revere the Talmud only for its historical value. But in all cases, the discussion of the issues raised by the Talmud does go on.

The Talmud is the authoritative source of Jewish law and tradition. The laws regulating dress, diet (laws of kashrut) and prayer, as well as the many other components of the law that are accepted as standard for Jewish life, are based on the Talmud. To this day, preparation for the rabbinate in Orthodox Judaism centers on exhaustive Talmudic study. But adherents of other denominations are encouraged to study the law as well. In fact, the study of the Torah may constitute the highest form of worship.

The Move to Spain and the Middle Ages

When Shi'ite Islam came to Persia in the seventh century A.D., Jewish culture in Babylon ceased flourishing. Judaism next took root and flowered on the Iberian Peninsula. The Umayad Muslim leaders of Spain (chapter three) focused their attention on fighting the Christian armies of Europe instead of suppressing a harmless Jewish minority at home.

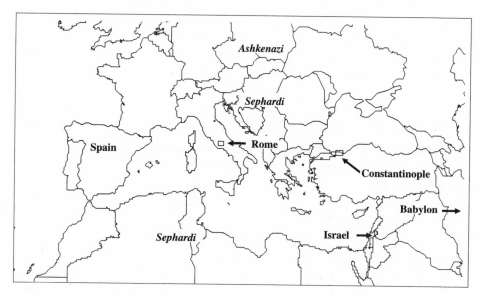

Map 2.1. Centers of Jewish culture

Throughout the European Middle Ages, Jewish culture and religion experienced cycles of tolerance and persecution. For example, when Christendom became en-thralled with the crusades, knights on their way to the Holy Land would practice their military skills by slaughtering Jews at home. The First Crusade (in the eleventh century) began with the murder of fifty thousand Jews in the Rhineland.

At the same time the Talmudic tradition continued to be expounded by leaders whose popularity is evidenced by the fact that they received lasting nicknames. Two of the most influential writers are known as Rashi and Rambam. Rashi (Rabbi Solomon ben Isaac) set the standard for literal interpretation of Scripture. He defended the traditional understandings of the origin of Scripture (for example, identifying Moses as the author of the Torah) and argued that a literal reading must always take precedence over an allegorical or a moral meaning. Rambam (Moses Maimonides) wrote the *Guide for the Perplexed* as an intellectual defense of Judaism. He was a scholar and scientist whose interests spanned many areas of medieval learning. His works were read and quoted by Christian philosophers as well. Thomas Aquinas spoke of him deferentially as "Rabbi Moses."[8]

Kabala

Mysticism has been a part of Judaism from the later years of the Second Jewish Commonwealth, and possibly before.[9] In fact, the name usually associated with Jewish mysticism, *kabala*, simply means "tradition." Wherever mysticism appears (within all religions and cultures), it constitutes the notion of attaining an unmediated link to the Absolute.[10] In Judaism this idea translates into having a direct vision of God.

Jewish mysticism is called *merkavah* mysticism, from the Hebrew word for "chariot" because God's throne in Ezekiel 1:26 was sometimes pictured as a celestial chariot. Scholars have tied it to the general trend of Gnosticism. Some have suggested that the experience described by the apostle Paul in 2 Corinthians 12 may be an early example of it.[11] The goal of this form of spirituality was to raise the soul through the various levels of heaven until it could finally see God on the throne of the third heaven.

Various schools of kabala developed during the Middle Ages and produced many mystical works. The most famous of the mystical treatises was called the Zohar, which literally means "book of splendor," but is often referred to as "book of lights."[12] Moses de Leon wrote this work in Spain. In an allegorical biblical style, the Zohar describes the universe in its relation to the being and glory of God. Another highly influential mystic was Isaac de Luria. He fled Spain when persecution by Christians broke out there. Later he set up a school at Safed in Galilee.

One aspect of kabala that has intrigued Jews as well as Gentiles for centuries, but is actually only a small part of it, is numerological mysticism, gematria (the word *gematria* is related to the word *geometry*). According to this tradition, each letter of the Hebrew alphabet is assigned a certain number value. Consequently, each word has a numerical equivalent, and simple arithmetical analysis of important words can yield spiritual insights that would otherwise remain unknown. In *The Chosen*, novelist Chaim Potok gives us a delightful example of gematria as it is practiced by the Hasidic rabbi, Reb Saunders:

> Listen. In gematriya, the words "this world" come out one hundred sixty-three, and the words "the world-to-come" come out one hundred fifty-four. The difference between "this world" and "the world-to-come" comes out to nine. Nine is half of eighteen. Eighteen is chai, life. In this world there is only half of chai. We are only

half alive in this world! Only half alive![13]
Kabala continues to be a potent force in Judaism.

1492 and Sabbatai Zevi

In 1492 Columbus sailed the ocean blue; in the same year the Jews in Spain experienced a great tragedy. Ferdinand and Isabella had recently unified Spain under Christian rule, and they issued a decree expelling all Jews from Spain. Ironically, a number of kabalistic scholars had predicted that 1492 would be the great year of redemption.[14] Instead, it turned out to be a year of horror. Once again, a whole population of Jews proceeded into exile. Many of these Jews from Spain settled in southeastern Europe, which at the time was under Turkish domination. There they led a relatively peaceful existence.

At this time there were two major groups of Jews in Europe: Sephardic Jews and Ashkenazic Jews. Sephardic Jews had Spanish roots, and their culture was influenced by the oriental customs of their earlier Arab and now Turkish neighbors. They spoke a language called "Ladino," which is basically a Spanish dialect written with Hebrew characters.

Ashkenazic Jews had roots in northern and northeastern Europe. They tended to keep a distance from the surrounding Gentile Europeans. Their vernacular was Yiddish, basically a dialect of German written with Hebrew characters.[15] The distinction between Sephardi and Ashkenazic Jews persists to this day. For example, the city of Indianapolis boasts a Sephardic synagogue. The distinction has also caused some social problems in the modern country of Israel, where Sephardic Jews feel that they are victims of discrimination.

The expulsion from Spain led to a renewed messianic expectation. The experience of persecution led to a desire for political as well as spiritual deliverance: a Messiah. Some mystics predicted that the Messiah would be revealed in 1666.

When Sabbatai Zevi arose in the seventeenth century, many Jews thought that the Messiah had come. Not since the days of Jesus or Bar Kochba had such a large group of Jews been overcome by messianic fervor. Jews in Europe, the Middle East and North Africa were all united in the belief that Sabbatai Zevi was the anointed one sent from God to redeem his people.

Sabbatai Zevi was born in Smyrna, now a part of Turkey. He studied the Zohar and other mystical literature, and eventually he came to believe that he was the Messiah. Apparently he suffered from bipolar disorder (manic-depressive illness), alternating between states of dark resignation and high euphoria. When euphoric, he often broke the law deliberately, even to the point of blasphemy. A circle of close followers, composed mostly of others who were steeped in kabala and naive believers, saw this behavior as a messianic sign. In 1665 a young man named Nathan of Gaza publicly proclaimed that Sabbatai was the Messiah. Sabbatian enthusiasm soared. Intense repentance and anticipation broke out among Jews everywhere, as people left their jobs, danced in the streets and ignored their personal responsibilities. Messianic fervor reached fever intensity when Sabbatai traveled to Constantinople, supposedly to convert the Turkish sultan to Judaism. But Sabbatai was captured and was invited to convert to Islam. Sabbatai agreed to convert, and thus in 1666 the supposed Messiah became a Muslim.

It is hard to overstate the impact that these events had on Jewish life for the next century or more. The failed movement gave rise to unprecedented despair and hopelessness. Yet many Jews continued to believe in the messiahship of Sabbatai Zevi. It is instructive for us to focus on this phenomenon as an example of how religion functions in the lives of many people. Just as Seventh-day Adventism got its start with the failed predictions of Christ's second coming by William Miller and Samuel Snow (October 22, 1844), and just as contemporary Christians have continued to support media evangelists after outrageous moral failings, Zevi's disciples interpreted his apostasy (along with his many earlier blasphemies) as a necessary stage in the life of the Messiah, leading to the redemption of the world. Right into the nineteenth century, marginal movements preached the need for Jewish apostasy in emulation of Sabbatai Zevi![16]

Nevertheless, the majority of those whose hopes had been raised and then crushed suffered horrendous disillusionment. This disappointment stimulated two new movements that arose in the eighteenth century, Hasidism and Reform Judaism. Both movements are characterized by an attempt to redefine the Jewish self-concept.

Torah scrolls in the main ark of Indianapolis Hebrew Congregation. The decorations include the "crown," the "breastplate" and the "yad," a finger-like pointer for reading.

Hasidism

The Sabbatai Zevi fiasco left Judaism in turmoil. The Talmudic orthodoxy, the continuing Sabbatian movement and various kabalistic influences all competed for people's attention. Eventually a certain order returned, and the rise of East European Hasidism was the product of that new order.

The central figure of this movement was a man named Israel ben Eliezer, who became known as Baal Shem Tov ("master of the good name" or "good master of the name"). He was affectionately referred to as the Besht. He was born in Poland in 1700. His youth and early adulthood were characterized by professional failure, since all he wanted to do was meditate in nature. But as he pursued his true calling as a miracle worker and link to God, he gained a large following among the Jews of eastern European countries.

At the heart of Baal Shem Tov's teaching was a new optimism. He claimed that God is not found in studying and obeying the law. Rather, God is found inside the person and is manifested through singing and dancing. Instead of pursuing old forms at all costs, Judaism should pursue the joyful expression of God in its midst. The Besht allowed up-to-date cultural forms. Thus, for example, he traded the old medieval kaftan (a long robe) for the stylish black coat and black, fur-trimmed hat of the Polish gentleman.

This new teaching subsequently followed a path that many other religious renewal movements have trod. Almost immediately the movement became stuck in the new outward forms. (Compare, for example, what happened with the Besht's contemporaries, the Amish.) The Hasidim traded in one set of obligatory cultural forms for an even more rigid code governing dress and other external aspects of life. Today Hasidism has become identified with a reactionary approach to Judaism, in complete opposition to Baal Shem Tov's original intentions. In dress and lifestyle, Hasidic Jews cling to eighteenth-century forms.

Even though the Besht did not regard the law as the doorway to God, he did not counsel antinomianism. Hasidism was (and still is) an Orthodox movement, and Hasidic Jews keep all of the Talmudic requirements. The popular press frequently refers to the Hasidim as ultra-Orthodox or fundamentalist. Calling them ultra-Orthodox is literally nonsense, since there cannot be degrees of orthodoxy; either you are orthodox or you are not. Referring to them as fundamentalist aligns Hasidism with fundamentalist Christianity, which is also problematic, since Hasidism has no "fundamentals" that correspond to the ones held by the Christian fundamentalist movement.

Shortly after the Besht's death, the Hasidic movement organized itself into various local communities named after villages. For example, the Lubavitcher movement was named after the Russian town of Lubavitch. At the center of each community was the rebbe, or zaddik, who was believed to have supernatural mystical powers. Since the zaddiks were able to effect miracle cures and predict the future, their communities gave them unconditional obedience.

Intense persecution drove many Hasidic groups to America and Israel, where they set up their communities as closely as possible to the original pattern. Most Hasidim who remained in Europe were exterminated by the Nazis. Some initially objected to the formation of modern Israel because it represented the restoration of the kingdom of God without the Messiah, but they have since accepted the state of Israel as an accomplished fact.

Reform Judaism

Reform Judaism also arose in the eighteenth century. Reform Judaism accepted western European cultural and intellectual fashions. Scholars recognize Moses Mendelssohn as the pioneer of this movement. He studied at the University of Berlin, abandoned outward Jewish forms and became an intellectual writer whose German works enjoyed broad popularity among German intellectuals. Mendelssohn came to symbolize a new approach to Judaism, one in which Jews saw themselves as being free to become part of the culture in which they lived.

This new movement spread quickly throughout the Western world, including Germany, France, England and the United States. For example, a Reform temple was founded in Charleston, South Carolina, early in the nineteenth century.[17]

Main characteristics of the Reform movement. Most fundamentally, the Reform movement does not see traditional forms as authoritative. Thus, for example, the Talmud is not considered the standard of Judaism. Following Orthodox practice is not considered wrong; it is just not binding. Religious practice is understood as being in a state of continuous development.

Reform Judaism is not looking for a messiah. If a messianic office exists, it is fulfilled by the people as a whole, who are working to make this a better world (and are, in this sense, "redeeming" the world).

Reform Judaism initially opposed the creation of a separate homeland for Jews, maintaining that Jews should be at home in their country of birth. In the wake of the Holocaust, however, Reform Jews became ardent supporters of the state of Israel.

Reform Jews refer to their meeting places as temples, having given up any expectation of a restored temple in Jerusalem. Reform worship services were deliberately modeled on Christian Protestant forms. Men and women sit together and participate in a liturgy that is mostly in the vernacular. (Recently some American congregations have started including more Hebrew in their services.) Services include congregational singing accompanied by organ music and an informational sermon. The temple in Charleston contains kneeling benches, even though kneeling is never a part of Jewish worship, as it is in the nearby Anglican church.

In terms of theological and social issues of the day, the Reform movement has generally been in the vanguard of modern liberalism. Reform theology accepts biblical criticism. Reform congregations are usually active in promoting political positions on the side of minority empowerment and social concern. For instance, the Reform congregation in Indianapolis supports abortions rights groups and a center that cares for AIDS patients.

Conservative Judaism

The Conservative movement was born out of the work of Zecharias Frankel in nineteenth-century Germany. If Orthodox Judaism is characterized by adhering to the law and Reform Judaism by accommodating contemporary culture, then Conservative Judaism is characterized by adhering to the law while adapting to contemporary culture. It attempts to maintain the basics of Jewish law (dietary laws, prayer, morality) while permitting more contemporary forms of dress and worship. For example, men and women sit together and most of the worship service is in the vernacular. Conservative Judaism has flourished in the United States. In smaller communities that can support only one synagogue, a Conservative congregation can meet the needs of Orthodox, Conservative and Reform members.

Reconstructionist Judaism was the innovation of an American rabbi, Mordecai Kaplan, in 1934. This small movement attempts to integrate religious Judaism into all aspects of Jewish life by viewing Jewish religion as a facet in the evolution of total Jewish culture. Of the four main branches of Judaism in the United States today, it is by far the smallest, possibly because of the abstract nature of its mission.

Reform	Orthodox	Conservative	Total
1,300,000	1,000,000	2,000,000	4,300,000
30%	23%	47%	100%

Table 2.1. **Membership figures for the three main branches of Judaism**[18]

Other Jewish Groups

Yemenite Jews existed in isolation in the southern part of the Arabian peninsula for many years, and they have preserved many of their own customs and culture. They dress in blue-and-white stripes, and most of them are short (allegedly because their Muslim overlords would not tolerate any non-Muslims who were taller than they were, and so they killed all tall Jews). They experienced a drastic initiation into modern technological society when they were transported en masse to Israel in the late 1940s.[19]

Karaite Jews rejected the Talmud back in the eighth century, when a remnant of Jews still existed in Babylon. They claimed that the only valid authority in Judaism was the Torah and thus denied the legacy of rabbinic interpretation. Karaite Judaism has persisted as a tiny movement into the present. Its headquarters are located in the Jewish quarter of the old city of Jerusalem.

Falasha Jews lived in a small community deep in Ethiopia, believing that they were the only Jews in the world. Cut off from the world at large, they had never heard of the worldwide Jewish community or Talmudic orthodoxy. They lived according to traditions that they had preserved from the earliest times of the second commonwealth. The world heard of the Falashas during the 1980s, when the government of Israel employed a massive airlift to rescue them from the Ethiopian famine.

Orthodox Judaism

All forms of Judaism (including the liberalizing movements) are ultimately variations on the theme of rabbinic orthodoxy. Let us look at Orthodox Judaism in more detail, remembering that just as the Talmud consistently reproduces dissenting opinions, so most issues in Judaism are still intensely debated.

At the heart of Judaism is belief in one God. God chose the Jews to be his covenant people. Being the chosen people includes the privilege of being particularly loved by God, but it also carries the responsibility of living up to that choice. God has provided the law so that his people can demonstrate to the world that living according to God's standards is possible and is beneficial. Gentiles are not obligated to follow the specifics of the law, but they must abide by certain basic directives, such as respect for life and truth.

Dress. Orthodox Jews dress in regular street clothes, to which they add a few things. The long black coats, white shirts and large hats often associated with the Orthodox are actually worn by the Hasidim. Additional garments that the Orthodox must wear include fringes, sidecurls and headcovering for both sexes.

As a reminder of God's commandments, the children of Israel were instructed to make fringes on their garments (Num 15:38, 39). This instruction has been incorporated into a special shirtlike garment worn under the shirt with the tassels hanging over the belt.

Leviticus 19:27 forbids cutting off the hair that grows on the sides of the head. Consequently, Orthodox Jewish men let a curl of hair grow in front of the ear. It falls down like a long sideburn, but it is not part of the beard hair.

An observant Jewish man always keeps his head covered. When he is not wearing a hat (or sometimes even under the hat), he wears a small skullcap called a yarmulke (Yiddish) or a kippah (Hebrew). A kippah can be either plain or ornate and frequently is matched to the rest of a man's wardrobe. A child may be seen wearing a kippah with popular cartoon characters embroidered into it.

Homes. A home may be identified as Jewish by the mezuzah, a small object installed on the doorpost of each room, the top always tilted slightly toward the room. It contains a small copy of Deuteronomy 6:4, 9, part of which is referred to as the Shema, "Hear, O Israel: The LORD our God, the LORD is one." Anyone entering or leaving the room greets the mezuzah by touching it and then kissing his or her fingers.

Diet. Dietary restrictions, the laws of kosher, play an important role in Jewish life. They are based on rules contained in Leviticus, along with a number of extrapolations. In this discussion we will look at some broad rules. In daily life many of these distinctions are defined more finely.

Leviticus divides the animal kingdom into clean and unclean animals. Among land animals, those that are clean have split hoofs and chew cud (ruminants), including cows, goats, sheep and not much else. Pigs, horses, dogs, cats, reptiles and invertebrates are all unclean. There are no specific rules in Leviticus for birds, but a list of excluded birds consists almost entirely of predators. Consequently, the list of allowable fowl does not go much beyond chickens, ducks and geese. Allowable aquatic animals must

have scales. Thus most common kinds of fish are permitted; shellfish and crustaceans are excluded. Plants are considered neutral (so, incidentally, are eggs). There are no basic restrictions on vegetable products.

An animal must be killed quickly, and all blood must be drained immediately. In order to do this, the animal carcass is frequently immersed in salt for a period of time.

The Torah (for example, Ex 23:19) warns against boiling a kid (baby goat) in its mother's milk. In rabbinic interpretation this injunction has led to avoiding consuming dairy products and meat products in a single meal. In fact, an Orthodox home has two sets of dishes and utensils—one for meat foods and one for dairy foods. Informal practice allows a person who has eaten a milk-based meal (for example, a cheese sand-

Opened Torah scroll.

wich) to consume a meat product in about an hour; but someone who has had a meat meal (for example, a hamburger) must wait until the next regular mealtime to consume any milk products.

In contemporary America it is not as difficult as it used to be to keep kosher. Approved food items are usually marked with a *U* or a *K*, frequently enclosed with a circle. The marks have the same meaning. Which mark the food item bears depends on the rabbinical group that issued it. Some products are marked *pareve,* which means that they are neutral and can be taken with either milk or meat. Kosher foods tend to be healthy because they are pure and have fewer additives than other foods. To a Jew who has been raised in Orthodoxy, eating pork or a meat-milk dish such as a cheeseburger is as revolting as eating dogs or flies. "We're not a religious kibbutz," a lady told me in Israel, "but we keep the dietary rules."

Prayer. Orthodox Jewish men pray three times a day (morning, noon, evening). If possible, they face in the direction of Jerusalem. Proper prayer on normal days begins with putting on the tallit, a large, fringed, blue-and-white prayer shawl, which is wrapped around the person's head or shoulders (depending on the tradition to which one belongs). Then the person puts on the phylacteries (English) or tefillin (Hebrew). This practice is based on the biblical injunction to bind the words of the law on the forehead and on the hand (Deut 6:8). A tefillin is a little black box containing four Scripture passages.[20] It is tied on the head with a leather strap and on the left hand with leather straps that are wrapped around the arm seven times and around the finger three times. On the sabbath the tallit is worn, but the tefillin are not. The prayer that is said at the regular prayer time is called the Amidah and consists of a series of blessings of God that is based on Scripture. As they pray, Orthodox men typically go through rhythmic bowing or swaying, symbolizing reverence as well as (possibly) moving between the two centers of attention: the Torah and the world.

Prayer for women is less formal, and they do not use tefillin. The traditional prayers are focused on women's traditional sphere in the home. Reform Judaism allows for full participation by women and dispenses with the traditional three prayers for men.

Synagogues. The synagogue is a house of worship, and much more. For Jews in the dispersion, the synagogue has become the center of the Jewish community. It is a house of prayer, study, education, social life and the arts (within the tradition's restrictions). The synagogue's sanctuary usually contains the ark, the bema and a menorah. Orthodox synagogues include a separate worship area for women.

The ark is a niche or a cabinet in which the Torah scrolls are kept. You will find it at the front of the room; the congregation usually faces it. The bema is a raised platform on which the service is conducted. It may be at the front of the room, but in many traditional synagogues it is in the center. The menorah is a the seven-branched candelabra that is lit at the beginning of the service. The menorah, more than anything else, has come to symbolize the Jewish religion.

The cantor plays an important role in synagogue worship. The cantor is the song leader, but his or her responsibilities extend beyond that. The cantor must be an expert on the music of his or her tradition, since the cantor plays the central role in special services such as funerals and weddings. In some ways it is the cantor more than the rabbi who brings the congregation together in worship. Women rabbis and cantors may be employed by Conservative and Reform congregations.

Special Days

The life cycle. Chapter one identified four nearly universal rites of passage: birth, puberty, marriage and death. Judaism takes all four of the basic rites seriously.

When a male baby is eight days old, he is circumcised, and infants of both sexes are officially endowed with their names. In contemporary American Judaism (for example, Reform), a child may receive a secular name such as Harry or Joanne and a Jewish name, perhaps Reuben or Sarah.

Traditionally, a boy becomes bar mitzvah (literally, "a son of the commandment") at thirteen years of age. The rite signifies that he is now accountable for keeping the law. A bar mitzvah celebration is big. The boy so recognized leads the blessing of the service, complete with the initial sip of wine, and reads aloud a passage of the Torah in Hebrew—which is to say the ancient form of the language that leaves out punctuation and vowel marks. Reform and some Conservative congregations also practice *bat* mitzvah for girls of that age, who thus become "daughters of the commandment."

Because the nuclear family plays a crucial role in Jewish culture and religion, weddings are very important. Bride and groom stand under a canopy. The wedding ceremony ends with the groom's crushing a glass under his foot. This act is a good example of a ritual looking for its explanation. The view held most widely is that the crushing of the glass is a sober reminder of the destruction of Jerusalem. Others say that its original purpose was to dispel demons from the new home or to bring good luck in some way. Despite the uncertainty regarding its meaning, the ritual is not likely to be abandoned.

In Jewish culture there is typically a very short waiting time between a death and the funeral (at most a day or two). Burial services include a reading from the Psalms. This practice expresses hope in a future resurrection.

The sabbath. The Fourth Commandment is particularly dear to the heart of Jewish people: "Remember the sabbath day by keeping it holy." An old proverb states, "It is not so much that the Jews have kept the sabbath as that the sabbath has kept the Jews." Feelings of chosenness and uniqueness are epitomized in this practice.

The sabbath begins with sunset on Friday evening. At dusk, the woman of the house lights the candles on the dinner table (one for each member of the household) and says a prayer with her face covered. Then the whole family gathers for its sabbath meal. Special attention is paid to the blessing of the wine and a loaf of braided bread that is eaten only on the sabbath.

Most synagogues hold a Friday-evening service and a Saturday-morning service. In Reform temples the Friday-night service is considered the main one. In Orthodox synagogues the Friday-evening service welcomes the sabbath, but the Saturday-morning prayer service is considered central. Ideally, the rest of Saturday is spent in family relaxation. The restrictions on work of any kind are supposed to make the day a time of rest. Orthodox families do not light fires of any kind (which by implication includes switching a light off or on or smoking a cigarette), answer the telephone, cook or go for a drive in an automobile (thus Orthodox families live in close proximity to each other and to their synagogue).

The sabbath ends at sunset on Saturday with a beautiful ceremony called havdalah, the official farewell to sabbath. In this ceremony a spice jar is passed around, a braided candle is lit, and everyone prays for the coming of Elijah. In modern Israel, Saturday night is a time when the towns come to life. Restaurants and shops open, and people throng the streets to enjoy a good time of socializing.

Rosh Hashanah. The Jewish New Year occurs in September or October, depending on how the Jewish calendar aligns with the secular one in any given year. The Jewish calendar is counted from a traditional year of creation; thus the year A.D. 1998 is 5758 in the Jewish tradition. The first month is Tishri, and the first day of the month is Rosh Hashanah. This day is considered a time of reflection and repentance. It is the first of ten days that are known as the Days of Awe. On Rosh Hashanah the congregation comes together for a lengthy service, the center of which is the blowing of the ram's horn, the shofar.

Yom Kippur. The tenth day of Tishri is Yom Kippur, the Day of Atonement. During the biblical period this was the day on which the high priest offered the annual sacrifice for sin: a bull on behalf of himself, a goat on behalf of the congregation and a goat that was sent into the wilderness symbolically carrying away the sins of the people. In rabbinic Judaism, Yom Kippur has become a day of personal repentance. In addition to the usual sabbath restrictions, Jews must abstain from eating, drinking, washing, wearing leather and engaging in marital relations. On this day synagogues of all branches are filled to overflowing for lengthy (possibly all-day) services.

Sukkoth. Five days after Yom Kippur is the Feast of Booths, called Sukkoth. This feast was established in the Torah to commemorate Israel's wandering in the wilderness. For a week everyone was to live in a temporary shelter for the purpose of remembering God's guidance and protection. Nowadays the practice is to build a booth with a frame of poles to which are added at least three walls and a roof made of leaves and straw. During the seven days of the festival, families eat their meals in their booths.

Simchat Torah. Directly after Sukkoth comes the day of the celebration of the Torah, Simchat Torah. In synagogues the entire Torah is read in the course of a year, and on this day the cycle is completed with the last few verses of Deuteronomy and the first few verses of Genesis. The congregation takes all its Torah scrolls (usually two to five) out of the ark and carries them around the synagogue seven times in a joyful procession. As many men as possible take turns holding the scrolls, kissing them and dancing with them. After all, they contain the revelation from God, the Father. Some rabbis have even said that a little inebriation is obligatory on Simchat Torah, just as it is at other joyous events. Simchat Torah completes the cluster of holidays that fall in early autumn.

Hanukkah. Falling sometime in December is the festival commemorating the purification of the temple by the Maccabees. In 166 B.C. Judas Maccabee and his brothers rebelled against the Seleucid overlords and established the Hasmonean kingdom. One of the first things they had to do was cleanse the temple, which had been defiled by Antiochus (who sacrificed a pig to Zeus on the altar). According to the legend, the priests had enough oil for only one day, although the ceremony was supposed to last eight days. However, the oil miraculously lasted for the full eight days. Thus the Hanukkah celebration is a kind of reenactment of this ceremony. It centers on the hanukiah, a special nine-branched candelabra (not to be confused with the usual seven-branched menorah). One branch and its candle is the "master." On each successive day one more candle is lit until all nine candles (one for each day plus the master) are burning brightly. Hanukkah is a time of family togetherness and fun. Observant Jews rightfully bristle at the common conception that Hanukkah is the "Jewish Christmas." Nevertheless, in the Western world many Jewish families whose children live side by side with Gentile children have adapted their Hanukkah celebration to more Gentile Christmas patterns, particularly with regard to exchanging gifts.

Purim. In February or March, Jews celebrate the festival of Purim. According to the Bible, Purim was instituted as a celebration of the events recorded in the book of Esther. Queen Esther was used by God to intercede successfully on behalf of the Jewish people, who had been scheduled for mass extermination by the Persians. The name Purim, which means "lots," is derived from the idea that the date of the genocide had been determined by the casting of lots. Purim tends to be celebrated as a social, cultural event with much music and dancing. It includes a public reading of the book of Esther.

Passover. Passover is a celebration lasting seven or eight days, depending on the specific tradition. In its biblical origins it commemorated God's protecting his people from the last plague on Egypt (the death of all firstborn sons), which led to the exodus. The Passover observance included three major components: the unleavened bread, the Passover lamb and the retelling of the story. Other practices included eating bitter herbs and taking formal sips of wine. Because sacrifices ceased in the second commonwealth, the sacrificial lamb is no longer a part of the celebration.

On the day before the celebration, all leaven and all foods containing leaven are removed from the house. On the first night the whole family gathers for the Seder, a formal meal that includes obligatory components and recitations. A typical Seder includes the following elements:[21]

☐ lighting the candles

☐ first cup of wine (cup of blessing)

☐ washing of the hands

☐ eating of the greens (parsley dipped in salt water)

☐ breaking of the unleavened bread (three matzahs—unleavened wafers—are placed in a container called a "unity;" the middle one [afikomen] is lifted up and broken; later on, everyone has a piece of it)

☐ the second cup of wine (cup of plagues—probably the one mentioned in Lk 22:17, 18)

☐ washing of the hands

☐ eating bitter herbs (horseradish)

☐ eating bitter herbs and charoseth (a delicious mixture of apple chunks, nuts and

grape juice; children look forward to this part, particularly after the horseradish)
□ the actual supper (no lamb)
□ hiding and finding a part of the afikomen (the broken middle matzah; the child who finds it wins a coin)
□ eating of the afikomen (of which Jesus said, "This is my body")
□ the third cup of wine (cup of redemption, of which Jesus said, "This is my blood")
□ opening the door for Elijah (a place setting has been left for him)
□ the fourth cup of wine (cup of praise)
□ conclusion with everyone reciting "next year in Jerusalem!" and singing a song.
Shavuot (Pentecost). The Hebrew name means "weeks" and the Greek-derived name means "fifty." The point is that this festival occurs fifty days (seven weeks) after Passover, the period between the original Passover and the giving of the law at Sinai. Thus this holiday commemorates the giving of the commandments. But it is also a harvest festival, celebrating the first harvest of the year. Shavuot is the third of the three pilgrimage festivals that the ancient Israelites were to celebrate in Jerusalem (the other two being Passover and Sukkoth).

Various Jewish groups observe additional minor holidays, Israeli national days and regional celebrations. Recently Jews the world over have designated April 19 (the day of the Warsaw uprising) as Holocaust Remembrance Day.

The State of Israel: A Third Commonwealth?

During the nineteenth century, Jewish families began to migrate to Palestine, their ancient homeland, which at the time was under Turkish rule. This early movement toward resettlement received impetus under Theodor Herzl, an Austrian Jew who coined the term *Zionism* and founded the World Zionist Organization. In 1895, while working as a newspaper correspondent in Paris, Herzl observed anti-Semitism at work in the Dreyfus trial (Dreyfus, a Jewish army officer, had been falsely accused of treason). It occurred to him that Jews would never be free from persecution as long as they existed as a minority group in non-Jewish countries. They needed a homeland of their own. Herzl suggested Uganda, Argentina and Palestine as potential Jewish homelands, but most Jews favored Palestine.

Jewish leaders in Palestine such as David Ben Gurion and Golda Meir were not primarily motivated by religious considerations. They intended to found a secular, socialist state. Nevertheless, many religious Jews supported them, including some (though not all) Hasidic groups. In 1917 the British took over Palestine from the Turks and officially gave the Jews permission to work toward a homeland (the Balfour Declaration). Under the stability of British rule many Jews (but also many Arabs) emigrated to Palestine. Inevitably, serious conflict between Jews and Arabs developed (for example, the Hebron massacre of 1929, in which sixty-seven Jews were slaughtered and many more injured).

World War II, a dark spot in the history of humanity in its own right, saw additionally the Holocaust, the extermination of six million Jews in Nazi death camps. In response to the atrocities, world opinion moved toward favoring the establishment of a Jewish state. When the British pulled out of Palestine in 1948, the state of Israel was established with the overwhelming sanction of the United Nations.[22]

The scope of this book does not permit telling the tumultuous story of the first fifty years of Israel's existence as an independent state. It has become clear that Herzl's dream of a truly secure existence for Jews in their homeland remains unrealized. Israel's legitimate needs and claims must be balanced against the legitimate needs and claims of Palestinian Arabs. It is hard to predict what long-term solutions to Israel's problems will be found, but one thing is certain: all simplistic solutions are bound to be wrong.

The face of Judaism has changed drastically with the reestablishment of the nation of Israel and has changed even more with the recapture of Jerusalem in 1967. Even without a temple in Jerusalem (although some radical fringe groups would like to rebuild the temple, the issue remains a hot potato for most Jews), Judaism again has a geographic center and a political identity. From 1948 on, the fate of Judaism has been

Mezuzah, apparently mismounted at first and then remounted at the required angle.

inextricably linked with a political unit that occupies a piece of land. The Passover slogan, "Next year in Jerusalem!" has become a reality. Consequently, it has been suggested that we are now in the beginning phase of a third Jewish commonwealth.

The Indeterminate Variable: Secular Judaism

"We are atheists, but we keep the holidays," a man told me on a kibbutz. Western Christians, particularly in a conservative or an evangelical context, tend to distinguish culture from religion. A person may be reared in a Christian home and may follow traditional Christian practices but is not considered a Christian until he or she makes a personal commitment to Christ. In Judaism there is no such dichotomy. Anyone who is born to a Jewish woman is recognized as being Jewish. Cultural and religious practices develop one's Jewish identity. Thus it is possible (indeed, necessary) to speak of "secular Jews," whereas "secular Christians" would be an oxymoron.[23]

Many Jews are not religious, but they affirm their identity as Jews, follow Jewish traditions and contribute generously to the Jewish community. It is essential to recognize that on the whole the relationship between the religious and the secular worlds of Judaism is seen as complementary, not antagonistic. Synagogues may support nonreligious political and charitable organizations, and nonobservant Jews may honor their heritage by supporting religious concerns.

■ *So You Meet a Jew . . .*
What You Might Expect
Misunderstanding and slander have long characterized relationships between Christians and Jews. Forget the stereotypes; they are false. Chances are that the Jews you meet are as much a part of your American (or British, Australian or Canadian) culture as you are. At least since the eighteenth century, Judaism in the West has integrated itself into Western culture. There seems to be an unwritten rule in the West nowadays that religion is a private, personal matter that ought to be kept out of casual contacts as much as possible, and many Jews abide by that rule as much as Christians do. Reform and secular Jews in particular seek to blend in with secular society and would be offended if a casual acquaintance called attention to their heritage or religion.[24]

Of course, Jews who abide by Talmudic laws distinguish themselves conspicuously from secular society in many ways. First, observant Jews keep kosher. This practice involves separating milk and meat meals and dishes, eating only pure, certified foods, maintaining the correct time lapses between milk and meat meals and avoiding all contamination in general. It is perfectly all right for a Gentile to share a kosher meal with a Jew, but the Gentile has to respect its kosher status and not do anything that would offend it.

Observant Jews keep the sabbath. Sabbath restrictions forbid talking on the telephone, turning on electric lights and driving cars. Gentiles need to be aware of these restrictions and need to avoid putting obstacles in the way of sabbath observance. For example, they should not be offended if even an important phone call is not returned.

Observant Jews keep the holidays. Of particular importance are Rosh Hashanah and Yom Kippur. Less observant Jews also wish to have these days off from school or work to attend services. Gentiles do well to abstain from facile comparisons of Christmas and Hanukkah.

Observant Jews wear required articles of clothing. Keep in mind that these items are seen as signs of devotion to God, not as indicators of holiness or spirituality.

If there is any one concept that might be applicable to most Jewish people you are likely to encounter, from Hasidim to secular Jews, it is the notion of "heritage." Being Jewish involves being endowed with a heritage, both culturally and religiously, that is different from the heritage of Gentiles. Being Jewish is (usually) not a choice, but a tradition into which one is born. All Jews are responsible to pass this tradition on to future generations.

Throughout history the Jewish people have suffered persecution for their heritage. Even the most thoroughly assimilated Jews have been betrayed by their neighbors and have found themselves victims of oppression. Thus even highly secularized Jews esteem their heritage as having been paid for with the blood and pain of their forefathers. Even Jews who do not practice the Talmudic obligations cherish their legacy.

Relating the Gospel

Many evangelical Christians tend to think that they understand Judaism because they know the Old Testament, but that may be a misconception. Many Christians look at Jews as deficient Christians, and such an attitude can only lead to misunderstandings. Finally—and again this is a point that applies to all encounters with members of another religion—do not ask a Jew to defend what you may find unacceptable in Judaism. Would you want to take personal responsibility for the crusades or for what some televangelist may have said about the doctrine of the Trinity? Similarly, it is not fair to expect someone to shoulder responsibility for everything an outsider may associate with his or her religion. In short, don't expect a Jew (other than perhaps a rabbi) to be able to defend some point of Talmudic law or some events in the Old Testament.

To repeat, modern Western Jews have been fully assimilated into modern Western society. Most of their concerns and activities are similar to your own. They like their religion, but they will manifest the same differing degrees of commitment to it as people everywhere. It is highly improbable that they are losing sleep worrying about the Messiah or the reestablishment of the temple in Jerusalem.

All attempts to evangelize Jews come under heavy suspicion. In the past, persecution and coerced conversion have gone hand in hand. Thus many Jewish people are offended by attempts at evangelism. They see a discussion of truth or falsehood in a religious context as an attempt to impugn the legitimacy of their culture and possibly even as a way of confirming the supposed inferiority of the Jewish people. These concerns will probably strike most Christians as excessively alarmist, but two thousand years of persecution, including the extermination of six million people in the Holocaust, are not easily forgotten.

Consequently, the Christian who is led to share the gospel with a Jew needs to make sure that his motives and attitudes are biblical. The apostle Paul said, "For I could wish that I myself were cursed and cut off from Christ for the sake of my brothers, those of my own race, the people of Israel" (Rom 9:3). This is an attitude of sacrificial love, not pride or arrogance. This attitude is a necessary prerequisite for all areas of evangelism, especially Jewish evangelism.

Jews need the Messiah. So do Hindus, Muslims, Buddhists, Baptists and Methodists. The reason for this need lies in our common sinful humanity, regardless of our religious upbringing. Nobody knows about Christ without being introduced to him (Rom 10:14). Some Christians react to Jews as though being Jewish entails knowing about Christ and deliberately rejecting him. But that is no more the case for Jewish people you meet than for anyone else. Jews need to know that they need a Messiah, and they need to know about Jesus, who is the Messiah. To convey that message requires a point of contact.

Because Judaism is as much a part of the Western world as Christianity, it is easy to find shared aspects of life (compared to, say, relating to someone in an Asian religion from a traditional Asian culture). For the most part, Jews and Christians share similar frustrations in life, and they tend to talk in pretty much the same terms. Christ is the solution to these life problems for Jews and Gentiles equally. Certainly there is a place for "Jewish evangelism" that zeroes in on particular aspects of Jewish culture. This is the practice of organizations such as Jews for Jesus. However, we need to keep uppermost in our minds that a Jewish person needs to find Jesus Christ as savior, not because the temple is gone and there are no more sacrifices but because he or she is a sinful human being who is alienated from God, a fact that has an impact on each person's interior life and relationships with others. Jews need Christ for exactly the same reasons that all other human beings need him. Pointing to Jesus' identity as the Jewish Messiah may be a helpful bridge to confirming Christ's role as savior. What is crucial is that the Jew finds salvation in Christ, which is offered to all, regardless of ethnic or religious background. But accepting Christ does not alter Jewish identity. Bernard B. Gair, past president of the Hebrew Christian Alliance of America, writes,

> When a Jew accepts the Messiah, Jesus, he is not less a Jew, but rather becomes a "completed" Jew, for he has found in his life and spirit the fulfillment of the promises made by God to our fathers. He becomes, together with all believers—Jew and Gentile—a redeemed son of God, a spiritual Israelite.[25]

Mastering the Material

When you have finished studying this chapter, you should be able to

1. avoid some basic misunderstandings Jews and Christians tend to have about each other;

2. make an outline of the events of the First and Second Jewish Commonwealths and describe how the religion developed during that era;

3. summarize the nature of the five first-century parties and explain how the events of A.D. 70 influenced their survival;

4. describe the development of the writings of rabbinic Judaism;

5. characterize the growth of Judaism in the Middle Ages with regard to physical survival, teaching and mysticism;

6. show how the Sabbatai Zevi affair was pivotal for the history of Judaism, both in terms of what led up to it and what followed it;

7. give a capsule description of each of the following branches of Judaism: Hasidism, Reform, Conservative, Reconstructionist, Orthodox, Yemenite, Karaite, Falasha, secular Judaism;

8. describe Orthodox practice in regard to dress, diet, homes and prayer;

9. list the distinctive features of a synagogue;

10. identify and give a capsule description of the special days in Judaism;

11. summarize the main events and issues concerning the founding of the modern state of Israel;

12. identify important concerns in encountering a Jewish person as a Christian.

Term Paper Ideas

1. Study the continuities and differences between the Judaism of the two commonwealths and later developments.

2. Describe the teachings of one rabbi or one school of rabbinic teaching in Judaism up to the development of the Talmud.

3. Trace a particular teaching of the law from its first biblical mention through its development in the Mishnah and the Talmud and in subsequent practices, for example, with regard to the sabbath, dietary laws, social regulations and so on. What adaptations have been made in the twentieth century?

4. Summarize the teachings and unique characteristics of a central figure in the history of Judaism. This can be a person out of the Halakic or the mystical tradition or someone who made a significant contribution in more recent times.

5. Choose one particular holiday and trace its development, unique practices associated with it, symbolism associated with it and any differing interpretations of its meaning. (Be warned, by the way, that in the library you will come across some interpreters who insist that every single Jewish holiday is in some way derived from a harvest/fertility celebration.)

6. Make an extensive list of more specific kosher regulations and compile an inventory of acceptable and unacceptable brands of food in contemporary supermarkets.

7. Visit one or more Jewish worship services, and compare and contrast their features with Christian services, as well as with services in other Jewish traditions.

8. Trace the role and status of women in Judaism. It hardly needs excessive belaboring to realize that in many Orthodox, let alone Hasidic, traditions women's status is not up to current expectations in the Western secular world. Instead, you might want to concentrate on the unique contribution women have made, even in those traditions, to the ongoing life of Judaism.

9. Do an in-depth study of a cultural contribution that came out of the Holocaust, for example, the work of an author, an artist or a particular school of thought.

10. Use research or interviews with Christians working in Jewish evangelism to write up a strategy for this kind of outreach.

Core Bibliography

Ben-Sasson, H. H. *A History of the Jewish People*. Cambridge, Mass.: Harvard University Press, 1976.

Danby, Herbert, trans. *The Mishnah*. Oxford, U.K.: Oxford University Press, 1933.

Encyclopaedia Judaica. 16 vols. New York: Macmillan, 1972.

Epstein, I., ed. *The Babylonian Talmud*. London: Soncino, 1935.

Fishbane, Michael. *Judaism: Revelation and Traditions*. San Francisco: Harper & Row, 1987.

Jewish Encyclopedia. 12 vols. New York: Funk and Wagnalls, 1925.

Scholem, Gershom G. *Major Trends in Jewish Mysticism*. New York: Schocken, 1946.

Trepp, Leo. *Judaism*. Belmont, Calif.: Wadsworth, 1982.

Chapter 3

Islam

Estimated Membership
Worldwide: 1,099,634,000
United States: 5,100,000

How can a religion completely focus on one man but not focus on that man at all? By being Islam. Everything in this religion is based on Muhammad's life and teaching, and yet Muhammad is not at all the center of worship and devotion.

How can a religion be both a religion and a political system? Again, by being Islam. True Islam functions within a community (the umma) that optimally carries its own political identity.

How can a religion espouse the highest monotheistic and ethical ideals while many of its adherents live in a state close to animism? Yet again, by being Islam. Every religion has to contend with a gap between its official teaching and what people practice in its "folk religion" version. Such a gap also exists in the world of Islam, to the dismay of many Islamic teachers.

How can a religion establish itself around the world and yet remain closely tied to one particular culture? One more time, by being Islam. It is making inroads into societies around the world, both Third World countries and Western industrialized societies. At the same time it still very much belongs to its original Arabic desert world.

Islam can be a paradoxical religion. Describing it requires that we constantly ask, Who speaks authoritatively? For example, even as the leader of an Islamic republic issues a decree in the name of the Qur'an that all women must wear the veil, an Islamic evangelist tells a group of American students that the veil is not mandated by the Qur'an and that only in Islam are women truly liberated. While the same Muslim apologist is insisting that the Qur'an forbids violence, the terrorist group Islamic Jihad may be bombing a building, killing innocent people. These observations are not meant to condemn Islam for failings that can ultimately be exposed in every religion. But there are ambiguities about Islam, which any study of Islam must take into account. In our attempt to understand Islam and all its complexity, we will begin with its beginnings.

The Life and Times of Muhammad

Muhammad was born in A.D. 570 in the vicinity of Mecca (see map 3.1). The indigenous Arabian religion of the time was a mixture of polytheism and animism. Mecca was a center of this religion and the focal point of pilgrims visiting its many idols and shrines. The first thing that greeted a pilgrim entering Mecca was a statue of God's (Allah's) three sensuous-appearing daughters (al-Lat, al-Manat and al-Uzza). A highlight of any visit to Mecca was a cube-shaped shrine (called the ka'ba, which means "cube") dedicated to the main god of this shrine, Hubal. Built into the side of the ka'ba was a meteorite that was considered holy because it had fallen from heaven. There were many other temples and holy sites, including the sacred well, Zamzam. Religious pilgrimages made Mecca a prosperous city.

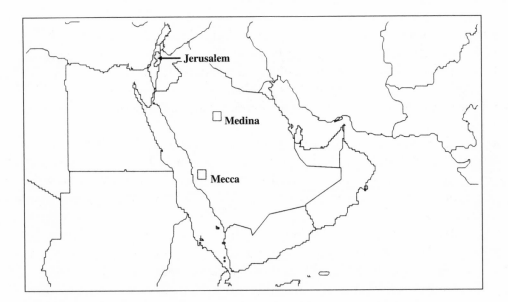

Map 3.1. The Arabian peninsula

(Religion can be a particularly gainful enterprise because it requires relatively little investment, and the merchandise [spiritual blessing] is an easily renewable resource.)

Until modern sea routes were opened by fifteenth- and sixteenth-century explorers, the Arabian peninsula was a significant thoroughfare for commerce, and so it was in Muhammad's day. Arabia has never existed as an isolated desert area out of contact with the rest of the world. In Muhammad's day Arabia was the site of extensive crosscultural interaction. There were Jewish, Christian and Zoroastrian merchants, as well as settlements of those groups, particularly in the northern part of the peninsula. In the city of Yathrib (Medina) dwelled a Jewish community numbering in the hundreds, which professed a strict monotheism.

A strain of native monotheism had survived independently in Arabian culture. A minority of people, called the hanif, or "pious ones," devoted themselves exclusively to the worship of one God, Allah. We see here a remnant of the original monotheism that is the universal starting point for the history of all religions (see chapter one for a discussion of original monotheism).

Muhammad was born into this culture as a member of a minor clan of the Quraish tribe. Orphaned at an early age, Muhammad was raised by an uncle. There was little opportunity for schooling, and the illiterate Muhammad subsisted as a camel driver. Eventually Muhammad came into the employ of a wealthy widow, Khadija. In the style of a storybook romance, they fell in love and married. For many years Muhammad and Khadija were devoted to each other, and when Muhammad started to receive his visions, Khadija immediately supported him. Muhammad was now a wealthy merchant himself, and he came into increasing contact with the many adherents of monotheistic religions. This contact helped shape his own spiritual development. However, it is a mistake to interpret Islam as nothing more than an adaptation of Judaism, Christianity and Zoroastrianism. We must leave room for the vestige of original Arabian monotheism as well as for Muhammad's own creativity.[1]

The unique twists of Muhammad's spiritual experience began in A.D. 610, while he was meditating in a cave located on what is now called the Mount of Light, overlooking the plain of Arafat outside Mecca. As Muhammad fell into a trance, trembling and sweating, the angel Gabriel spoke to him. "Recite!" the angel proclaimed to him.[2] At this moment the brooding, introspective merchant turned into the stern prophet who refused to compromise his convictions and suffered for his steadfastness.[3]

Now began Muhammad's career as a prophet in Mecca. His message encompassed two main points: (1) there is only one God to whose will people must submit, and (2) there will be a day of judgment when all people will be judged in terms of whether or not they have obeyed God. Converts were slow in coming at first. Khadija believed Muhammad immediately, but others were skeptical at best. Many people were hostile or derisive. Muhammad's revelatory experiences continued, as they would throughout his life, not on a regular basis but from time to time as the occasion demanded. Eventually Muhammad gained a small group of followers, and after about ten years the group had become fairly sizable, numbering in the thousands.

Muhammad's followers referred to their belief as Islam, which means "submission to God." They came to be identified as Muslims, "those who submit to God." These terms are still the correct designations. Muslims consider the term Muhammadanism and its variations offensive because it implies to them that they worship Muhammad, which they certainly do not.

Eventually Muhammad's group of followers grew so large that the city fathers in Mecca found their presence undesirable. After all, nothing ruins the business of idol worship like the incessant claim that there is only one God. Persecution escalated until in A.D. 622 Muhammad and a group of his followers fled Mecca for Yathrib.

This flight from Mecca is called the hijra (meaning "flight"), and it is used as the beginning of the Islamic calendar, for at this point an independent Muslim community, the umma, was born. Islamic dates are reckoned A.H., "anno hegirae." Thus 1998 is the year A.H. 1418.[4] Khadija had died by this time, and Muhammad found solace with a number of new wives.

Muhammad and his followers moved to Yathrib, and there they were received with open arms; in fact, Muhammad was put in charge of the town with the responsibility of resolving certain disputes. He made a special pact with the Jewish community in Yathrib, recognizing that Jews were not expected to become Muslims. Unfortunately, the relationship broke down when some Jews attempted to assassinate Muhammad, and he ordered the execution of hundreds of Jews.

Throughout this time Islam continued to grow in numbers and influence. Many Arabian tribes swore allegiance to Muhammad, adopting his religion and his leadership. Eventually he and his army became strong enough to capture Mecca. Muhammad removed all idols from the city and cleansed the ka'ba of all statues in a special ceremony. However, he retained Mecca as the center for pilgrimage and maintained some of the external sites, such as the ka'ba and the well Zamzam, as holy places. By the time Muhammad died in A.D. 632, he was the religious and political head of much of the Arabian peninsula.

The Caliphate and the Shi'a

An understanding of the events that occurred right after Muhammad's death is crucial to an understanding of the contemporary Muslim world. The report of Muhammad's demise was received by many with incredulity. Some people wanted to confer immediate divinity on him. It was Abu Bakr, Muhammad's father-in-law and close friend, who took charge and settled the issue. He appeared before the crowd and said, "If anyone worships Muhammad, Muhammad is dead; but if anyone worships Allah, he is alive and does not die," thereby assuring at least passing stability.

However, there was no escaping the pressing question of who would succeed Muhammad as leader of the political and religious community. The search was on for the caliph, the successor. Because Muhammad had no surviving son, the obvious choice was his son-in-law Ali, husband of Muhammad's favorite daughter, Fatima. Ali had distinguished himself in his devotion and enthusiasm for Muhammad's cause. Furthermore, Ali claimed that Muhammad had endowed him with his designation (*'ilm*) and spiritual knowledge (*nass*). Ali, like Muhammad, would be able to speak directly from God.

Unfortunately, Ali did not enjoy the confidence of many people. He was seen as hotheaded and unreliable. A general consensus (*sunna*) was established that Abu Bakr,

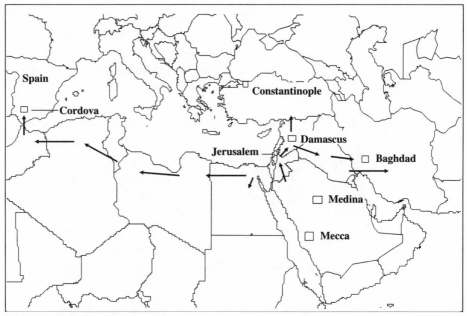

Map 3.2. Early Muslim expansion

Muhammad's father-in-law, would be the caliph. Ali's supporters were disgruntled, and at that moment the seeds of a dissenting party were sown. The Arabic word for this splinter group was *shi'a*, and thus we have the origins of Sunnites (the majority) and Shi'ites (the minority).

This process repeated itself two more times, as Abu Bakr was replaced by Umar in A.D. 634 and Umar was replaced by Uthman in 644. Uthman was the first of many caliphs from the tribe of the Umayyads. Each time Ali was bypassed. During this time the Islamic world grew rapidly, but internal tensions increased as well. None of the leaders after Abu Bakr ruled for long or died a natural death. Umar was poisoned and Uthman was stabbed to death.

Uthman did not enjoy a strong political base, but he made a major contribution to Islam prior to his death by collecting all of Muhammad's revelations and issuing the authoritative edition of the Qur'an. Muhammad himself did not write anything down. It was left to his followers to record his utterances on whatever material happened to be handy at the moment—a piece of parchment, a palm leaf, maybe even a piece of wood. Uthman brought together all of this material along with whatever compilations were already in circulation. He and his associates carefully sorted out all that was authentic and destroyed the rest. The resulting collection became the Qur'an, in the same form that we have today. Of course, there is now no way of reproducing what might have been committed to the flames by Uthman. Some Shi'ites claim that Uthman did some deliberate tampering because the present Qur'an is devoid of any references to Ali as Muhammad's designated successor or to Ali's immediate family.

When Uthman died in A.D. 656, Ali finally became caliph. However, his caliphate did not last long. Another Umayyad, Mu'awiyah, also laid claim to the caliphate. Hostilities increased to the point that armies were arrayed against each other. When Ali offered to allow for mediation at the last moment, some of his own followers killed him in disgust.

Sunni leadership, representing the overwhelming majority of Muslims, was passed down through the tribe of Umayyads for another hundred years. Their capital city was

Muslims at prayer in the mosque of the North American Islamic Center, Plainfield, Indiana.

Damascus, and the Islamic empire included all of the Middle East, extending through Persia (Iran) and encompassing Egypt, North Africa and Spain. In A.D. 750 the Umayyads were replaced by the Abbasids, named after Muhammad's uncle, who moved the capital to Baghdad. This dynasty eventually gave way to the Shi'ite Fatimid kingdom, which had become established in Egypt. The real political end of the Abbasids, however, came with the Seljuk Turks in the eleventh century. The Seljuks suffered the loss of Palestine during the crusades, but the crusader state was in turn defeated by Saladin and the Sunni Mamelukes, who carried the mantle of Islamic leadership for about two hundred years. After the Mamelukes were destroyed by the Mongols, the longest-running Islamic dynasty came into being by way of the Ottoman Turks. The Ottoman Empire, which at one time included all of the Middle East, Egypt and Europe up to the gates of Vienna, finally collapsed in 1917 under the double pressure of internal corruption and World War I.

While Sunni Muslims experienced a certain amount of stability under the Umayyads, the Shi'ite struggle was just beginning. With Ali's death a permanent split between Sunna and Shi'a was inevitable, but it was highly uncertain who was to carry the Shi'ite banner. Ali had two sons, Hasan and Husayn, who were also Muhammad's grandsons. Hasan, the older, abdicated his claim due to illness and died almost immediately thereafter (poison was suspected). In A.D. 680 Husayn rallied his troops to battle the Sunni Umayyads in the vicinity of the Iraqi town of Karbala, whose inhabitants had identified with his cause. But in a classical maneuver of desert warfare, the Sunnis managed to deprive the Shi'ites of water and then massacred them in their weakened condition. When Husayn's head was thrown over the city walls, his supporters picked it up, mounted it on a lance and carried it about in a procession of anguished mourning.

The day of Husayn's death (the tenth day of Muharram on the Islamic calendar) continues to be commemorated by Shi'ites, particularly in Iran. It is a day marked by universal mourning and reenactments of his martyrdom. Many people lash themselves with chains and knives to identify with Husayn's martyrdom, which they see to have been on their behalf. On this day Shi'ite mobs are easily moved to acts of revenge against all outsiders, since they consider virtually all non-Shi'ites a threat to their existence. For example, it was on this day—November 4, 1979—that the Shi'ite radicals in Teheran usurped the American embassy and took its personnel hostage.

Shi'ite belief centers on the idea that the special line of succession through Husayn continues. Each person in the succession receives the 'ilm, a direct designation of succession from his predecessor, and the nass, the supernatural spiritual knowledge to carry out the prophetic leadership. These successors are called imams, a term that carries different meanings in different contexts (for example, it is also the term for the prayer leader in a Sunni mosque). In the present context it refers to the spiritual and political leader of the Shi'ites. The imam's interpretation of the Qur'an is considered infallible. Sometimes this infallibility is seen as implying personal sinlessness as well.

Those who live by splits and divisiveness die by splits and divisiveness. The subsequent history of the Shi'a is one of continual strife and schism. There are three main Shi'ite groups as well as numerous smaller ones. The major ones are identified by their understanding of how many original imams there were and when they branched off. They include the Twelvers (Imamites), the Fivers (Zaidites) and the Seveners (Ismailites).

The Twelvers (Imamites) have come to the attention of Americans most frequently over the last twenty years. They make up the majority of the people of Iran and Iraq (the Iraqi leader Saddam Hussein, however, is a Sunni). The Twelvers are also strongly represented in Lebanon.[5]

The Twelvers are so called because they recognize twelve imams in the line of succession, counting Ali, Hasan, Husayn and nine others. The twelfth imam, Muhammad al-Muntazar, disappeared when he was only five years old. According to the tradition, he withdrew into a cave and continues to live in concealment. Some day he will return. Then he will be known as the Mahdi and will establish universal Islamic rule.

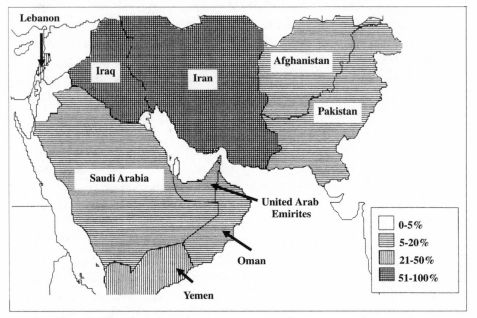

Map 3.3 Distribution of Shi'ites

Until the coming of the Mahdi, the place of the divinely designated imam is held by a caretaker who is also known as "imam." Americans who watched the news during the Iranian hostage crisis may remember that the followers of the Ayatollah Khomeini referred to him as "imam." There is a hierarchy under the imam that consists of a handful of other ayatollahs. Below the ayatollahs are many mullahs.[6] The imam's decisions in regard to any issue—religious, social or political—are considered binding.

The Fivers (Zaidites) make up a smaller body of Shi'ites that is located primarily in Yemen. They recognize a different fifth imam, named Zaid, through whom they continued a different line of succession for a time. He is also considered to be living in concealment for the time being. On the whole the Zaidites are less extreme than the other Shi'ite groups.

The Seveners (Ismailites) are the most radical theologically. They branched off with the seventh imam. Today they are found mainly in India, Pakistan and East Africa (the population of Kenya, for example, includes a large group of Indian people and consequently many centers of Indian religions). The Seveners believe that the true seventh imam was Ismail, the incarnation of Allah (a notion that is totally unacceptable to all other Muslims). Ismailites claim that it was Ismail who disappeared into concealment and will return as the Mahdi (although some say it was his son).

For a time the Ismailites held ascendancy over all of Islam. They ruled through the Fatimid dynasty (named after Muhammad's daughter Fatima) in Egypt from A.D. 909 to A.D. 1171. As mentioned earlier, they took over preeminence from the Abbasids, but

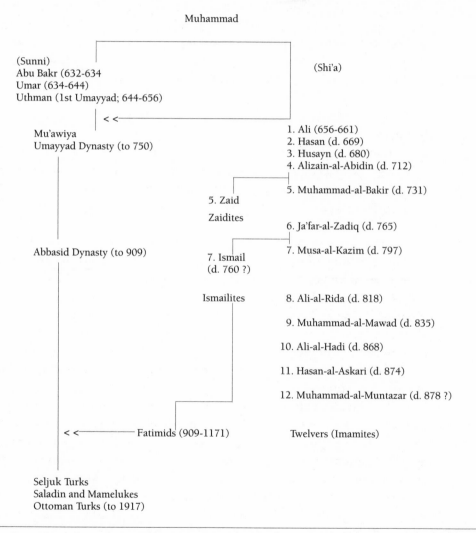

Figure 3.1. Islamic lines of succession, adapted from Noss

they too lost most of their territory to the crusaders and the Seljuk Turks. Eventually they were displaced by the Sunni Mamelukes under Saladin. During the twelfth and thirteenth centuries A.D., a radical subgroup of Ismailites in Persia provided young men with hashish and then induced them to kill political leaders. They became known as the Hashishins, from which we get our word *assassins.*

All Shi'ites are united by the dispute over the line of succession and by the idea of divinely appointed imams. There are other traits as well that distinguish the Shi'a from Sunni Islam. For example, they recognize other holy places in addition to Mecca, such as the tombs of the imams, particularly those of Ali and Husayn. Sometimes the fervor of their devotion for these places exceeds that for Mecca. The Shi'ites have an authority structure that focuses on the interpretation of the Qur'an by their holy leaders. The more radical groups (Ismailites and Imamites) curse the first three caliphs—Abu Bakr, Umar and Uthman—every Friday in the services at the mosque. Shi'ites are theoretically bound together in their awaiting the coming of a Mahdi.

Authority in Islam

The Qur'an. The highest authority in Islam is the Qur'an. As we have seen, Muslims believe that the angel Gabriel divinely revealed the Qur'an to Muhammad. Essentially it is the earthly version of a heavenly book, the um-al-kitab (mother of all books). Muhammad was privileged to convey this earthly version along with specific instructions.

The Qur'an is about as long as the New Testament. It is divided into 114 chapters, called *suras,* with each sura being divided into verses *(ayat).* The suras are arranged roughly by length, from longer suras to shorter ones, which leads to a kind of reverse chronological order. The older suras are relatively short and focus on the basic theological themes of God and judgment; the longer, later ones contain many detailed instructions for the Islamic community as well as historical and biblical references. The Qur'an begins with al-Fatiha, the opening sura, which is recited at all important prayer times. All but one sura begin with the formula "in the name of Allah, the most gracious and most merciful."

The Qur'an maintains its authoritative character only in Arabic, the language in which it was revealed. All translations of necessity involve interpretation (and thus distortion), and so no translated version can be the authentic Qur'an. Schoolchildren are encouraged to memorize the entire Qur'an in Arabic, even in countries where Arabic is not the dominant language (or possibly is not understood at all). Recitation of the Qur'an is considered an art form, with high acclaim going to those who can do so exceptionally well. A professional reciter of the Qur'an has mastered the technique of making each ayat ring out as a well-shaped musical line.

The Qur'an contains many references to biblical materials. Conventional opinion holds that Muhammad borrowed these stories from his Jewish and Christian contacts. But these stories receive new twists in the Qur'an. For example, Sura 2 tells about Adam and Eve. Adam ate the fruit and came under God's wrath, but God's displeasure was quickly tempered by his mercy. There was no enduring judgment. After a time God forgave Adam, who was then reinstated to God's favor.

The sunna and hadiths. For any issues that are left undefined by the Qur'an, the prophet's life and informal sayings are the ultimate authority. These traditions are called the *hadiths,* and they were vigorously collected and evaluated in the first generations of Islam. As *sunna* (here again meaning "consensus"), the hadiths point to Muhammad's actual life as indications of how Muslims should act. When in doubt, do as Muhammad did! The hadiths also include many sayings that are attributed to Muhammad. These may be used to clarify the revelation of the Qur'an, and thus their authority comes close to that of the Qur'an. Among the hadiths are various miracle stories, including Muhammad's ride to Jerusalem and back to Mecca in one night and his ascent to heaven, while in Jerusalem, for receiving a night of revelations.

The shari'a. Theoretically, the sources discussed above are sufficient for all occasions. All that remains is to apply the information. In practice, however, that means that the Qur'an and the hadiths must be interpreted correctly in order to obtain the correct application.

The mihrab is a niche at the front of every mosque, indicating the direction toward Mecca. Sultan Mosque, Singapore.

Therefore the concept of *shari'a,* or "Islamic law," developed. Four different schools of shari'a arose in the context of Sunni Islam between A.D. 750 and A.D. 850: (1) the Hanifite school, which bases itself essentially on a loose interpretation of the Qur'an alone, (2) the Malikite school, which loosely combines Qur'an and hadith, (3) the Shafi'ite school, which has formal criteria for adjudicating between Qur'an and hadith, and (4) the Hanbalite school, which is both the latest and the most conservative; it attempts to base itself on rigid interpretations of the Qur'an alone.

It needs to be emphasized that these are not four schools of theology that maintain compilations of beliefs. Although minor variations in beliefs are unavoidable, the schools basically represent different ways of delineating morals and practices. We could also add the Shi'a as a fifth school, although in the Shi'a the authority of the imam is the final point of reference. Shi'ite Islam rejects many of the hadiths.

The mystical tradition: Sufism. Islam glories in the fact that it has these written sources of authority. However, in a move not all that dissimilar to the rise of kabala in Judaism, Islam also developed a mystical tradition in an attempt to find a spiritual reality beyond laws and commandments.

Islamic mystics have been called Sufis, a term that originally referred to the woolen garments worn by the mystic practitioners. Sufism arose as a recognizable movement in the eighth century and has continued as a spiritual force in Islam to this day. At the heart of Sufi teaching is the mystical quest for a direct experience of Allah, possibly even to merge one's soul with him. Needless to say, Muslim authorities viewed these notions with suspicion and even hostility, particularly in the early stages. In the tenth century the Sufi al-Hallaj was executed. Two of the most famous Sufis are Rumi, the Persian poet, and al-Ghazali, a scholar who provided a comprehensive theology of Sufi thought. Sufism also gave rise to numerous monastic orders, among whom the ecstasy-seeking "whirling dervishes" have attained notoriety in their own right.

Essential Beliefs

To repeat a comment made in connection with Judaism, Islam is primarily a religion about practices, not beliefs. That does not mean that it is possible to have Islam without certain beliefs or that beliefs are irrelevant. It means that the central question is whether or not a person submits to Allah. Nevertheless, five or six core beliefs have been identified as essential (the difference being in the grouping, not the content).

The oneness of God. Allah is not a proper noun in Arabic, even as *God* is not a proper noun in English. It is simply the word for God, and if you were to talk in Arabic about the God of the Bible, *Allah* is the word you would use.

As already noted, the historic roots of Muhammad's understanding of Allah lie in original monotheism, as preserved by Judaism, Christianity and an Arabian vestige. Thus we can expect a lot of similarities to other monotheistic religions, as well as some differences. A perennial question in religious discussion is, Do Christians and Muslims worship the same God? Because of the imprecise nature of the question, the answer depends on the questioner's perspective: historical origin or theological description. In terms of historical origin, the answer is clearly yes. In terms of theological description, there are many general points of similarity, but when it comes down to specific details, the answer has to be no. After all, what is the Christian God if not the Trinity: Father, Son and Holy Spirit? And what is the Muslim God if not the revealer of the Qur'an? But these two descriptions are mutually exclusive.

The Qur'anic conception of Allah is strictly unitarian, since God is seen as one and one only. Muhammad considered the very notion of a "fatherhood" of Allah, which he associated with a sexual procreation of a son, as highly blasphemous. Keep in mind that a grossly sensualist version of Allah and his daughters was a part of the pre-Islamic Meccan religion. It conveyed notions of sexual activity on the part of God. Consequently Muhammad had no use for the idea of Christ as the Son of God or for the Trinity.

Apparently Muhammad did not understand the Christian doctrine of the Trinity (how many Christians do?). One verse in the Qur'an (5:116) suggests that he may have thought that the Trinity consisted of God the Father, Jesus the Son and Mary the Mother. It is a fact that most of the Christians with whom Muhammad would have had contact would have been technically heretical on christological issues,[8] but neither of these two groups would have held that peculiar version of the Trinity. Some Christians seem to think that Muhammad would have embraced belief in the Trinity if only he had been exposed to its orthodox formulation. But this strikes me as highly naive.

In all forms of theism (including Christianity, Judaism and Islam), God combines the two characteristics of being transcendent (greater than the world, and not limited by it) and immanent (active within the world). In Islam, by far the greater emphasis goes to Allah's transcendence. One should never identify Allah with any finite, created being. To do so would be *shirk* (idolatry), which is the most serious of all sins.

Angels and spirits. The reality of Allah does not exclude the reality of other spiritual beings. Muhammad received the revelations of the Qur'an through the angel Gabriel. Islam recognizes three other archangels and a large hosts of angels. There are also many evil spirits (the jinn) that are led by the devil. They are relatively weak entities but can cause trouble. The believer must maintain constant vigilance because the jinn can cause physical harm. They can also tempt the believer into compromising his or her obedience to Allah.

Many common believers are preoccupied with the spirit world. Here we have a classic example of the difference between the standard version of a religion and its folk counterpart. Folk Islam tends to be highly animistic. Although standard descriptions of Islam (such as this one) focus on Islamic history, the Qur'an, the five pillars and many idealized practices, the common nomad or villager may be occupied mainly with warding off evil spirits. Facets of Islam such as the five pillars may become subordinated to this animism and may come to be thought of as tools for dealing with the spirits rather than aspects of submission to Allah in their own right.

Many Islamic teachers are working hard to raise all Muslims out of animism; after all, Islam arose as a rebellion against animistic religion. Furthermore, Islam is certainly not the only religion to experience this decay. We can remind ourselves of the "second law of thermodynamics" of religion (chapter one). Even Christianity has not been immune on this point. Perhaps this crypto-animism is so noticeable in Islam because many of its adherents still live in technologically undeveloped cultures in which animism and superstition can easily rear their heads.

Prophets. According to Islam, from time to time God has disclosed his will to the world through prophets. These prophets are human beings who have won victory in their struggle against sin; God has directed them by his inspiration. A prophet (*nabi*) is also considered an apostle (*rasul*) if he provides a book for his community to live by. All the prophets preach the same basic message of submission to the one God and an impending judgment.

The Qur'an provides no definitive list of prophets. In fact, it makes clear that there have been prophets who are not now remembered (90:78). Most of the twenty-five prophets mentioned in the Qur'an (for example, in 3:33, 34; 4:163; 6:83-86) are biblical figures, including Adam, Noah, Abraham, David and Jesus. The Qur'an refers to three prophets—Hud, Shu'aib and Salih (7:66-93)—who are not biblical but whose roots may be in the independent Arabian monotheistic tradition.

If Moses and Jesus were prophets from God, why are there discrepancies between the Bible and the Qur'an with regard to their lives and teachings? The traditional Islamic answer is that all the prophets taught the message that Muhammad taught. But subsequently people tampered with the writings they left behind and distorted the truth of the original message. As one drastic example, Muslims say that Christ did not claim to be God. Passages in which he apparently did so (for example, Jn 10:30) they claim to be later fabrications by the Christian church.

Muhammad had great respect for Jesus, seeing him as a prophet. The Qur'an even teaches his virgin birth (3:45-47), his many miracles (3:49) and his ascension (4:158). However, two points are nonnegotiable in Islam. First, Jesus Christ is not God (5:117). As we saw already, the only view of God acceptable to Islam is a purely unitarian monotheism. Any notion of the Trinity or of Christ's being the Son of God is rejected vehemently. Second, Christ did not die on the cross (4:157). Muslims consider it unthinkable that God would allow one of his messengers to die a death of shame and torture. Also, Muslims reject the doctrine of Christ's substitutionary atonement as barbaric and contrary to the nature of God. The Qur'an asserts that the Jews believed they had crucified Jesus. Either Allah deceived them into that belief, or (as many Muslims believe, even though it is not a part of the Qur'an) Simon of Cyrene was accidentally crucified in Christ's stead.

For some Muslims the line of the prophets will be completed only when the Mahdi appears. As has already been observed, Shi'ite Islam expects the last in each specific line of imams (fifth, seventh or twelfth, depending on the school) to return as the Mahdi. Since it is very much a part of human nature to expect a future redeemer who will set all things straight, the Mahdi idea has also manifested itself in Sunni circles at certain times. In the 1880s a fanatic named Mohammed Ahmed rallied Muslims of the Sudan around himself as the Mahdi. His intended mission was to throw off the recently acquired British colonial masters (and thereby revive the slave trade, which European colonialists were forbidding in Africa). Oblivious to European might and resources, thousands followed him into battle, gaining a temporary victory and occupying the city of Khartoum. Eventually the rebellion was put down and the Mahdi was executed, though not before the legendary British general Charles "Chinese" Gordon[9] was killed.

In 1979, shortly after Shi'ites took over the American embassy in Teheran, a small group of Saudi (Sunni) extremists, proclaiming one of their number, Muhammad Abdullah al-Qahtani, as the Mahdi, attempted to take over the grand mosque of Mecca by force. They were all killed. The American news media, having vainly attempted to establish a Marxist link to the Iranian revolution, now sought to lay this act at Ayatollah Khomeini's doorstep. This explanation was also in vain, since this was not even a Shi'ite group. Khomeini himself blamed Zionists and Americans.

Despite occasional Mahdi fever, the only approved Sunni Muslim view is that Muhammad was the final prophet. Even in Shi'ite circles, anyone claiming to be the Mahdi was more likely to be rejected than accepted, a fact that gave rise to the religion of Baha'i (chapter four).

Books. Prophets who were also apostles left books for their people: Zoroaster recorded his revelations, Moses revealed the law, David gave us the psalms and Jesus left us the gospel. Thus Jews, Christians and Zoroastrians have their holy books, just as Muslims have the Qur'an. These groups are known as "people of the book," and Muhammad allowed them privileges and protections not available to pagans. Upon paying a tax, they were supposed to be allowed to practice their religion and lead an unencumbered life. If they were not full citizens, they were not a persecuted minority either. Muhammad also left room for "people of the book" to enter heaven. Human nature being what it is, it is hardly surprising that these ideals often went unfulfilled in practice.

Judgment. One of the earliest components of Muhammad's teaching was impending judgment. In subsequent embellishments of this core belief, Muslims borrowed descriptions from other faiths, particularly Zoroastrian apocalyptic myths. But the essence of the Qur'an's teaching on the judgment is relatively plain and sobering (20:102-127; 18:101-104; 23:105-115). On the appointed day (known only to God), the trumpet will sound and a general resurrection will follow. The living and the dead will appear before God, and everyone will be confronted with the deeds done in life. All persons will be given a book in which has been recorded all of their deeds. The wicked will receive their books in their left hands (traditionally the unclean hand), while the righteous will hold their books in their right hands.

The basis of judgment is a sincere submission to Allah's will. Did the person recognize God alone and endeavor to live by Allah's commands? Merely professing Islam is not enough; in fact, some of the severest punishments are reserved for hypocrites. Conversely, a Christian or a Jew who sincerely lives by all the right obligations may enter heaven. Allah is considered to be "most gracious" and "most merciful," so he will probably forgive otherwise devout people certain sins. There is even a hadith that says that Muhammad may intercede on behalf of some people. In distinction to Judaism, which ultimately enjoins obedience to the law simply out of devotion to God, Islam focuses on heaven as a reward and on hell as a punishment. In contrast to Christianity, which also emphasizes outcomes, Islam is not a redemptive religion. Whereas the Christian's faith in Christ provides absolution from all sins, the Muslim's confession of faith is only the first step in a life that may eventually be rewarded with heaven.

In general, Islam frowns on claims to certainty of salvation. Claims of assurance regarding entry into heaven are considered presumptuous because that attitude is seen as dictating what God must do. God's mercy gives reason for optimism, but never complete assurance. Suzanne Haneef emphasizes that

> no Muslim, even the best among them, imagines that he is guaranteed Paradise; on the contrary, the more conscientious and God-fearing one is, the more he is aware of his own shortcomings and weaknesses. Therefore the Muslim, knowing that God alone controls life and death, and that death may come to him at any time, tries to send on ahead for his future existence such deeds as will merit the pleasure of his Lord, so that he can look forward to it with hope for His mercy and grace.[10]

Wall hanging depicting the ka'ba at the Durga Shrine, Singapore.

Yet some Muslims do profess assurance. One evening in Singapore I gave an introductory talk on Islam to a small group of Christian workers. I made comments to the effect that Islam cannot provide absolute certainty of salvation. When we visited a mosque the next day, a young Muslim man told us that he would no doubt go to heaven. When we asked him to explain what he meant, he said that *as long as he kept his thoughts on Allah and obeyed his commandments every second of every day,* he could be sure of his salvation. In other words, he was saying that he had assurance of heaven as long as he kept an impossible standard. On that basis there was no particular assurance after all, which brought him back to the usual Muslim attitude of hoping that God in his mercy will forgive occasional trespasses. Such claims to assurance are useful in that they tell us what would be the case *if* human beings were not sinful. In light of human shortcomings, though Muslims have good reason to hope for God's forgiveness, they think it would be wrong to bank on it.

Heaven and hell are depicted in the Qur'an as places of physical pleasure and torment (56:1-56). Muslim scholars are quick to point out that these descriptions are intended to be symbolic. Nevertheless, to Muhammad's audience in the context of a desert culture the appeal must have been highly sensual. Heaven is an ideal desert oasis with fruit trees, shade, refreshing drinks and beautiful companions. In hell the damned drink boiling, fetid water.

The decree of God. Allah is sovereign; all that Allah wills comes to pass. Whatever Allah does not will does not happen. All that has happened must have been willed by Allah. This is the core belief on the infallible decree of God. Its intent is to proclaim the sovereignty of God; its effect has been to promote at least the appearance of determinism. Apathy can also result. Since all that happens is decreed by God, there is no reason to try to change anything.

Many Muslim teachers are unhappy with the notion of determinism and the apathy it can engender. Throughout Islamic history the freedom-predestination issue has been debated, numerous scholars claiming that the sovereignty of God is not intended to preclude human free will. Human beings are responsible for their choices, and they will be judged on the basis of the choices they make.[11]

The Five Pillars

Some of the core practices of Islam have been grouped together into the five pillars of Islam. These five obligations are essential but not exhaustive. There are many other obligations, such as those involving food and modesty, which are crucial as well. The five pillars summarize Muslim worship.

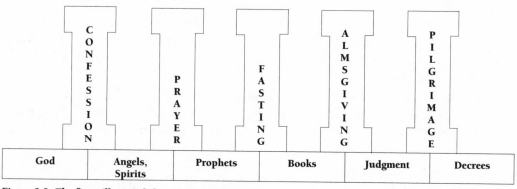

Figure 3.2. The five pillars and the six essential beliefs

Confession (shahada). The first pillar is the idea that carries the rest of Islamic belief. It is the shahada, which is the fundamental confession of Islam: "There is no God but God, and Muhammad is the apostle of God." In English translation this statement is often rendered, "There is no God but *Allah*." But in Arabic the word *Allah* is used both times: *la ilaha illa allah*—"no God but God." This is an assertion of the fundamental unitarian monotheism that is crucial to Islam.

The second part, *Muhammad rasul Allah,* commits the Muslim to undivided allegiance to God's commandments. The believer recognizes Muhammad as God's spokesman. Muhammad is *rasul,* the apostle who speaks God's message. What Muhammad says, God says. Thus to confess this statement sincerely is to submit to all other teachings of Islam.

All that is necessary to become a Muslim is to repeat the confession and mean it. This act does not guarantee salvation, but it is the first step on the road to salvation. The shahada is a part of all crucial junctures of life. The first sound a newborn baby hears is someone whispering the shahada. The last sound a dying person says or hears is the shahada. Thus this confession encompasses all of Muslim's life.

Prayer (salat). Each Muslim is supposed to perform the required ritual prayers five times a day: (1) at sunrise—as soon it is possible to distinguish a white thread from a black one, (2) at noon; (3) in midafternoon, (4) at sunset and (5) one hour after sunset. A first-time traveler to an Islamic country may notice that some mosques post six, not five, prayer times. The additional prayer time, set for midmorning, serves as time for people to undertake additional devotion for special concerns.

Prayers may be performed anywhere, but men are encouraged to pray at a mosque. A mosque is at a minimum a room or building designated for prayer; frequently it is a more elaborately designed house. Westerners learn to recognize mosques by the towers, called minarets. These towers traditionally have little balconies from which the official caller, the muezzin, invites the people to prayer. Nowadays in urban areas this task is done by means of a public address system, but the mosques retain minarets for decorative purposes.

A crucial facility in any mosque is water for ritual washing. Modern buildings include shower and bathroom facilities, although ritual washing must be performed subsequent to toilet functions. In more traditional settings, there may be a well or a set of outside faucets.

The most important part of the mosque is the prayer hall, which is essentially an empty room with varying degrees of decoration. One looks in vain for pictures, altars or sacred precincts. The most important part of the mosque is the niche at the front of the building *(mihrab)* that indicates the direction toward Mecca *(qiblah).* Other features may include a pulpit, a few copies of the Qur'an with wooden stands on which to place them for reading and a separate area (balcony or back room) in which women pray. Many modern mosques have carpets with decorations marked out in rows so that the worshipers can easily arrange themselves in straight lines to pray. Some mosques contain so many clocks that there can be no excuse for missing the correct prayer time. To enter a prayer hall, the worshiper must remove his shoes (and preferably rinse his feet). Apart from its religious implications, cleanliness is essential because Muslim prayer requires the supplicant to place his forehead on the carpet.

The sequence of salat is highly structured. Shortly before the actual prayer time, the muezzin (or his recorded voice) issues the official call to prayer. This call is a melodic repetition of a stylized formula. It includes several repetitions of "Allahu akbar!"— "God is most great!"—and the shahada as well as numerous exhortations to "come to prayer!" and "come to devotion!" Visitors to Muslim countries find themselves constantly accompanied by the call to prayer. It rings in memory long after they return home.

The Muslim faithful prepare themselves for prayer by ablution. This involves rinsing hands, feet, eyes, ears, nose and mouth three times with water. Representative gestures using sand may be substituted in the desert. Now they are considered ritually pure. They must avoid any contact that could cause defilement, for instance, bodily excretions or contact with a member of the opposite sex.

Women by and large pray at home, and men, if possible, pray in the mosque. But prayers can be said anywhere as long as a space has been sanctified, which can be accomplished by laying down a prayer rug. When men pray in a mosque, they line up in straight horizontal rows facing the mihrab. One person serves as prayer leader. Women do the same, but out of the men's sight. The reason advanced for the segregation of the sexes is preserving the dignity of women. Since a part of the prayer ritual is to prostrate oneself with the forehead touching the floor, it would be uncouth for men to line up alongside or behind women in this position. (We will discuss the role of women in Islam later in this chapter.)

The actual prayer is a formalized ritual that combines sequences of postures with recitation. People begin the prayer standing upright with briefly cupped ears, showing Allah that they are available to hear him. The first sura of the Qur'an (*al fatiha*, "the opening") is prayed, followed by further prescribed recitations. At appropriate moments the posture changes: bowing, standing, prostration, kneeling, prostration and standing again. In general, the prayers are recited in an undertone, but the changes of posture are accompanied by the leader's call of "Allah." Each such sequence is called a *rak'at*. Every prayer time has a designated number of them (two to five), with the larger number coming later in the day and evening when presumably more time is available. The participants line up and carry out these activities in unison side by side in long even rows, indicating the equality of all people before God. This custom is distinctive to Muslim prayer.

After prayer the people greet each other informally and then return to their regular activities. On Fridays there are special prayers in the mosque. Families often attend together, though men and women pray separately. Young children of both sexes may be allowed to roam the prayer hall. The actual prayer time is shortened to two rak'at, but it is preceded by a sermon preached by the prayer leader (imam, in the non-Shi'ite sense). This is the time for any announcements concerning the life of the congregation to be made. After Friday prayers there may be fellowship activities.

Despite all of this focused religious activity on Fridays, it would not be correct to consider Friday the Muslim sabbath. There is no requirement to abstain from work. Stores in Muslim towns are usually closed through afternoon prayer time, but they may open afterward. There is no religious mandate to refrain from work, but there is a duty to attend prayer services.

In many industrialized countries, the pillar of prayer has necessitated some adaptation in practice, if not in the interpretation of the requirement. Busy people pray when they can; prayer times are shifted to occur more regularly before and after common work times instead of being tied to the daily sun cycle. For instance, morning prayer may be held at 5 A.M., which in the winter comes long before sunrise. Prayers may be broadcast over loudspeakers in their entirety so that people who cannot get away from their activity can still pray along silently.

Fasting (sawm). Muhammad received his first revelations during the month of Ramadan. In commemoration of this event, Muslims are required to fast during daylight hours throughout the month. As usual, daylight begins when a white thread can be distinguished from a black one. No form of refreshment may be taken for the entire day, not even a sip of water. It is permissible to eat and drink in the morning when it is still dark and at night after sunset. But the key is to be moderate even then; all forms of indulgence are forbidden. This prohibition includes sexual relations and various forms of entertainment.

Since the Muslim calendar is lunar, it is approximately twelve days shorter than the standard solar calendar. This means that Ramadan (along with the entire calendar) cycles through the solar year in the course of a person's lifetime. When Ramadan occurs during the short, relatively cool days of winter, fasting is comparatively easy. But when Ramadan falls in the long, hot days of summer, it constitutes a serious challenge. People must moderate their routine activities in order to preserve their stamina.

Observance of Ramadan may be postponed if absolutely necessary. Young children are obviously exempt. People who are seriously ill or soldiers on military duty may do their fasting when they are out of danger. In extreme cases, when it will be impossible ever to make up the fast, it is possible to substitute a major act of mercy, for example, a donation to the poor.

On the first day after Ramadan, Muslims celebrate *eid-al-fitr* with a special service in the mosque. Families decorate their homes, feast together and exchange presents.

Almsgiving (zakat). The Qur'an commands all believers to practice regular charity (2:43), but it does not specify formal procedures. In the shari'a this commandment has been elucidated as a formal obligation of standardized annual giving to the poor, called the zakat. In theory this is a voluntary gift made out of liberality; in practice, in some Islamic communities, it has become a clearly defined obligation collected by the representative of the community on behalf of the poor. Although it is not called a tax, it has taken on that character at times.

Zakat is not excessive. The various schools of Islamic law have worked out the detailed requirements meticulously. All possessions—real estate, jewelry, livestock and so on—are assessed. The basic principle for cash assessment is one fortieth (2.5 percent) of any net profit (not the total worth). Thus the zakat does not pertain to gross income, and it is nowhere near the biblical tithe.

Early in the history of Islam the zakat provided Islamic countries with a clear program of social welfare. Islam instituted this pillar while Europe was in the so-called Dark Ages, and it set a uniform measure to take care of the poor.

Pilgrimage (hajj). If at all possible, a Muslim should visit Mecca at least once in his or her lifetime. The last month of the Islamic calendar, called *al-hajj,* has been designated as the official period of pilgrimage. Muhammad originally decreed that his followers pray facing Jerusalem. In Medina after his conflict with the Jews, he made Mecca the geographic focal point of Muslim devotion. Pragmatically, retaining Mecca as the center of pilgrimage helped smooth the transition into his theocracy once he retook that holy city.

Mecca is not the only holy city of Islam. Right behind it in prestige are Medina, where Muhammad is buried, and Jerusalem, where he supposedly ascended to heaven one night. The Dome of the Rock, built in the seventh century, marks the site from

An individual Muslim prostrate before Allah during prayer.

which Muhammad made his temporary ascent (the Jewish temple having been destroyed over six hundred years earlier). When the caliph Umar built the first mosque in Jerusalem, he placed it next to the rock. This mosque became known as al-Aqsa, "the farthest," because at the time (though not for very long) it marked the farthest extent of the Muslim empire. Shi'ites have some of their own holy cities, including Qum and Karbala. In addition, Muslims the world over have designated other centers of pilgrimage. For example, in Indonesia devotees make regular pilgrimages to graves of distinguished holy men. No other pilgrimage center, however, rivals the sacredness and importance of Mecca.

The requirement to visit Mecca applies to both men and women. Anyone who is unable to make the pilgrimage may designate someone else do it on his or her behalf, though this provision is not actually specified in the shari'a. I have a Palestinian Muslim acquaintance who has traveled to Mecca three times—the first time to fulfill his own obligation, the second time on behalf of his mother, who had become too old to go herself, and the third time for his wife, who was unable to go due to ill health. (I think he enjoyed going to Mecca.) A man who has journeyed to Mecca receives an honorary title, Hajji, and his accomplishment is recognized in different ways, depending on his home culture. In Palestine his house is marked with an ornate sign testifying to his status, while in Malaysia he may trade the traditional black hat (songkok) for a white one.

It would be hard to overestimate the emotional impact that Mecca has on a Muslim when he first sees it. All of his life he has prayed toward that city. Pictures of the ka'ba have adorned his environment. Now he is finally there, at the very center of his faith, the place where Muhammad lived and taught. And being there with two million of his fellow Muslims instills a feeling of mission and solidarity.

The hajj has seven main components, the first one being arrival and preparation. Mecca itself is located inland and has no harbor or airport. Pilgrims arrive at the coastal city of Jidda, located about an hour's bus ride from Mecca. Pilgrims from all over the world must comply with the formalities of entering the country of Saudi Arabia.

Before entering Mecca, Muslims must enter a state of purity. Men bathe, shave their heads and don two triangular pieces of linen—their only clothing—which symbolizes the twin themes of ritual cleanliness and equality. Women wear the traditional Islamic robe and veil. From this point on, until the end of the most important activities, all ritual restrictions must be strictly observed.

The second major component of the hajj is tawaf, the first required act of walking around the ka'ba seven times. Ideally this walk occurs in a spiral pattern that culminates in touching the sacred stone, embedded in the wall of the ka'ba. The third major component is running between Marwa and Safa. According to tradition, Abraham's expelled concubine, Hagar, ran frantically back and forth between two hills known as Marwa and Safa until an angel provided her with water from the well Zamzam. These two points are part of the structure of the grand mosque now and are connected by a long hallway. The pilgrim emulates the jog between the two sites seven times. Before leaving this area, the pilgrim may also have water from Zamzam to drink.

The fourth component is the greater pilgrimage. From here the entire mass of pilgrims moves out of the city of Mecca. On the ninth day of the month of al-hajj, they assemble on the Plain of Arafat at the foot of the Mount of Mercy (where Muhammad delivered his last sermon). From the afternoon prayer until sunset, the pilgrims stand in the presence of Allah—meditating, praying, reading the Qur'an, chanting and so forth. This "day of standing" is considered the spiritual high point of the pilgrimage. The fifth component is sacrifices at Mina. That evening, the company moves back to the little town of Mina, halfway between Mecca and Arafat. All of the pilgrims live in a tent city for about three days. In the evening animals (sheep or goats) are slaughtered as offerings to God and then are consumed in joyous feasts. Muslims do not offer these sacrifices as atonement for sin. They are expressions of gratitude to Allah; specifically, they commemorate Abraham's sacrificing an animal as a substitute for his son Ishmael (not Isaac, as in the Bible).

The sixth main component of the hajj is stoning the devil. The pilgrims take turns throwing stones at three pillars representing the devil (Iblis). Each pilgrim is supposed to throw nine rocks at these pillars. The seven component is the final tawaf. The pilgrim moves back to Mecca, walks around the ka'ba one more time, and the pilgrimage is complete.

Further Requirements
The five pillars represent the central ethical obligations of Muslims, but not the only ones. The Muslim's entire life is focused on living up to the requirements of righteousness, including such universal expectations as honesty, respect for property and marital fidelity. According to Muslim ethical thought, actions fall into one of three categories: (1) *fard*—actions that are obligatory, such as the five pillars; (2) *haram*—actions that are expressly prohibited, such as idolatry, and (3) *halal*—actions that are permitted.

Diet. The Islamic counterpart to the Jewish kosher system is the concept of *halal* (permitted) foods. Only halal foods may be eaten. Consuming pork or products derived from pork is forbidden. Since many Western foods contain pork products of which the average consumer may not be aware, Muslims must be careful in what they accept from well-meaning hosts and hostesses. The Qur'an also forbids drinking wine (2:219); this injunction is interpreted as prohibiting all intoxicating drinks.

Modesty in dress. Although Islamic dress is associated with Middle Eastern cultures, there are no specifically required garments. What is required is modesty. The stereotyped view of Islamic modesty conjures up visions of women draped in robes and veils with nothing showing but their eyes (if those). It is true that in some Middle Eastern cultures robes and veils have been designated as the proper Islamic mode of dress for women, called *purdah*. In the 1980s the government of Iran imposed it on Muslim women as a sign of true Islam. Yet many Islamic scholars contend that this practice is going too far; the Qur'an does not expect a woman to be completely shrouded.

The Qur'an counsels that a woman should dress in public in such a way that she does not call attention to her physical beauty (24:31). The interpretation of this directive is that her body should be entirely covered, including her legs and arms. Her face may be visible, but her hair and the sides of her head need to be covered. There are also modesty expectations for men. They should not expose their skin above their elbows or knees. A head covering, though not mandated by shari'a, is a permanent part of dress in many Islamic cultures. These restrictions do not apply within the home, where a woman can be much freer in her dress.

Marriage and the status of women. The status of women in Islam is controversial. Many people regard this issue as the weakest point of Islam, since Muslim women seem to be highly inferior to men in status. Muslims insist that this charge rests on misunderstanding and flawed assumptions. What is the reality?

A fair answer to this question must take several different viewpoints into account and, for the outsider at least, will remain ambiguous. It is impossible to talk about women in Islam without beginning with the topic of marriage. First, the Qur'an teaches that a man may have up to four wives as long as he provides for them equally in terms of love and material goods. Muhammad himself claimed in the Qur'an that this limitation did not apply to himself (33:50-52). His marriages were supposed to be a part of his total prophetic ministry and they deviated from the norm set for others. His marriages to Aisha, Abu Bakr's nine-year-old daughter, and Zainab, his cousin and the wife of his adopted son, Zaid, were controversial.

Second, divorce is extremely simple but not be taken lightly. It is considered halal, the lowest level of permitted actions. A hadith states that it is "hateful in the sight of God." Nevertheless, the Qur'an provides for it (2:228-242; 115:1-7). According to the shari'a, all a man has to do is to say "I divorce you" three times publicly, and the marriage has been dissolved. The usual expectation in the Qur'an is that these three statements of repudiation are not made at one time. Before the third statement, particularly, there should be a waiting period of three months (to allow for possible reconciliation and to make sure that the woman is not pregnant). Thus women seem to be little more than chattel—easily acquired and disposed of. However, this is only a part of the story. Muslim apologists ask us to look at these regulations in their total context.

At the time when Muhammad issued his standards, the status he espoused for women actually placed them ahead of women in most other parts of the world, certainly in western Europe. The Qur'an gives women specific property rights and legal rights. Before, during and after marriage, a woman is entitled to material provision; if her husband does not comply, she can bring charges against him. Furthermore—and this was revolutionary at the time—in case of divorce, the man could not send the woman out penniless. She was entitled to have enough property to exist on an acceptable level. Finally, women were allowed to receive inheritances in their own right. Some of these rights did not become law in Europe until the nineteenth century.

But that was then. What about now? Is it not true that now the Western world recognizes women as equals under the law and accords them the freedom to choose their own lifestyle, career and mate, while in Islamic countries women continue to live as virtual slaves of their fathers and husbands? Here it is necessary to distinguish between what is truly Islamic and what just happens to be a part of a local culture. Many Muslim scholars maintain that some of the restrictions placed on women in these countries, for example, veiling (purdah), treating women as chattel and maintaining closed harems, are excessive. They do not comply with the Qur'an, and they ought to be discontinued.

The Muslim response to secular women's liberation is, Look what liberation got you! Women have been wrenched out of the security of being allowed to be women and have been forced to earn their own living, compete in an unfair job world, and relegate their children to the care of strangers. Not to mention the continuing abuse they suffer at the hands of men! Furthermore, their so-called equality has resulted in rampant immorality and broken families. By recognizing the fundamental difference between men and women, the Qur'an liberates women to be themselves within guidelines that supply security and happiness. The so-called restrictions are actually guidelines that emancipate women to be women. Truly Islamic women are happy women. When a class that I was teaching visited an American mosque, a young woman told us, "I became a Muslim because only in Islam are women truly free."

Nevertheless, a non-Muslim may remain puzzled on this issue. For one thing, where restrictions on women are enforced, they are promulgated in the name of Islam. Thus in the minds of many Muslims, they are a part of Qur'anic piety. Furthermore, many Muslim

The mihrab of the Durga shrine, Singapore, gives evidence of deep East Asian influence on some indigenous Islam.

women yearn to be released from some of these limitations without giving up their Muslim faith. It is one thing for men to discuss these issues on a theoretical basis; it is quite another for women to live in a dominantly Islamic country where life for women is circumscribed from beginning to end by men.

Clearly, this issue is far from settled within the Islamic world itself. In my capacity as a religion professor, I receive a steady stream of literature from various Islamic groups. Much of it attempts to paint a rosy picture of the place of women in Islam. It may be that this picture is the one the Qur'an intends to bring about. However, many

Muslims (of both sexes) would say that this picture has not yet been attained.

Holy war (jihad). Another issue that has been controversial for Islam is the matter of "holy war," jihad. Islam has been stereotyped as a religion spread by the sword. Particularly in its first one hundred years, Islam seemed to expand through methods that were political, not religious. According to this stereotype, the onward march of Islam was the progress of the Islamic army, sometimes in a nonviolent takeover of new territory, sometimes with many bloody battles. Let us see how much truth this stereotype holds.

No one in the contemporary world likes to be accused of imperialism or of using force to impose a belief system. Muslims also want to be viewed as tolerant. In a theological sense, Islam may be more vulnerable to charges of intolerance than, say, Christianity is to the embarrassment of the Crusades (among many other misadventures). As a Christian, I can say that yes, the Crusades did happen; yes, they are an embarrassment to Christendom, and yes, I wish they had not happened. Spreading Christianity by means of the sword, let alone the barbaric cruelty that accompanied the Crusades, is opposed to the teachings of Christianity. But Christian teaching affirms a doctrine of original sin; there is no reason we should expect the European princes of the high Middle Ages to have been pure in all of their actions even if they had been genuine Christians (which is doubtful). This is no excuse, but it explains why the Crusades, for all their ignominious character, did not prove Christianity false.

However, Muslims cannot take this line of defense. First, Islam has no doctrine of original sin. The early caliphs in particular, though merely mortal, were supposed to have been "companions" of Muhammad (which became a regular title) and "rightly guided." Second, they themselves compiled the Qur'an and laid down the original interpretations of it. If they violated the teachings of the Qur'an, Islam would have a serious credibility gap on that point. And third, the Qur'an does expressly forbid the conversion of anyone by force (2:256). No wonder, then, that Muslims are eager to tell their side of the story; it certainly deserves a fair hearing.

In responding to this issue, Muslims frequently point out that some Qur'anic passages (for example, 61:11) referring to jihad need to be understood as referring to internal spiritual striving. This jihad is the war against one's own evil inclinations to bring oneself to full submission to Allah. This is the most important war, and it should not be misunderstood as military warfare.

The concept of jihad as physical war does nevertheless play an important role in Islamic history and in the shari'a. There are five basic principles of holy war.[12] First, physical violence may never be used to advance the cause of Islam. An Islamic country may never initiate international conflict. Second, Islam should be propagated by means of rational appeal and persuasion only. Third, if another nation commits an act of aggression against an Islamic country, the Islamic country is justified in using military force to defend itself. Fourth, if a non-Islamic country uses physical force to repress the free exercise of Islam, including the propagation of Islam, those actions constitute physical aggression against Islam or a particular Islamic country. This judgment would also apply in the case of suppression by laws (which would include any physical punishment, such as being jailed). It would then be appropriate for Islamic nations to liberate the oppressed Muslims by force of arms. This principle was in evidence when Ayatollah Khomeini of Iran declared the war against Iraq to be a jihad. Even though Iraq is also an Islamic country, its laws clearly discriminate against its Shi'ite population. Thus the ayatollah, the leader of the Shi'ites, saw Iraq as suppressing Islam.

The fifth basic principle of holy war applies to Islamic territories that have been taken over by non-Muslim powers. Once a country has come to belong to Dar-al-Islam (literally the "House of Submission"), it may never be allowed to revert to non-Muslim hands, since reversion would be a form of aggression against Islam. It must be reclaimed for Islam by jihad. This principle has been invoked countless times by Muslims as the reason why they cannot ever recognize the state of Israel and why Muslim political leaders who have compromised on this principle (King Abdullah of Jordan and President Anwar Sadat of Egypt) wound up paying with their lives for their actions.

Thus we need to understand the military expansion of Islam in terms of these principles. Islam sent out emissaries to invite people to join the Islamic community (which would, of course, have involved a shift of political allegiance to the Islamic umma). If the government, for example, a local vassal of the Byzantine Empire, tried to stop the emissaries, their resistance could be construed as the violent suppression of Islam. Then military action was legitimate. Thus the Muslim armies marched on and on, annexing an enormous amount of territory in a very short time, always construing this movement as defensive action protecting the right of Muslims to spread their message.

Usually there was very little resistance to the spread of Islam. Whole towns willingly threw open their gates to the advancing Muslims, more than willing to take their chances on the new overlords who replaced the corrupt and oppressive Byzantine rulers. Even many Christians freely welcomed the Muslim army.

Thus there are at least two different interpretations of the spread of Islam: the popular stereotype that Islam spread by violence alone and the Islamic construal that the spread of Islam was primarily peaceful, although defended in accordance with the rules of jihad. If non-Muslims find the Islamic interpretation of the Muslim advance strained, it is important nevertheless to hear and understand the Islamic version of the story. An open mind is essential to the study of history. The worst thing anyone could ever do would be to rewrite history to suit a set of preconceptions in either direction.

The Black Muslim Movement
In 1930 a momentous meeting took place between Elijah Poole, who had just taken

a job at a Detroit automobile factory, and W. D. Fard (calling himself Master Wali Farrad Muhammad), who had for the previous few years been preaching his version of Islam as the true religion for African-American people. Poole changed his name to Elijah Muhammad and started to popularize Fard's teachings; they soon had a sizable following. Fard disappeared in 1934. Elijah Muhammad interpreted his disappearance as a Shi'ite imam's going into concealment. The movement became known as The Lost/Found Nation of Islam. Five key teachings constitute the fundamental beliefs of the radical Black Muslim movement. First, W. D. Fard is an incarnation of Allah himself and is thus worthy of prayer and worship. Second, Elijah Muhammad is a prophet, proclaiming anew the message of God. Third, black people are descended from a tribe called the Shabazz, the ancient inhabitants of Mecca and the original keepers of the ka'ba. They are by nature good, pious and peaceful. Fourth, white people are by nature evil, sneaky and oppressive. They are the creation of a mad scientist named Yakub who did not want to submit properly to Allah. Thus white people are not fully human.

This mosque in Singapore is made entirely of wood. Its Malaysian style of architecture provides an interesting contrast to the modern city.

The fifth teaching is that black people ought to return to their roots by submitting to the five pillars of Islam and by taking care of each other in the face of white oppression. They should not take political action. Sixth, by Allah's will, the time is at hand when black people will again come to their rightful place of dominance in the world, and white people will get what they deserve. This brief summary reveals some points of tension. On the one hand, these principles espouse some clearly unorthodox concepts, particularly the idea of an incarnation of Allah and a new prophet. But on the other hand, these ideas are combined with orthodox Islam, such as the five pillars and a traditional Islamic lifestyle. This tension arose from the fact that the Black Muslim movement was not originally intended as a mission for Islam. Rather, it was a new message of hope to oppressed black Americans.

The same tension surfaces on the political side of the movement insofar as stridently militant rhetoric was used to counsel people to assume an almost quietistic political attitude. That this tension should have spawned practical consequences is not surprising. Whereas Black Muslims were not allowed to serve in the American armed forces (which came to the American public's attention in the celebrated case of boxer Muhammad Ali), the movement wound up with its own military arm, called the Fruit of Islam.

Whatever its tensions or ambiguities, the Nation of Islam became a potent force for good in the American black community. It gave hope and identity to many people, and it provided relief in the fight against drug abuse and poverty. But it did so with a message that was clearly divisive for the United States as a whole.

In 1960 a leading Black Muslim sowed the seeds of significant change for the movement. Malcolm X (Malcolm Little, calling himself Malik Shabazz) went to Mecca and there witnessed people of many races praying together in peace and harmony. This experience triggered a new vision: not one race lording it over another race but all races living together under God. Malik was assassinated shortly after this event, sadly, but his new message became increasingly influential in Black Islam.

Elijah Muhammad died in 1975, and his son Warith (Wallace) took over. He undertook some radical revisions by (1) aligning black Islam to mainstream Sunni Islam by repudiating all heretical doctrines and adopting mainstream beliefs and practices; (2) dissolving the Fruit of Islam and permitting American Muslims to participate in the political process; (3) changing the name of the movement to The American Muslim Mission; (4) cooperating with worldwide Islam. This revision coincided fortuitously with the influx of large amounts of Arab oil money. Islam centers consequently sprang up all over the United States, serving increasing numbers of immigrants from the Arab world as well as the American Muslim population.

The radical, racially oriented Nation of Islam was revived soon after the realignment. In 1978 Louis Farrakhan reclaimed the heritage of the Nation of Islam as a separate (and smaller) movement. He reappropriated the racist message that originally informed Fard's teachings. Farrakhan rebuilt the Fruit of Islam and occasionally made headlines with his incendiary rhetoric, particularly as directed against Jews. Recently Farrakhan called attention to himself and his movement with the Million Man March, a rally in Washington, D.C., which ostensibly called African-American men to personal responsibility but may have had its greatest effect in enhancing Farrakhan's fame and bank account.

The average African-American Muslim probably belongs to the mainstream American Muslim Mission. Nevertheless, the Nation of Islam is still an active participant in the contemporary American scene.

■ *So You Meet a Muslim . . .*

What You Might Expect

The first step many Americans must take in meeting Muslims is to overcome the pernicious stereotype of Muslims as terrorists. Unfortunately, the last few decades have seen numerous acts of world terrorism carried out in the name of Islam. Television newscasts devote extensive coverage to fanatics claiming that their doings are the will of Allah on behalf of Islam.

Of course, the majority of Muslims repudiate these misdeeds by a demented minority, which they condemn as criminal acts. When you encounter a Muslim, it is very unlikely that you are meeting someone who supports terrorism, openly or covertly. Be prepared, however, to receive a slant on international politics that may differ drastically from what you are used to hearing, not just with regard to the state of Israel and Palestine but also with regard to the role that the West plays on the international stage.

Muslims generally take their practices very seriously. Of course, there are hypocrites and superficial people in every religion, and Islam is no exception. Nevertheless, since Islam focuses more sharply on practice more than on labels, any Muslim who takes his or her religion seriously will maintain careful observance of all obligations.

Two issues in particular may come up in extended social or vocational contacts. One is diet. The Muslim halal code is not as finely tuned as the Jewish kosher laws, but a large percentage of Muslims take it seriously. While many nonobservant Jews do not keep kosher, all Muslims at least in theory abide by the Quran's dietary restrictions. Thus a non-Muslim host must be very careful not to embarrass Muslim guests by serving food that has pork or pork derivatives in it.

Non-Muslims should see that their Muslim friends, associates or employees have opportunity during the day to say their prayers. Of the five prayer times, only the afternoon prayer can hinder a person's work schedule. The noon prayer can be easily accommodated during a lunch period. Employers can create a lot of goodwill if they make sure that their Muslim employees have this opportunity, especially if they permit a late lunch hour on Friday to permit the worker to participate in Friday services in the mosque.

Relating the Gospel

Evangelizing Muslims is a notoriously difficult undertaking, particularly since Islam is also a missionary religion. Do not think that every Muslim you meet is out to convert you. But if the conversation runs to the topic of religion, be prepared to get some stiff debate. In its most basic form Islam is a very rational religion, and it is not easy to counter some arguments on their own ground. Furthermore, most Muslims living in Western countries are trained to know why they do not believe in the Trinity or in Christ as God. There are four basic points in Muslim apologetics. First, God is one. The Trinity does not make sense, and it is blasphemous to think that God can have a son. Second, Christ cannot be God. It is contradictory to think that any human being could be God. Third, the Bible is demonstrably full of errors whereas the Qur'an is direct revelation from God, passed down in its original, pure form. Fourth, instead of holding on to such absurd beliefs, it makes sense to accept the very simple faith of Islam: submit to the one God and keep his commandments.

How should a Christian respond to such argumentation? First, let me emphasize as strongly as I can that Christians need to know the fundamentals of their own faith. The Muslim interpretation of the Trinity explains it as polytheism—Christians worship three gods. Christians should be able to respond, at a minimum, that they do not. Christianity is a monotheistic religion; Christians worship one God in three persons—never three gods. Ideally, Christians should be able to go on and explain roughly why this model was chosen to summarize the biblical picture of God, not by use of some lame analogy but precisely in order to preserve belief in the essential unity of God.

More likely than not, the Muslim will reply that the doctrine of the Trinity does not make rational sense (and he or she would not be alone in that judgment). However, that point is a totally different issue. After all, being incomprehensible intellectually does not make a belief polytheistic. As a matter of fact, the doctrine of the Trinity is a very reasonable model to make sense out of the scriptural data.[13] But even if it were not, it would still not be polytheism, the primary point under consideration.

The same consideration applies to the Christian belief in the incarnation. Muslims charge that worshiping any human being as God is idolatry, which is true as far as it goes. But Christians do not worship a man as God. They say that God, the second person of the Trinity, joined himself inextricably to the man. Christians worship the God who is present with the man in the one person of Christ. Since the fifth century—based on the definition of the Council of Chalcedon—the accepted understanding of Christ has been that he is one person with two natures, a human one and a divine one. Again, the question I am addressing here is not whether the doctrine does or does not make sense, but whether Christians commit idolatry in worshiping Christ. The actual teachings of Christianity do not promote idolatry.

Clearly the matter cannot rest there. The Muslim will invariably respond that even at its best the Christian understanding is a horrendous tour de force, cramming some highly unlikely considerations into pretty questionable contentions. How much simpler, how much more rational, to believe that there is only one God with no further differentiations and that the prophets were human beings and nothing more.

I have no problem conceding the force of that point. But simplicity can hardly be the sole or even the primary criterion for truth, and my imaginings alone cannot decide what reality must be like. For example, it would be easier to accept the much simpler world of Newtonian physics without all the complexity of quantum mechanics and relativity. But scientists must bow to the realities they encounter, no matter how complex their theories must become in order to describe those realities. In the same way, thinkers in the field of religion cannot merely opt for the simplest doctrines. They must accept the realities that have been revealed by God and then express them as lucidly as possible so as to do justice to them. In short, Christians do not accept the doctrine of the Trinity or the status of Christ as the God-man because they are the simplest (how could they?) but because they express revealed reality.[14]

The preceding consideration raises the question of where the authentic revelation of God is to be found. The Christian looks to the Bible; the Muslim points to the Qur'an and claims superiority for it. My point here is not to make a case for the inspiration of the Bible per se[15] but to identify a possible response to the Muslim disparagement of it. Muslims point to many supposed flaws in both Old and New Testaments, which they read about in the works of people (claiming to be Christians) who apply negative critical scholarship to the Bible. If so-called Christians do not believe that their book is flawless, why would anyone accept it as divine revelation or base their beliefs on it? Ancient manuscripts of the Bible display many different textual variations, and the Bible is said to contain many apparent contradictions. By contrast, Muslims assert, the Qur'an has been preserved in a form identical to its original version, and it is free from error.

In response to the issue of God's preservation of the Bible, it can be pointed out that if someone had burned all textual variants of the Bible, as Uthman burned Qur'an variants, then there would be a single version of the Bible as well. Furthermore, the very existence of so many variant readings allows us to recover what the original must have said with a great degree of confidence. By contrast, it is impossible to restore the Qur'an to what existed prior to Uthman, since we now have only one version of the Qur'an—the one Uthman wanted us to have.[16]

Concerning the many alleged discrepancies in the Bible, evangelical Christians must do their homework and focus on the problem passages with diligence and integrity. The Qur'an is essentially the product of one man. Its content spans a little more than twenty years within a single cultural context. By contrast, the Bible spans about fifteen hundred years in several different languages and highly divergent cultures. This fact makes it much more difficult to interpret and correlate biblical information correctly, a point sometimes missed by critics and defenders alike. Christians who want to defend the inerrancy of the Bible incur the liability of knowing both sides of the coin: the critics' case as well as the data that support the believer's case. Again, if a Muslim points to a possible problem passage in the Bible, the Christian needs to have studied the issues involved. Having said as much, I can hasten to add that as a matter of fact there is every good reason to believe that the Bible is not full of errors or contradictions. Adequate study has produced and will continue to produce reassuring results.[17]

Needless to say, such religious discussions with a Muslim are never an end in themselves, for either the Christian or the Muslim. Both sides are concerned for the other's salvation—for the Muslim by submitting to Allah, for the Christian by receiving Christ in faith. In that sense winning an intellectual debate is in itself fruitless for both. The Christian's intent must be to show the Muslim (1) what the realities of the cross and salvation are and (2) that the realities are graciously provided by God to give us salvation. Since Islam relies on an unattainable standard of perfection, it can never in the final analysis provide certain assurance of salvation. Christians are allowed to say that our salvation is assured, not because of our righteousness but because we can trust God to keep his promises (for example, Jn 1:12; 3:16). It is on the basis of Christ and his work alone that we can we know for sure that we are saved. Christians must demonstrate this truth to Muslims through their lives as well as their words.

Christians living in Muslim countries need to realize that the rules may be very different from the ones stated by Muslim apologists in the United States. Many Islamic cultures are characterized by harshness and intolerance. Many Muslims themselves may decry these conditions, but that does not make them disappear, and Christians ignore them to their peril.

In many Muslim countries, openness to persuasion is a one-way street. Christians may be prohibited by law from carrying out any evangelism (for example, in Malaysia) and may be prohibited from practicing their religion publicly (for example, in Saudi Arabia and Iran). Further-more, there are Muslim communities where public conversion to Christianity automatically results in complete ostracism, possi-bly even the forfeiture of the convert's life. These are the realities—denying them does not make them go away. Western Chris-tians need to be aware of the risks that go along with making a Christian com-mitment in those societies.

Similarly, many Muslim countries are not culturally tolerant. Western women

Purification prior to prayers at the Abdul Aziz Mosque in Nairobi, Kenya.

visiting some Muslim countries will simply have to live with the fact that, all disclaimers aside, they will be treated as second-class people. A recruiter for a Christian mission group to Islamic countries has lamented that many women who sign up for mission work in a Muslim context get discouraged and return home when they are confronted with the social realities. He does not blame them but points out that they might be able to make a long-range contribution by calling attention to the liberating power of the gospel if they stayed. Nevertheless, there is a sacrifice.

In Islamic countries, as everywhere, folk religion prevails, often to the chagrin of the educated leaders. The Islamic practices of the common people (for example, reciting the Qur'an or praying) tend to be carried out to keep the jinn at bay, not to worship God. Sometimes practices that have no foundation in the Qur'an or shari'a prevail, such as commemoration of saints and pilgrimages to holy sites other than Mecca. This is particularly true of Southeast Asia, where Islam has adapted itself to prevailing customs in some ways. For example, in Singapore there are several mosques of unusual architecture in the vicinity of some Chinese and Hindu temples. In my ramblings through the neighborhood I saw a sign pointing out the "Durga Shrine." Immediately recognizing Durga as the name of a Hindu goddess, I expected to see a small Hindu temple. Instead, the building was a mosque unlike any I had ever visited before. I knew that this was not a typical mosque the moment I entered and smelled incense, which reminded me of Asian temples, not mosques. The small building was divided into several open rooms with a narrow corridor leading up to the mihrab, the niche facing Mecca. The mihrab was partitioned off with an iron gate, and behind it was a display of lights and incense sticks burning as a sign of devotion to Allah. There was probably nothing in direct violation of Islamic law, but this form of devotion certainly does not fit the traditional pattern. It is an example of a culturally adapted Islam, which is more prevalent in Southeast Asia than standard descriptions of Islam are likely to reveal.

Christian Missionary Strategies

Christian missions to Islam have long been some of the least fruitful. Many people have labored for long periods of time without seeing results. Consequent review and rethinking of mission strategies have led to the identification of three potential mission strategies. The first is an emphasis on "tentmaking." The apostle Paul worked as tentmaker during the course of his missionary journeys (Acts 18:3). Similarly, Christians are encouraged to enter Islamic countries that are closed to missionaries by plying some other profession and using their physical presence as an opportunity to share the gospel.

The second recommended strategy is cultural contextualization. If Christianity is rejected, it should be rejected for the right reason—for its message, not for the Western culture frequently associated with it. This goal is attainable, at least to some extent. There is no reason why Christian workers cannot dress in local style, worship on the floor in empty buildings or pray five times a day.[18] However, such workers need to be careful not to compromise any essential Christian beliefs or create the impression that they are Muslims. Sharing the outward forms of Islamic piety with their Muslim friends can build a bridge for sharing the unique Christian message.

The third strategy is the "fulfilled Muslim" approach. Some Christians have taken this approach a step further, reasoning that since a Muslim is someone who submits to God and since Christians submit to God, Christians are Muslims. Furthermore, just as Christians out of a Jewish context are "fulfilled" Jews, that is, Jews who have found the true Messiah, it is possible for Christians to call themselves "fulfilled Muslims." They claim to be Muslims and worship in mosques along with other Muslims in the hope of being able to persuade Muslims to accept Christ as Savior.

The "fulfilled Muslim" approach is clearly inappropriate. Since the Qur'an explicitly denies certain essential Christian doctrines (for example, Christ's deity and atoning death on the cross), Christianity can never be a fulfillment of Islam; it is Islam's contradiction. Christians can never accept Muhammad as an authentic prophet. Finally, if I go to a mosque and call myself a Muslim, the people I am talking to have every right to interpret that claim as acceptance of the belief that the Qur'an is true, that Muhammad is a true prophet and that Christ is no more than a prophet. Regardless of what I think in my head, that is what my words would communicate to people, and consequently I would be denying Christ.

On the other hand, a culturally contextualized approach to missions to Islam seems highly appropriate, mandated by the apostle Paul's own cultural adaptations in his mission to Gentiles. Any approach to Islam needs to recognize the dignity and worth of Muslims as human beings and needs to try to separate the message of the gospel from cultural factors. This recognition (which is appropriate for all groups) rules out intentional deceptions, but it facilitates displaying the gospel message in such a way that people can understand it within their own frame of reference. Thus it should also keep us focused on the main concern: that Muslims, like all people, need the hope and assurance that is possible only through Jesus Christ.

Mastering the Material

When you have finished studying this chapter, you should be able to

1. narrate the important events of the life of Muhammad;

2. summarize the events of the struggles for succession, including the first four caliphs, the Sunni dynasties, the first three Shi'ite imams, the different groups of Shi'ite Islam, the specific points of difference between Sunna and Shi'a;

3. describe the written sources of authority in Islam as embodied in the Qur'an, the hadiths and shari'a;

4. outline the distinctive doctrinal beliefs of Islam, as expressed under the headings of God, angels and spirits, prophets and Scripture, judgment and decree;

5. summarize the main obligations associated with each of the five pillars of Islam: confession, prayer, fasting, almsgiving and pilgrimage to Mecca;

6. describe Islamic requirements concerning diet and clothing;

7. explain how the status of women is said to be enhanced in Islam and describe the criticisms of that view;

8. explain jihad and the Muslim view of the Islamic advance;

9. summarize the main events of the Black Muslim movement;

10. be able to respond intelligently to a Muslim apologetic against Christianity;

11. state some of the important issues in a Christian mission to Islam.

Term Paper Ideas

1. Undertake a detailed study of the life of Muhammad; show how specific events were formative for his beliefs and the subsequent history of Islam.

2. Research the specific beliefs and practices of one Islamic subgroup or in one geographic location, for example, the distinctives of Ismailite Shi'ite Islam or Islam in Malaysia.

3. Do an exposition of one sura or one group of suras in the Qur'an for their meaning and implications.

4. Trace how one particular issue in Islam has been treated in hadith and shari'a.

5. Compile a comprehensive picture of Islamic teaching about Jesus Christ.

6. Make a detailed analysis of how one of the five pillars would function in the life of one Muslim individual.

7. Treat the subject of women in Islam from the testimony of Islamic women in various Muslim countries.

8. By using reports contemporary to the events in newspapers and magazines, paint a portrait of how Black Islam has been perceived at various points in time. For instance, research reports on the assassination of Malcolm X or the refusal by Muhammad Ali to serve in the armed forces.

9. Analyze a specific armed conflict involving Islam and show how the concept of jihad was applied.

10. Make a thorough study of the principles and practices of one Christian missions group to an Islamic group or country.

Core Bibliography

Ali, A. Jusuf, trans. *The Holy Qur'an*. Brentwood, Md.: Amana, 1983.

Denney, Frederick M. *An Introduction to Islam*. 2nd ed. New York: Macmillan, 1994.

———. *Islam and the Muslim Community*. San Francisco: HarperSanFrancisco, 1987.

Encyclopedia of Islam. 7 vols. and supplements. New York: E. J. Brill, 1993.

Haneef, Suzanne. *What Everyone Should Know About Islam and Muslims*. Chicago: Kazi, 1979.

Martin, Richard C. *Islam: A Cultural Perspective*. Englewood Cliffs, N.J.: Prentice-Hall, 1982.

Chapter 4

Zoroastrianism

Estimated Membership
Worldwide: 189,000
North America: 1,000[1]

Compared to many of the other religions in this book, the religion of ancient Persia is little known among people today. We know little about its beginnings, far less about its time of growth and not as much as we would like about its time of flourishing.[2] Its present membership is a small minority, most of whom live far away from its land of origin. Furthermore, claims to its influence on other religions have been exaggerated. Then why study it? For our purposes there are several reasons to look at Zoroastrianism, such as historical interest and fascination with the religion of this admittedly small group of adherents. Above all, this religion is a case study in the claims I have made for the development of religion and ritual.

In brief, Zoroastrianism is the religion of ancient Persia. It received its name from the Greek form of the name of its founder, Zoroaster, who lived sometime in the sixth century B.C. It survives today as the religion of the Gabars in Iran and the Parsis in India and in locations around the globe to which Indian people have emigrated.

Period	Dates	Form of Religion
Aryans	? to 600 B.C.	Polytheism, fire sacrifice, haoma
Zoroaster	628 to 551 B.C.	Ahura Mazda and Amesha Spentas, opposed by Angra Mainyu, moral dualism, sacrifice
Achaemenid	558 to 330 B.C.	Zoroastrianism mixed with polytheism, administered by magi
Greek	330 B.C. to A.D. 226	Zoroastrianism dormant, Mithraism
Sassanid	A.D. 226 to 637	Zoroastrian orthodoxy, Ohmazd vs. Ahriman, ceremonial dualism; also Zurvanism, Manichaeism
Modern	A.D. 637 to present	Gabars in Iran, Parsis in India and places of immigration, fire temples, orthodox Zoroastrianism passed on through tradition and practice

Table 4.1. Periods of Zoroastrian history

The Religion of the Aryan Invaders

To understand the origins of Zoroastrianism, we need to go back into earliest prehistory. This requires a bit of detective work and a lot of detailed data. But it will be worth it. We will find evidence that there was a religion with roots that go back as far as five thousand years. Tribes holding to this religion eventually settled in various locations of Europe and Asia. Zoroastrianism is a descendant of that ancient religion.

A group of tribes, collectively called the Aryans, came from somewhere in southeastern Europe—possibly the southwestern Asian steppes, possibly the area of the Aral Sea. They were related to various European tribes, a fact that is evident today in the similarities that exist among languages.[3] Linguistics recognizes an Indo-European language family. Many words and grammatical functions that we use in English today are similar to words used in India (in Sanskrit) three thousand years ago. These similarities show up in culture and religion as well.

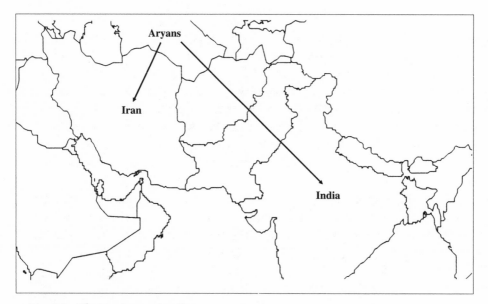

Map 4.1. The two Aryan migrations

The Aryans were nomads who raised cattle as they wandered over the plains. Around 1500 B.C., for reasons kept to themselves, they undertook one of the mass migrations that occur from time to time in ancient history. Some of them went as far as India; the ones who are the subject of this chapter wound up settling on the Iranian plateau (whence we get the name Iran—the land of the Aryans). We can extrapolate some of their earliest religious beliefs and practices from (1) early Hindu scriptures, the Vedas, which became the extension of ancient Aryan religion in India, and (2) the reaction *against* Aryan religion found in Zoroaster's writings. For example, from the fact that

Zoroaster exhorted his converts to cease slaughtering animals as sacrifices to the daevas, we can reasonably infer that up to this point people were sacrificing animals to daevas.

Monotheism and the lesser gods. In both the Indian and the Iranian versions of Aryan religion, we find two kinds of spiritual beings. Of primary day-to-day importance were the devas (Indian) or daevas (Iranian); these beings were the recipients of regular worship. The root word for the names of these gods is *div,* which literally means "to shine." Thus the daevas are "the shining ones." The same root is preserved in English in the terms *divinities, deities* and (paradoxically) *devil.*[4] Some of the daevas worshiped in Iranian religion included Mithra, a god of truth and light (Indian Mitra); Intar (Verethragna), a god of war and power (Indian Indra); Arta (Asha), a god of truth, justice and order (Indian Rita, compare our word *right*) and Vayu, a god of wind.

Competing with these beings was another group of spirits, called asuras (Indian) or ahuras (Iranian). This term meant "lords," and its meaning was ambiguous. In one sense it referred simply to a second group of spirits, but Ahura was also an honorific title applied to particularly great gods.

Behind this pantheon, however, we find the remnants of an original monotheism, although it had undergone several changes. The same root word, *div,* which became the source of the word *daevas,* originally served as the word for a single God, known in Indian as Dyaus Pitar, which means literally "father god" (note how the stem of *pitar* survives in words such as *paternal*). In various permutations, this name survived into Greek mythology as Zeus Pater or its Latin form, Jupiter. This god was believed to live in the sky; by the time of the Aryan invasions, his identity had merged into the sky itself, and so we have the sky god Varuna in India or his counterpart Ouranos in Greek mythology. We meet him in Iran under the name of Uruwana; here he is also called Ahura Mazda, literally the "wise lord."[5] Ahura Mazda is the creator and preserver of the natural order.

Thus we find in Iran, as elsewhere, the remnant of an original belief in one God. Though displaced by layers of religious development, this deity remains part of the religious heritage. The eventual move back to monotheism thus did not have to be either a brand-new invention or the result of some external influence. It was a return to what was already a part of the culture.

The sacrifice. In chapter one it was pointed out that original monotheism, as it may have been understood in Genesis 4:26, included animal sacrifice—animals were burned on stone altars. Animal sacrifice was the focal point of Aryan religion in its Indian and Iranian forms. However, it had become far more complex than whatever its original form was.

The Aryan fire sacrifice became the exclusive province of a professional priesthood. The priests, who had several enigmatic titles, including *magi* and *karpans,* were the only ones who knew the proper method and formulas. They alone had the right to perform the sacrifices and to insist that the populace comply with their demands. It is crucial for the entire history of religion that in the millennium from about 1500 B.C. to 500 B.C., an exclusive priesthood held a position of prominence in virtually every civilized culture around the world. The sixth century saw a worldwide rebellion against this priestly aristocracy.[6] It was one of their own number, the priest Zoroaster, who led the revolt in Persia.

Description	Indian	Ancient Iranian	After Zoroaster
gods	devas (good)	daevas (good)	daevas (devils)
lords	asuras (capricious)	ahura(s) (good, exalted)	Ahura Mazda is Wise Lord
Father God	Dyaus Pitar	Equated with Ahura Mazda?	Ahura Mazda
Sky	Varuna	Uruwana	Equated with Ahura Mazda
King of Gods	Indra	Intar	Verethragna
God of Truth	Rita	Arta (Asha)	Asha is an Amesha Spenta
fire sacrifice	animals sacrificed God Agni	animals sacrificed God Atar	fire, but no animals sacrificed
sacred drink	soma	haoma	forbidden by Z., later restored

Table 4.2. Ancient Indo-Aryan religion

The sacrifice was an animal such as an ox that the worshiper provided. As the priest uttered the prescribed words, he sacrificed all or part of the animal with fire. Because the Aryans considered fire such an important force, they recognized it as a divinity in its own right—the fire god Atar (Iranian; Indian: Agni—compare our word *ignition*). In addition, the priests provided themselves with a drink from a sacred plant called haoma (Iranian; Indian: soma). Apparently this drink contained an intoxicating, possibly psychedelic, drug. The Aryans thought it could confer immortality. Haoma itself became personified as a deity.

Thus by the time of Zoroaster, ancient Aryan religion was a complicated polytheistic religion involving many intricate rituals, and it was concentrated in the hands of a professional priestly aristocracy.

Zoroaster's Life

The Persian form of Zoroaster's name was Zarathustra. Zoroaster was the Greek form of the name, and it has survived as the main term for the man and the religion.[7] Because of the force of Zoroaster's eventual influence on the world, ancient writers embellished his legend with imaginary dates, such as 6000 B.C. Contemporary scholarship has produced highly divergent dates, with one writer going as far back as possibly 1700

B.C.8 The sources that we have (the Pahlavi scriptures) are far more prosaic. They state that his mission occurred "258 years before Alexander." Filling in the details (Alexander's defeat of the Persians in 330 B.C.; Zoroaster's first successes at age forty; his life span of seventy-seven years) produces a popularly accepted set of dates: 628 B.C. to 551 B.C.9 Thus Zoroaster was a contemporary of the Hebrew prophets Jeremiah and Daniel (among others) at the time of the Jewish exile in Babylonia. Then the Persians took over Babylonia. At that time Persia was experiencing serious political conflict as various tribes attempted to establish ascendancy over each other. The Medes have achieved the most power as our story begins.

The birth of Zoroaster is shrouded in mythology. Surviving writings contain various stories of prophecies and attendant miracles. The sources agree that he left his family at age twenty to become a member of the priesthood, which gives him unique status among founders of religions, most of whom come from social strata that have been successfully subordinated to and by the priests. According to tradition, he spent a lot of time meditating in the mountains, although he also officiated at priestly rituals.

When he was thirty years old,[10] Zoroaster had his first vision of God. The legend tells us that when he was on the bank of the Daitya River, an archangel, Vohu Manah ("good thought"), appeared to him as a human figure that was nine times bigger than an ordinary person. Vohu Manah asked Zoroaster to lay aside his body for the time being and ascend with him to heaven. There the prophet entered the presence of Ahura Mazda, who instructed him in what he was to teach from that time forward. Back on earth, he complied with the vision immediately. Over the next eight years he had six more visions.

At first Zoroaster experienced opposition. This was not surprising, since much of Zoroaster's teaching cut at the livelihood of the professional priesthood as well as beliefs and practices that were dear to the common people. Eventually he came to the court of King Hystapes (also called Vishtaspa).[11] Although the king initially went along with his priests and imprisoned Zoroaster, he accepted the prophet's teaching when Zoroaster supposedly cured Hystapes' favorite horse. The king's conversion provided Zoroaster with a base of support that would safeguard his message for the future.

The extent of Zoroaster's success for the remaining thirty-three years of his life is unclear. The entire empire never converted to his teachings, but then his message did not remain confined to just a handful of individuals either. Apparently many people accepted Zoroaster's teachings, and many rejected them as well. According to the traditions, Zoroaster was killed during an invasion as he was kneeling before the fire altar.

Zoroaster's Teachings

The sources. Zoroastrianism has a collection of holy scriptures called the Avesta. Like the Bible, the Avesta is composed of many different writings that originated in various periods of time. Its main body is called the Yasna. The Yasna's most ancient component is the Gathas, which are supposed to contain hymns by Zoroaster himself. The very ancient form of its language demonstrates the antiquity of the Avesta. The other components of the Avesta reflect different time periods and views that sometimes conflict with the teachings of the Yasna, though they are put into the mouth of Zoroaster. In addition, there are later writings, particularly the Pahlavi scriptures,

Figure 4.1. The Zoroastrian scriptures

which date from the ninth century A.D. Thus they are very late, but they seem to incorporate ancient authority.[12]

God. The most crucial aspect of Zoroaster's teaching was the return to monotheism. Ahura Mazda was to be thought of as supreme, the only god worthy of worship. By contrast, the daevas are evil spirits and should not be worshiped.

God is working in the world through Spenta Mainyu, his holy spirit. In addition, he manifests himself through his Amesha Spentas, the "holy immortals." These beings, if that is what they are, have been the subject of much debate. There are six of them, and they seem to have been accepted as angels or even deities in later developments. There is good reason to believe that Zoroaster saw them as attributes of Ahura Mazda himself, not as separate beings. They are divided into a father side and a mother side, and their names reflect desirable qualities for proper devotion.

Father Side	Mother Side
Vohu Manah (Good Thought)	Haurvatat (Perfection)
Asha (Righteousness)	Armaiti (Piety)
Kshathra (Power, Dominion)	Ameretat (Immortality)

Table 4.3. Amesha Spentas

According to one Zoroastrian scholar, "It must never be forgotten that all these six are not *different* Beings, nor even the 'creations' of the Supreme. They are in very truth *aspects* of *Ahura Mazda*. . . . These six 'Holy Immortals' together with *Ahura Mazda* made a *Heptad,* who are known in later literature as the 'Seven Amesha-Spenta.' "[13]

Thus Ahura Mazda may be analogous to the Christian Trinity (one God in three persons), consisting of one God in seven Amesha Spentas. In any event, the doctrine of the Amesha Spentas should not be interpreted in any way that compromises Zoroaster's monotheism, although it would eventually change in exactly that way after the passing of Zoroaster himself.

Ahura Mazda has all the characteristics typically associated with the God of original monotheism. As his name ("Wise Lord") implies, Ahura Mazda is all-knowing, and he is the creator of all that exists. Most important, he is the author of the standards of righteousness by which his creatures must live.

The evil spirit. Ahura Mazda is opposed by an evil spirit, Angra Mainyu, who seeks to divert creatures from following the commands of Ahura Mazda. The existence of Angra Mainyu in Zoroastrianism has caused this religion to be called dualistic, meaning a religion based on the opposition of two spirits, one all good and one all evil, with the outcome of the conflict depending on the believer's choices. Strictly speaking, Zoroaster's own teachings are not dualistic, since the evil spirit is not equal to Ahura Mazda in any respect. In true dualism the two spirits are of equal stature, and the outcome of their cosmic struggle is in doubt. But Angra Mainyu is inferior to Ahura Mazda; he is derived from God (as creature or in later descriptions as offspring); he does not share Ahura Mazda's high attributes—for example, he is stupid, not wise, and he is going to lose the war. Thus Zoroaster's belief about God and Angra Mainyu fits the pattern we see in the monotheistic faiths of Judaism, Islam and Christianity with regard to the role of Satan.

Although Ahura Mazda will certainly win the war, the outcome of the individual battles within particular persons remains uncertain. It is up to each human being to come into alignment with Ahura Mazda. Preeminently, this means that each person must be on the side of Truth (*Asha*) and must be opposed to the Lie (*Druj*). Human beings are free to choose, and each action furthers either Ahura Mazda's truth or Angra Mainyu's lie. All of these deeds are accumulated over a lifetime. The person who has supported Truth will receive rewards on earth and in heaven, but the person who has supported the Lie will receive punishment.

Although Zoroaster did not teach a metaphysical dualism, we can speak of a "moral dualism" in regard to the practical implications of his teachings. Each person's life consists of an ongoing series of choices between right and wrong. The opposition that occurs here is moral, involving right and wrong choices. In later Zoroastrianism this moral dualism was rivaled by a ritual dualism that involved a conflict between spiritual cleanness and uncleanness.

Ritual practice. Zoroaster opposed the system of animal sacrifices because he saw it as inherently cruel to animals as well as part of the worship of the evil daevas. Furthermore, he denounced the use of haoma as corrupt and decadent. But he did not abolish all the practices of his day. Most importantly, Zoroaster retained the centrality of fire as representing the truth and purity of Ahura Mazda, and he continued to practice a fire ritual as an act of worship of God alone.

The Achaemenid Period (558-330 B.C.)

Although Zoroaster's teaching has not been lost, there is no evidence that it was ever consistently implemented on a large scale. The fragmentary information we have in regard to Persian religion in the centuries before the coming of Alexander the Great shows that Zoroaster's lofty monotheism was soon accommodated to the prevailing polytheism. The principle of decay explained in chapter one applies: a religious culture, left without strong guidance, will tend toward increased ritual and magic. The history of Zoroastrianism after the prophet is a good case in point.

There is no good reason to believe that any of the great Persian kings (referred to as the Achaemenid dynasty) were genuine followers of Zoroaster (or, if any were, they left no record of it). Cyrus the Great identified himself specifically as a worshiper of the Babylonian god Marduk.[14] Three kings referred to Ahura Mazda in their inscriptions, but never as the only God. Xerxes specifically mentioned the god Arta (Asha) as one that he worshiped, Artaxerxes praised Mithra and Anahita (a fertility goddess), and Darius I thanked Ahura Mazda "and the other gods."[15] Thus Ahura Mazda, the one true God of Zoroaster's reform, became the greatest of gods within a larger Persian pantheon.

During the time of the Achaemenid kings, the apparent custodians of Zoroaster's teachings were the magi, the very group Zoroaster opposed. They showed no willingness to give up their privileged position as ritual experts. Although they paid lip service to Zoroaster's teachings, they incorporated the worship of Ahura Mazda into their larger heritage of polytheism and ritual. Because the Aryans had been in the land for a long time and had replaced a nomadic culture with an agrarian economy, the supply of animals for sacrificial purposes was drying up because of the ongoing demand. Consequently, the magi dispensed with the traditional sacrificial patterns but retained other aspects of worship practice, including the haoma ritual that Zoroaster had thoroughly detested.

Reliable information on the magi is scant. This is not surprising, since there are few reliable sources for this period in general. We meet the magi in a later period as astrologers coming to Bethlehem to worship the King of the Jews (Mt 2), but how this event fits into their larger sphere of activities is unclear.[16] They apparently served as priests, astrologers, magicians (they gave us the word *magic*) and all-around leaders in religious matters wherever they found a niche to exert their influence. From what we can tell, they incorporated Zoroastrianism only insofar as it did not detract from their other functions.

The Greek Period (330 B.C.-A.D. 226)

From Alexander the Great's victory over the Persian Empire in 330 B.C. until a true Persian kingdom was reestablished in A.D. 226, Zoroastrianism existed only in a state of dormancy, practiced by common people without much influence on society at large. The sole worldwide impact of Persian religion (though hardly what Zoroaster would have wanted) was the cult of the god Mithra, which Roman soldiers picked up and spread throughout the Roman Empire. Mithra was seen as the supreme god that all other gods worshiped, even Ahura Mazda! He was symbolized by the "invincible sun" and was associated with truth and light. This religion, which at its height rivaled Christianity in popularity, particularly attracted men, possibly because it held secret ceremonies in mountain caves that included sacrificing bulls to Mithra.

Zoroaster. Photograph: Corbis-Bettmann.

The Sassanid Dynasty (A.D. 226-637)

A new dynasty took over the Persian kingdom in A.D. 226. It survived until the Muslim conquest of 637. Possibly for political reasons, these rulers reinstated the ancient religion of Zoroaster. Zoroastrianism flourished for the next four hundred years, although not in the pure form that Zoroaster intended. During this period the collection of scriptures that we know as the Avesta was completed. This was Zoroastrianism in its prime.

Deities. Ahura Mazda, now called Ohrmazd, reigned supreme during the Sassanid dynasty. Some of the worst polytheistic influences were purged. Nevertheless, older, secondary gods were still present. Among deities that still received recognition were Mithra, Asha, Vayu and Verethragna. Still lesser spirits were also acknowledged: the angels, the evil daevas and a collection of ancestral guardian spirits called the fravashis. However, Ohrmazd's supremacy was not questioned.

Tendency toward dualism. The mythology of Angra Mainyu, now called Ahriman, also developed further. Although Ahriman was theoretically inferior to Ohrmazd, he was credited with a lot more power, particularly the power to create. He was seen as producing an evil countercreation to Ohrmazd's good creation. For each good, beautiful and beneficial thing that Ohrmazd made, Ahriman made something bad, ugly and destructive. Whereas Ohrmazd was aided by his angels, Ahriman, now endowed with an evil counterpart to the Amesha Spentas, was supported by the daevas.

On the practical level, this development meant that Zoroaster's battle between good and evil, originally fought out on the personal, moral plane, became increasingly focused on the spiritual, ritual sphere. Living by the Truth and avoiding the Lie was no longer enough. Increasingly, it became necessary to be protected from all the potentially evil influences in the world. Thus Zoroastrians became preoccupied with maintaining ceremonial purity and warding off evil spirits.

Ceremonial (or ritual) purity is different from moral righteousness. In highly simplified terms, a moral act involves intentionally keeping or intentionally breaking a rule, whereas ceremonial purity is concerned with avoiding contamination from contact with an unclean object or person. Thus killing someone in violation of a commandment results in moral impurity, while touching a corpse results in ceremonial impurity. The one violation renders someone wicked, the other, unclean. If a moral violation is unintentional (for example, you did not mean to break your mother's vase), it may be excused. But ritual contamination is objective: someone who touches a corpse becomes unclean, whether or not the contact was intentional.

All religions (at least on the folk level) have a category of ceremonial purity.[17] In late Zoroastrianism, ritual concerns overshadowed moral injunctions. The domain of the daevas was particularly associated with corpses and, by logical extension, with any part of a human body no longer connected to the living person, such as hair, nail clippings, bodily excretions or anything that came into contact with a menstruating woman.

Disposing of corpses presented a particular difficulty. Interment would defile the earth; cremation would defile the fire, the symbol of Ohrmazd himself. Therefore the Zoroastrian culture resorted to an ancient practice of the magi: mounting corpses in such a way that scavengers would dispose of them, a practice that continues to this day. Zoroastrian communities in Iran still maintain "towers of silence"—walled open-air platforms of circular shape where vultures feed.

Warding off the daevas also became an ongoing concern. The last component of the Avesta, the Videvdat, was a collection of spells intended to ward off the daevas and the defilement that they caused. The power of these spells lay in the proper recitation of them, and the spells became the content of their own ritual ceremonies. Chanting the proper phrase or sentence, called a manthra (Indian mantra), was considered a powerful weapon against Ahriman's hordes.

Future expectations. Zoroastrianism also developed widened expectations for the future, including (1) personal judgment after death, (2) the coming of future prophets and (3) the end of the world.

After a person dies, the soul spends three days sitting at the head of the body contemplating his or her deeds. This is a time of intense, agonized reflection. The soul of a good person is already being comforted by an angel, while the soul of an evil person is already being tormented by demons. Then the soul must cross the Chivrat bridge, which is essentially the blade of a sword. If the person was good, the blade flips onto its broad side and the soul crosses into paradise with ease; if the person was bad, the blade flips onto its sharp edge. The evil soul, already spooked by horrible apparitions, cannot keep its balance and falls into the torments of hell.

Zoroaster prophesied that his coming had occurred at the beginning of the final age of humanity, which would last three thousand years. As each of the three remaining thousand-year periods closed, another prophet, Zoroaster's direct offspring, would make his appearance. A legend developed that Zoroaster had deposited sperm into a lake, and in each of the predicted time periods, a pure virgin would bathe in the lake, become impregnated with Zoroaster's sperm and give birth to his son, who would be the next prophet. The three prophets (Aushetar, Aushetarmah and Saoshyant) would lead the world in their age; for Saoshyant this would mean presiding over the end of the world.

The end of the world will come with a cosmic flood of hot molten metal. To righteous people it will feel like a bath of warm milk. But evil people, on earth and in hell, will feel all the agony and torture the image implies. In the end all will be brought back to purity. The wicked will survive, cleansed of all evil and retaining whatever good they possessed. Ahriman will be defeated for all time.

Extremes in dualism. During this time Zoroastrianism spawned two further religious movements, Zurvanism and Manichaeism, both of which carried dualistic tendencies to their logical extremes. Orthodox Zoroastrians considered them heretical.

Zurvanism attempted to explain the origin of evil. Despite a tendency to place Ohrmazd and Ahriman increasingly on a par, Zoroastrianism had been hesitant to make them completely equal. But it was only a matter of time before someone took that step, and the followers of Zurvanism took dualism to this extreme. Ohrmazd and Ahriman, the "twins" (an expression used metaphorically by Zoroaster himself), were considered equal in all respects, in origin as well as in power. This was genuine dualism, not a dualism in which the good being is intrinsically superior to the evil one, as in mainstream Zoroastrianism.

How did the twins originate? How could there be two coequal gods, one good and one evil? The answer was that both were the offspring of the god Zurvan. *Zurvan* originally meant "time"; in an extended sense it came to mean the total space-time continuum. In the hands of these religious thinkers it took on the characteristics of a god with personhood. The Zurvanites then worshiped Zurvan, the god of space-time, as their highest god, the father of Ohrmazd and Ahriman. Zurvanism made a strong showing for a while during the Sassanid period. Eventually it was suppressed by the orthodox followers of Ohrmazd.[18]

A second dualistic movement began in this period under the prophet Mani. Mani, who lived in the third century A.D., combined ideas from Zurvanism, Christianity and even Buddhism in his teachings. He gave Persian dualism a new twist—a dualism of spirit and matter. Traditional Zoroastrian dualism focused on the distinction between good and evil in the realms of morality, spiritual forces and ritual. It was assumed that this battle was being waged in both the physical and the spiritual world. But Mani described the battle as the result of the cleavage between spirit (good) and matter (evil). Spirit consists of light that is entrapped in the darkness of evil matter. God is the father of light, and the soul's yearning is to be reunited with its source of light. Manichaeism, which is classified with other Gnostic philosophies, also established itself throughout the Roman Empire for many centuries. The best-known adherent of Manichaeism achieved fame when he eventually deserted Mani's teachings. Augustine of Hippo, arguably the father of

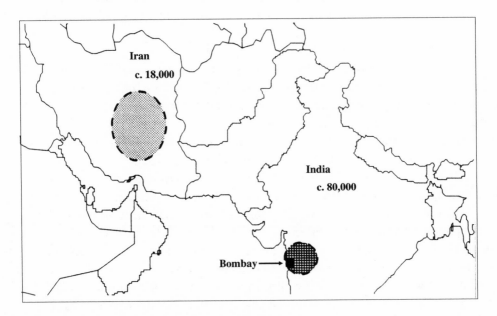

Map 4.2. Largest Parsi regions in Iran and India

Western Christian theology, began his intellectual and spiritual journey as a Manichaean.[19]

Demise and Dispersion

The Muslim conquest of Iran in the seventh century ended the era of Zoroastrian ascendancy. Although theoretically Zoroastrians were entitled to the protection accorded to "People of the Book," in practice the religion was oppressed. Under Islamic rule their official title was *Gabars,* which means "infidels" or "unbelievers." Their self-designation is *Zardushtins* or *Iranis.* It is estimated that they now number about 18,000.[20] Recent reinstitution of an intolerant Shi'ite regime in Iran has precipitated further persecution.

Most of the two hundred thousand Zoroastrians in the world today live outside of Iran. Within a hundred years after the Muslims took over their homeland, many Zoroastrians realized that they had a better chance of surviving somewhere else. The majority of those who left settled in Bombay, India, where a small but active Zoroastrian community has survived to this day. In India Zoroastrians became known as the Parsis, the Persians. It is customary to refer to living Zoroastrianism as the Parsi religion (the terms will be used interchangeably from now on). The last one hundred years have seen large waves of emigration from India. The Indian emigrants have taken their religions with them and have established their own temples around the world. That pattern applies to the Parsis as well. Thus, for example, there are Parsi fire temples in Nairobi, Toronto and Chicago.

Contemporary Zoroastrianism

The contemporary development of Zoroastrianism is geared as much to insuring the survival of the community as it is to propagating its beliefs.[21] Like Judaism, the Parsi religion is tied to one particular ethnic group. As the number of ethnic Parsis in the world declines, so does the number of Zoroastrians. Nevertheless, Zoroastrians have resisted the idea of accepting converts from the outside. Even today many adherents feel that converts would contaminate their faith.

Contemporary Zoroastrianism closely approximates the ideals of the prophet. Ohrmazd is clearly recognized as the only God; all inferior deities are neatly designated as archangels (*yazdat*) or angels. Ahriman continues to be seen as the evil counterpart to God, but of unambiguously lower stature. The daevas, though potentially dangerous, are nothing more than low-level spirits. Rites and worship services abound with symbolism, but without the extremes that Zoroaster criticized.

The life cycle. Each of the four standard rites of passage—birth, puberty, marriage and death—is important in the life of Zoroastrians. When a child is born, a lamp is lit. This rite seems highly appropriate for a religion in which light and fire are symbols for God. The lamp, traditionally fueled by butter, is kept burning for at least three days. A special thanksgiving ceremony is performed at the child's first birthday.

The *navjot* ceremony, which is performed at puberty, initiates young people into the Zoroastrian faith. Boys and girls undergo the ritual sometime between the ages of seven and fifteen (earlier in India, later in Iran). At this time the children declare themselves to be full adherents of Zoroaster's teachings. The ceremony can take place at home or on a ceremonial stage. After purificatory prayers, the child receives presents and auspicious objects and then makes a public declaration of adherence to the faith. The ceremony reaches its high point as the child is invested with the sacred shirt (sudra) and the sacred belt (kusti), articles that will be worn throughout life.

The sudra, the sacred shirt, is an undershirt made of white cotton. On the front of it is a small pocket that symbolically collects the person's good deeds over the course of a lifetime. The kusti, the sacred belt, is a long cord consisting of six white woollen threads, each of which is made of twelve threads, a total of seventy-two threads symbolizing the seventy-two chapters of the Yasna. The belt is wrapped around the body three times so as to be knotted in front and in back twice each. The kusti belt is untied and then retied at each prayer time. The navjot ceremony closes with the recitation of blessings.

Parsis are monogamous. Marriage is considered a religious rite as well as a social institution. The wedding ceremony includes prayers and exorcisms. At one point in the ceremony a thread is wrapped around the couple. The bride and groom sit before the priest, separated by a screen of thin cloth hung between them. They join hands, and the priest wraps a thread, first around their hands and then around the entire couple. They remain linked in that fashion through the remainder of the official ceremony, which is followed by a celebration feast.

Wherever possible, Parsis have retained ancient customs. But in modern societies outside of Iran, Zoroastrians have replaced the towers of silence with cremation. Nevertheless, Zoroastrian beliefs continue to stress the notion that death marks the soul's entrance into the next life, where it is judged on the basis of good and evil deeds performed in this life.

Daily practice. Zoroastrians attempt to make devotion to Ahura Mazda the center of their lives from beginning to end and around the clock each day. The day is divided into five "watches," which constitute prayer periods. During each watch the adherents are supposed to say a ritual prayer.[22] The prayers involve purification, untying and tying the kusti belt and reciting certain passages from the Avesta. A prayer is considered particularly helpful when it is said in the vicinity of water, perhaps facing the rising sun over the ocean. Evening prayers are traditionally said in front of the fire altar in the home. This is a small altar on which a tiny sandalwood fire is lit in honor of God.

Zoroastrians attempt to lead lives in compliance with Ahura Mazda's commands. Their adherence to high moral standards has earned them high regard in their larger communities and, on the whole, success in the modern business world. They also abide by the demands of ritual purity, which include necessary ablutions such as a daily morning bath, and recite manthras as necessary to ward off evil. There are no elaborate dietary standards. Contamination with ritually unclean substances (for example, hair or nail clippings) is not considered terribly serious, except for contact with corpses or carrion.

Temple ceremonies. Zoroastrian temples are known as fire temples. For reasons of community survival, the temples bear little identification on the outside. Usually the only decoration is a winged wheel. This decoration, commonly identified as the sign of Ahura Mazda, is more likely the symbol representing the fravashi, the ancient ancestral guardian spirit. Fire temples are considered extremely sacred; most of them are completely closed to outsiders as well as ritually unclean Parsis. Their ceremonies,

Parsi women participating in the World Parliament of Religions, Chicago, August 1993. Photograph: Reuters/Corbis-Bettmann.

however, are not secret; Parsi books include detailed descriptions of temple practices.

The interior of a fire temple, except for the sacred precinct, is essentially bare. Worshipers should attend every day, though four times a month is an accepted minimum. Worship services consist of ceremonies performed by the priest for the benefit of whoever may be present. Routine temple attendance consists of entering, performing ablutions, approaching the threshold of the sacred precinct barefoot, receiving ashes from the sacred fire on the eyelids and forehead, reciting a prayer and leaving.

Two major ceremonies, Yasna and Videvdat, are performed in fire temples on a regular basis. These rituals can be done only by a priest since they are extremely complex and demand perfection—the smallest deviation from the prescribed practice nullifies the ceremony.

The priesthood is hereditary. Contemporary priests are theoretically descendants of the original magi. Only males in the line of succession are eligible for the priesthood (priests clearly are not celibate). Becoming a full priest with supervisory authority (*dastur*) requires many years of learning. A priest has to know all the requirements of ritual purity and the various intricacies of the temple rituals. He must be able to recite extensive passages from the Avesta, which is a demanding task because he probably does not understand a word of the ancient Avestan language he is reciting. Priests are trained from boyhood in the necessary skills. They must wear a mouth veil and avoid unnecessary speaking (let alone coughing and sneezing) as they carry out their functions in the temple to avoid contaminating the sacred fire.

The main rite is the Yasna ceremony, which is a dedicatory service. The fire, contained in a small vaselike stand, is fed with sandalwood and is supposed to be maintained twenty-four hours a day without interruption. During the Yasna ceremony, wood is added to the fire while the priests recite Avestan manthras. Haoma twigs are pounded, and their juice is added to a mixture of milk and water. Sacred bread and butter are displayed on the altar and are imbued with spiritual power through recitations. The priests consume parts of the haoma and the bread. Then the elements are passed to the worshipers, who partake of them as a kind of communion service.

The Videvdat is the part of the Avesta that consists primarily of instructions on how to guard against the daevas, both by the invocation of manthras and by the observance of the proper rituals. The Videvdat ceremony performed in a fire temple centers around reading passages from the Videvdat in order to ward off these evil spirits. Since a mistake in performing the ceremony could have disastrous consequences, the passages are read, not recited from memory. Because the ceremony is usually carried out during the fifth watch, midnight to dawn, special copies of the Videvdat with extra-large print are used to facilitate reading at a time when there may not be much light. The sacred fire and the drinking of haoma are again a part of the service.

Special days. Modern Zoroastrians have a calendar of 365 days, divided into twelve months of thirty days and a special five-day period before each new year. There are at present three schools of thought on when the new year is supposed to begin: Iranian, Indian and a compromise that suits neither. Depending on the school, the new year begins in August, September or March. There is, however, agreement on the major holidays. The thirty-day months are not subdivided into weeks. Each month is named after one of the holy beings (an Amesha Spenta or a yazda). Each month has a holiday in recognition of the holy being for whom the month is named.

Several feasts occur in the first month of the year (Farvardin). New Year's Day (No Ruz) is a major feast that begins with solemn reflection and ends with joyful celebration. Zoroaster's birth is commemorated on the sixth day. The nineteenth day is dedicated to the angel Farvardin, for whom the month is named. Since he is in charge of departed spirits, it is believed that ancestors return to their homes during this festival, and special offerings are laid out for them.

Reflections. As a non-Zoroastrian outsider, I am in no position to judge what true Zoroastrianism is supposed to be. However, there is a pattern in the development of this religion that reflects exactly the kind of tension between original monotheism and its decay into ritual and animism that was described in chapter one. Zoroaster himself clearly taught monotheism. In following centuries his insights were merged into polytheistic and animistic patterns. Even in a phase that may be true to Zoroaster's intentions (the present phase) we nevertheless find a great preoccupation with rituals, reverence for inferior beings and techniques to subdue evil spirits. Worship of Ahura Mazda is definitely the center of the religion, but on the level of daily life this focus is constantly in danger of being swallowed by animistic concerns.

Zoroastrian Influences

Scholars commonly observe that the real significance of Zoroastrianism lies in the influence it has exerted on the development of other world religions, specifically Judaism, Christianity and Islam. For example, it has been suggested that Jews picked up the concepts of Satan, angels, demons and the apocalypse (resurrection and judgment at the end of the world) during their exile in Babylonia and immediately thereafter. Notions of Zoroastrian influence were particularly popular during the early twentieth century. Even though scholarly support for them has eroded, they continue to be propagated on the popular level and in introductory textbooks.[23]

There is nothing intrinsically pernicious about the idea that one religion may have influenced another one. A case in point lies in the origin of Islam in the life of Muhammad. We know that Muhammad came into contact with established versions of Judaism, Christianity and Zoroastrianism. We know what those adherents believed for the most part, and we can show exactly how some of those beliefs showed up (and how they were modified) in the Qur'an. Thus it makes sense to think in terms of the influence that these three religions exerted on Muhammad. I have argued that we must leave plenty of room both for Muhammad's own creativity and for the vestige of original monotheism present in Arabian culture at his time. The idea does become objectionable when the identification of a supposed influence is used to eliminate all originality (or even truth—the "genetic fallacy") from a religious belief simply by showing that it was derived from some other source.

We can use the example of influences on Muhammad to establish criteria by which we can judge whether Zoroastrianism could have influenced Judaism. In order to conclude reasonably that such an influence occurred, the following points have to be true:

1. Zoroastrianism must have been established in the form in which it was supposed to have influenced Judaism.

2. There must have been sufficient opportunity for the Jews to absorb the doctrines.

3. There must be sufficient resemblance between the Zoroastrian version of the doctrines and the biblical version to make influence a reasonable conclusion.

4. There must be a clear indication that the influence went from Zoroastrianism to Judaism and not the other way around. This criterion is particularly incisive if there is some evidence that the beliefs in question may have been present in Judaism before the period of supposed contact with Zoroastrianism.

A relief from Persepolis most likely showing King Darius and his son Xerxes. Photograph: Courtesy of the Oriental Institute of the University of Chicago.

As it turns out, not one of these criteria supports the notion of Zoroastrian influence.

1. Zoroastrianism had a particularly tough time getting established in Persia. Even the kings we know as Zoroastrians worshiped Ahura Mazda along with other gods. All these kings ruled at a time later than the period of the exile. Cyrus, who sent the Jews back to their own land, was not Zoroastrian. If Zoroastrianism had influenced Israel at this time, then the Jews must have been more open to the message of Zoroaster than the Persians themselves were.

2. The kind of intimate contact necessary for assimilation of foreign beliefs cannot be demonstrated for the Jews in the mainstream of biblical Judaism. As stated above, Persia did not become Zoroastrian until after the exile. So the influences (if any) must have come much more indirectly. An interesting sidelight to this discussion is that the ten northern tribes were indeed transported by the Assyrians to the region roughly identical with Media, the sphere of Zoroaster's activity. But the northern tribes had no concrete influence on the development of Judaism (in fact, they basically vanished). It would be far more likely that their presence in Media might have influenced subsequent thought there, but we have no evidence for that hypothesis either.

3. By and large, the supposed resemblances between Zoroastrianism and Judaism

are superficial at best. Beyond the idea that Jewish biblical writings show evidence of Satan, angels and apocalypse, there is very little similarity in the details. It must be kept in mind here that (1) we know very little about the Zoroastrianism of the Achaemenid dynasty; (2) much of what we do know comes from sources considerably later than biblical writings; (3) what we do know reflects the garbled, magic-obsessed, syncretistic religion of the magi—hardly the Zoroastrianism necessary for the Jews to use as source for the biblical version. The Talmud (itself a very late source—A.D. 400) states that the Jews brought the names of angels back with them from Babylon;[24] we can also allow for the idea that they may have been stimulated in their thinking about God, Satan, angels, demons and so on (in fact, common sense tells us that they must have done so). Nevertheless, such broad strokes are a far cry from proving that the Jews directly *borrowed* the actual concepts from Zoroastrianism. The Old Testament depicts Satan as a very inferior being, not as a dualistic opponent of God. We find only the sketchiest references to angels. They are definitely not objects of worship, and it is apparent that the apocalypses of the two cultures differ in all details other than *that* there is a resurrection and a judgment.

4. Finally, beyond resemblances, there are no particular data to support the assertion that Zoroastrianism influenced Judaism rather than the other way around. The very idea of foreign influences on Judaism has its basis in a dogmatic commitment by Western biblical scholars of the early twentieth century to explain Judaism in terms of the supposed evolution of religion (see chapter one). Thus all claims to an original revealed monotheism needed to be rethought in terms of either evolutionary development or foreign influences such as Zoroastrianism. Wherever such scholars find an apparent resemblance to another religion or culture, they immediately infer that the other religion was the source that influenced Judaism. This tendency also shows up in the ascription of Zoroastrian influence, though the data really do not support the arrows going in that direction (just as it would be difficult to make them point the other way). It becomes apparent that in tracing the supposed influence the question is frequently begged in favor of Zoroastrian influence on biblical writings. A quote by James H. Moulton is telling for this whole enterprise:

> It is perhaps as well to remember that these theories do not come from Iranian experts, but from scholars whose fame was achieved in other fields. Were we to count only the Iranists, we should even doubt whether the Parsi did not borrow from the Jew, for that was the view of [the Iranian scholar] Darmesteter![25]

In sum, the story of Zoroastrian influence on other religions has been greatly exaggerated. The resemblances are more superficial than real, and even where they are close, there is no good reason to infer direct influencing or borrowing. The real significance of Zoroastrianism does not lie in its influence on other religions but on what we learn about this religion in its own domain, as well as what we learn about the experience of monotheistic religions by its example.

■ *So you meet a Parsi . . .*

What You Might Expect

You are a privileged person, since there are not many Parsis to meet.[26] Furthermore, their tradition has developed in the direction of not advertising itself. Fire temples are hardly recognizable as such from the outside, and the people themselves do not usually call attention to their religion. Non-Parsis are not admitted to fire temples. They will be treated politely but with great reserve.

When the British came to India, they recognized the Parsis as a hard-working, able minority and enabled them to make above average economic strides. Thus today's Parsis are, on the whole, relatively well-off. In North America Parsis have established small communities in larger population centers such as Chicago. Parsis in the West tend to be professional people who take great pride in being recognized for their achievements by non-Parsis. Zubin Mehta, the well-known orchestra conductor, is a Parsi, and the entire Parsi community claims a share of his fame.

Integration into the secularized Western world has led the Parsis to deemphasize the religious side of their heritage in favor of their ethnic and cultural legacy. They have deemphasized ritual observances such as the shirt and the belt and the honoring of angels,[27] and many contemporary Parsis are no more preoccupied with a serious struggle for moral purity than any other people are.

Zoroaster	Aushetar		Aushetarmah	Saoshyant
Creation				*Possible Victory*

Figure 4.2. Parsi view

Theologically, many Western Parsis have adapted their thinking to current ideological fashions. Instead of seeing themselves as followers of the exclusive way of Ohrmazd as taught by Zoroaster, they consider their religion an important part of their cultural heritage, just as other people do. However, many Parsis do cherish their religion for the cultural legacy it represents, even if they no longer practice it rigorously.

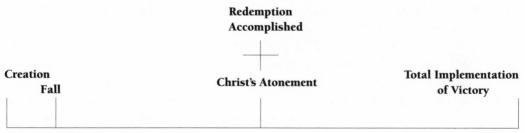

	Redemption Accomplished	
Creation		Total Implementation
Fall	Christ's Atonement	of Victory

Figure 4.3. Christian view

Relating the Gospel

A Christian attempting to share the gospel message with a Parsi needs to be prepared to go in one of two directions. First, even though the textbook version of Zoroastrianism displays the grand dualism of Ohrmazd versus Ahriman, a modern Western Parsi may be more inclined to believe in a pluralism that sees many religions (including Zoroastrianism and Christianity) as equally valid ways to God. Then the strategy the Christian must pursue has actually very little to do with Parsiism per se and much with modern relativism. The Christian needs to be able to show the person of Parsi background the uniqueness of the Christian gospel. Such a basic strategy might include demonstrating (1) the impossibility of showing that all religions are equally valid in light of the fact that many religions contradict each other; (2) the unique grounding of the Christian gospel in historical events; (3) the exclusive claims made by Christ for himself because he alone has atoned for our sins.

Second, many Zoroastrians continue to see themselves as especially designated adherents of good in the cosmic battle between good and evil. This is particularly true of Parsis who are in India or Iran. They look forward to the future defeat of all evil. In that case, Christians have the privilege of sharing the fact that evil has already been defeated in history in Christ's victory over Satan on the cross. For the Parsi, the hope of God's victory is still future and depends on each person's compliance with God's commandments. But Christianity teaches that the decisive battle has already been won. What remains is the implementation of the victory. In the meantime, those who are on the side of the victor are supplied by God with the power to resist evil supernaturally.

Mastering the Material

When you have finished studying this chapter, you should be able to

1. summarize the important features of the religion of the Aryan invaders, including their gods (Iranian and Indian);

2. describe the life and teaching of Zoroaster;

3. identify the Achaemenid dynasty and what we know about Persian religion during that time;

4. portray the important changes in Zoroastrianism during the Sassanid period;

5. point out in what ways Zurvanism and Manichaeism departed from orthodox Zoroastrianism;

6. describe contemporary Zoroastrianism in terms of its distribution, practices, rituals and special observances;

7. make the case why it is unlikely that Zoroastrianism influenced Judaism to a large extent.

Term Paper Ideas

1. Do a detailed comparison between the early phases of Aryan religion in India and in Iran.

2. Trace the origin and development of Indo-European peoples through history.

3. Compile a detailed biography of Zoroaster, based on history and legend.

4. Research the descriptions of Persian religion in classical Greek writers, for example, Herodotus.

5. Inventory Zoroastrian writings of the Sassanid period; provide a bibliography of what is available in English translation.

6. Trace Mithraism, Zurvanism or Manichaeism through its history in the ancient world.

7. Undertake a detailed study of one aspect of contemporary Parsi religion, for example, a worship ritual, a rite of passage or a special day observance.

8. Defend a position, pro or con, regarding the direct influence of Zoroastrianism on another religion, for example, one particular phase of Judaism, early Christianity or Sufi Islam.

Core Bibliography

Boyce, Mary. *Zoroastrians: Their Religious Beliefs and Practices.* London: Routledge & Kegan Paul, 1979.

Duchesne-Guillemin, Jacques, trans. *The Hymns of Zarathustra: Being a Translation of the Gathas Together with Introduction and Commentary.* Boston: Beacon, 1963.

Jackson, A. V. Williams. *Zoroaster: The Prophet of Ancient Iran.* New York: Columbia University Press, 1898.

Moulton, James H. *Early Zoroastrianism.* London: Williams & Norgate, 1913.

Nigosian, S. A. *The Zoroastrian Faith: Tradition and Modern Research.* Montreal: McGill-Queen's University Press, 1993.

Taraporewala, Irach J. S. "Zoroastrianism." In *Living Schools of Religion,* edited by Vergilius Ferm, pp. 19-43. Paterson, N.J.: Littlefield, Adams, 1965.

Zaehner, R. C. *The Dawn and Twilight of Zoroastrianism.* London: Weidenfeld & Nicolson, 1961.

———. *Zurvan: A Zoroastrian Dilemma.* New York: Biblo and Tannen, 1972.

Chapter 5

Traditional Religions
Introduction & African Religion

Estimated Practitioners in Africa: 72,777,000

Oone of the major themes of this book is that animistic and ritualistic concerns tend to displace monotheistic religion. Now that we have looked at three clearly monotheistic religions, Judaism, Islam and Zoroastrianism, we move on to discuss religions in which spirits, magic and ritual are prevalent. Many different labels have been applied to this kind of religion, including primitive religion, primal religion, basic religion, stage 1 religion, animistic religion, ancestor worship religion and indigenous religion.

None of these terms is particularly satisfactory. All but the last two seem to imply that such religions are older than monotheistic religion, a throwback to the evolutionary view that we have shown to be erroneous. *Animism* and *ancestor worship* can be used legitimately to describe certain spirit-oriented religions, but the religions under discussion are not limited to these traits. *Indigenous* expresses how much these religions are tied to specific cultures and locations, but this term does not sufficiently distinguish these religions from many other religions, such as Hinduism in India, that are indigenous to their country of origin. The worst misconception is to think that these religions are somehow simplistic or childish. They are extremely complex sets of beliefs and practices that have grown into place over long periods of time.[1]

We shall settle on the term *traditional religions*. This term has several advantages. For one, it has become standardized by some adherents (for example, in Africa) who reject the term *primitive* as demeaning. Second, it captures the fact that these religions are the products of long periods of cultural development. Third, it reflects the idea that these religions are primarily rooted in tradition rather than scriptures. Although such religions sometimes include books and writings (for example, a collection of spells or chants) as part of their standard ritual, these writings do not constitute the basis of authority in the religion. The essential vehicle of transmission is oral tradition. Myths and ritual instructions are memorized and transmitted orally from generation to generation.

It must be emphasized that oral transmission is usually a very rigorous process. In many cases every word counts in telling the story the way it has always been told. In short, we need to abandon the notion that oral tradition is a sloppy, happenstance process. More often than not it is extremely precise.

Common Traits of Traditional Religions

It would be foolhardy to try to come up with a standardized picture of traditional religions. In fact, it was precisely this error that perpetuated the notion of religious evolution for so long. A close look at traditional religions reveals immense diversity. It is wrongheaded to read magic into a culture where it is absent or to claim animism where a culture is actually theistic. This point should go without saying, but we must emphasize it due to the imperialistic methods of past generations.

Nevertheless, it is possible to draw up some generalizations that are applicable to most traditional religions. Fair generalizations can be helpful as we try to make sense out of the bewildering array of information that we amass when we examine religions that do not have scriptures. Still, we must avoid making the pattern take precedence over the data (here as everywhere else).

The powers. Some evolutionary scholars view mana as the first stage in religious development (see discussion in chapter one). There mana is seen as an impersonal spiritual force that can be manipulated by magic. But Wilhelm Schmidt has pointed out that in its original context the word *mana* simply refers to superior power and does not carry a predominantly spiritual connotation.[2] According to the Melanesians (whose culture gave us the term *mana*), material objects contain power. Anyone who has ever eaten a candy bar for quick energy, drunk a cup of coffee to wake up or filled a car's tank with gasoline subscribes to a limited, prosaic form of mana.

As a religious concept, however, mana implies something broader (universal and "transcendent")—a mysterious spiritual energy in all things. People who recognize this organize their entire lives around relating to that energy. Such a mana-centered worldview by itself is extremely rare and is more likely to be a part of enscripturated religions than traditional ones.

Most traditional religions venerate two kinds of spirits—ancestors and nature spirits. These powers were discussed briefly in chapter one and will be considered at greater length later in this chapter.

Practically all traditional religions recognize the god of the sky, even religions that lack some other characteristics that are common among traditional religions. This recognition is expressed in a wide variety of ways, but it is rarely (probably never) absent. Traditional religions usually understand spiritual powers as a triangular configuration, with human beings in the center trying to placate all three powers as required by their specific traditions.

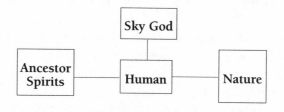

Figure 5.1. Spiritual powers in traditional religions

There may also be a goddess, subordinate gods, various powers and people mediating among each other, not to mention different levels of access to the spiritual powers granted to human beings.

Rituals and magic. There is within traditional religions a proliferation of ritual and magic. The absence of a written authority means the lack of a permanent standard of what is essential and required and what is not. Each generation only knows what it was taught by the previous generation. Consequently, if a new ritual is added, there is no external standard to use in judging its appropriateness. Thus any ritual that accrues becomes a permanent part of the tradition. In this way ritual balloons into the greatest component of a traditional religion.

Magic is essentially a subset of ritual, the key difference being that magic is directed more immediately toward the spiritual powers. Magic frequently comes in two flavors: good and evil. Consequently, many descriptions of magic in traditional religion distinguish between good magic and evil magic through the use of different terms, such as *magic, sorcery* or *witchcraft.* But each group defines these terms in its own context with a particular eye toward how destructive the powers are. In a certain context, magic may be considered good and witchcraft evil. The general reader needs to be aware that there is *no standardized terminology* in this respect, though different writers frequently use these words as though there were.

Most traditional communities have resident experts on ritual and magic. If they function as a group in some public facility, we may consider them priests. When they function as single individuals, we usually call them healers (medicine men) or shamans. Again the English terms represent arbitrary substitutes for the words used in the traditional culture's own setting. However, we can draw basic distinctions between two or three different categories of function.

A healer (medicine man), as the name implies, usually seeks to heal diseases in the community. Since most traditional societies believe that illnesses are caused by spiritual forces, it takes a person trained in spiritual powers to deal with them. The healer uses magic rituals, chants, fetish objects and whatever else it takes to redirect the spirits that are causing problems. These persons do not occupy themselves exclusively with what we would consider physical health matters. They may also influence the spirits in other areas of life, including agriculture, interpersonal relationships and warfare.

A shaman, on the other hand, is a medium for the spiritual powers. Usually the shaman allows himself or herself to become possessed by the spirits through a ritual. Once he or she is in a trance, the spirits work directly though the shaman. The word *shaman* comes from traditional Siberian society. The healer differs from the shaman in that the healer manipulates the spirits whereas the spirits possess and manipulate the shaman.

Despite the extreme variations from culture to culture, traditional communities include people who function as priests. Since spirits are usually considered a part of the community, those who are elders, chiefs or clan leaders are almost invariably expected to represent the living physical community in relationships with the spirit world. Most of the time these functions are transacted externally (analogously to the healer) rather than through possession (analogously to the shaman).

Rites of passage. Rites of passage are observed in Judaism, Islam and Zoroastrianism. These rituals possess even more importance in traditional communities, where life tends to be highly regulated according to age and social status. The principle that a particular transition in life has not been attained until the proper ceremony has been observed tends to become irrevocable in many traditional societies.

Within traditional religions, the onset of life is usually the moment at which the birth rite of passage is performed. Before the ceremony takes place, children may not be considered fully alive. Yet in numerous traditional cultures, the actual ceremony may be delayed for quite a long time after birth, from a few days to as long as a year. The reason for the delay probably is found in the high infant mortality rates in such cultures. If a baby dies after the rite has been performed, the family has to cope with the death of a fully human being. On the other hand, if the child dies prior to the ceremony, it has never really entered into full human life, and so the family's grief is presumably lessened. Some cultures believe that infants who die before initiation are actually disguised spirits who come to play pranks.

The transition from childhood to adulthood tends to be crucial in traditional cultures. The rite of passage may involve ordeals and tortures. However, the young man or woman who passes satisfactorily receives a new identity as well as all the honors of adult standing in the society.

Marriage in a traditional culture may be matrilocal, patrilineal or exogamous, to name but a few options. In most traditional societies, a wedding is primarily a legal and social event. Since the spirit world is part of the extended family, it is almost invariably considered to be involved in the occasion.

As odd as it may sound, in many traditional societies a death is not recognized until the correct ritual has been performed. For example, among the Toraja of Irian Jaya, Indonesia, a person is not considered dead until the body has been shifted from lying along an east-west axis (indicating that the person is considered to be sleeping) to a north-south axis (marking death). The video series *The Long Search* chronicles how the death of a high priest among the Toraja required a full year of elaborate funeral preparations. All this time the corpse, rolled up in a mat, was considered seriously ill and was left lying in a hut. The body was shifted at the proper moment. Then the deceased was officially dead, and the mourning began.[3]

Psychologists say that funerals help us accept the loss of a loved one and cope with grief. But this rite of passage seems to have far more basic purposes in traditional religions. Here the purpose of funerals tends to be threefold: (1) to make sure that the deceased is truly dead and will remain dead and will not harm the living; (2) to process the deceased into the appropriate status as ancestor (which is frequently the means of meeting the first purpose) and (3) to bring the community together, to reaffirm its unity in the face of the loss of one of its members and to reenter life on a renewed basis.

Taboo. Another trait common to traditional religions is the recognition of some objects as taboo. We use this word as a synonym for forbidden, usually in a context of morality. For example, among fundamentalists smoking and drinking are taboo. The idea is that the practices in question are evil and must be avoided at all costs.

However, the term *taboo* has a somewhat different meaning in the context of religion. Let me explain the difference with an example. The Old Testament (1 Chron 13) describes David's efforts to bring the ark of the covenant to Jerusalem. The ark is mounted on an oxcart (contrary to instructions in Ex 25:14) and slowly transported up a hill. Along the way, the oxen step on an uneven section of the road and stumble. The cart starts to tip over. Uzzah, the cart driver, turns back to steady the ark lest it smash to the ground. The instant his hand touches the ark, he falls over dead. The ark, representing God's holiness, is never to be touched.

This untouchability has nothing to do with moral impurity. It is God's holiness that makes the ark untouchable. On the other hand, something may be considered untouchable because it is so pervasively evil. But it is the nature of the object, not a person's moral action, that renders the object untouchable. This untouchability is the essence of taboo. Zoroastrianism includes the concept of ritual purity (chapter four); taboo is an extreme case of ritual impurity.

In a traditional culture many things may be considered taboo: a physical object (possibly, though not necessarily, related to ritual practices), a person or a place. Common taboos can include the place of offering, which may be entered only by the person designated for that function, a fetish or a woman at the time of her menses. To violate the taboo is to invite drastic consequences. As a case in point, in the Toraja culture, touching a statue commemorating a deceased person will cause one to swell up and explode.[4]

Totem. Think of a fairly large tribal group and divide it into a number of clans (a clan is larger than an extended family but smaller than the tribe as a whole). Each clan sees itself as being related to a particular animal or some other life form. This being is its totem. The clan's relationship to the totem is considered to be based in genetic descent. Consequently, the members of the clan (called the moiety) see themselves as biologically related to the animal that serves as the clan totem and as therefore enjoying the special traits of that animal. A moiety that has a hawk for its totem might think of itself as embodying a hawk's swiftness, whereas the moiety of bears could believe that they are as strong as bears.

Zulu woman dancing in front of warriors and taunting them to deeds of bravery. Photograph: UPI/Corbis-Bettmann.

The native tribes of northwest America are famous for their totem poles. These poles, commonly misunderstood as idols, are actually pictorial genealogies describing physical and spiritual descent. They reveal the lineage of animals embodied in the particular totem moieties. Of course, since traditional families also include the extended spiritual family, the totem poles do carry concomitant religious function as well. Totemic moieties have devised many different kinds of ritual to express their bonding with their totem. There are no truly universal practices associated with totemism.

Ritual aside, a primary function of totemism is the prevention of inbreeding. Most of totemistic cultures are exogamous, which is to say that people must marry someone outside of their moiety. For example, a bear may marry a hawk, a deer or a wolf, but never another bear. Whether the new unit is then counted with the husband's or wife's moiety depends on whether the culture is patrilineal or matrilineal. Though there is no universal rule, totemism on the whole tends to be patrilineal.[5]

A second function of totemism is to assure food distribution among all members of the tribe by forbidding members of a clan to eat its totem animal. This is the case among several Australian groups. Let us imagine a tribe that eats only two animals: buffalo and deer. Now let us say that this tribe consists of two moieties, the buffalo moiety and the deer moiety. Neither moiety is permitted to eat its totem animal. In that case the buffalo moiety can eat all the deer available, and the deer moiety can eat all the buffalo available. The system prevents one moiety from getting all the food. For a totemic moiety, its own animal *may be* taboo (although there is no universal rule to that effect).

Many descriptions of totemism refer to a totem feast, a special occasion on which moiety members may partake of their animal, as though it were a universal practice.[6] Once a year at a special ceremony, the moiety slays the animal and each member ritually consumes a piece of it, thereby ingesting some of the special qualities of the totem animal. But totem feasts are very rarely part of totemic cultures. Wilhelm Schmidt reports that "of the many hundred totemic races of the whole earth there are just four who know any rite even approximating [the totem feast], and they all belong . . . to the most modern totemic peoples."[7] In short, the overwhelming number of cultures that have totems do not have totem feasts.

The idea of totemism, particularly the totem feast, captivated the minds of European scholars as soon as they learned about it. The concept soon became distorted beyond all reason. Hypothesis followed hypothesis until the idea of totemism became disconnected from physical reality. Sigmund Freud, in particular, incorporated the idea of a totem feast into his argument that all religion originates with the need for a father figure.[8] According to him, the first totem feast involved the father of a particular primordial moiety. His sons killed him because they desired his women (the Oedipus complex), and then they consumed his body. In an ineffectual attempt to assuage their guilt feelings, they continued to reenact this event in ritual form. As the ritual continued throughout human history, a God figure was eventually substituted for the primordial father. Thus Christian Communion is really a continuation of this original cannibalistic totem feast.

However, there is no evidence of any cannibalistic totem feasts, past or present, let alone the patricide invented by Freud to deal with his personal complexes. Totem feasts occur in only a tiny fraction of totemic cultures. But Freud's theory must have fulfilled a psychological need, since it has been repeated over and over again despite the absence of supporting evidence.

Introduction to African Traditional Religion

It has become standard practice among many writers to abbreviate "African traditional religion" as ATR, and we will follow suit. Still, we need to acknowledge the presumptuousness of subsuming the hundreds of specific religious traditions on an entire continent under one heading. This discussion will draw on that variety for specific examples throughout. That having been said, there are enough common points that it is possible to make cautious use of *African traditional religions* (ATR) as an umbrella term referring to the traditional religions of the inhabitants of sub-Saharan Africa. The elements that these cultures hold loosely in common include (1) the recognition and worship of the high god, (2) the importance attached to relationships with the ancestors; (3) the importance attached to age grades and rites of passage and (4) a philosophy of life that focuses on this-worldly concerns and present spiritual agencies. These elements are not unique to traditional religions, of course. But as they combine with each other, they provide the overall pattern of similarities among the many African religions that distinguish them from other regional groups of traditional religions.

There are hundreds of African tribal groups. Each has its own specific culture, its own language and its own religion. Once we get beyond the broad generalities, we find a myriad of details of beliefs and practices. Reason demands limiting examples to a few tribes that are representative of the whole. The peoples primarily referred to include (1) the Kikuyu of Kenya, representing an East African agricultural people;[9] (2) the Maasai of Kenya and Tanzania, representing an East African herding people;[10] (3) the Yoruba of Nigeria, representing a West African agricultural people;[11] (4) the Zulu of South Africa, representing a South African herding people.[12] These four tribes will serve as our guides in illustrating the unity and variety in ATR.[13]

The Social Setting

By their very nature, traditional religions are incorporated into the full life of the culture in which they are practiced. In the case of ATR this means that the religion is bound to be an intrinsic part of the two most dominant allegiances in the lives of African people: the immediate community and the tribe. By way of contrast, since I am an American of European extraction, presumably my two highest social allegiances are to my immediate family and my country. Africans typically think of their intimate loyalties as extending to the whole village or compound. But their primary allegiance stops on the level of the tribe, far short of the modern innovation of national identity. Again, to make the contrast, I as an American surrender my ethnic interests to those of my country as a whole. For African people, even relatively "Westernized" ones, the interest of the tribe tends to take precedence over allegiance to the nation. Thus a Kikuyu tribesperson is Kikuyu first and Kenyan only second.

Most important, Africans are not nearly as individualistic as North Americans tend to be. Shakespeare's Polonius advises Laertes, "This above all: to thine own self be true" *(Hamlet)*. But Africans "above all" are members of a community. As John S. Mbiti puts it, "Whatever happens to the individual happens to the whole group, and whatever happens to the whole group happens to the individual. The individual can only say, 'I am, because we are; and since we are, there-

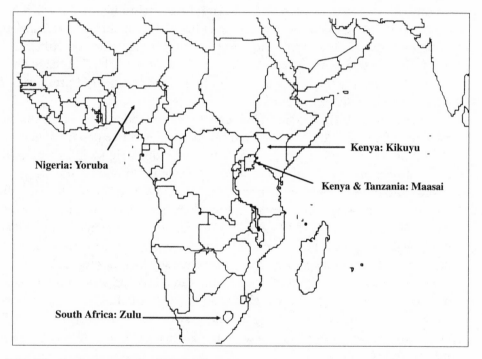

Map 5.1. Four representative African tribes

fore I am.'"[14] In short, African religion is about what a community believes and practices and about individuals participating in something that belongs to the community as a whole.

God

All African tribes recognize the supreme God, some with elaborate theological development, others with very little reflection. The amount of direct worship that God receives also differs drastically; nevertheless, virtually all forms of ATR include at least minimal recognition of one God.

The God of ATR fits the picture of the God of original monotheism. God is thought to be (1) associated with the sky, (2) all-powerful, (3) all-knowing, (4) eternal, (5) spirit (not having a physical body), (6) a person, (7) good, though he can be capricious (unpredictable), (8) creator of the world, (9) provider.

It would be a mistake to interpret these attributes within the categories of traditional Christian theology, which were formulated through centuries of abstract philosophical reflection. The picture of God in ATR is expressed in narrative mythology and explanations of ritual. Nevertheless, the points of comparison speak for themselves.

Do traditional Africans worship the God of the Christians? In terms of historical origin, yes; in terms of present understanding, including all the ways in which this concept of God has become incorporated into ATR, probably not. This ambiguity needs to be considered by people who want to communicate across cultures. Missionary practice by and large is to call God by his name in the tribal language and to work in terms of correcting the tribe's understanding of God instead of presenting the biblical God as a totally different being.

The Kikuyu call God "Ngai." He is creator and provider. Ngai keeps his distance from the daily affairs of people and should not be bothered needlessly by petty requests; he should never be approached directly by an individual. He manifests himself in various celestial phenomena like the sun, moon, stars, rain, rainbows, lightning (which is his sword) and thunder (which is the cracking of his joints). Because the sky is his domain, it is considered taboo to look up to heaven during a thunderstorm. He is worshiped only in times of great distress (for example, a drought or an epidemic). Then an entire family group gathers under a huge tree and sacrifices an animal, perhaps a sheep, to him. It is believed that the family gathering for this ceremony includes the ancestors.

It is not clear what the traditional Zulu name for God was. Some researchers insist on the name Inkosi Yezulu, which simply means "chief of the sky."[15] However, many writers use the name Unkulunkulu, and that is the name used by many Zulus today and by the modern Zulu New Testament.[16] He is known by other names as well, which may be praise names.

One may approach Inkosi Yezulu, the creator, only in dire situations. In Zulu tradition, God may be approached by an individual supplicant. His worship and requests are mediated by someone who specializes in relating to God. This person, known as the heaven herd, also controls the weather. Becoming a heaven herd requires a specific call from God, such as being almost struck by lightning. When the supplicant comes to the heaven herd, the two worship God underneath the open sky on an unoccupied hill. Inkosi Yezulu manifests himself particularly through lightning. Thus any individual who is killed by lightning is thought to belong to God and will not be mourned or considered an ancestor spirit.

A number of West African religions, including the Yoruba, have added numerous subordinate gods to their belief systems. Thus "God" is synonymous with "supreme God" in these contexts. The highest original God for the Yoruba is Olorun, a term that simply means "owner of the sky." Olorun is the source of all power, but he is distant and has no direct relationship with the world. He supplied the power and instruction for creation to the god Orisa-nla, who then carried out the task. Olorun is never worshiped directly; Orisa-nla is worshiped as the supreme god. In this case the original supreme God has been displaced by a new deity, but at least the memory remains.

On the other extreme is Engai, God of the Maasai. Engai means "rain" and "sky." God is creator, and the Maasai particularly thank God for giving them cattle. The

West African warriors dancing. Photograph: UPI/Corbis-Bettmann.

Maasai believe that God has placed all cattle under their proprietorship. If cattle are held by someone other than a Maasai, they have a religious duty to liberate them.[17] Because their lives are inextricably intertwined with the cattle and because Engai is the giver of the cattle, the Maasai invoke God on a daily basis as well as on special occasions. Maasai usually refer to Engai by two colors: black, when he is seen as good and benevolent, and red, when he is angry and causes harm, such as by lightning. References to Engai are usually in the masculine gender grammatically, but forms that are grammatically feminine may also be used.[18]

These four conceptions of God demonstrate the unity and the diversity in African religion. God is acknowledged by all but is revered in many different ways. But even if a religion seems to display a monotheistic understanding of God, we should not think that it focuses on God in the way that Judaism and Islam do.

West African Divinities

West African tribes recognize many different gods that are subordinate to the original supreme God. Among the Yoruba, Olorun has been practically displaced by Orisa-nla. In fact, the Yoruba have hundreds of such subordinate deities called the "orisa" (estimates vary from 400 to 1,700). It is difficult to ascertain an exact number of gods, because many of them may be known by several different names.

Orisa-nla carried out the actual work of creation. There is a further tradition that he did not finish the work but that it was actually completed by another orisa, Oduduwa, when Orisanla's got drunk on the job. Then there is Orunmila, the god of knowledge and wisdom, possibly also the patron of divination. Ogun is the god of metals and war; he is also considered the first king of the city of Ife, and thus the original ancestor of all human beings (though it is not clear how that myth fits in with the idea of Orisa-nla's having created human beings). Esu is known as a trickster and a practical joker. His main function is to mediate human worship to other orisa. To ignore him is to court seriously negative consequences. Thus there is a great diversity of orisa among the Yoruba. Although different orisa may be worshiped at different shrines, Esu is a constant presence.

Up to now the term *god* has referred to the orisa (a common scholarly practice).[19] If the use of this terminology is correct, Yoruba religion is polytheistic; other scholars, however, dispute the appropriateness of this label.[20] They would rather refer to the orisa as "divinities," thereby indicating that they are something less than gods. This understanding maintains the idea that ATR is uniformly monotheistic. If that assessment is correct, it could still be true that in these cultures ATR is at least on the brink of losing its monotheistic status.

The Ancestors

For most people who practice ATR, however, the concept of God is not particularly relevant to their lives. The religion they practice is animism. Of the two types of spirits usually present in animistic religion, nature spirits and ancestor spirits, it is the ancestors who receive the most attention in ATR.

It has been pointed out with some justification that the word *ancestor* in this context is a misnomer and that a better term would be the *living/dead.*[21] This term points to the fact that even though the people in question are dead, they are considered to be a continuing, living presence in the community. It is not necessary to have been someone's progenitor to qualify as an ancestor. An unmarried person, though technically no one's ancestor, is eligible to be a living/dead. However, because the term *ancestor* is in such wide usage for religions all around the globe, it is best to stick with traditional terminology and just be aware of the inexact nature of the term.

In general, the pattern of ancestor recognition is less diversified among different African cultures than the concept of God. A person who has died belongs to the realm of the spirits. The spirit world is visualized in many different ways, but it is usually pictured as a spiritual counterpart to the physical world, complete with relationships. However, the ancestor is still involved in the world of living people, is still considered a member of the family and is still deserving of the respect given any senior family member. Anyone who personally remembers the departed person will venerate, consult and give a share of food and drink to him or her. Once everyone who had direct knowledge of the person has passed on (perhaps after five generations), the ancestor loses contact with the earth. If the departed person had great standing in the community, he or she could conceivably be revered for a much longer time, possibly becoming the subject of myths and permanent tribal recognition.

For the Zulu, the ancestors live in the earth under the kraal (the circular arrangement of huts). They protect the social order, helping those who respect traditions or hurting people who do wrong. Each hut contains a little shrine, the unumzane. There daily rituals are conducted that are directed toward the ancestors. The head of each clan functions as priest, representing his extended family before the ancestors. Male ancestors are considered more important than female ancestors.

The Yoruba also pay close attention to their ancestors. In keeping with the many levels of spiritual beings in that culture, there is a sizable number of ancestors of greater tribal importance. In fact, the orisa Ogun may be considered an ancestor spirit at the highest level of importance.

Every Kikuyu ceremony contains references to the ancestors. Again the clan has become the provenance of spirits. Kikuyus also recognize spirits that have taken on particular age grades or the tribe as a whole. Interestingly, in Kikuyu belief, wayward nature spirits may actually be neglected ancestor spirits. These spirits can responsible for large-scale disasters such as epidemics.

Any tribal member can receive a personal visit from an ancestor, usually in a dream. Ancestors may come with demands, warnings, encouragement or advice. It is up to the living person to understand their messages and take them seriously, since to ignore them could lead to severe punishment.

The relationship between living person and ancestor is courteous but uneasy, like the feelings of a motorist who gets pulled over by a police officer. Once an officer pulled me over to inform me that there was something dangerously wrong with the rear wheel of my truck. On another occasion an officer pulled me over to tell me that the road ahead was flooded and I needed to take a different route. Both encounters elicited my gratitude. There have been other times when getting pulled over meant trouble. On every occasion, however, I found myself being extremely courteous and maintaining a superficial smile, even though inwardly I was wishing the policeman would just go away.

By and large, people's attitude toward visits from ancestors seems to follow the same line: outward courtesy and formality, inward anxiety. Contemporary (Western!) writings tend to romanticize the living-ancestor relationship in terms of love and affection in the larger community. But even Mbiti, who is not above glamorizing ATR a bit himself, has to acknowledge that contact with ancestors is not based on affection. He states that

there is no affectionate warmth such as one witnesses when relatives or friends meet in this life. There is no exchange of greetings, which in African societies is an extremely important social means of contact; and when the living/dead departs, human beings do not give greetings to other living/dead.[22]

The one word that characterizes the attitude of the living toward ancestor spirits is *fear.* Most Africans living in the context of ATR exist in perpetual fear of what the ancestors may do or demand.[23]

For Africans, religion consists of complex interplay between different spiritual powers. God, divinities, ancestors and nature spirits all demand their share of attention, though different tribes apportion this attention variously. African religion can be described as monotheistic, but only on a purely theoretical basis. With few exceptions (possibly the Maasai), the single God is virtually irrelevant to people's day-to-day existence. Mbiti attempts to salvage the monotheistic label by claiming that offerings made to spirits and ancestors are "regarded as intermediaries between God and men, so that God is the ultimate Recipient *whether or not the worshippers are aware of that.*"[24] But Gehman responds that such a claim goes "beyond the bounds of reasonableness." He adds an all-important caution for the study of any religion: "When we study ATR we must learn what in fact the peoples traditionally believed and practiced and not what we as academic scholars think they ought to have believed and practiced."[25] It is true that in most tribes the word that is used for revering the ancestors is not the same as the one for worshiping God. What that really means is that many African people rarely, if ever, worship. Their lives are occupied with revering the ancestors.

Rites of Passage

African societies attach supreme importance to the distinct phases of life. In addition to family and clan memberships, age grades are crucial demarcations for communal loyalties. Many tribes practice circumcision at puberty, and your "graduating class" for initiation becomes one of the most important features of your identity. The diversity in how the rites of passage are practiced fits in well with each particular tribal culture.

The Yoruba are one of those extremely rare peoples who do not have a puberty rite of passage. They do observe the three other standard rites: birth, marriage and death. Yoruba religion emphasizes divination, and so it is not surprising that divination also figures prominently in the most crucial stages along life's way. Prior to a child's birth, the expectant mother visits the diviner to learn the pertinent information concerning her child's future. The instructions she receives include a list of food taboos to be observed as the child grows up. The infant receives a name on the seventh day of life (for girls) or on the ninth day (for boys). Boys are circumcised sometime before the age of two. This is not a major ceremony, but it is an essential precondition for marriage later in life. Marriages are arranged between families through a matchmaker. Again divination figures prominently, ensuring a successful marriage. Only when the plans have been settled and approved may the young people meet and speak. The actual wedding ceremony takes several days. On the last day the bridegroom is permitted to see his new wife for the first time since the ceremony and to begin the marriage. Burial is by interment on the family compound. Divination is again important, since death is rarely, if ever, seen as natural. The cause of death, usually some form of magic, must be identified. The burial ceremony is carried out by some priests of the various orisa. It concludes with turning the grave site into a new shrine for this, the latest ancestor.[26]

The Maasai practice more than four rites of passage, and cattle figure prominently in each. When a child is born, the father is informed of its sex while he waits outside the hut. For a boy, the father draws blood from a bullock, and a boy collects the blood in a container. For a girl, the father draws blood from a heifer, and this is collected by a girl. Someone then takes the blood and mixes it with warm milk, and it is given to the new mother to drink. The entire birthing process and ceremony are accompanied by invocations of Engai and ritual exhortations to the child to take responsibility for his or her life. The child receives a name within days of birth. A second name is added between the ages of eight and twelve.

The Maasai practice circumcision as the puberty rite of passage. A girl is circumcised as soon as she shows signs of entering puberty. After circumcision (clitoridectomy) she is considered ready for marriage and childbearing. Girls are not considered part of an age-group ranking as boys are. For boys, circumcision means entry into adulthood as part of their age group. When a time for circumcision has been declared, boys up to the age of sixteen undergo the ritual. It is preceded by a ceremony that involves selecting a leader for their age group and endowing their generation with a name. The actual circumcision is done on an individual basis. The boy is teased by his peers during the process and is expected to bear the pain without crying. Until the wounds are healed, he dresses as a girl, wearing ostrich feather decorations. Then he is ready for his new stage in life: warriorhood.

Maasai warriors, long known for their fierceness, live a life of privilege. They are recognized by ochre-colored long hair and their spears and shields. Living communally in specially designated kraals, the warriors enjoy the love of girls who have not been circumcised and feasts of meat and milk taken together. But this idyllic life does not last forever; eventually they need to let go of warrior status and become junior elders, usually in their thirties. This transition is traumatic and is attained through a four-day ceremony that includes shaving the head, drinking milk by oneself and eating meat for the first time in front of circumcised women. As a junior elder, a man is allowed to get married. His wife, usually procured through family arrangements, will be from among the newly circumcised girls. Thus he will be substantially older than his wife.

Another Maasai rite of passage marks the transition to senior elderhood. This is celebrated with a large communal feast, again lasting several days. The new generation of elders receives a new name, cattle sticks are blessed, and a ritual is enacted in which the senior elder drinks blood directly from a slit in the dewlap of an ox. A final transition into the highest level of senior elderhood can be attained years later. It requires personal purification. Everyone looks forward to this ceremony because it includes a hilarious mock battle between men and women using branches and twigs as weapons. The death ritual involves copious weeping, anointing the body, dressing the person with sandals and cattle stick (for a man) or with sewing needle and calabash (for a woman) and then leaving the corpse outside the kraal for scavengers to dispose of. Thus the stages in a Maasai man's life include birth, childhood, circumcision, warriorhood, junior elderhood, senior elderhood, advanced senior elderhood, death.[27]

West African healer. Photograph: UPI/Corbis-Bettmann.

The Kikuyu observe basically the same stages in the context of an agrarian culture. The ceremonies involve beer, vegetable products and an occasional roasted sheep or goat. Circumcision is the most important rite, as it marks each individual's initiation into the life of the tribe. Among the Kikuyu it is performed as a group ritual. All the boys and girls of the same age in one location become men and women together. The young men become warriors, but the social distinction is not as rigid as it is as among the Maasai.

Kikuyu marriage is based on the personal choice of a marriage partner, although the parents negotiate the bride price after the young people have announced their wishes. If the first wife consents, a man can add several more wives to his household. Each wife owns her own plot of land and is in charge of her subsection of the family. In the latter years of warriorhood, a married man joins the council of elders. Once he has children old enough to be circumcised, he is initiated into junior elderhood and from there eventually into the two higher grades of elderhood.[28]

Maasai and Kikuyu elders are responsible for both ceremonial and governmental leadership. Neither group has priests or other professional officiants at their various religious rituals. Thus becoming an elder involves learning all the ceremonial techniques and the lore associated with them. In addition, until colonial times, both tribes practiced an informal democracy in which decisions were arrived at in long meetings of representative elders on the appropriate levels. When the British came to Kenya, they could not understand how "native tribes" could function without a "chief," so they appointed chiefs to be in charge of various clans, a concept that was utterly foreign to the Kikuyu.

Zulu society is more autocratic, being headed by a chief. Thus Zulu rites of passage do not include the various levels of elderhood. When a child is born, an ox is sacrificed, and cow's milk is given to the child before mother's milk. Naming follows a period of purification for the mother. In the middle of childhood there is an important ceremony in which the child's ears are pierced. Circumcision is the central ritual of initiation into the tribe. After a boy experiences his first nocturnal emission, he hides his family's cattle as an unmistakable sign that he is ready for manhood. After this important ceremony he can become a warrior, and once initiation into warriorhood and training have taken place, he can marry the bride of his choice. His parents then make the arrangements for the marriage. The young man declares his intentions publicly by exchanging the cattle in his family's kraal with cattle in the kraal of his future in-laws. The last rite of passage occurs at death, when the deceased is transformed into a respected ancestor. Thus the important rites for the Zulu man are birth, ear piercing, circumcision, warriorhood, marriage, death.[29]

Rites of passage are important in ATR. Sociologically they delineate roles and provide the means of governance; psychologically they endow members of a community with the self-worth that comes with having attained a new stage in life. Religiously they steer the community in a unified direction, and they provide a system for the transmission of their heritage from one generation to the next.

Ritual and Magic

In ATR, as in any traditional setting, life is defined by ritual. The ritual does not merely

Tribe	Sequence
Maasai	Birth, child, circumcision, warrior, jr. elder, marriage, sr. elder, adv. sr. elder, death
Kikuyu	Birth, child, circumcision, warrior, marriage, jr. elder, sr. elder, adv. sr. elder, death
Zulu	Birth, ear piercing, circumcision, warrior, marriage, death
Yoruba	Birth, circumcision, child, marriage, death

Table 5.1. Rites of passage in African cultures

decorate an event in life, it actually gives the event its significance and meaning. Compiling an inventory of all the different rituals that are a part of traditional African life would be impossible, so this discussion will make do with representative examples.

Kikuyu land sale ritual. One ritual is of particular interest because Western ignorance of it resulted in disastrous consequences. In the 1950s the world learned of the Mau Mau rebellion in Kenya. The Kikuyu tribe in particular instigated a revolt against their British colonial overlords. Many white people were killed, but even more Africans lost their lives during the suppression of the rebellion. One of the issues that triggered the rebellion was the use of land. British settlers had bought large tracts of land from the Kikuyu. They permitted the tribespeople to continue to live on their land as "squatters" governed by the settlers' rules and restrictions. The friction generated by this arrangement eventually resulted in rebellion.

This scenario gives us occasion to look at the ritual that is involved in the sale of land in the Kikuyu tradition. The sale of land is extremely rare to begin with. Land is passed from generation to generation. Land is the only means of subsistence in this agrarian culture. No one has the right to dispose of it, since it secures the livelihood of his progeny. Women usually work the fields. They own the land that they receive with their marriage alongside the land owned by the men.

But let us suppose that someone actually has a piece of land to sell and someone else is in the market to purchase it. Kenyatta tells us that before any deal can be concluded, a preliminary conversation must take place between the two parties. The intended purchaser visits the hut of the seller and brings him a little container of beer. Then the two men pursue a somewhat scripted conversation in which the topic of "buying and selling land" is disguised with references to paying the bride price for a beautiful girl. The men barter in this way for a while. When they have agreed on terms, they set a date for the actual transaction.

On the day of the sale, the two parties gather with a group of elders on the field in question. The leading elder asks both persons to take an oath, the seller to the effect that the land is his and that he is sticking to the asking price, the buyer to the effect that he is buying the land, at the agreed price, of his own free will. Then a ram is slaughtered and the contents of its stomach are removed. Now the whole group takes a walk around the perimeter of the property. They all join in a chant on the fertility of the soil while the leading elder sprinkles the undigested food from the ram's stomach onto the ground and the other elders plant trees and lilies along the boundary. When the procession is completed, elders announce curses against anyone moving the markers. The buyer and seller each put a small piece of ram's flesh on their wrists and refer to each other as in-laws. The ceremony concludes with a feast.[30]

Such is life in a traditional culture. It seems cumbersome to Westerners, but it cements relationships and takes the dreariness out of subsistence. All other observations concerning ritual, anxiety and animism (true as they are) notwithstanding, there is a poetry in this kind of ritual that does not show up in modern secular life.

Against this background, consider the actions of the colonists. The British appointed chiefs (as mentioned above) and then gave those chiefs (who had no formal standing in the Kikuyu tradition) money for large tracts of land that was not theirs to sell. Events like the Mau Mau uprising result from the interaction of complex forces. But the Kikuyu were certainly right in claiming that as far as they were concerned they had never sold the land; none of the traditional obligations had been observed.[31]

Kikuyu healing. Another important example of ritual in ATR is the practice of healing. Human bodies are frail, and advancing age means greater effort must be exerted to maintain or improve health. In Africa these efforts are tied into the ritual systems (as indeed is all of life). These rituals are performed by the person known in his particular culture as healer, medicine man or herbalist (the term *witch doctor* is officially repudiated but commonly used).

Kenyatta has given us a thorough description of the medical ritual used by the Kikuyu healer (whom he calls the magician, a point to which we shall return). After divination has revealed the particular kinds of spirits causing an illness, the healer comes and stands outside the patient's hut dressed in his official garb. The patient is seated or propped up in front of the healer, who opens his medical bag and takes out his implements: the healing magic, a horn or a small gourd into which he places the magic and a small bell. The patient has to lick the magic or spit into it, thereby opening up channels of communication with the spirits. The healer chants an incantation, accompanied by the tinkling of the bell. He declares that the patient will vomit out all of the evil that is in his body.

The healer then digs a hole in the ground and lines it with banana leaves. He fills it with a solution made of an herbal compound mixed with water. Now the patient kneels in "vomiting position" with his or her head over the hole, and the healer squats in front of him. The healer recites a long incantation in which he declares that the evil spirits are leaving the body. After each sentence the patient licks the healing magic in the horn and spits into the hole, symbolically vomiting out the evil.

Now the healer enters the patient's hut and with some magical leaves sweeps out the evil spirits that may still be in the hut, chanting all the while. As he tinkles his bell, he removes the swept-up dust from the hut and deposits it in the water in the hole. Now the patient uses the same leaves to sweep his body, and the healer drops the leaves into the hole as well. As the last major part of the ritual, the fire in the hut is extinguished, and the healer ignites a new one. Now he declares the patient to be cured; all that is left is to wait for the body to recover. The healer receives a small token for his services. A more substantial payment will be made if and when the patient completely recovers.[32]

What everyone wants to know is whether this procedure works, and, if so, how? Kenyatta himself attributes its efficacy to psychological influences. Skeptical Westerners might point to certain hygienic procedures and possibly the physical effects of the herbs used in the process. Anyone believing in supernatural causes would not want to disregard possible spiritual influences. But for traditional Africans, these are analytical questions that really do not matter. They see all of these factors together in a total picture that we can subsume under the term *magic* (hence Kenyatta's description of the healer as magician).

Witchcraft. Magic, as defined in chapter one, is the manipulation of spiritual powers to achieve an end. In the traditional African setting, magic is involved in all of human existence, sometimes in the routine transactions with the spirits that are part of life, sometimes in applications such as healing and divination, but sometimes also as a force for evil and destruction. In African contexts the negative use of magic is usually called witchcraft.

The relationship between general magic and witchcraft varies from tribe to tribe. By and large, magic is accessible to every member of a tribe, although someone who wants to become a healer receives much more intense training. In some tribes the role of witch is left exclusively to women, while other cultures (for example, the Kikuyu) recognize both male and female witches. Magic can sometimes have harmful effects, but witchcraft (as the word is used here) is always irremediably evil.[33]

Africans living in traditional cultures exercise constant vigilance against witchcraft. Amulets and spells are considered helpful but not completely efficacious. A neighbor or even a total stranger can cause great harm through witchcraft. Kenyatta claims that witchcraft is actually nothing more than the administration of physical poison.[34] But in most contexts it is considered a destructive spiritual force as well. As a general rule, whenever harm befalls a person, it is thought that there must be a spiritual cause. The concept of a "natural" death is not part of the traditional African worldview. When someone dies, particularly if the death is inexplicable, it is almost invariably seen as the result of witchcraft. If that is the case, the witch must be sought out and destroyed. Traditional cultures specify the ordeals and the means of execution for witches. Mob execution can be the fate of suspected witches even in the modern African state. When I was in Kenya in August 1993, I noticed a report in the newspaper about an incident in a remote town. A man and his son had been accused of being witches. The people of the village locked them in their hut and burned it down. This incident brought the known total of such executions in Kenya to forty-one for that year.

ATR in the Modern World

The success of Christian and Muslim missions, as well as the ongoing secularization that comes from contact with Western culture, increasingly seems to discourage practices associated with ATR. However, it would be a mistake to think that ATR is vanishing from the scene; it is simply becoming less visible. A recurring phrase in contemporary discussions of the fate of ATR is that it is "in the people's blood." Richard Gehman has explained convincingly why ATR continues to be a force in modern Africa:

it provides the basic presuppositions of life; it becomes a refuge for people in times of crisis (even when they have made a profession of Christianity); and it frequently makes comebacks under the heading of reviving national cultural identity.[35]

ATR has found a new place in a synthesis with Christianity in the so-called independent churches of Africa.[36] These churches represent a form of Christianity that was produced by African nationalism working together with the ever present need for contextualizing the gospel.

Christianity was taken to Africa by European and American missionaries who introduced their Western culture along with the gospel. The process

Kikuyu warrior. Photograph: UPI/Corbis-Bettmann.

of contextualizing the gospel is tricky. Ideally speaking, missionaries should be able to extract the pure gospel message from the biblical message and pass it on untouched by their own culture to the converts, who then incorporate the gospel into their culture without polluting it. In practice this is impossible. The gospel message comes to us embedded in the culture of biblical times. Missionaries can try their best to separate true Christianity from its expression in their own culture, but no one can do so perfectly. The gap between the missionaries' and the hearers' cultures will cause misconceptions. The only way to avoid "cultural pollution" would be to stop sharing the gospel altogether.

All evangelical missionaries of the twentieth century doubtlessly know that they are supposed to export the gospel, not their culture. The problem is that the missionaries' understanding of the gospel is larded with products of Western culture, which are alien to the African setting. Thus, for example, the main Christian denominations in Kenya today are the legacy of Western missionary societies, and their services tend to follow traditional Western patterns: people in Western clothes (including suits and ties) sit on benches under a steepled roof, sing Western hymns in African translation, listen to sermons and so on.

Throughout this century there have been efforts to establish an African Christianity that combines the Christian message with African culture. Why not sing African songs accompanied by African instruments and worship in African style? Some large movements, such as the amaNazaretha Church founded by Isaiah Shembe and many other small congregations, have attempted to claim Christianity using African forms. These churches have been called independent (as opposed to missionary) churches.

In many cases the result has been syncretistic. Christian words are used in conjunction with traditional practices. A lengthy study of the independent churches of Kenya led Professor Murikwa to compile the following list of typical beliefs: (1) God is remote and capricious; (2) the ancestors are mediators between God and humans; (3) Christ is an example of the perfect life with God (with little mention of the atonement); (4) various degrees of initiation into stages of life, typically including levels of junior and senior elderhood; (5) a ministerial focus on healing and dream interpretation.

Clearly, the features that characterize ATR are reproduced in the beliefs of the independent churches; one looks in vain for the gospel message. In most cases the embodiment of the gospel in traditional African culture has swallowed up Christian doctrine and the gospel itself. As of the mid-1990s, the independent churches are dwindling in size, since the causes that spawned the movement are disappearing. The independent churches were originally part of the political independence movements, but political independence has been achieved. Churches founded by missionaries have for the most part been turned over to national leadership; there is no need for separate national churches. If ATR is indeed "in the blood of the people" and if it is no longer expressed in either the old tribal forms or the independent church movement, is syncretism next for the missionary-originated denominations?[37]

So You Meet a Traditional African . . .
What You Might Expect

Cultural differences inevitably complicate encounters with adherents of traditional religion. But a discussion of those differences would be a book in its own right. Still, a few words will give a bit of help. As an American visiting Africa, I had to make a fairly drastic adaptation that turned out to be a very pleasant task. I had to learn that African people love to have strangers drop by their houses unannounced to share a meal and visit. Relationships with people take far higher priority than time constraints or tasks.

When I visited Kenya, for example, my hosts suggested that I talk to Samson A., who had just returned from a trip to Tanzania. By then I knew better than to ask if I should call ahead. I got directions and walked to find his house. When I showed up on his doorstep, he welcomed me with "Karibu! Karibu!" Samson invited me in, and we sat and talked for a while. Only after about ten minutes of friendly conversation did I have a chance to introduce myself. Stating my name and my intention in visiting immediately upon arriving would have been impolite.

We went on talking as Samson's wife, Eunice, worked in the kitchen and outside. As Samson was sharing with me what he had experienced in Tanzania, I was distracted by the antics of the monkeys outside the back of the house. When some of Samson's friends dropped by, we shared tea and some roots. By lunch time, I made motions to leave, but Samson would have none of that; I stayed for lunch, which consisted of rice cakes *(ugali)*, more rice, fish and vegetables, and the conversation went on. By midafternoon, Samson said that I was free to go. Following African custom, he walked me to the main road.

As you can see, Africans do not view time as Westerners do. (Anyone reading these words who has lived in Africa will chuckle at the understatement.) We divide time into neat packages in which everything optimally begins and ends at a certain point. In the African setting, events do not have to start on the hour; they do not need to end until they are done.

Traditional African cultures are narrative oriented. They consider a point much better communicated if it comes embedded in a story instead of being expressed as an abstract principle. That fact also implies that the Westerner needs to take his time in conversation. To be in a hurry to get one's point made is considered discourteous and possibly unintelligent.[38]

In the religious dimension, ATR can appear as the central part of a tribal culture, or it can express itself in new ways, such as with the independent churches. Most important, it is not a set of doctrines or necessarily a standardized set of practices but a way of life that ultimately is "in the blood" of the people.

If you meet an African traditionalist, you will not necessarily see signs of it such as labels or characteristic practices. Instead, look for the person's relationship to the ancestors. Is he or she wearing amulets to defend against spirits? In case of illness, does the patient prefer to be treated by the local healer? My point is this: when you meet a traditional African, you may not at first see signs of his religious practices, not because they do not exist but because they are such an all-pervasive part of life.[39] It is hard to see some things because they are so scarce; other things may be hard to see at first because they are so fundamental. The latter is the case with ATR.

Relating the Gospel

Africans live in a religious environment, not only within ATR and established Christian churches but also through the efforts of Islam and various new syncretistic movements. Urbanized areas are filled with preaching and proselytizing. Thus Africans have heard Christian terminology, although they may not be aware of the true meaning of Christian beliefs.

The greatest barrier to true Christianity is the element of fear. The caprice of the ancestors combined with the threat of witchcraft is enough to keep many people from trusting Christ. An African mother, for example, may seriously consider responding to the gospel, but not if it means taking off the amulet bracelet her baby is wearing as protection against the spirits. What is needed is time, patience and a careful sharing of the gospel. Genuine Christians need to show through the story of their lives that Jesus Christ is real.

Missionaries to Africa have been criticized for a lack of sensitivity to African culture. Many of these criticisms are no doubt based on anti-European attitudes that it would not be possible to satisfy under any terms. Other criticisms may be based on facts. The need for contextualization has already been addressed, as well as the fact that it is not easy to accomplish. In Africa, as well as every other place on the globe, any attempts at evangelism need to be true to the message but also intelligible to the hearers.

Mastering the Material

When you have finished studying this chapter, you should be able to

1. give a meaningful definition of traditional religion;

2. delineate the main powers that typically are a part of traditional religion;

3. indicate the roles played by magical rituals in traditional religion;

4. describe the four nearly universal rites of passage and their vestiges in today's secular society;

5. characterize the nature of taboo;

6. depict the genuine nature and function of totem;

7. summarize the distinctive traits of ATR;

8. indicate the nature of the high God in ATR and illustrate his function in our four representative cultures (Kikuyu, Maasai, Zulu, Yoruba);

9. identify the nature of divinities in West African cultures;

10. draw together the function of the ancestors in ATR;

11. show how the rites of passage are integrated into our four representative cultures;

12. indicate the importance of ritual and magic, particularly healing, in ATR;

13. display the difference between general magic and witchcraft in ATR and its importance in African society;

14. expose the need for and difficulties with contextualization of the Christian gospel; show how it was attempted by the independent churches and explain what happened as a result.

Term Paper Ideas

1. Pursue an in-depth study of how Western scholarship has interpreted one aspect of traditional religion, such as magic, rites of passage, totem, taboo.

2. Compile a comprehensive summary of ATR in one African tribal culture.

3. Do an in-depth report on one aspect of ATR in one African tribal culture.

4. Trace how historical influences, such as trade, colonialism and independence, have influenced ATR in one culture.

5. Write out a summary of the history and beliefs of an independent church movement.

6. Trace how motifs typical of ATR have been carried into African-originated cultures in the Americas, for example, Haiti.

7. Describe the missionary philosophy and method of one organization or individual ministering in Africa.

Core Bibliography

Drewal, Henry John, and John Pemberton III. *Yoruba: Nine Centuries of African Art and Thought.* New York: Abrams, 1989.

Gehman, Richard J. *African Traditional Religion in Biblical Perspective.* Kijabe, Kenya: Kesho, 1989.

Kenyatta, Jomo. *Facing Mt. Kenya: The Tribal Life of the Gikuyu.* New York: Random House, 1965.

Lawson, E. Thomas. *Religions of Africa.* San Francisco: Harper & Row, 1985.

Mbiti, John S. *African Religions and Philosophy.* Nairobi, Kenya: East African Educational Publishers, 1969.

————. *Concepts of God in Africa.* New York: Praeger, 1970.

Newing, Edward G. "Religions of Pre-literary Societies." In *The World's Religions,* edited by Sir Norman Anderson, pp. 11-48. Grand Rapids, Mich.: Eerdmans, 1975.

Saitoti, Tepilit Ole. *Maasai.* New York: Abrams, 1980.

Sawyerr, Harry. *God: Ancestor or Creator? Aspects of Belief in Ghana, Nigeria and Sierra Leone.* London: Longman, 1970.

Schmidt, Wilhelm. *The Origin and Growth of Religion: Facts and Theories.* Translated by H. J. Rose. London: Methuen, 1931.

Chapter 6

Native American Religion

Estimated practitioners: 47,000

Sometimes you know someone who lives far across town better than your next-door neighbor. Similarly, many Americans have only a vague notion of the culture and religion of Native Americans. What we think we know about the "Indian" way of life comes mostly from Hollywood's depictions of it. You are more likely to encounter someone who knows something about Asian Indian religion than someone who knows something about the traditional religions that are still to some extent practiced within the boundaries of our own country.

Accurate information concerning Native American religion has not always been easy to come by, even for scholars. There are several reasons why this is so. First, many religious beliefs died with the people who were killed in genocidal actions. Second, those who managed to survive have often adapted their beliefs to prevailing beliefs or have kept their ancient practices secretly. Third, there is a tremendous amount of diversity in the beliefs and practices of Native Americans, making reliable generalizations about them difficult to establish. Fourth, the information provided frequently is skewed in favor of a particular preconception, either by the one who investigates and reports the information or by the Native practitioner who states what he or she thinks the researcher wants to hear.

This problem of distortion needs further elaboration. Information concerning the religion of the Native Americans has often been filtered through certain preconceived notions. Many early reports were provided by Christian missionaries who were likely to distort the picture they presented in one of two ways. First, they sometimes began with the presupposition that the "Indians" were heathens and thus nature worshipers or idolaters. In that case their reports were extremely negative, often ascribing to Native Americans beliefs or practices that the tribespeople themselves would have been appalled to hold. Second, they sometimes began with the philosophical presupposition that they would discover a natural common religion that centers on worship of a Great Spirit who punishes wicked behavior and provides a blissful afterlife for those who obey him. Even though there is some belief in a supreme being among Native Americans, a pure natural theism is quite rare.

Another distortion of Native American religion has been a series of variations on the theme of the "noble savage." An outgrowth of nineteenth-century romanticism, the notion became popular that races untouched by Western civilization lived in a state of purity and innocence, in harmony with the world of spirit and nature.[1] Descriptions arising from this context drew an idealized picture of Native American beliefs and practices that simply was not true. This approach has been revived recently as Native American beliefs are forced into alignment with currently fashionable political conceptions. Native Americans are extolled as being in complete harmony with nature, peaceful except when needing to defend themselves and sharing all things with each other as provided by Mother Earth.

A realistic appraisal shows that Native Americans' religious patterns are similar to the ones in the rest of the world, including the existence of a gap between espoused theory and lived practice. Though living in harmony with nature is crucial for many Native American societies, like everyone else, they have economic issues to consider as well. When Europeans colonized North America, many tribes were the second or third layer of occupation in their territories, each layer having displaced the previous occupants. Property rights varied within specific tribal cultures and toward outsiders. In short, although some Native American societies espoused ideals that the rest of the world would do well to emulate, on the whole Native cultures manifest the mixture of good and bad found in all human cultures. For our purposes, a description of Native American religion needs to be fair and evenhanded.[2]

Distribution of Native American Tribal Cultures

We need to begin with a brief survey of Native American distribution in North America prior to the European conquests.[3] By and large anthropologists agree that this population originally came to America from Asia during the last ice age. Some of these groups moved into Central and South America early on while others settled in various locations in North America. Further migrations and conquests occurred from time to time, and peaceful cultural interchanges took place as well. One line of evidence for the constant shifting of the population lies in the distribution of language groups. In various parts of the continent, versions of Athabascan, Algonkin and Aztec-Tanoan are spoken by tribes that live side by side. This fact seems to indicate different ethnic origins. Yet their cultures are very similar economically. It seems fair to conclude that geographic location and economic culture (for example, agriculture, hunting-gathering or bison hunting) influenced many external components of these cultures independently of each group's specific ethnic derivation.

Consequently, most introductory descriptions (such as this one) have used a geographic key to classify Native American cultures. A geographic key is not entirely satisfactory, but it is less unsatisfactory than other keys, for example, language, aboriginal ethnic origin or cultural evolution. The similarities from group to group within a particular geographic setting create enough order to permit some fairly reliable regional generalizations. For reasons of space this chapter focuses on North American tribes, the so-called American Indians, only. Thus it excludes Arctic peoples (Eskimos and Aleuts) and Meso-Americans. Six major regional groupings are evident among Native peoples living in North America. We will look briefly at each region and then zero in on specific beliefs and practices.[4]

Region	Representative Tribes	Culture and Economy	Religious Features
Northwest coast	Tlingit, Haida	totemism, fish, kelp	shamanism
West	Nez Perce, Ute, Shoshone	hunter-gatherer	shamanism, nature spirits
Southwest	Zuni, Navajo, Hopi, Apache	agriculture, pueblos	fertility, healing
Great Plains	Sioux, Dakota Mandan, Omaha	bison hunting or agriculture	shamanism, sun, Wakan Tanka
Eastern woodlands	Cree, Miami Iroquois	hunter-gatherer, fish	shamanism, Manitou
Southeast	Creek, Natchez Cherokee	corn agriculture	shamanism, medicine men

Table 6.1. Regional groupings of Native Americans

The Northwest coast. The peoples who inhabited the coastal areas of Alaska and British Columbia included the Tlingit, the Haida and the Tsimshian. They derived their sustenance mainly from the sea. Their society was organized on the basis of a matrilineal totemism (see chapter five). Their religions tended to be shamanistic.

The West. This region encompasses three subregions, each of which could be treated separately: the plateau (Oregon and Washington), which housed the Nez Perce and others; the basin (Utah, Nevada and northern New Mexico), which included the Ute and Shoshone; and California, home of the Hupa and the Mohave as well as some others. These tribes tended to live a hunter-gatherer existence. Where they came in contact with bordering tribes, they were likely to adopt some elements of those cultures. Specific geographic variations influenced regional specializations. For instance, in California acorns became a staple food, while in the basin the Shoshone's staple was pine seeds. The religions in this region focused on nature spirits. Shamans tended to have great influence.

The Southwest. Arizona, New Mexico and the surrounding area were home to the Zuni, Navajo, Hopi and Apache tribes (among others). Many, though not all, of the tribes in this area were agricultural. Those that were tended to have permanent dwellings (for example, the pueblos). Their religions centered around the fertility of the fields (Hopi and Zuni) and healing rituals (Navajo).

The Great Plains. The bison-hunting Natives of the Great Plains provided the stereotype for the "American Indian," with their feathered headdresses and teepee villages. And yet the tribes that fit into this broad pattern (Sioux, Cheyenne, Comanche, Kiowa, Teton Dakota) shared their territory with agricultural, sedentary tribes (Mandan, Omaha, Kansa, Missouri). No doubt the bison-hunting component received a great impetus with the arrival of the horse in the seventeenth century, which may have prompted the influx of some groups from the basin region and possibly some abandonment of agricultural practices. The religions of these groups focus on the sun and on a "great spirit" (Wakan Tanka) as well as spirits and shamanistic practices.

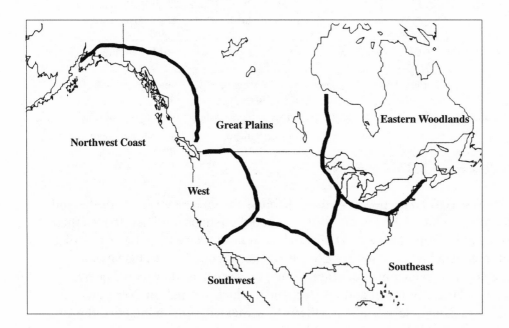

Map 6.1. Major areas of Native American settlement

The Eastern woodlands. This region extends from the northeast to the Great Lakes and the Ohio Valley all the way up to James Bay (including a region that could also be classified by itself as eastern subarctic). Representative tribes included the Ojibwa, the

Miami, the Cree and the Iroquois Federation. Hunting/gathering was supplemented by some fishing and agriculture. In terms of religion, many members of this group had a well-developed belief in a supreme God, Manitou, in addition to the usual shamanic occupation with spirits.

The Southeast. The Creek, the Natchez and the Cherokee were among the peoples of this area. Their economy included some corn agriculture, and their religion reflects this occupation. Shamans and medicine men directed the life of the spirit world.

The rest of this chapter looks at typical features of various Native American religions. There is no all-encompassing "Indian religion." The purpose of the depictions in this chapter is to draw attention to some of the features that are unique or particularly interesting among the many religions. Some of them are more typical for Native practices—shamanism comes to mind. Others are relatively rare but take on special significance in their limited areas, such as the vision quests of the Great Plains tribes.

The Supreme Being

Traditional Native American religions recognize the usual three levels of spiritual beings—supreme god, nature spirits and ancestor spirits—to varying degrees. In addition, superior spirits with godlike qualities often enter into the mix. Tribes may emphasize one or more of these components to the point of virtually ignoring the others.

To what extent did Native American religions include the recognition of a supreme god of the sky (in terms of the pattern associated with original monotheism)? Many of the descriptions included in writings on this subject were informed by a commitment to the evolutionary model of the origin and development of religion. For example, a scholar with impeccable credentials and enviable field studies to her credit places virtually all Native religions on the plane of belief in impersonal mana and writes, "Only in two or three highly developed Indian groups do we find the idea of an all-good Being."[5] As a matter of fact, this statement errs in two ways. First, it ignores the evidence of theism among the least developed tribes.[6] Second, it casts the evidence in more developed tribes into a framework not at home among the people themselves.

Belief in a Creator God has been found among tribes in California that existed at the lowest level of a hunter-gatherer economy. These groups include the Maidu, Yuki and Wintun. Extensive studies of their culture[7] have shown that "contrary to the animistic and preanimistic theories of the late development of a high god, these very tribes had a clearly developed Supreme Being and an idea of a real creation much more decidedly than any other Amerindian peoples, despite the relatively great advances of the latter in other aspects of culture."[8] In short, belief in a supreme god shows up in very undeveloped contexts and seems to diminish as the cultures develop further.

Many tribes testify to belief in a supreme power and the being that wields it. Several tribes of the plains speak of *wakan;* the Iroquois refer to *orenda.* Both Native American words apply first to a spiritual power that is found on all levels of existence, from rocks and grass to spirit beings. An Oglala man by the name of Sword told an investigator, "Every object in the world has a spirit and that spirit is wakan. Thus the spirits of the tree or things of that kind, while not like the spirit of man, are also wakan."[9] Such statements, along with the expectation of finding these people on the lower rungs of religious evolution, have led scholars to interpret wakan and orenda as examples of mana, the impersonal spiritual force.[10] However, neither wakan nor orenda is actually believed by the people themselves to exist autonomously as an impersonal force. Rather, they constitute the power wielded by personal spiritual beings.[11] The stronger the spirit, the stronger the force, and vice versa.

The logical extension of this idea is that supreme power is wielded by a supreme being, and this is exactly the case. The same Oglala also said, "*Wakan* comes from the *wakan* beings. . . . *Wakan Tanka Kin* signifies the chief or leading *Wakan* being, which is the Sun. However, the most powerful of the *Wakan* beings is *Nagi Tanka,* the Great Spirit who is also *Taku Skanskan. Taku Skanskan* signifies the Blue, in other words, the Sky."[12] Thus in some tribes at least there is a remembrance of a supreme being in relation to the powers of the world. In other tribes, however, it has virtually vanished.

A large number of woodland tribes have a highly articulated understanding of God. Among these are tribes of the Northeast that share the Algonkin language family, including the Algonkins, the Cree and the Ojibwa. They differ among themselves as to the ramifications of their understanding of God, but they also have a lot in common. God is referred to as Manitou or Gitche Manitou ("Great Spirit" or "Old Spirit"). Manitou is invisible and resides in the sky. He is creator of all, but he is particularly responsible for providing food. Thus to waste any food, such as parts of a slain animal, is to incur the wrath of Manitou and probably to starve to death. Any slain animal, including the smallest bird killed by a child, must be consumed completely. Meat may never be carried outside without being covered. To varying degrees, Manitou also guards the moral obligations of the tribe. In some cases he is opposed by an evil spirit, Matchi Manitou.[13] Similarly, the southeastern Natchez hold to a clearly defined belief in a supreme spirit who is creator. However, in distinction to the California tribes mentioned earlier, all of these groups have developed progressively away from theism and have supplemented their religious observances with a great amount of animism and shamanism.

In keeping with the pattern of religious development away from monotheism, many tribes have supplanted the invisible creator with a more concrete figure. For them the highest spirit may be the eagle, the crow or the sun. Quite a few tribes also have a second divine figure who plays the role of trickster (compare the Yoruba Esu in chapter five). The trickster, often pictured as the coyote, is not purely evil. He may do good, as he did when he assisted in creating the world, but he is unreliable. Suddenly the trickster may do something to harm the people, and so they must keep him at arm's length. Thus we see the transition from recognizing a creator god to placating a capricious spirit. Whether or not they recognize a high god, virtually all Native American religions function in the context of various spirits.

Spirits

Nature spirits. Though most traditional religions recognize the triad of god, nature spirits and ancestor spirits, they tend to attach varying importance to each. Most Native American religions grant the highest recognition to nature spirits. The world for them is made up of living personal spirits, not inanimate matter. Each plant, animal, unusual rock or body of water may be sacred because there is a spirit in it. Many cultures promote the practice of informing a deer, for example, of its impending fate before killing it in a hunt. This custom is frequently interpreted in terms of maintaining harmony with the natural world, but the fear of retribution from the spirit of the animal is no doubt relevant as well.

Alaskan Indian shaman. Photograph: Corbis-Bettmann.

The religion of the Teton Sioux, a plains group, recognizes the diversity of spirits in the natural world.[14] The Sun and the Sky are considered the highest spirits; both are envisioned as male. Their counterpart is the female Mother Earth. It would be a mistake to think of an orderly hierarchy of spirits, but roughly on a second level are the main spirits of the East, North, South and West Winds, the Whirlwind, Moon, Buffalo and Bear. The Thunder spirit occupies a special place among the Tetons (as with numerous other tribes). He is often pictured as a huge bird and is both feared and adored for his power. Then there are the multitudinous other spirits of the natural world, not all of whom are considered good. All spirits are considered wakan. Human spirits do not form a distinct category but are a lesser part of the total complex of spirit beings. The individual experiences life as one member of this spirit world. When he or she has a hard time finding the way, particularly when misfortunes occur, shamans are available to rectify the course.

Agricultural spirits. Many Native American cultures are agricultural. It is possible that a few plains tribes abandoned agriculture in favor of hunting when the horse was introduced by the Spanish. What is more likely, however, is that the hunting tribes of that region adopted the horse for greater efficiency while the agricultural tribes continued in their way of life.

Growing corn (as well as beans and squash) was an important part of many eastern tribal economies, north and south. This occupation is reflected in the eastern tribes' religious focus. Many of them (for example, Iroquois, Creek, Seminole and Cherokee) observe an annual festival known as the Green Corn Ceremony (or "busk"). This festival is observed when the corn ripens in August. The new year begins at this time and all of life enters a new cycle. It is a time of repentance and forgiveness, reflection on accomplishments and formulation of new year's resolutions, purification and feasting. Most importantly, it is a time of thanksgiving for the sustenance that has been provided. The Iroquois, whose economy is also largely dependent on hunting, thank the Great Spirit for the harvest; however, the Cherokee, who are firmly settled in an agricultural economy, express their gratitude to Selu, the corn goddess.

The most elaborate agricultural rites occur among the Natives of the Southwest, who have long been established in an agricultural way of life. Both the Hopi and the Zuni recognize the Kachina spirits that sustain their livelihood. In addition to corn, beans and squash, which are grown by both tribes, the Hopi also grow cotton. Agricultural pursuits in a relatively arid land require a lot of supernatural assistance. This help is thought to be provided by the Kachinas, the spirits of children who were lost in the mountains. They return to the villages each year to bring rain and make the crops, particularly the beans, productive. A feast lasting several days marks the Kachinas' return from the mountains. Kachina men, dressed up in colorful costumes and large masks, perform ritual dances. A sideshow is provided by the all-important Kachina clowns, who always appear in black and white outfits and amuse the crowd with actions that range from silliness to breaking taboos. The Kachina spirits remain in the villages until harvest time. Then they return to the mountains for the winter.[15]

Ancestor spirits. Most Native American religions do not have an elaborate belief system concerning departed human beings. Some of the northern tribes refer to the aurora borealis as the "dead dancing," but no further mythology is usually attached to that belief. The Creek, on the other hand, have a somewhat more elaborate view of life after death. The supreme spirit, known as the Breath Holder, is in charge of all human spirits, and he superintends the realm of the dead who have attained bliss. Only those who have led a righteous life are eligible for this honor. After they die they must fight their way through many dangers along the Milky Way until they finally attain the state of contentment.[16] One of the most developed thanatologies was held by the Natchez, also of the Southeast and now virtually extinct. They believed in a firm set of rewards and punishments, a rarity among Native Americans. They thought that evil people went to a barren land covered with water and infested by mosquitoes. People who lived by the code of the tribe, on the other hand, would rise to a land of fertility and bliss characterized by ease and serenity.[17]

Native American cultures hold generally vague conceptions concerning the dead. Although burial customs can be elaborate and burial sites can be considered sacred, funeral customs focus on taboos and rituals for the living as much as on preparing the departed for a life to come. Frequently favorite objects are buried along with the dead (a custom among the Tlingit of Alaska), but again, there is no great mythology attached to these preparations. By and large, the departed are just that—departed—and if all goes well, they will remain there. But most tribal cultures do not close the door on special manifestations originating from a departed spirit. A disgruntled dead person may come back as a ghost. Among a few tribes, especially the Navajo, the fear of ghosts has become extreme. In instances of haunting, the shaman can diagnose and treat the problem.

The Shaman and Healing Practices

The vast majority of Native American religions practice shamanism. A shaman heals through contact with the spirits. Once they possess the shaman, he or she becomes the medium through which the spirits work. Thus we make a distinction between a healer ("medicine man") who uses magic to manipulate the spirits and a shaman who is used by the spirits. Although the term *medicine man* is closely associated in the popular mind with Native Americans, technically the function carried out in most tribes is shamanism. But there are some examples of healings without shamanistic possession as well.

The specific nature of shamanistic culture varies from tribe to tribe. There are examples of both male and female shamans. In general, someone becomes a shaman on the basis of a supernatural calling, which frequently manifests itself through illness. A vow to become a shaman may be required in order to recover from the illness (the same pattern occurs in the context of Japanese religion). Black Elk was an Oglala Sioux whose life encompassed Custer's defeat at the Little Big Horn, Buffalo Bill's Wild West Show in London and life on a reservation.[18] As a child, Black Elk had been frail and sickly. He was also extremely fearful, which was a serious flaw for a member of his tribe. When he was nine, he came down with an illness that caused his extremities to become inflamed and swollen. At one point he fell into a trance and had an elaborate vision. Black Elk recovered from this sickness but did not regain full health. Eventually a shaman named Black Road diagnosed the problem. To cure it, he had the tribe act out a large part of Black Elk's vision. This ceremony put him in direct contact with the spirit beings, including the thunder beings of the west who had always frightened him severely. Once the rite was performed, Black Elk gained physical and psychological strength. A short while later he became a shaman himself and performed cures for a number of years.

The Algonkin tribes of the Northeast (for example, the Ojibwa and the Cree) share a special shamanistic rite called the shaking tent ceremony. The shaman performs this ritual as a service for clients of his tribe. First he purifies himself in a ceremony that includes the sweat lodge. Native American rituals almost invariably include time spent in a sweat lodge—a small, tightly closed hut in which water is poured on hot stones to create steam. After he leaves the sweat lodge, the shaking tent shaman enters the sacred tent by himself and begins to commune with the spirits. Among the spirits may be some pretty fearful beings whose power is essential for success. As the spirits take control of the shaman, they manifest themselves through many different noises and eventually by shaking the whole tent (hence the name of the ceremony). When the ordeal is over, the shaman emerges and announces what the spirits have revealed to him, perhaps how to cure an illness, how to succeed in love or where find a lost object or person.[19]

Among the Tlingit of the Alaskan coast, shamans are designated as such from birth. In order to maintain their powers, they may never do anything to adorn their hair, including combing it or cutting it. If their hair is ever cut, their power (like Samson's) will be lost. These shamans perform the usual functions, but one of their main duties is to expose witches. The shaman's word is usually considered infallible in this regard. Like many traditional Africans, the Tlingit believe that every misfortune has a spiritual cause. Serious problems are usually the work of a witch (male or female). The shaman identifies the witch, who is promptly killed, usually by drowning. People who are exposed as witches tend to live on the margins of the community and have little social protection. Or they are people for whom the shaman already bears animosity. Not surprisingly, shamans are greatly feared by common people. Sometimes shamans expose each other as frauds or witches. If the identification sticks, the accused shaman dies. Shamans' remains are preserved in special houses that are considered strictly taboo.[20]

Some healing rituals involve a medicine man, or healer, rather than a shaman. The first step in the healing is identifying the cause of the ailment. Among the Creek, this work is performed by a "knower," who reveals what is wrong with the person. The medicine man then carries out the treatment. One commonly used technique, particularly in the Southwest desert, involves sucking the disease out of the person's body.[21] Incantations, amulets, sacred smoke and the ever present sweat baths are frequently employed. Some healings involve both medicine men and shamans.

A method of healing that originated among the Navajo has become popular in holistic medicine.[22] The disease is thought to have a spiritual cause, possibly being instigated by a witch, a ghost (former human being) or one of the many spirits known as "holy people." (The holy people are nature spirits who can do good or cause mischief. Among these beings, only Changing Woman—the original provider of corn—is considered entirely beneficent and reliable.) Illnesses caused by spiritual beings are treated by a spiritual counterattack. The patient may be placed in the center of an elaborate diagram (a dry painting with pollen and other organic substances in the sand; often called a "sand painting"), and lengthy chants are pronounced on his or her behalf. A full-blown ceremony can take several days. As the ceremony is conducted, all spiritual impurities are removed and health is restored.

Totemism

Totemism, the practice of dividing society into distinct groups bearing the names of animals or plants (as described in chapter five), is widespread among Native Americans. For example, it is found among the Hopi of the Southwest, the Creek and Cherokee of the Southeast and the tribes of the Northwest coast. Their elaborately carved totem poles are familiar to people everywhere. These poles are commonly thought to be idols, but experts point out that they represent genealogies, not idols. Neither opinion is strictly accurate.

Totemism as practiced by the Tlingit of Alaska fits the standard patterns associated with totemism in many ways, but it includes some interesting departures. The entire Tlingit tribe consists of two main moieties: the Eagles and the Crows. Each person belongs to one or the other. Each moiety consists of numerous subgroups called phratries that also bear the names of various animals. Table 6.2 illustrates this structure.[23]

Moieties	Eagle	Crow
Phratries	Eagle	Crow
	Bear	Beaver
	Wolf	Frog
	Whale	Salmon
	Shark	Seal

Table 6.2. Totemistic structure of the Tlingit

A person belonging to the Eagle moiety also belongs to one of the phratries listed below the Eagle. Someone of the Eagle moiety can be an Eagle pure and simple or can be a Bear, a Wolf, and so on. The same pattern applies to the Crow moiety. There are more phratries than the ones listed in the illustration.

The hierarchy of phratries constitutes a permanent caste system in Tlingit culture. This practice is mythologically justified in terms of the qualities of the animals involved. A beaver is greater than a frog in terms of strength and intellect. Consequently the Beaver phratry would be higher than the Frog phratry. These caste distinctions are supposed to be strictly observed in terms of the social life in general and of marriage in particular. Marriages take place only among persons of equal phratry.

The totemic system of the Tlingit, as with virtually all such systems, is exogamous. Persons of the same phratry and moiety may not marry each other. In terms of table 6.2, someone in one of the Eagle phratries may only marry a person in one of the Crow phratries. In our example above, a Wolf can marry a Frog, but not a Bear. Breaking this rule involves the severest penalties. Of course, along with the proper moiety distinction, the correct caste association must also be observed. Thus, the Wolf should probably not marry someone of the Seal or Crow phratry.

If someone in the Wolf phratry married someone of the Frogs, to which phratry would the new family, particularly the children, belong? The answer depends on the wife's phratry. Since Tlingit society is matrilineal, the family counts for the wife's totem and the children belong to her phratry, although the husband does not lose his own totemic affiliation as an individual. Thus, if the wife is a Frog, so are the children. Property rights and inheritance rights all belong to the wife's side of the family. Legally the children belong to the wife's brother more than to their biological father (though the biological family unit lives intact, barring disruption).

Among the Tlingit the totem animal is not considered taboo. In chapter five it was mentioned that totemic taboos insure equitable food distribution within a tribe. But a member of the Whale phratry is permitted to eat whale meat without compunction. Thus in strict terms Tlingit totemism does not carry out this function directly with regard to the totem animal. Nevertheless, other totemistic aspects of Tlingit culture do have a distributing function.

Most ceremonial offices must be awarded to members of the opposite moiety (Crow or Eagle, with their phratries). Virtually all jobs associated with funerals, weddings or other special occasions must be given to someone of the other moiety, who is paid handsomely. For instance, making a casket, carrying a casket or carving a totem pole can only be done across moiety boundaries. Thus there is a built-in system for economic distribution. Furthermore, wedding or funeral feasts may be partaken of by members of the moiety opposite to the groom or the deceased only. Whatever is not eaten on the spot will be taken home by these guests.

A great event among the Tlingit is the occasional "potlatch," an extended feast that includes a lot of dancing. The person who hosts the potlatch gives presents to a large group of people, thereby demonstrating high economic status (even if he starved himself and his family for many years). Presents are given to members of the opposite moiety, so the potlatch also serves to distribute food throughout the society.

In the absence of Native writing, picture carving serve to transmit tradition. Different kinds of totem poles function in different ways. One writer has distinguished four different types of poles:[24] (1) genealogical—recording the ancestry of an important person; (2) historical—recording the ancestry of a clan; (3) legendary—recounting an epic, usually about the clan's origin (for instance, it may tell how the Wolf phratry was founded by the great Wolf spirit in the remote past); (4) mortuary—

Snake war dance of the Flathead tribe in Montana. Photograph: UPI/Corbis-Bettmann.

functioning as a grave marker, indicating the deceased's totemic affiliation. It is probably best to think of this information as mythological rather than as embodying historical facts.

In a traditional society, information is never neutral; it is always charged with religious content. Thus it would be false to think of these poles as doing nothing more than relating information. Having a special relationship to one's clan animal implies being related to the nature spirit embodied by that animal. The great ancestors depicted on the pole need to be revered. The poles are not idols, since no one prays to them. But neither are they *merely* genealogies; they do not simply provide a registry. They are visual representations of the spirits to which a particular group owes its special allegiance and thus they bear religious significance.

Sacred Objects

Many Native American cultures consider certain objects sacred. An object may be sacred because it has a special ceremonial function or because it possesses great spiritual energy. In the latter case it would be considered a fetish by modern scholars. Fetishes can be personal or communal. In some tribes an individual may possess something that he or she considers a special "medicine." This object is guarded carefully, and it may even be ritually fed. It can be any natural object (organic or inorganic). Sometimes it is carried about, but often it is stored at home in a safe place. A young warrior belonging to one of the plains tribes, which emphasize the quest for visions, may be shown a special object that he must then find and never abandon.

Certain tribes or communities may also possess sacred objects that belong to the people at large. These objects are venerated at tribal ceremonies. For example, Hopi and Zuni cultures venerate certain perfectly formed ears of corn. An individual or special society maintains physical possession of the objects. These keepers are also endowed with greater spiritual power. However, they are only stewards of these objects on behalf of the community.

Among other tribes, for example, many plains tribes, there are special objects called bundles. These can be personal or tribal. Bundles may contain natural objects or even weapons, and they function like fetishes, that is, they are charged with spiritual energy. Sometimes they provide links to departed members of the tribe. In that case, caring for the bundle properly keeps the ancestors from coming back as ghosts.

An object that is sacred primarily because of its ceremonial function is the sacred pipe, called calumet in the Southeast. Pipe ceremonies extend west all the way through the plains. Even though there are differences in terms of pipe construction and ceremonial details, there are also similarities. In the ritual use of the calumet, smoke is inhaled and then expelled toward heaven, earth and the four winds. The tobacco used by Native Americans in former days had a powerful narcotic (possibly even hallucinogenic) effect.

In tribes such as the Oglala, which used the pipe for many different purposes, the form of the pipe varied with the particular function. Special occasions, such as sealing a treaty, required a two-part pipe. The head was made of clay, usually quarried from a sacred place in Minnesota, and the stem was made of wood. The two pieces were joined only at the time of the special ceremony. It is clear that the sexual union symbolized by the construction was intended to enhance the spiritual union that was effected.

Vision Quests

Receiving and implementing visions is an important aspect of Native American religion, particularly among the plains tribes. For example, each member of the Crow tribe hopes to receive a vision.[25] A person who has received such a visitation has a greater chance of success in life. A vision may assure health or prosperity, but many of the reports given to researchers have linked the reception of a vision with later heroic deeds in tribal warfare. Among the plains tribes, greater honor went to a warrior who had accumulated many coups than to one who had slain many enemies. A coup is made when a warrior does something risky, like touching an enemy in battle or stealing his weapons. Thus in former days, a vision predicted that a man would be able to count many coup in the near future.

Visions can be attained in different ways. A vision may come at a tranquil moment or a moment of great stress. More often than not, a vision must be induced. A warrior may stay in the wilderness without food or drink for four days or sit in the snow without clothes for a long period of time. He may even inflict an injury on himself such as cutting off a finger. In some tribes such an ordeal is an integral part of the attainment of warriorhood. Women also seek and find visions. Among the plains cultures, their quest is less important than men's quests. In the Southeast, on the other hand, visionary activity by women may take precedence over men's activities.

The actual content of visions varies, of course. Among the plains tribes, the visionary sees an extraordinary animal being, perhaps a huge buffalo or a weasel, entering his or her body. But it may also be a person (or a group of persons) who comes to see the individual in order to pass on a cryptic message. The person who has received the vision feels reassured of the success about to befall him or her. There usually is no great shame associated with returning empty from a vision quest (except when it is tied into a mandatory puberty rite). But someone who has not had a vision may feel spiritually unfulfilled and pessimistic about the future.

Rites of Passage

Of the four nearly universal rites of passage (birth, puberty, marriage, adolescence), the puberty rite has perhaps provided the most unique coloring among Native American cultures. All four stages are amply represented in various tribal settings. In this connection we can also address the matter of special societies and special observances, such as the sun dance of the plains. Since there are so many variations, we shall use the Tlingit of Alaska as our primary pattern; however, we shall supplement as warranted from other cultures.

Birth. Some cultures seclude pregnant woman for a long time before they give birth. Among the Shoshone, whose social organization centers around the immediate family (which is then very loosely aggregated with a clan), the father undergoes certain restrictions as to diet and activity along with the mother. Among the Tlingit, however, women continue to function in society up until the time of birth has come. Both boys and girls are welcomed: boys because they represent superior strength[26] and girls because inheritance rights descend through them in this matrilineal society.[27] Nevertheless, some children are not wanted. Children born out of wedlock violate the social system, and twins represent an evil omen. Such infants are taken to the woods, where they are suffocated with moss. Other tribes besides the Tlingit practice infanticide.

Various tribes undertake ritual precautions intended to protect the child from harm in the coming life. The Teton Sioux preserve a piece of the umbilical cord and leave the placenta on a tree to "die." In the agricultural Zuni and Navajo societies, the child is blessed with an ear of corn and with the sprinkling of corn pollen.

Among the matrilineal Tlingit, the child receives its name a few days after birth, usually the name of a recently departed relative. This practice conforms to an informal belief in reincarnation (in that the departed person has apparently come back as the new child). Different ways of naming a child appear in various tribal cultures. The Zuni make a special effort not to give a child a name (and thus to treat him or her as a real person) until the child's survival is assured.

Virtually all Native American cultures use some form of the cradle board for their infants. The child is tied to a board and then wrapped, creating the effect known commonly as the papoose. The baby usually remains confined, except for its daily hygienic care, until it learns to talk. Before the time of European influence, the pressure applied to the forehead by a strap on the board caused members of Southeastern tribes (for example, Creek and Cherokee) to have permanently flattened foreheads.

Early childhood is a time of indulgence. Babies are usually fed whenever they ask for food, and discipline seems rare. By the time a child is six years old, an informal training process has begun. For boys in particular, in many tribes, the process of strengthening courage and hardening the body against physical dangers commences. The Zuni have a special procedure for boys aged five to nine. Sometime around this time the child is initiated into the Kachina cult. He and his age mates are awakened in the night and carried to a special place where two Kachinas (costumed men—but the child does not know this) give them instructions and a ritual whipping.

Puberty. On the whole, this rite of passage seems to be one of the most crucial in many tribes. But that fact ought not to blind us to the clear distinctions among the various groups. For example, for boys in the Tlingit culture, the whole affair is smooth and painless. Around age ten, a potlatch is given for him, and he moves into his maternal uncle's household. Other than that, there is no special ritual observance.

At the other end of the spectrum is the initiation of boys in the Great Plains tribes, such as the Tetons. At the time of puberty, a boy sets out on his first vision quest. After receiving preparation from a shaman, he purifies himself with a sweat bath. Then he undertakes a four-day ordeal to receive his vision. He finds a place all by himself in the wilderness, usually on top of a hill or some other exposed area. He does not eat or drink all this time as he waits for a spirit to reveal itself. He gashes his arms and legs from time to time with a knife in order to enhance the process. The spirit that eventually shows itself will be the boy's guardian spirit for the rest of his life. The physical item associated with this spirit becomes the young man's special "medicine," and he carries it with him in a pouch for the rest of his life. If the boy has a vision of the thunder beings, he is expected to join the Heyoka society, members of which often live by reversing the social norms of their tribe; for example, they might wear furs in the summer.[28] There is no particular record that the young men try to influence their vision in the direction of the thunder beings, which are considered to be fierce. Vision quests may be undertaken later in life to enhance the relationship to this guardian spirit or to involve further spirits.

The puberty rite for boys among Zuni and Hopi tends to go in the direction of demystification. The boys are given a second audience with the Kachinas. But this time, the spirit impersonators take off their masks and place them on the faces of the shocked boys. Thus they are taught that the spirits in human form are merely costumed human beings. Although the boys are at first terribly disillusioned, they eventually learn the lesson that the Kachina spirits are not just "out there," but are present and active among real people in common society.[29]

When girls attain puberty in Tlingit society, they undergo more serious restrictions than boys. They have their ears and lips pierced, and for several weeks their diet is limited. It is taboo for them to touch anything that could be a weapon. Similar restrictions are enforced whenever a woman has her menses.

Puberty rites for girls among the Shoshone are more rigorous. Depending on the particular clan, a girl may be confined in a small hut from five to thirty days. During this time she may not talk or laugh. She is frequently combed and deloused. Her diet is severely restricted, excluding all animal products. During this time the girl may not touch her body except with her scratching stick. From time to time she is allowed to leave the hut, but then she must put on a veil and perform some act of hard labor, maybe carrying wood. Successfully completing this trial renders her attractive for marriage.[30]

Marriage. The Tlingit are an exogamous totemic matrilineal society, meaning that people can marry only outside of their totemic moiety and that the genealogical line is traced through the mother's totem. Selecting a marriage partner can be a matter of personal choice or family arrangement. Romantic love and courtship seldom play a role. It is crucial to observe proper channels and taboos. Marriage is first and foremost an arrangement between clans. Sometimes a bride and groom do not meet until the day of their wedding.[31]

Traditional Tlingit marriages are settled by the transfer of the dowry from the groom's family to the bride's family. If the wife is unfaithful to her husband, the family must return the dowry, so there is a lot of pressure on her to remain faithful. On the other hand, the husband can dismiss the wife at any time. Thus this matrilineal society does not coerce men into unwanted affiliations.

The Zuni people are also exogamous, but they are matrilocal. The husband goes to live with his wife on the wife's property (a physical requirement that is not present among the Tlingit where house ownership is variable). A Zuni woman can divorce her husband simply by placing his belongings outside the house. He then moves back into his parent's dwelling.

A practice found among the Tlingit, but not the Zuni, is levirate and sororite marriage. In a custom reminiscent of Old Testament biblical culture, when a man dies his brother is obligated to take his widow for a wife. Correspondingly, a woman must marry the widowed husband of her sister. Since Tlingit society is primarily monogamous, the replacement spouse must get divorced in order to marry the survivor left behind by the brother or sister. Furthermore, if there is no brother or sister, a nephew or niece must carry out the function of replacement spouse, which can make for some highly drastic differences in age. To a less stringent degree, levirate or sororite marriage is practiced by some other tribal cultures as well.

Special societies and ceremonies. Many Native American cultures have various societies that carry out important social and religious functions. In totemic cultures, it might be a special association centered around the spirit of the totem. Such is clearly the case in the Southwest among the totemic clans of the Hopi and Zuni. Different clans have precise functions with regard to agricultural ceremonies. The role of the Kachina impersonation is performed, for example, by the men of the Kachina society, who are members of the Kachina phratry. Other tribes have dancing societies or healing societies. In each case, membership in the group requires an initiation.

Dancing societies are fairly common among Native Americans. The intricacies of ritual dance require extensive preparation. At important festivals the necessary dances may be performed by the particular societies holding proprietorship over them. Among the Tlingit, the dancing societies provide contact with the spirit world, which turns the otherwise materialistic potlatch into a religious event.

A well-known healing society is the Iroquois False Face Society. According to legend, the good great spirit and the evil spirit had a strength contest. The evil spirit, which is the bringer of disease, lost the contest and was left with a twisted mouth and a broken nose. Because he lost, he had to show human beings how to cure the illnesses that he inflicts on them. These prescriptions are carried out by the False Face Society, whose membership consists primarily of men who have been healed previously. When someone becomes ill, members of the society don masks that are replicas of the disease bringer's face (with individual variations decreed in personal dreams). As they approach the house of the sick person, they begin to chant and dance, entering the house after several false starts.[32] Then they carry out the usual procedures associated with traditional healing: dancing, chanting, shaking rattles and blowing smoke into the patient's face. This process involves no shamanism. The cure is attained on the basis of technique alone, apart from direct spirit possession. Patients who recover are expected to make a gift to the society.

The sun dance of the Great Plains tribes is of central importance to a great number of bison-hunting cultures. It signifies tribal unity and facilitates interaction among the clans that make up the larger unit. Some researchers maintain that this ceremony, as crucial as it has become in the lives of the tribes, was not fully developed until about A.D. 1800, when these cultures had changed into horse-dependent hunting societies.[33] I suspect that the roots, at least, go back much further. But if this late date is accurate, it certainly provides evidence for our contention throughout this book that rituals can proliferate very quickly. The rite also functions as a kind of initiation into superior warriorhood. It is difficult to isolate one overarching purpose of the sun dance; it combines elements of worship, communal identification, reintegration into the religious dimension of life, as well as the initiatory aspect, which is our concern here.

Apache "Devil Dance." Photograph: UPI/Corbis-Bettmann.

Some version of the sun dance is practiced by many tribes, but once again the specific forms vary.[34] For the most part, the ceremony takes eight days. The participants, who are seeking initiation under the direction of shamans or other mentors, will undergo a prolonged ritual that includes purification, dancing and incessant gazing at a central object (a pole or the sun). Although physical self-torture is not intrinsic to the dance, in practice it is more the rule than the exception.

As the bands of the tribe come together, they set up the physical facilities for the ceremony while each initiate receives instruction from his mentor. He needs to learn the dances and undergo extensive purification. The sweat lodge once again figures prominently. In the meantime, one of the most important preliminary rituals concerns finding the tree that will serve as the center post for the ritual lodge. It must be a straight cottonwood tree. In the ceremony of felling it, the tree is taunted as an enemy. Often the job of hacking it down is given to a woman. Once the tree is felled, it is carried to the ceremonial ground where it is erected, and an open lodge is built around it. The dancers are by now fasting and trying to purify their minds. Whereas the rest of the tribe is engaged in joyful social activities, the dancers must remain taciturn and aloof.

Those participating in the dance form a circle around the pole, singing the traditional chants, raising and lowering themselves on their toes, blowing whistles and keeping their gaze constantly fixed on the pole. This procedure may go on from sunrise to sunset, and it has been known to continue for days. In that case the participants are permitted certain short breaks.

What has made the sun dance so famous among Natives and non-Natives is self-torture, which has become standard practice among several tribes. Among the Oglala, for example, the participants insert little wooden pegs, with leather straps attached to them sideways, into their backs and chests. Objects fastened to the straps cause pain as the participant dances. The straps in back may be attached to buffalo skulls. Straps in the chest may be tied to four outside poles, the center pole or a crotch in the center pole so that someone can raise and lower the participant by pulling the straps, leaving the initiate dangling in the air. From time to time, one of the dancers attempts to stare at the bright sun without showing any evidence of pain. In the full-blown Oglala version of the ceremony, at the end of the dance the participants are expected to leap so that the pegs tear out of their flesh. Those who succeed bear the scars with pride and receive many honors, one of which is automatic eligibility to participate in the sun dance again next year.

Death. Although Native American cultures as a whole do not have many explicit beliefs concerning an afterlife, disposal of the dead frequently involves elaborate rituals and taboos. No human culture has ever freed itself entirely from the fear of ghosts, and such notions are also a part of Native American thought patterns. Fear of ghosts has taken on extreme dimensions for the Navajo, whose apprehension over the return of the departed has been termed a "tribal phobia."[35] Once the Navajo had burial performed by slaves, who would then be killed on the spot. Today the task is given to non-Navajo whenever possible.

Among the Tlingit, totemic concerns permeate practices surrounding the disposal of the dead.[36] In traditional practice there is also a strong taboo concerning physical contact with the dead. For that reason, if possible, a dying person dresses in grave clothes so that no one has to touch that person's body after death. A coffin is constructed from rude boards, frequently before the eyes of the nearly departed to provide reassurance that he or she will be properly treated. If possible, the person is moved to someone else's house in order to confuse the spirit in potential future visits. Once the person has died, a vigil with lights is held, waiting for people to show up for the funeral. Relatives of the deceased of the same totem prepare an elaborate feast. All the people involved in the actual burial (those who dress the dead, make and carry the coffin, dig the grave, carve the totem pole and so on) are members of the opposite moiety.

On the day of the burial, the body is removed through a breach broken into the wall or roof. Sometimes a dog is carried through the hole as well, presumably in order to further confuse the spirit. Pallbearers carry the coffin to the grave site. The body is buried along with some of the deceased's favorite possessions and a jug of water. In case of cremation, the remains are placed in a special "dead house" owned by the family. In either case, a marker, traditionally a small totem pole, is left to indicate the rank of the departed person.

Now follows the feast, which is given by members of the deceased's phratry for members of the opposite moiety. This feast has three purposes:[37] to honor the dead, to feed the departed spirit and—perhaps most importantly—to make good on all debts that could presumably be laid against the departed. In particular, anyone who had any part in funeral preparations expects a handsome reward at this occasion.

The amount of pomp and circumstance accompanying a Tlingit funeral depends on the social standing of the deceased. Funerals of chiefs are major occasions; less auspicious persons receive more modest ceremonies. Shamans are never buried, but are laid to rest in houses that are isolated from the community and are considered severely taboo.

In terms of social rank, the Natchez of the Southeast draw strong distinctions between nobility and commoners, referring to them as "suns" and "stinkards" respectively.[38] Ancient funerary practice demonstrates this drastic distinction. Funerals for commoners consisted of burying the deceased with his or her possessions. The bereaved cut their hair in mourning. On the other hand, the funeral for a "sun" might include being escorted into death by relatives, slaves and volunteers. The path to the burial site was lined with dead infants, sacrificed by parents of slaves and people of inferior social standing. Presumably the volunteers sought to insure themselves entry to a blissful afterlife, a belief that was well developed among the Natchez.

Shoshone disposal of the dead is relatively simple. Their fear of the dead prompts them to keep the disposal process as simple as possible. The corpse is washed by a member of the same sex and then burned. Often the hut in which the corpse is laid out serves as a funeral pyre. Sometimes the corpse is simply abandoned as the band moves on to another location. The possessions of the deceased are destroyed. Widows may not eat meat or wash anything for a certain period of time. And no one is allowed to mention the name of the dead.

The Tetons seem to have no particular fear of the dead, even if they have reason to believe that someone has reappeared as a spirit. The corpse is initially mourned in a special lodge for that purpose. Then it is wrapped, together with the person's belongings (such as pipe, medicines and implements) and stored on a tree or platform, together with some food offerings. Eastern tribes (for example, the Huron) practice similar elevated disposal, but follow it up with secondary interment every twelve years.

Despite their fear of the dead, Native Americans demonstrate little fear of death. Individuals usually accept imminent death with astounding equanimity. Desecration of Native burial grounds has been a political issue lately. Early in this century, anthropologists frequently took articles from burial sites for scholarly investigation or for display as curiosities. A resurgence of tribal identity has caused Native Americans to lobby the government for the return of such articles. In 1990 President George Bush signed a bill into law that mandated the return of certain Native articles found on federal land or stored in national museum holdings (for instance, the Smithsonian Institution).

Modern Syncretistic Movements

As Native Americans came into increasing contact with the religions of Europeans, they incorporated some Christian concepts into their own beliefs and practices. This process was encouraged by the political protection that traditional practices could receive if they fit the label of "religion." Because of their importance, we shall look at two such movements: the ghost dancing religion of 1890 and the Native American Church.

Ghost dancing. The ghost dance movement that occurred in 1890 was the offshoot of similar movements, including one in 1870 that had gone by the same name and had carried a similar message. As Native American tribes faced defeat at the hands of the U.S. military and as they were pushed into conditions resulting in starvation, epidemics and the loss of their homes, messianic movements arose that promised supernatural military victory and the restoration of pristine conditions.

The movement of 1890 was begun by a Paiute named Wovoka, who had grown up on a reservation and then worked on a farm, where he was given the name Jack Wilson. Wovoka became seriously ill and received a vision. In it he was given a message to spread to all Native people that would renew their lives. His teachings included five major points. (1) He, Wovoka, was the messiah, the son of God. He had come once before to the white people, but they mistreated him and killed him. Now he had come to the red people in the expectation that they would treat him better.[39] (2) God would redeem the red people. In the spring of 1891 he would send a flood that would wipe out all white people, but he would spare the red population. (3) All people must live peaceful, moral lives. No one may lie or steal; no one should accomplish anything by force of arms. (4) Until the time of final redemption, the red people must work to bring their ancestors back to earth. They can do this by holding five day-long dances. These dances would bring visions, healing, supernatural power and contact with the departed who would then be able to join in the new world to come. This aspect of the movement gave it the name ghost dancing. (5) When the Great Spirit has finished his work, all faithful red people will live in a paradise with plenty of food for all. Most importantly, there they will be permanently reunited with all of their departed family members.

Within a few months, Wovoka's teachings spread throughout the tribes of the plateau and the Great Plains. Everywhere on the reservations people were adopting the dance and assimilating its message. Individual tribes added their own cultural traits to their performances. Some wore special "ghost shirts," which were supposed to make them bulletproof; others devised special ways of coloring their skin; still others performed the dance around a pole.[40] Native celebrities, including Sitting Bull, Black Elk and Big Foot, joined the movement.

The American government saw in the ghost dance movement a threat to prevailing conditions. The tribes had finally been secured on reservations, but trouble seemed to be breaking out again. So the ghost dance was outlawed. On December 29, 1890, Colonel James W. Forsyth and his regiment attempted to disarm a camp of mostly sick men, women and children at Wounded Knee, South Dakota. One warrior's rifle went off, probably by accident, possibly when someone tried to wrest it from him. The waiting soldiers immediately opened rifle and artillery fire on the helpless camp. Several hundred people died, and with them the hope of the ghost dance. Wovoka, who lived in Nevada, continued to function as a shaman until his death in 1932. The fact that his predictions had not come true apparently did not cause him to lose confidence in his personal spiritual powers.

The Native American Church. Another modern syncretistic movement centers around the sacrament of the peyote cactus. It combines elements of Native religion, Christian beliefs and traditional practices. Ceremonies involving the peyote cactus originated in Mexico and the adjoining region of the American Southwest. However, in the twentieth century these practices have been adopted by members of tribes as far away as Canada. Since peyote is a hallucinogenic drug, its use has come under various restrictions. However, tribal groups have obtained protection for this practice under the First Amendment right of freedom of religion. The largest body to have received such sanction is the Native American Church of North America.[41]

There are several versions of Peyote religion. Indigenous Mexican forms of it contrast with early versions practiced in the United States, which may not have begun until the nineteenth century. In the American versions, the ceremony is carried out in a specially designated lodge where a large button-shaped piece of peyote, called the chief peyote, is displayed on a crescent or horseshoe-shaped altar. Small peyote buttons are passed to the participants as a form of communion. The ceremony includes singing and other purification rituals (with smoke and water) to the accompaniment of Native drums. The peyote is intended to provide knowledge and insight but not visions. Some versions of the ceremony even include Bible reading and a Christian liturgy as part of the observation.

The Native American Church and some of its smaller counterparts see themselves as incorporating Native ritual into the broader context of Christianity. Their charter of 1918 provides that the church "teach the Christian religion with morality, sobriety, industry, kindly charity and right living."[42] All peyote movements ban liquor and restrict tobacco to ceremonial use only. The U.S. government has upheld the legality of the peyote ceremonies on condition that it is limited to people of Native American descent and that the use of peyote can be shown to be a legitimate sacrament within the group.

■ So You Meet a Native American with Ties to the Traditional Religion . . .
What You Might Expect
Many Native Americans have adopted European culture and religious forms and have integrated themselves to varying degrees into non-Native society. Political ramifications concerning the status of Native Americans in the United States at the turn of the millennium continue to abound. Native groups seek redress for the genocide of the past as well as incorporation into the society of the future. The religious heritage of the various tribes at times figures prominently in the legal issues involved in this process.

The United States is now experiencing a surge in the philosophy of multiculturalism, as many different ethnic groups are reasserting their unique cultural heritage. This effort is taking hold among people of Native American descent as well. Some people, having lived as whites among whites for many generations, are rediscovering their Native roots, affirming their tribal heritage and meeting with similar-minded folk in regular powwows. In many such cases, the intentions overshoot knowledge and practice by a wide margin. People of woodland descent mix with people of plateau descent at ceremonies of Californian derivation under decorations from the Great Plains. Everything comes together under the benign umbrella of the "Indian way," which frequently consists of highly inaccurate but very idealistic depictions of Native belief and practice. In encountering people who have adopted this cultural identity, it is important to realize that for them the spirit of identifying with one's heritage takes precedence over truly finding one's own tradition.

Nevertheless, many Native Americans have continued to practice their religion as well as they can without interruption, particularly, though not exclusively, on reservations. They may have added some Christian forms to their practice, but it remains in essence that which was carried out in the nineteenth century. For these people, religion is not the cultural affectation referred to in the previous paragraph, but continues to be an integral part of their lives.

Clearly conditions of life at the end of the twentieth century will not allow any Native American, let alone an entire tribe, to return to a full-fledged traditional lifestyle. Insofar as it is being done, it happens on a smaller scale and in the face of constant pressure toward secularization. Practices from their religious past that some Native Americans are attempting to hold on to include

☐ sweat baths for purification rituals (prison inmates have sued states to have such baths provided in order to carry out their religious practices),

☐ various religious implements (for example, pipes or totem poles) as being entirely in the custody of the appropriate tribes,

☐ classification of various tracts of land as holy and thus not subject to any form of development,

☐ recognition of tribal practices (for example, the sun dance or peyote ceremony) as being as legitimate as any Christian or Jewish religious observance.

Relating the Gospel

Behind any encounter between a person of European descent and a Native American lies the undeniable fact of the genocidal actions that continued late into the nineteenth century. Whether ancient tribes may also have eliminated their own competition, whether the European conquest of America is only one such instance of many in the history of humanity, whether present-day people on both sides need to learn to surmount the past—none of these considerations will make that item disappear from the table.

Rightly or wrongly, this fact of history also colors religious dialogue. Outsiders wishing to engage with Native American religions need to tread carefully. On the one hand, Native Americans covet recognition of their ancient ways as legitimate forms of religion that are on a par with Christianity and other faiths. On the other hand, they fear the exploitation of their tradition for mass consumption. For example, many European Americans are attempting to find spiritual realization by adopting aspects of Native traditions. Some Native American leaders, rather than being flattered by the imitation, object to such spiritual explorations by non-Natives. They see them as stealing the last remnant of Native American heritage, possibly even for financial gain. Having taken their land, their food and their livelihood, white people now seem to be appropriating their religion as well.

This deeply rooted suspicion extends to Christian evangelistic efforts, which are sometimes interpreted as efforts to eradicate Native culture for good. The fact that some nineteenth-century missionaries willingly participated in the genocide does not help matters. Native Americans face a situation in which the practice of their traditional religion requires a decision in the face of pressures to the contrary, including secularization as well as forms of Christianity. Still, Christian efforts to present the gospel to Native Americans (and all other people) continue. Evangelical Christians realize that all people need Christ and that the truth claims of the gospel must, in the final analysis, supersede political boundaries and barriers. Clearly the key in regard to Native Americans is showing that true, biblical Christianity absolutely opposes genocide or exploitation.

Once again, the key word is contextualization. The Christian worker must learn to meet the Native American in terms that make the gospel accessible and credible. An important aspect of such an effort on behalf of Native Americans on reservations is the provision of social services. For complex reasons many people on reservations live in abject poverty. Even the necessities of life are often hard to come by. A Christian coming to help without expecting something immediately in return and without trying to turn

"Sweat house" ceremony on the Grindstone Reservation in northern California. Photograph: UPI/Corbis-Bettmann.

his or her presence into a political statement is more likely to get a hearing than someone who comes with empty hands.

Contextualization remains a difficult enterprise. Cultural factors can impede the communication of the gospel on the part of the evangelist and the hearer. Many Native Americans have adopted outward Christian forms, sometimes in conjunction with syncretistic beliefs. The Christian worker must do his or her best to clarify the nature of authentic Christianity as based on Scripture alone. At the same time, it might not hurt for the Christian to concede that Christianity as practiced in many white suburbs is also a syncretistic mix of biblical religion and Western materialism. A self-consciously decontaminated Christianity may be easier to hold up as a model for biblical belief than one that comes with a lot of dross.

Mastering the Material

When you have finished studying this chapter, you should be able to

1. summarize some of the main obstacles to a thorough understanding of Native American religions;

2. state the basic categories of tribal distribution in the United States with some examples;

3. defend the existence of belief in a creator in Native American religion;

4. describe the understanding of spirits in Native American religion with some examples;

5. summarize the nature of shamanism and some of its variations;

6. delineate the nature and practice of totemism, using the Tlingit as an example;

7. give examples for the wide variety of rites of passage practiced among Native Americans;

8. show how ghost dancing and the Native American Church are attempts by Native Americans to respond religiously to prevailing cultural pressures.

Term Paper Ideas

1. Trace the distribution of language families among Native Americans and describe hypotheses that have been suggested on that basis in terms of historical origins.

2. Choose one particular tribe and undertake a detailed explication of its religious culture.

3. Compare and contrast the institution of shamanism between Native American practices and their Asian counterparts.

4. Prepare a summary of legal decisions involving one particular topic of Native American religion, for example, the use of peyote or the protection of sacred sites.

5. Describe the various forms or uses of the sacred pipe, either within one tribe or across various tribes.

6. Put together a portfolio of creation myths or afterlife myths held by Native Americans.

7. Demonstrate how Native American beliefs or practices have been absorbed or distorted in contemporary American culture at large.

8. On the basis of interviews, research or personal experience, write up a summary of Christian strategy used in evangelistic work among Native Americans.

Core Bibliography

Collins, John James. *Native American Religions: A Geographical Survey.* Lewiston, N.Y.: Edwin Mellen, 1991.

Hirschfelder, Arlene, and Paulette Molin. *The Encylcopedia of Native American Religions.* New York: Facts on File, 1992.

Krickberg, Walter, Hermann Trimborn, Werner Müller and Otto Zerries. *Pre-Columbian American Religions.* Translated by Stanley Davis. London: Weidenfeld & Nicolson, 1968.

Spencer, Robert F., Jesse D. Jennings et al. *The Native Americans: Ethnology and Backgrounds of the North American Indians.* New York: Harper & Row, 1977.

Underhill, Ruth M. *Red Man's Religion: Beliefs and Practices of the Indians North of Mexico.* Chicago: University of Chicago Press, 1965.

Chapter 7

Hinduism

Estimated Membership
Worldwide: 780,547,000
United States: 910,000

The history of the religion that we commonly refer to as Hinduism illustrates what was said in chapter one about the changes a religion can undergo. This religion (or, maybe better, religious culture) has moved back and forth through various phases of monotheism, henotheism, polytheism and animism, with each stage retaining at least a vestigial presence in the ensuing one. There is no set of core beliefs that remains constant throughout. The name itself, actually a label devised by Westerners, simply means "the religion of India."

Yet paradoxically, not every religion at home in India is regarded as part of Hinduism. In fact, Buddhism and Jainism may be referred to as "heretical" schools of Hinduism. How can that be so? The one criterion a Hindu religious phase has to meet is to fit into the traditional culture of India. There are almost no restrictions on personal beliefs, but in order to qualify as "Hindu," a religion has to (1) regard the Vedas (the early sacred writings) as divinely inspired and authoritative, (2) accept the caste system and (3) respect the veneration of the various levels of deities and spirits, including the protection of cows.

The requirement to generally recognize the Vedas as divinely authoritative does not mean accepting them as literally true and practicing exactly what is commanded in them. Accepting the caste system is the most crucial requirement. Religions such as Buddhism and Jainism have a lot in common with general Hindu beliefs, but because they renounce the caste system they are automatically excluded from Hinduism. Venerating the various deities is also not required, but must be recognized as being valid for others in the society.

These loose requirements are really social expectations, not obligatory beliefs or truly mandatory religious worship practices. In the history of Hinduism, rejecting them carried social sanctions for their violators. For our purposes, they set the limits of what is properly contained in a study of Hinduism.

This study is organized according to the three major phases of Hinduism. Even though these three phases originated in a historical sequence, once they were in place they influenced each other while continuing to exist as three separate threads. We can refer to them as three "ways": (1) the way of works, (2) the way of knowledge and (3) the way of devotion.

The *way of works* refers to the first phase of Hinduism. It is based on ritual and legal requirements and is administered by the professional priesthood, the Brahmins. It can also be called Brahmanism or Vedic Hinduism because it retains the ritualistic emphasis of the Vedas. The *way of knowledge* is the ascetic and mystical path that arose around 500 B.C. From the names of the scriptures associated with this movement, we can also refer to it as Vedantic (supplement to the Vedas) or Upanishadic (from the Upanishads) Hinduism. The *way of devotion* developed in spurts in the first millennium A.D. This phase focuses on devotion to one's own god within a pantheon of available deities. Much of contemporary Hinduism fits into this phase, but only within a broad mixture of elements from all three.

Way	Origin	Scriptures	Practice
Works	c. 1500 B.C.	Vedas, Sutras, Brahmanas, Code of Manu	Detailed observance of laws and rituals, governed by priests
Knowledge	c. 500 B.C.	Upanishads (Vedanta)	Mystical recognition of Atman-Brahman identity, withdrawal
Devotion (Bhakti)	c. 200 B.C. and A.D. 800	Bhagavad Gita, Tamil poetry, Puranas	Attachment to one god or goddess; three main schools

Table 7.1. The three ways

The Way of Works

Aryan origins. The story of Hinduism began with the Aryan peoples who migrated into the Indian subcontinent. Their conquest started with the northwestern corner of India, the Indus Valley, which already contained a thriving civilization. Archaeologists have excavated a number of cities in that region, but we know relatively little of their history because their system of writing remains undeciphered. Based on the towns they built (Harappa, Kalibangan and Mohenjo-daro), we do know that they had a highly developed agrarian culture. Our knowledge of their religion is also sparse. Certain figures that have come to light are probably images of gods, possibly fertility deities.

Their actual beliefs and myths remain a mystery.

Around 1500 B.C. the Aryans moved in and began their slow, thousand-year process of conquering the entire Indian subcontinent. The religion that the Aryans brought with them was similar to what their cousins took to Iran, the difference being that it underwent no Zoroastrian reform. All we know about the Iranian form of Aryan religion is what we have been able to piece together about the beliefs and practices Zoroaster was preaching against. In India we have writings that accumulated from the time of the invasion. We can infer that no large-scale reversal such as the Zoroastrian

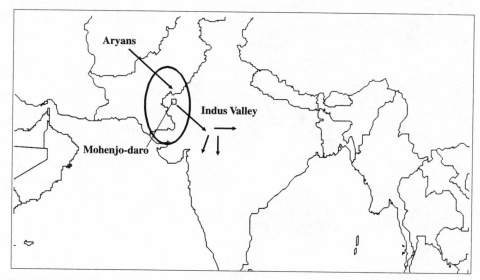

Map 7.1.   The Aryan invasion of India

one ever occurred in India from the fact that in Hinduism the good gods are referred to as the devas (compared to the evil daevas of Iran), whereas the asuras are considered malicious (in contrast to the Iranian concept of ahuras as good).

The Vedas. The term *Vedas* can have numerous references. In Western scholarly circles, the term usually refers to the four sacred scriptures that came out of the early Aryan culture. Hindus often include the later Upanishads and their commentaries under the term *Vedas.* It is not unknown for Vedas to be used collectively for all Hindu sacred writings.[1] In this discussion it refers to the four sacred scriptures.

The four Vedas—the Rig-Veda, the Yajur Veda, the Sama Veda and the Atharva Veda—are compilations rather than unitary works. The term *Veda* literally means "knowledge," so these are the records of religious knowledge as it developed over centuries of Aryan religion in India. In Hindu mythology, the Vedas were revealed to a group of holy men, the rishis, who wrote them down for posterity. The Rig ("verses")

Veda is dated as early as 1500 B.C., frequently later. It is a compilation of 1,028 prayerful hymns addressed to various gods (devas). Many hymns seem to suggest that one particular god is supreme, but in context a complex and flexible pantheon emerges that shows signs of development even over the period of collection.

The Yajur Veda is a somewhat later collection that consists of mantras—short, specific verses to be recited by priests in the context of their duties at sacrifices. The Sama Veda, which has a somewhat later date of composition, contains songs or chants, again for use by priests. They are thought to refer particularly to the ritual associated with soma, the sacred drink. The Atharva Veda is thought to be somewhat inferior to the first three Vedas. It consists of magic spells and incantations. Thus a picture more closely associated with the folk religion of the common people than the official functions of the priesthood emerges from this Veda. Each Brahmin priest specializes in one of these four Vedas. Part of the priest's responsibility is to memorize the assigned Veda and all of its associated commentaries and rituals.

The depiction of Balarama, brother to Krishna, incorporates elements of an early snake deity. Sri Mariamman Temple, Singapore.

The Vedic gods. The collection of deities in the Vedas, particularly the Rig-Veda, is a fluid pantheon consisting of many gods (the figure 33 is used as a symbolic representation of their number) whose significance increases and decreases over time. (Compare the discussion of Iranian gods in chapter four.) Dyaus Pitar was the original sky god. His importance had already been usurped by the time of the Rig-Veda. He is at times associated with Prithivi Mater, "mother earth." Varuna is the god of the sky; in the Vedas his position of supreme importance deteriorates to a lesser status. Indra is the "king of heaven." This god seems to have been supreme during the Vedic period. Indra is a warlike ruler, the perfect god for a people in the process of conquering a subcontinent. In later mythology Indra served more as a title than as a name. A god that defeats the titleholder assumes the title himself, becoming Indra.

Mitra was a sun god associated with moral and ritual purity. Rita was a god of truth and right. Vishnu was a minor god in the Vedas, possibly associated with the sun. Eventually, after Vedic times, Vishnu emerges as one of the three highest gods and becomes known as the "preserver." Rudra was a capricious, sometimes malicious mountain god. Originally he was more feared than worshiped. Subsequent to the Vedic period, people attempted to pacify him by giving him a pleasant name, so they called him Shiva, the "auspicious one." He became one of the main gods of later Hinduism, the "destroyer." Agni was the god of fire, originally referring to the fire used in the sacrifice. The fire later became personalized into a powerful spiritual being.

Soma was the god of the sacred drink. Since the drink conveyed feelings of immortality, it became personalized into the god of immortality and rapture. *Brahmanaspati* was the word spoken at the sacrifice. Since the efficacy of the sacrifice depended on the proper words, the word itself became a god, eventually the highest conception of God in Hinduism. The word *brahman* has several different spellings and meanings, including

- *Brahman:* the impersonal and pantheistic form of God
- *Brahma:* the personal creator god
- *Brahmin:* the priests and the priestly caste
- *Brahmanas:* priestly commentaries on the Vedas

Deity	Features
Dyaus Pitar	Original supreme sky god, losing significance
Pritivi Mater	Mother earth
Varuna	Later sky god, losing significance
Indra	King of gods, supreme during Vedic period
Mitra	A sun god; ritual and moral purity
Rita	God of truth and right
Vishnu	A sun god; later the Preserver
Rudra	Capricious mountain god; later Shiva
Agni	God of fire
Soma	God of drink or immortality
Brahmanaspati	Spoken word; gaining significance

Table 7.2. The Vedic deities

A fairly clear line of development emerges in the history of Vedic religion. Apparently the Aryans worshiped the one high god of the sky with fire offerings of animals before they divided into Iranian and Indian groups. By the true Vedic period, a professional priesthood has taken ownership of the rituals. There are many gods, and they are worshiped with fire sacrifices. As the number of gods and the complexity of rituals increases, the power of the Brahmin priests in society also increases.

Further writings: Brahmanas, Sutras, Code of Manu. As Vedic religion developed, so did the writings associated with it. The Brahmins developed a special language used for holy writings—the language of Sanskrit. In a sense, Sanskrit is a purely artificial language. No group has ever used it as a vernacular. It is closely related to the language of the Vedas (though a little less complex), and it fits into the overall linguistic patterns of Indo-European languages and modern Hindi. Sanskrit has been called the Latin of India, but unlike Latin, pure Sanskrit never was a living language.

The writings subsequent to the Vedas were for the most part Sutras and Brahmanas. Sutras (literally "threads") were originally delineations of the obligations that come with Vedic religion for both priests and common people. In later phases that term expanded to include all kinds of religious expositions. The Brahmanas were commentaries on the Vedas. They constituted further instructions for the priests as well as information on the mythological and theological underpinnings of the rituals.

A crucial writing for the history of Hinduism, composed sometime in the later Vedic period, was the Code of Manu. Manu is one name for the mythical ancestor of humanity; this book is supposed to be the revelation of the divine will for all human beings. It is primarily a compilation of the laws governing the ideal Hindu society, including the obligations of individuals to their families and to society at large. Thus the Code of Manu gives official sanction to the caste system.

The caste system. References to the basic four castes already exist in the Vedas. They are amplified in subsequent writings, particularly the Code of Manu, as well as through social inertia. Clearly, the castes holding higher power will use that power to perpetuate their privileged standing. The word that is used in Sanskrit for a caste is *varna,* which literally means "color." Although the caste system has received layers of religious justifications, it is difficult to get away from the idea that it originated in the light-skinned Aryans' attempts to retain their superior status over the dark-skinned vanquished people.

Brahmins	Priests, scholars	Twice born
Kshatriyas	Warriors, rulers	
Vaishyas	Merchants, land owners	
Shudras	Workers	

Table 7.3. The four castes

The first three castes are considered "twice born." They are permitted full participation in Hindu life, including study of the Vedas, puberty initiation and social leadership. The lower caste exists to serve the upper three, and members of that caste are restricted in their religious obligations and privileges. The members of the twice-born castes can be recognized by a cord that is looped around one shoulder and hangs down to the waist: the thread of the twice born.

The Brahmins are the priests, the ones devoting their lives to the Vedas and Vedic ritual. It is important for the beginning student of Hinduism to realize that most of the priests officiating in Hindu temples are not Brahmins; they are not even necessarily twice born. To this day, Brahmin priests hold themselves apart from the routine service of the gods in temples, focusing on the fire ritual and on personal services, such as the rites of passage.

The Kshatriyas originally formed the warrior caste. It then settled into the caste of rulers, those who hold political power. Unsurprisingly, the decision as to whether the Brahmins or the Kshatriyas should be considered supreme was not made without a long struggle. It is a commentary on the power of religion in people's lives that the Brahmins emerged victorious.

The Vaishyas constitute the merchant caste that includes business owners and land owners, and the Shudras are the common laborers. The Shudras exist for the sake of the other three classes. They are considered impure, and someone from the upper castes who has physical contact with them will be defiled.

The Code of Manu asserts that these castes are inflexible. It is not possible to switch castes or to marry outside one's caste. As the caste system proliferated, it became increasingly rigid and specific. The lower castes in particular became subdivided into numerous subcastes *(jati),* and social contact between different jati was forbidden. Today there are hundreds of such jati.

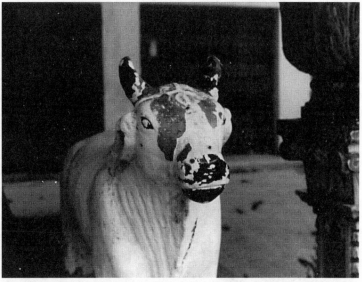

The trident on the forehead of this bull in the courtyard of a temple in Nairobi shows that it is a depiction of Shiva's riding animal.

The very lowest groups have virtually no standing in society; they are the "outcasts" or "untouchables." These are the people whose very life work, perhaps as tanners or corpse removers, renders them unclean. Even the shadow of such an untouchable has the power to pollute a higher-caste person. Since Mahatma Gandhi referred to them as *harijan,* "children of God," their status has improved in modern India. Technically, discrimination on the basis of caste is considered illegal; ingrained attitudes are, however, hard to abolish.

Reincarnation. Reincarnation is an important source of support for the caste system.

No trace of this belief appears in the Vedas, nor is there any evidence of belief in reincarnation in the Iranian counterpart to early Aryan religion. Presumably this belief came into Hinduism in conjunction with the spread of the religion throughout India. Possibly the concept was assimilated from the religion of the original population.

In recent years reincarnation has become widely accepted in the West under the influence of New Age thought. Reincarnation is seen as reason for optimism: there is always another life to attain what you could not do in this one. It is important to understand that in Indian thought reincarnation is a highly negative concept. It is a burden because to live is to suffer, and multiple lives mean going through multiple lifetimes of suffering. Reincarnation does not give hope for life after death. It is a threat of continuing misery.

Reincarnation is called *samsara*, which literally means "wanderings" or simply "existence." It refers to a seemingly endless cycle of lives encompassing the entire realm of beings, from the lowest animals to humans.[2] To die as one being means to come back as another being. We need to see that the various beings are ordered into a hierarchy, with male humans of the highest caste at the very top and inferior animals, such as worms and slugs, on the bottom. A wealthy and comfortable human being may return in the next life as a worm that gets eaten by a fish.

Durga, the goddess whose main function is the destruction of evil, is worshiped simply as *mata* ("mother") among the Hindus of Nairobi.

What level of being one returns as is determined by the law of karma. *Karma* is best translated as "cause and effect." The idea is that whatever one does in this life exercises an impact on the next one, or even several, incarnations. The person who lives a good life may return as a higher form. Someone who breaks rules in this life may return as a far lower being. The law of karma guarantees that all people get exactly what their actions merit.

The meaning of karma may be clarified by distinguishing it from similar concepts. Karma is not fate in the sense that whatever happens is destined, regardless of human effort. In contrast, karma teaches that whatever happens to people is the result of their personal actions in a previous existence. Karma is not judgment; no divine decree is required to bring about the consequences that actions deserve. The results occur with all the inevitability of a natural law. Finally, karma is not sin in the sense of being an offense against some deity. There can also be good karma, though the negative side is usually emphasized.

The concept of reincarnation does not specify the rules that apply to the next life. It is not possible for humans to know what will happen to them in the next life. This uncertainty is part of the reason samsara engenders anxiety and dread. For all that anyone can know, an apparently small slip in this life may cause a thousand rebirths as a cockroach. All one can do under such circumstances is suffer passively until the negative karma has been worked off. A return to a higher state then follows.

Samsara and karma provided the primary support for the caste system. A high-caste Brahmin must have merited such a fortunate incarnation by the quality of his previous lives. On the other hand, a Shudra[3] must have done some bad things in his earlier existence, and so he must work them off by present suffering. To shortcut the system and attain a higher standard of living would violate the strictures of caste and thereby only incur worse karma. Furthermore, if the Brahmin helped the Shudra, he would only make things worse for both of them by opposing karma's dictates. Thus it is best for all people to live strictly within the rules of their caste, whether in comfort or in agony, and thereby merit a better incarnation.

Thus the goal of Hinduism became finding release from samsara. Initially, under the auspices of Brahmanic religion, that meant complete obedience to all of the ritual obligations in the Sutras and the Code of Manu. Furthermore, it meant total submission to the authority of the Brahmins, for they alone held the key to such release. The word for "release" is moksha, which is sometimes translated as "redemption." But keep in mind that its initial meaning is to find some way off the wheel of samsara.

The Way of Knowledge

By the sixth century B.C., Brahmanism, the Vedic phase of Hinduism, was well established throughout India. The Brahmins were able to dictate how the gods should be worshiped. Through their ownership of the rituals, they held the destiny of millions of souls in their hands. By this time, the system had developed the characteristic typical of a ritualistic, priest-centered religion: the ritual, as carried out by the experts, took precedence over explicit beliefs. Neither the laypeople nor the priests needed to understand the rituals. As long as the right words were being said and the right actions were being performed, the rituals would be efficacious. With an elite group holding this kind of power, it is not surprising that a revolt against the established priesthood took place in the sixth century. In effect, this revolt replaced Brahmanic ritualism with a belief system of mystical contemplation; in the words of one scholar, "words without meaning" (the ritual) were replaced with "meaning without words" (a deeper mystical reality).[4]

These mystical beliefs were first recorded in a group of writings called the Upan-ishads, which literally means "to sit down," reflecting the idea of a pupil sitting at his master's feet to learn. The twelve major Upanishads were written as commentaries on the Vedas. Thus each Upanishad corresponds to one of the Vedas. Eventually they became part of the official collections of the four branches of Vedic learning. The teaching of the Upanishads is often called Vedanta, which means literally "supplement to the Vedas."

The entry to the Sri Mariamman Temple in Singapore.

Although the Upanishads are part of Vedic literature, their teaching diverges from it somewhat. Whereas the Vedas emphasize priestly ritual, the Upanishads seek a deeper spiritual reality. At the heart of Vedantic teaching is the idea that there is only one true reality, namely, Brahman. Brahman is God, conceptualized as an impersonal, all-pervasive being; in English it is sometimes called the "world soul." Brahman is infinite, beyond all categories and beyond all human thought. Brahman is actually all there is.

Everything that is not Brahman is not truly real. It is called maya, which literally means "play" and is related to the word *magic*. The life that we experience day in and day out is simply magical play arising out of Brahman; it does not possess genuine reality. Subsequent Vedantic Hinduism thought of maya as illusion, though it is not completely necessary to say that maya has no reality whatsoever. It is sufficient to say that maya's reality is completely derived from Brahman. Therefore it is self-destructive to consider maya as having reality in itself. We may think of maya as the image created by a movie projector or as a dream: real, but insubstantial. If we immerse ourselves in the projection or the dream as genuine reality, we will live in complete ignorance (*advaita*), and this state will keep us from finding true reality.

Everything that we experience or think about rationally belongs to maya. Maya encompasses all physical objects, including our bodies. Our feelings and emotions are maya; so are our thoughts. Even religion is part of maya; the gods and their worship are all merely manifestations of Brahman. Thus there does not seem to be anything trustworthy, for it is all maya.

Deep inside the human soul, however, under all the intellectual, psychological and religious faculties, there is a reality that is not maya. It is called Atman, sometimes translated as the "true self." It has reality apart from maya's deceptions, for Atman is identical with Brahman. Thus in the farthest reaches of the soul, where the true self resides, there is God.

"Atman is Brahman." More than anything else, this slogan becomes the message of the Upanishads, and it needs to be understood as literal identity. It is not just that Atman is related to Brahman or that Atman is a part of Brahman, Atman is identical with Brahman. Thus Atman is the same infinite world soul that is beyond all thought and distinctions. A phrase that typifies this Vedantic teaching is *tat tvam asi,* "that art thou." *Tat* refers to Brahman, a reality so deep it can be expressed only with an impersonal pronoun; *tvam asi* means "you are," showing that this is one's own personal reality.

The key to Vedantic thought, then, is to transcend the world of experience, which is only maya, and to uncover one's identity as Atman-Brahman. This goal can only be attained through a life of strict separation from the world and deep contemplation. The best thing to do is to leave one's regular environment and renounce all previous attachments. This requires adopting the life of a complete hermit, a *sannyasin,* seeking one's true identity apart from the world. Liberation comes as one attains moksha, the release from samsara and all of maya. At death the Atman-Brahman reality is fully recovered. The soul reenters Brahman as a drop of

Kali stands center stage among other goddess representations.

water coming back to the ocean. Nirvana, a state of supreme bliss, has been realized.[5]

It is important to keep in mind that moksha can be attained only through rigorous pursuit of this true knowledge by a life of renunciation and discipline. Thus common people, preoccupied as they must be with the need to obtain the necessities of life, do not have access to moksha. They must wait until a further incarnation puts them in a position to undertake the life of a sannyasin.

Vedantic philosophy has been a part of Hindu tradition since the first Upanishads. It received a strong boost through the work of the philosopher Shankara, who lived around A.D. 800, and it has continued into present times. However, because of the abstract nature of its speculations and the demands placed on its followers, it has always remained a minor part of Hinduism.[6]

The Way of Devotion

A second revolt against established Hinduism took hold in the southern part of India in the mid-second millennium A.D. Even though the seeds of this movement went back many centuries before, it was only at this time that it blossomed as a popular movement. Southern India was still populated by its original (non-Aryan) inhabitants, who were referred to as Dravidians. (They were not directly related to the people of the ancient Indus Valley civilization.) Today they are known as the Tamil people. It was the poets of Tamil India who spread the idea that moksha can be found through a loving relationship to one god, not through the virtually impossible way of works, let alone the unattainable secrets of the way of knowledge. This school of thought became known as Bhakti, which means "loving attachment." The essence of its teaching is that the love of a god or goddess provides salvation to those who love him or her alone.

The roots of Bhakti Hinduism go back as least as far as the Bhagavad-Gita, a poem that forms a part of the Mahabharata, a lengthy epic composed around 200 B.C. In the Bhagavad-Gita we find the heroic archer Arjuna about to lead his army into battle against the army of his enemies, some of whom are his cousins. Arjuna feels torn about what will happen to his karma because of these actions. He is about to turn away from battle when Krishna, his chariot driver, starts to talk to him. In the course of a long discussion, Krishna makes two important points. As a member of the Kshatryia class, Arjuna is obligated to go to war. He should perform his caste duty, but in a state of detachment from any results of his actions, whether they cause pleasure or pain. Regarding Arjuna's eternal destiny, Krishna counsels him to attach himself solely to him. Devotion to Krishna alone is necessary for moksha. At the end of the discourse, Krishna displays himself in all his glory as the god Vishnu. Then the battle commences (Arjuna's side eventually wins).

The idea that total devotion to one god is sufficient for salvation eventually became the cornerstone of Bhakti Hinduism. In a broad generalization it can be said that Bhakti is at the heart of most of contemporary Hinduism. A Hindu typically recognizes one god as his or her highest god (or, of course, goddess). But this devotion need not exclude recognizing and serving many other gods, mixing ritual of Vedic origin and possibly a smattering of Vedantic thought.

Most Hindus acknowledge Brahman as true reality and possibly even the Brahman-Atman distinction, but among the masses at least, these beliefs are inconsequential. People who are given to speculation may acknowledge a kind of divine trinity: the Trimurti. As originally conceived, it consisted of Brahman manifesting itself as three gods: Brahma, the creator; Vishnu, the preserver; and Shiva, the destroyer. The idea is that Brahma creates the universe, Vishnu preserves it as long as possible, and Shiva destroys it when it has become irreparable so that a new universe can be made. Modern Hinduism does not pay much attention to Brahma, and a goddess is viewed as the third in the triad.

Sorting out the Hindu deities is a virtually impossible task. First of all, it is popularly said that there are 330 million gods (a wild increase from the thirty-three devas of the Rig-Veda). Just saying all of their names at the rate of five seconds a name would take fifty-two years. Of course, this figure is an exaggeration meant to emphasize the multitude of the gods. The problem is that many of these gods go by many different names. Various gods are identified with each other in different parts of India. Local deities are merged into Vedic gods; the same myth is recounted about different gods; epic and national heroes become deified. The main source of popular mythology are the Puranas. Which gods appear in a particular version depends largely on the devotional allegiance of the writer.

What follows is a brief overview of some of the main gods and goddesses. Bhakti Hinduism is divided roughly into three schools. The Vaishnavite school recognizes Vishnu as the highest god, the Shaivite school worships Shiva as highest god and the Shaktite school gives primary allegiance to a goddess. Further variations are possible within each school.

Each male god is associated with a female deity, his shakti. The shakti can be called the god's wife, though in many cases consort is more appropriate. Shakti means literally the "source of power." In this form of Hinduism it is the goddess who infuses the god with the energy to carry out his tasks. In the Shakti school the goddess is venerated directly.

In addition to having a shakti, each god has certain symbolic representations and a riding animal, thereby making it possible to recognize their statues in a temple, given enough familiarity. Hindu gods are typically shown with multiple arms; this depiction is intended to illustrate their great power.

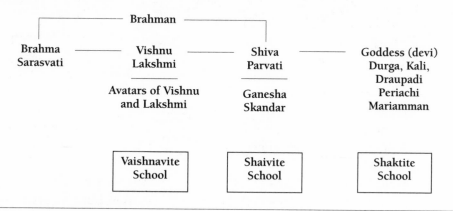

Figure 7.1. Main Hindu gods

Brahma, as already noted, is the creator. Representations of him can be recognized by his four-faced head, each face looking in a different direction. The four faces represent four heads. According to the mythology, Brahma originally had five heads, but Shiva cut one off in combat. Brahma's image is found in many temples, but few temples are devoted to him exclusively. He is not a major Bhakti god. Sarasvati, on the other hand, is a very popular goddess. She is associated with learning and the arts, and thus she is the goddess of the schools and receives much veneration on her appointed day. Her representation usually includes a musical instrument, such as a sitar.

Devotion to Vishnu constitutes one of the three main branches of Bhakti Hinduism. The followers of Vishnu, the Vaishnavites, look to Vishnu or one of his incarnations (discussed below) for their salvation. One can recognize the devotees of Vishnu by a vertical decoration on their foreheads (the *tilaka*), usually two vertical lines that converge on the bridge of the nose. Vaishnavite spirituality tends to be gentle and serene, emphasizing chanting, dancing and meditation.

In the Trimurti, Vishnu is known as the preserver, but to his followers he is simply God. In his representations he can be recognized by having four arms, among which are distributed a conch shell, a lotus blossom, a discus and a mace. His riding animal is a bird, but he is often shown reclining on a serpent. Vishnu is most concerned with maintaining the *dharma,* the true ways of the gods. Thus, whenever it

This worshiper earns merit by walking around the shrine of the nine planets.

appears that the world is particularly out of sync, he lets himself be born in the world, either as a heroic animal or as a human hero in order to straighten things out. He lives a complete life and eventually dies, but he is always be ready to come again if needed. These incarnations of Vishnu are known as his avatars. They are generally counted as ten in number.

Lakshmi is known as the goddess of fortune and beauty. She is particularly popular with married women. Some of her statues have only two arms, but four arms are also popular. She always holds a lotus blossom in one hand, possibly also a conch shell.

When Vishnu is incarnated as one of his avatars, she also becomes incarnated as the wife of the avatar.

Number	Name	Form, identity
1	Matsya	Fish
2	Kurma	Turtle
3	Varaha	Boar
4	Narasimha	Man-Lion
5	Vamana	Dwarf
6	Parashu-Rama	Rama with ax
7	Rama	Hero of Ramayana (wife Sita, Hanuman)
8	Krishna	Teacher of Bhagavad Gita (wife Rada)
9	Buddha Balarama	Founder of Buddhism Alternate, brother of Krishna
10	Kalki	Horse, future avatar

Table 7.4. The avatars of Vishnu

All of the figures included in table 7.4 are associated with various Hindu myths. Rama has become one of the main gods of Vaishnavite devotion. He is the hero of the epic Ramayana, which tells the story of how the demon king Ravana abducted Sita, Rama's wife, and how Rama and his companions fought to recover her. Rama is usually pictured in a group consisting of himself, Sita, his brother Lakshman and the monkey god, Hanuman. The dominant color is green, and Rama usually holds a long bow. Hanuman, the monkey, played a leading role in the epic due to his swiftness and craftiness. He is a popular object of worship today. Sita is worshiped as the ideal woman because she was willing to sacrifice her life to avoid defiling herself.

Rama Bhakti emphasizes the love and grace of Rama in granting people salvation. Two schools of thought concerning how Rama brings this about have developed. They are named for the way a mother animal carries her young. According to the monkey school, the believer must cling to Rama just as a baby monkey holds on to its mother. The cat school attributes all work and preservation to Rama alone, just as a mother cat transports her kittens by holding them in her mouth.

This emphasis on divine grace prompts some contemporary Christians to look for Christian influence on Bhakti Hinduism. This is unlikely for three reasons. First, the similarities between Rama Bhakti and the Bible are entirely superficial beyond the basic notion that there is a god that performs the work of salvation. Second, there is no record of strong Christian influence at the time when these schools developed (though there may have been a minimal Christian presence at the time). Third, even if there had been a strong Christian element in the culture at the time, there is no particular reason to believe that those Christians would have understood the New Testament doctrine of grace.[7]

Krishna is one of the most popular Bhakti deities. Even though he appears in the Bhagavad-Gita as a profound teacher, his usual characterization in the mythologies is as a young cowherd who has lively relationships with the cow maidens. He too was victorious over a demon king. In his representations he is colored black or dark blue and plays a flute. He is usually shown in the company of his wife, Radha.

The so-called Hare Krishna movement, officially known as the International Society for Krishna Consciousness (ISKCON), is a legitimate form of Vaishnavite Bhakti Hinduism. Its origins go back to the teacher Caitanya in the sixteenth century. He proclaimed that Krishna was the highest form of personal godhead. This teaching became popularized in the United States in the 1960s under the direction of A. C.

Ganesha, the elephant-headed "remover of obstacles" is one of the most popular Hindu deities.

Bhaktivedanta Prabhupada, a retired pharmaceuticals salesman who came to America when he was seventy years old. ISKCON is characterized by five essential teachings.

First, Krishna is the supreme form of personal god (thus ISKCON is essentially monotheistic). Interestingly, devotees of this group hold that Vishnu is an avatar of Krishna. Second, salvation can be obtained by continually chanting the Krishna mantra ("Hare Krishna"). This mantra must be chanted a thousand times a day. Special worship consists of daily singing and dancing sessions (arati). Third, the Bhagavad-Gita is inspired scripture. Fourth, devotees must observe a life of pure devotion to God (Krishna). This includes abstaining from meat, caffeine, sweets and sex for pleasure. On the other hand, devotees are encouraged to eat their fill at the community meal (the prasadam). Fifth, distributing literature that disseminates the message of Krishna consciousness is important. At the height of Hare Krishna's popularity in the United States, robed, head-shaven devotees could be found at airports around the country selling Back to

Godhead magazines.

ISKCON was immensely popular in the United States in the early seventies, numbering adherents in the tens of thousands. Although its numbers have declined, the movement continues to be a steady presence. Since returning to India, ISKON has developed a large organization with several huge temples.

It might surprise you to see the Buddha listed as an avatar of the Hindu god Vishnu. Hindu thinkers incorporated Buddha as an avatar as a response to competition from Buddhism. They told the people, "Yes, Buddha is a great teacher; after all he is an incarnation from God. But as Buddha he is deliberately teaching falsehood in order to call followers of the dharma back to the truth." Did this ploy work? There are few Buddhists in India today.[8]

Numerous Hindus today count Krishna's brother, Balarama, as the ninth incarnation, instead of Buddha. In contrast to Krishna, the "dark one," Balarama is known as the "white one." He is pictured with a light complexion and—possibly as a result of a confusion of myths—snake's teeth.

The tenth avatar, Kalki, is a messianic figure. It is thought that he will appear at the very end of the age and will preside over a period when the dharma will be supreme and universal. He will appear riding on a horse; in the iconography he is pictured with the head of a horse.

The largest number of Bhakti Hindus recognize Shiva as the highest god. Shaivites decorate their foreheads (tilaka) with three horizontal stripes. In contrast to Vaishnavism, Shaivite worship is a little harsher, emphasizing austerity and leaving more room for self-inflicted extremes of devotion.

Shiva is traditionally called the destroyer, a notion that is generally interpreted in terms of destroying evil, but that has not been totally purged of the connotation of causing harm from time to time (a throwback to Shiva's early days as Rudra). The Puranas sometimes picture Shiva as deliberately violating the taboos established by some of the other gods; he is also known for his fiery temper. Nevertheless, his devotees love and worship him as their God. Popular piety tends to minimize the more alienating aspects of his mythology.

Shiva is represented in many different ways. A very popular representation shows him as Nataraya, the lord of the dance. His arms form a circle as he destroys the cosmic serpent by dancing on it. This aspect of Shiva's form is worshiped in dance performances.

The most common depiction of Shiva is as a pointed, conical, nonhuman form, clearly a representation of the penis. Called the *lingam*, this phallic symbol is frequently surrounded by the *yoni*, the representation of the vagina. The lingam-yoni is common in temples associated with the worship of Shiva. Even though there is no question that it represents the spiritual energy engendered by the god in conjunction with his shakti, it is not treated as particularly sexual in popular worship today. There are no sexual rituals associated with the lingam-yoni in normal Shaivite worship.

Shiva rides on a bull, and his main symbol is the trident. He is associated with each of the female deities as his shakti, depending on the context. However, when he is pictured as being married to a goddess, she is called Parvati. Parvati is worshiped for her exclusive devotion to Shiva; she is not usually pictured completely apart from Shiva.

Devotees of Sait Baba in Singapore chant before their god's picture.

Shiva and Parvati have two sons in their divine family, but the mythology is not entirely clear as to the sons' parentage. The older of the two is Ganesha, easily the most recognizable god of Hinduism because he has the head of an elephant. In the mythology, Shiva severed Ganesha's head in a fit of jealous rage. When he calmed down, he vowed to present Ganesha with the first head he came across as a replacement. That turned out to be the head of an elephant. Ganesha is worshiped as the remover of obstacles; people turn to him at the outset of any new undertaking. He is always the first god worshiped in any temple service. His riding animal is a rat.

The younger son of Shiva and Parvati is Skandar, a god of war. Skandar is known entirely by local names, such as Kartikeya and Muruga.[9] Despite his variable names, Skandar is easily recognized by his long spear, which has a broad, almost heart-shaped point, and his riding animal, the peacock. Tamil worship of Muruga is a good example of Shaivite practices. They observe the Taipusam festival in honor of this god. Devotees take a vow to undergo particular austerities on this day. They pierce their tongues and cheeks with skewers and carry large, decorated frames, the *kavadis*, by having their pointed ends penetrate their skin.

On the whole, the identities and mythologies of the goddesses are less developed than those of the male deities. A female deity is commonly referred to as "goddess," or simply *mata,* "mother." The personal identities of goddesses are a little more interchangeable than those of the gods. But this observation is only relative; the identities of male gods are also frequently in flux, and a great deal of mythology centers on goddesses.

Shaktism is the school of Bhakti in which the goddess has become the principal object of worship. It is much smaller than Vaishnavism or Shaivism, but it has exerted significant impact on Hindu history. When we refer to worship of the Shakti, the identity of the goddess is usually either Durga or Kali. Both of them are at times considered Shiva's consorts but are not thought to be faithful, loving wives.

In the mythology, Durga overcame a buffalo-headed demon. Her representations typically show her in that conquering pose; one of her ten arms holds a trident, the others hold various other war implements. She may be shown standing on top of her riding animal, a lion, and the severed head of a buffalo may be displayed at her feet.

Kali's depiction is intentionally gruesome. Her face is contorted into a grimace with the tongue sticking out and down. The only clothing covering her black body and sagging breasts is a necklace of skulls and a belt of severed arms. She too holds weapons, though with only four arms. Kali stands either on a tiger or, more frequently, on Shiva's prone body. In short, everything about Kali's representation enforces the idea that she is a goddess of violence and cruelty. Yet all that force is supposedly directed against evil.

Both Durga and Kali are given blood as worship offerings. This practice gave rise to the cult of the Thagis, who presented Kali with regular human sacrifices.[10] This cult was prohibited by the British in the late nineteenth century, but its name survives to this day in the English word *thug*.

Another aspect of Shaktism is its use of sexual motifs. The celebration of the Shakti's union with Shiva has given rise to its emulation in worship rituals, both symbolically and physically (the kind of practice that Shaivism avoids). Known also as tantrism, the ritual emphasizes the spiritual energy released through the fusion of opposites. In the school of left-handed tantrism, the breaking of taboos (such as eating meat) culminates in ritual intercourse that sends the practitioner on the way to moksha. Such practices have never been widespread.

We have just begun to scratch the surface of the world of Hindu gods and their mythologies. All these gods and goddesses have their own relationships and subsidiary beings. (Remember, it supposedly adds up to 330 million!) In many cases, local deities from pre-Hindu times were invested with new Hindu identities and then were added to Hindu mythology. One such example is the South Indian goddess Mariamman, who has a long history as a village goddess. She wards off smallpox, but she may cause the disease if she is not pleased. Today Mariamman is the main goddess in many Tamil Hindu temples.

Another category of popular gods includes the main characters from the epics. Earlier we mentioned Arjuna, the warrior who received instruction from Krishna in the Bhagavad-Gita. Today he is worshiped in many temples. Particularly popular is Draupadi, Arjuna's wife, who also married Arjuna's four brothers. She has gained the status of a goddess.

The process of discovering new deities is endless. Times of life, ages of the universe, aspects of food and work—there is nothing that has not been personified and deified. Many temples have representations of the Hindu nine planets,[11] the last two of which are considered inauspicious. They need to be appeased. In addition, living and recently deceased human beings, such as Mohandas K. Gandhi or one's personal guru, are recognized as gods. Finally, there are the many malevolent spirits, the asuras, who populate the spiritual universe of Hinduism.

Hindu Temple Worship

Hindu worship is carried out in the home and in the temple. A Hindu temple is the earthly residence of the gods. Let us be crystal-clear about this point: in Hinduism the statues are not just visual representations of spiritual beings. The gods live in their statues. It is true that a physical statue by itself is not a god, but it definitely is considered the special abode of the god. The god will continue to reside in the statue as long as he is properly cared for, namely, washed, clothed, fed and worshiped. Thus caring for the statue insures the favor of the god inside.

At the conclusion of a puja, the worshiper receives some ashes and flower dust.

Each Hindu temple is dedicated to one particular god or goddess. That deity is housed in a special sanctuary of the temple, the *rajagopuram*. The temple also houses other deities, the number depending partly on the financial status of the temple. Well-to-do temples have statues that are reserved for birthdays or other special days for the gods with regular statues in the temple. They may be housed in a separate section, but they need regular daily care as well. Most Hindu temples are decorated with images of gods, such as roof decorations, but people do not believe that gods reside in these images.

Temple service is called *puja*, meaning "sacrifice." It falls generally into three categories: scheduled daily services, routine individual worship and special celebrations. Normally congregational puja is performed three times a day: morning, noon and evening. In preparation for this the statues are cleaned and decorated, and the rajagopuram is covered with a decorated curtain. The worshipers, usually only a handful of people, wait in expectation as the musicians line up. When the priest and his assistant enter, the service begins.

A notion that came out of the Vedantic phase of Hinduism is that the essence of Brahman can be captured in the mystic syllable *OM*.[12] *OM* has no meaning as a word. Its meaning lies in its sound as it is pronounced or chanted. The vibrations produced capture the essence of Brahman and put the chanter in touch with it and thereby with his Atman-Brahman identity. In the same way, the sounds produced by the temple music are supposed to create a spiritual aura that purifies and edifies the worshiper. The usual instruments for temple puja are a drum, an Indian trumpet and a bell on a rope. Sometimes a deep resonator is added. The music produced, with complicated rhythms and somewhat jazzy melodic phrases, can be quite intriguing to Western ears.

When the priest and his assistant enter the worship area, the music commences and the puja begins in earnest. The first statue worshiped is always the elephant-headed Ganesha. The priest has a bell on his left hand that he rings continuously. With his right hand he alternately waves incense and oil lights in front of the statue. Then he places marks of flower paste on the god's forehead. There is no chanting in the routine puja of a god.

Next may be the puja for the main god in the rajagopuram. The priest and his assistant disappear for a moment behind the curtain, and the music ceases. All eyes are fixed on the curtain. Then the curtain is drawn back suddenly, and the priest stands before the god with a tall "Christmas tree" candelabra. The music resumes at full volume, and the worshipers throw themselves prostrate to the ground. The overall effect is very dramatic. Then the priest completes the service for the main god, after which he continues through all of the gods in the temple, repeating the basic procedure for each. When the entire process is done—usually within about fifteen minutes—the music ceases, and the worshipers line up to pass their hands through the fire and have their foreheads marked with ashes and flower paste.

The temple is also available for individual worship. A devotee enters the temple, leaving his or her shoes outside and being careful not to step on the threshold, and rings a small bell to warn spiritual beings. The worshiper declares his or her concerns to an attendant priest and pays a small fee; a rite that includes coconut costs extra. The priest performs a brief ceremony before the appropriate deity. This service, which does not usually last longer than a minute or so, includes the chanting of certain Vedic passages. At the end of the rite, the individual is again marked with flowers and ashes. In the Vaishnavite context, the worshiper also drinks a sip of holy water and has a silver bowl with two miniature feet on the bottom inverted on his head, a ritual known as "walking in the footsteps of God."

A Hindu temple during open hours can be a busy place, with many individuals lining up to have their needs attended to. Some people may be carrying out vows, such as measuring the entire temple with their prostrate bodies. They stand, lie on their stomachs, stand up, move ahead a step, lie down and so on. The atmosphere in the temple, except during puja, is not particularly worshipful. Idle chatting and casual attitudes are not considered out of place.

The temple becomes crowded during the many festivals that are observed. In addition to the major holidays, each god has a "day of descent," informally referred to as the god's birthday. Throngs of people participate in these celebrations. When a god has his birthday, his statue is decorated in special ways, possibly with fancier clothes. The priests observe a longer puja that may include some special chanting to the god. The highlight of such a celebration is the procession of the god, either carried around the temple area or, very frequently, mounted on a special cart that is drawn through the village. A famous example of this kind of celebration is the annual procession for the god Jagannatha in eastern India. This parade uses a chariot that is forty-five feet tall and provides the origin of our word *juggernaut.*

Periachi, the goddess of children, protects the unborn from evil spirits while in the womb. Sri Kaliamman Temple, Singapore.

Modern Developments in Hinduism

With little or no mandatory doctrine, Hinduism is always open to the new and the different. The history of Hinduism includes many movements initiated by important teachers. One of many examples is the founder of the Krishna-consciousness movement, Caitanya, in the sixteenth century. The last hundred years have been no exception. I will briefly highlight two such developments: the Ramakrishna mission and the Sai Baba movement.

Ramakrishna (1836-1886) was a priest of the goddess Kali who was dissatisfied with his spiritual experiences. Eventually he achieved union with Kali in meditative trance, along with many other Hindu gods and goddesses, plus Jesus, Allah and the impersonal Brahman. On each occasion, he discovered, he had truly become the object of his meditation. Thus Ramakrishna believed that he had shown experientially that all religions were one and that he was a manifestation of the one God. He gathered a group of followers about him who recognized both him and his wife, Sarada, as avatars.

Ramakrishna had a disciple called Swami Vivekananda (1863-1902). Together with four other disciples, he founded an ascetic order called the Ramakrishna Mission. Vivekananda vaulted to world attention when he spoke on behalf of Hinduism at the so-called World's Parliament of Religions, which was held in Chicago in conjunction with the 1893 World's Fair. He riveted those in attendance with his pleas for universal tolerance and acceptance, although by his third speech many listeners had became a little annoyed by his obvious purpose of subsuming all religions under a Vedantic pattern of philosophy.[13] In India and in Western circles inclined toward pantheistic mysticism, Vivekananda was a great hit, and his influence was instrumental in establishing societies in league with the Ramakrishna Mission all over the world. In the United States, centers of the Swami Vivekananda Vedanta Society are located in many major cities.

The worship hall of such a center has an altar on which are placed, left to right, pictures of Jesus Christ, Vivekananda, Ramakrishna (in the center), Sarada, and the Buddha. All these persons are worshiped in Hindu fashion as manifestations of God. Christmas is a major celebration, not only because it is Jesus' birthday but also because it is the day of the founding of the Ramakrishna Mission. The Vivekananda society holds Sunday morning services which are essentially lectures that begin with invocations of OM and Ramakrishna. The teaching is essentially a modernized version of the Vedantic Atman-Brahman identity in which all religions are seen as ways toward achieving this goal. The Ramakrishna movement has also taken a step unique among most Indian religions in establishing hospitals and educational centers.

The Sai Baba movement centers around an original holy man who lived around the beginning of the twentieth century and his supposed present incarnation. Although the present Sai Baba is virtually unknown in the United States (as of this writing) and little known in Europe, he has devoted followers throughout Asia. The original Sai Baba, now known as Sai Baba of Shirdi, had a local following of Indian devotees who saw him as avatar. He was reputed to have performed miracles, such as being able to be present in several places at the same time. Sai Baba of Shirdi died in 1918.

Satya Sai Baba, the new incarnation, was born in 1926 and is still active. In addition to his teaching, which advocates a return to traditional Indian values, he mesmerizes his followers with alleged miracles. Many healings are claimed, though his reputation rests primarily on being able to materialize objects such as wristwatches and endless mounds of sacred ash (vibhuti) out of his empty hands. Sai Baba goes about wearing a pink robe. He is easily recognizable by his teased black hair. His followers accept his claim that he is God, revere him as such and look to him for success, healing and wisdom. They worship him in regular weekly meetings as the congregation sits before a large picture of him. If possible, the devotees wear something pink, even if it is just a scarf, as they sing melodious hymns to their avatar.

Religious Observances

Hindu religious observances are highly varied. Major distinctions in practice are derived from the particular school and are based on local tradition, caste and, of course, personal preference. In general terms, what unites Hindu practice is a set of three obligations called the "three debts": debts to the *rishis* (the ancient recorders of the Vedas), debts to the gods and debts to the ancestors.[14] Specific responsibilities are carried out within this broad understanding of duty.

Lifelike representation of A. C. Bhaktivedanta Prabhupada, the founder of the Hare Krishna movement in the United States.

Daily rituals. Classical teachings instruct high-caste Hindu men to perform devotional prayers three times a day: at sunrise, noon and sunset. Only the sunrise meditation remains a widely practiced observance. It includes a few small purification rites, a bath and recitation of a Vedic passage.

All households that keep a god must carry out a morning puja. The god must be washed, dressed and decorated. The deity receives his portion of food at every meal and needs to be prepared for sleep at bedtime. In terms of overall Hindu life, puja at home is more important than temple puja. The duties of caring for puja are usually performed by the father of the family (although in wealthy homes they are carried out by a Brahmin priest).

Women occupy a rather low status in traditional Hindu society, but they do perform important religious services on behalf of the family. It is their obligation to keep the home free from destructive spiritual influences and to forge positive ones. They will have learned how to make intricate diagrams out of colored rice *(kolams)* that are placed at the front threshold and consumed by ants. Women take vows, visit the temples and make pilgrimages on behalf of the whole family in order to maintain spiritual harmony at home. Nevertheless, their main role in traditional patterns focuses particularly on domestic activities, primarily through bearing and rearing children.[15]

The life cycle. Hinduism cultivates numerous rites of passage, with particular traditions going in their own directions. Most Hindu traditions promote several methods of ensuring that the pregnant mother and unborn child are protected from negative spiritual influences. The husband may apply red flower paste to the part in the wife's hair. This sign is supposed to ward off evil spirits. Hindu women frequently observe rituals in order to make sure that the new child will be a boy. (These rites are effective approximately 50 percent of the time.)

The birth of a child may be superintended by a Brahmin priest as well as a midwife. One of his obligations is to make sure that there are no knotted cords in the house. The infant receives a public name and a secret name within a few days of birth. After a few months, several other rituals are observed: the first bite of solid food and, at about one year of age, the first haircut. Tamil Hindus dedicate one-month-old babies to the goddess of children, Periachi. She is a gruesome-looking deity usually pictured standing on a disemboweled demon and chewing on another demon's intestines as blood runs down her face. Her fierceness is supposed to ward off destructive forces. The parents place the child, whose head has been shaved and covered with yellow sandalwood powder, in front of the goddess on the ground. Everyone (except older siblings) steps back, acknowledging that the infant was protected by the goddess while it was in the womb and for the first few months of life. Then a priest performs the usual acts of worship for Periachi.

For the male members of the top three castes, the beginning of "twice-born" life occurs sometime around the age of ten (before puberty), when the boy is officially initiated. Up to this time he had the standing of a Shudra. Now he becomes a full-fledged member of his caste. There are two central aspects to this initiation rite. The boy begins, at least symbolically, the study of the Vedas

The high point of puja for Hanuman on the occasion of his "birthday."

(which usually goes no further than this token symbolic recitation), and he receives the "thread of the twice born." He will wear this cord looped over his left shoulder for the rest of his life. The cord is replaced once a year at a renewal ceremony. The Code of Manu, which divides Hindu life into four stages, considers this initiation the beginning of the first phase, that of a student.

In traditional Hindu culture, marriage is arranged and is confined to one caste. A wedding ceremony can be performed either at home or in a temple. It is usually officiated by a Brahmin priest. The most important part of the ceremony involves the sacred fire. The bride and groom, with their clothes knotted together, walk three times in seven steps around the fire. The groom applies a red dot to the bride's forehead. This mark identifies her as a married woman. The Code of Manu sees marriage as the beginning of the second stage of life, that of householder, when people are expected to be occupied with the material side of life: earning wealth, raising a family, acquiring standing in the community.

After raising a family and securing material prosperity, the couple are expected to begin pulling out of the mundane activities of everyday existence. The Code of Manu suggests that a man should by now be disgusted with a physical life of material gain and should be ready to move out of that cycle. Together with his wife, he should withdraw from his village and move into the forest to apply himself to religious pursuits, studying scriptures and worshiping gods as well as undergoing self-appraisal and meditation. In more practical terms, this stage occurs as an older person makes the natural shift toward greater religious intensity. In most cases, there is no actual physical withdrawal, but the older generation, now that the household has been turned over to the younger generation, is able to do more praying, worshiping and meditating. In addition, the older generation at this point has time to be with children and socialize them into the proper traditions of Hindu life.

Step four of the Code of Manu is the point of complete renunciation. This stage is the ideal pursuit of the Vedantic seeker after moksha. The code states that at some point an old man should totally renounce all of his life up to then, take on a new name, repudiate all family connections and live by himself in total absorption of the final goal of life, the dissolution into Brahman. Needless to say, in everyday life this stage is seldom attained. People who do attain it are considered extremely holy.

In Hinduism funeral rites are performed soon after a person dies. The body is bathed with water, milk, honey and coconut milk. Then the family transports the body to the site of the funeral pyre, where it is cremated. The person's soul is considered to have returned to its origin. Not all descriptions of this are reconcilable with each other. In addition to the hope that the person has joined with Brahman and the fear that he or she may have entered a lower incarnation, there is the expectation that the deceased, now an ancestor, will remain in contact with the family for a while. Memorial ceremonies are performed for the departed person once a month for the first year and annually thereafter.

Classical Hinduism endorsed the practice known popularly as *sati*, in which a surviving wife would let herself be cremated with her deceased husband's body. Having a wife of such devotion was considered highly meritorious (for the man) and thereby enhanced his prospects for future incarnations. Performing this act might allow the wife to come back as a man in the next life. Sati has been outlawed since British colonial times in the nineteenth century, but it continues to occur on rare occasions.

Festivals and Holidays
Hindus love festivals. Because of great geographic and devotional diversity, there is

considerable variation among the celebrations. Each goddess has a "day of descent," or birthday, which is celebrated in the temples that house their images. Village-wide festivals are held for gods that have special community significance. A popular festival is Holi, the celebration of Krishna. In the Bengal area, Ganesha's birthday celebration takes several days. Schools take a day or more to observe the annual festival of Sarasvati, the patroness of learning.

Some festivals are associated with physical demands. In one temple with which I am familiar, the annual day of Draupadi is observed with a fire-walking ceremony. I already mentioned Taipusam, the annual festival of Muruga in Tamil Indian observance, which is characterized by body skewering. Similar rites are performed in honor of Kali in the Bengal region. In fact, many Hindu subcultures have designated a day for self-immolating practices in honor of some important deity. The god or timing varies, but the practices are similar, at least in outward form.

There are a few days that receive universal observance. New Year's Day closely follows the beginning of the Western new year. Temples and homes are decorated with mango leaves, and women draw auspicious diagrams on the temple floor. Divali (also known as Dipavali) is the "festival of lights." It is held in the autumn in honor of the goddess (usually Lakshmi). Families light lamps in their homes in order to guide Lakshmi to their abodes so as to provide them with prosperity.

■ *So You Meet a Hindu . . .*

What You Might Expect

Knowing that someone is Hindu tells you little about that person's beliefs and practices. Hinduism includes a tremendous amount of diversity in what people actually believe and practice. The same is true in some of the other large Asian religions as well (for example, Buddhism).

Hinduism has arrived in the United States in sporadic waves that have become linked increasingly with traditional Indian culture. The first foothold of Hindu thought in the Western world came about through the modified version of Hinduism spread by the Theosophical Society. This organization, begun by Helena Blavatsky and Henry Olcott in New York in 1875, attempted to popularize Vedantic monism. To this end it provided the service of issuing English translations of Hindu scriptures. However, even after moving its headquarters to India, the Theosophical Society has continued to be a group of Westerners flirting with Eastern thought more than an actual extension of Hinduism. The coming of the Ramakrishna movement, as embodied in the Vivekananda Society, fortified interest in Vedantic thought.

During the early part of this century, those who immigrated from India were often people of professional standing, such as scientists, doctors and businesspeople. As relatively Westernized individuals, these people had either abandoned their Hindu roots or had found all they needed among the movements of Vedantic orientation. They observed traditions as they could and tended to relegate the rest to superstition.

However, immigration patterns into the United States have changed drastically over the last twenty years. With fewer restrictions to limit immigration from Asia, there has been an influx of Indians bringing their entire culture with them—dress, language and religion. These people are continuing to observe the god-centered forms of Hinduism in temples that have been erected in the larger cities of the United States. Families worship together in informal settings in the absence of a temple.

With a skewer already through his cheeks and in his forehead, a devotee of Muruga has a skewer inserted through his tongue at the Taipusam festival. The many narrow skewers in his chest support the kavadi.

Thus, we come back to the lack of clear definition. Of course, not every Indian is Hindu. An Indian who is Hindu may be part of the broader, more philosophical pattern of earlier immigration or may fit into a traditional pattern of worship and practice. The point is for you to be aware, for example, that an educated Hindu may consider the self-inflicted wounds of Shaivite ceremonies to be barbaric, or that for a more traditionally oriented person the Atman-Brahman philosophy may represent irrelevant abstraction.

Many Hindus are vegetarian. Vegetarianism is not an integral part of Hinduism, but in many traditions it has become obligatory. When you are planning to share a meal with a Hindu, it is good to know in advance whether he or she is vegetarian and to avoid foods that could prove embarrassing. Be aware that in Indian vegetarianism eggs are usually considered meat.

Relating the Gospel

Hinduism prides itself on its tolerant attitude toward all world religions.[16] Just as Hinduism includes many different ways and multiple paths within each larger way, so religions outside of Hinduism are also allowed as ways to God, even if they are considered inferior. In this context, getting a Hindu to become a Christian externally is extremely easy. If you are already worshiping 330 million gods, it requires no particularly big effort to add one more to the group. "Recognize Christ as Savior and invite him into your heart? Why not? It can't hurt."

The problem is, of course, that adding Jesus to a pantheon of Shiva, Krishna, Kali and the rest is not what biblical Christianity is about. Christianity comes with some exclusive demands, and at that point for a Hindu a big barrier goes up. Christians claim that there is no way of salvation outside of Christ, that a person can find forgiveness in Christ's death alone, and that abandoning all other religious commitments is part of genuine faith in Christ. These ideas are extremely difficult for someone from a Hindu context to accept. Frequently such claims by Christians are ascribed to Western arrogance and are linked to intolerance and persecution.

The fact of the matter is that Hindu inclusivism is more apparent than real. All human beings, including Hindus, need to live on the basis of a firm truth-falsehood distinction that carries through into the religious arena as well. Three thousand years of dispute among the various forms of Hinduism have been carried out with the idea that one school was indeed truer than or superior to another one. Also, Hindu culture has consistently attempted to establish its dominance in regard to other religions. The Hindu kingdom of Nepal currently has a law forbidding anyone from interfering with its Hindu way of life. My point here is to demonstrate that Hindu claims of inclusivism do not necessarily run very deep. There are some clear limits as to what is being accommodated; a Christian claim to the exclusive truth of biblical salvation will be received with intolerance.

Then why make such an exclusive claim? Why should not the Christian simply hold up the gospel as one option for the Hindu to explore if he or she finds a lack of fulfillment in Hinduism? Why do Christians have to insist that theirs is the only way to fulfillment?

The answer is that Christianity is not about fulfillment but about salvation from sin and its effects. Biblical Christianity concerns itself with some objective facts—namely, the fact of sin, which bars a person from a relationship with God, the fact of Christ's atonement on the cross as God's provision for salvation and the fact that we can receive this provision by trusting God in faith. Christianity makes such exclusive claims because only the death of Christ has made such a provision; only Christ, who rose again, is Savior. As mentioned above, even though Bhakti Hinduism has a loose concept of grace, there is no atonement or redemption in the biblical sense, as payment for sin. Even if Rama had been a historical person, he did not die for anyone's sins. Even if Sai Baba were a manifestation of God who did genuine miracles and taught great wisdom, a person following him would be just as sinful after years of being his devotee as before. Christ did not claim to be the only way because he was arrogant, but because he alone alleviated the human condition of sinfulness.

Christians should not feel intimidated in sharing the gospel with Hindus (or anyone else). Obviously, any such conversation calls for tact, patience and the guidance of the

Holy Spirit. Yet it is another fact that despite the many theoretical obstacles, Christian missions have been quite successful in a Hindu context. There are three basic reasons for this success. First, the practical demonstration of Christian love. Westerners came to India as Christians and engaged in economic exploitation as well as colonial oppression. Western missionaries, however, came with hospitals, educational facilities, food and a willingness to reach out to the people on the lowest rungs of the caste system. Hindu caste society can be heartless, and twentieth-century efforts by Hindus to reach out to the needy (Ramakrishna hospitals, Gandhi's preaching) would probably not have taken place apart from some Christian influence. Many Hindus have responded to the open hearts of Christian missionaries. Of course, that point implies that the Christians will come and live, possibly even suffer, with the local people. Brief mass rallies in themselves rarely provide that kind of influence.

Second, Hinduism makes too many promises that cannot be fulfilled. The promise to find God within yourself does not stand up to our human consciousness of sin. None other than Prabhupada, the popularizer of the Hare Krishna movement, who was worshiped as avatar by his disciples, realized on his deathbed how short he fell of perfection. He expressed the realization that "in this world, unknowingly you commit offenses."[17] His disciples talked him out of that mood by insisting that he could not commit offenses, but it seems that he knew something that they did not want to accept. But if he was divine, how could he be wrong about anything—including his sense of sinfulness? Many Hindus, aware of their inability to cope with sin, have come to Christ for genuine redemption.

Third, Hindu worship rituals, with all their colors, sounds and intriguing mysteries, are addictive. They are also enslaving. In many ways Hinduism, like traditional religions, is based on fear: fear of capricious gods, malevolent spirits, never-ending rituals and another billion reincarnations at the least slip-up. Many Hindus have found liberation from this enslavement in Christ.

Mastering the Material

When you have finished studying this chapter, you should be able to

1. identify the Vedas and what they teach us about the religion of the Aryans who invaded the Indian subcontinent;

2. name the main Vedic deities, their history of development and their functions;

3. summarize the caste system;

4. describe the system of reincarnation (samsara) and how it is driven by the law of karma;

5. portray the innovations in Vedantic philosophy as it arose out of the Upanishads;

6. show what is distinctive about Bhakti Hinduism and how it originated out of the germinal ideas of the Bhagavad-Gita;

7. identify the Hindu gods mentioned in this chapter (except for the first six avatars of Vishnu);

8. summarize the different activities carried out in a Hindu temple;

9. describe the basic history and main teachings of ISKCON, the Ramakrishna movement and the Sai Baba movement;

10. outline the important rites of passage in Hinduism with their distinctive practices;

11. explain the nature of the ambivalence in relating to a Hindu in the United States.

Term Paper Ideas

1. Research one of the many Hindu-derived cultic movements that have entered the United States; show where its roots in Hinduism are and where it may have deviated. Possibilities include the Divine Light Mission or transcendental meditation.

2. Read one of the Upanishads in translation and outline its main teachings.

3. Read and make a summary of one of the Hindu epics or puranas.

4. Demonstrate the interplay of ritual and magic in Hindu practices.

5. Write a history of the caste system in India (perhaps focusing on the recent history of the untouchables).

6. Explain in depth the understanding of karma in Hinduism.

7. Describe the ideal Hindu family.

8. Summarize the teachings of an important teacher in Hinduism from ancient times to the present.

9. Locate a Hindu group in your area and write up a set of interviews with members of that group.

10. Research Christian missionary strategies and successes by one group or an individual ministering to Hindus.

Core Bibliography

Danielou, Alain. *Hindu Polytheism.* New York: Random House, 1964.

Doniger, Wendy, and Brian K. Smith, trans. *The Laws of Manu.* London: Penguin, 1991.

Hume, Robert Ernest, ed. *The Thirteen Principal Upanishads.* New York: Oxford University Press, 1971.

Knipe, David M. *Hinduism: Experiments in the Sacred.* San Francisco: HarperSanFrancisco, 1991.

O'Flaherty, Wendy Doniger, trans. *The Rig Veda.* London: Penguin, 1981.

Thomas, P. *Epics, Myths and Legends of India.* Bombay, India: D. B. Taraporevala, n.d.

Wilkins, W. J. *Hindu Mythology: Vedic and Puranic.* Totowa, N.J.: Rowman & Littlefield, 1974.

Zaehner, R. C., trans. *The Bhagavad-Gita.* New York: Oxford University Press, 1969.

Chapter 8

Buddhism

Estimated Membership
Worldwide: 323,894,000
United States: 780,000

Diversity persists as we continue to look at religions originating in India. The designation *Buddhist* without further qualification conveys virtually no insight into what a person believes or practices. There are as many schools of Buddhism as there are Christian Protestant denominations, but the teachings of many of these schools appear to be irreconcilable beyond a very general core.

With their exposure to the Western world, people in Asia, particularly the Chinese, have learned that they are supposed to have some kind of official label for their religion, and so, if asked, they politely reply that they are Buddhists. However, in many such cases, they are really adherents of a Chinese popular religion that includes Buddha among the deities worshiped but has virtually nothing to do with traditional schools of Buddhism. This chapter restricts its focus to the traditional schools of Buddhism.

Life of Buddha

Any discussion of Buddhism must begin with its founder, Gautama Buddha. Yet it is important to realize that the Buddha is not crucial to the essence of Buddhism. He is the teacher and the initiator, and he is venerated by millions of Buddhists. But millions of other Buddhists worship different Buddhas and spiritual beings; still others say that worship of any being has no place in Buddhism. Zen Buddhists even treat Gautama Buddha disparagingly at times. The point is that a teaching lies at the core of Buddhism, not a person. The teaching came through a person, and he is revered for it, but the teaching ultimately does not depend on the teacher.

Reliable information concerning the Buddha is scarce, but we can safely place him in the sixth century B.C. in northeastern India about the same time as the development of Vedanta Hinduism and the worldwide revolt against priestly religions. For the greater details of his story, we need to rely on the legend as it has been handed down in the history of Buddhism. There is no good reason to believe that the essential elements of the legend are not anchored in facts. There is great diversity in regard to specific elements, for example, whether the famous chariot ride took place on one day or on four days. I am going to recount one version; the reader must be aware that other versions are not necessarily wrong.[1]

According to the legend, the person now commonly known as the Buddha was a prince named Siddhartha Gautama. His father, Suddhona, was ruler of the Sakya clan. Siddhartha's birth was attended by many unusual events. Shortly prior to the birth his mother, Queen Mahamaya, dreamed that a white elephant entered her womb. The child's birth took place painlessly in a grove of blooming trees, at which point he immediately proclaimed his exaltation. At the palace a great prophecy concerning this child was pronounced, first by an itinerant sage and then by the court astrologers. They predicted that Siddhartha would become either a great king or a great religious monk. Queen Mahamaya died a short time later.

The Venerable Dr. C. Phangcham of the Wat Dhammaram, a Thai Buddhist temple, lectures to a group of students.

King Suddhona wanted Siddhartha to become a great king, so he took every precaution to ensure that his son would not be influenced in the direction of religion. He ensured that the boy would not see any examples of old age, disease, death or religious renunciation. Despite growing up in this very protected environment, Siddhartha showed early signs of spiritual proclivity, for instance, by being unbeatable in martial skills and by falling into deep meditation that resulted in levitation. Eventually Siddhartha married, and his wife, Yasodhara, gave birth to a boy, Rahula.

Siddhartha grew increasingly curious about the outside world and persuaded his father to allow him to take a chariot ride through the countryside. Suddhona agreed to the outing but purged the area of any evidence of the four elements that could induce Siddhartha to consider religion. All old and sick people were hidden away, funeral processions were prohibited, and all religious mendicants were removed. However, at this point the gods involved themselves in the situation. The devas of Hindu mythology took an interest in Siddhartha's becoming a religious leader. They assumed the forms of the four banished influences, and Siddhartha saw successively an old man on the verge of death, a man with a disfiguring disease, a funeral procession for a decomposing corpse and a holy monk displaying the serenity of a life of renunciation. These four sights left Gautama extremely troubled. He began to see that the life of luxury he was leading would only end in death and decay.

Not too long after this experience, Siddhartha Gautama, now almost thirty years old, abandoned his life of comfort and ease. Disgusted with the futility of carnal pleasures, he bade his sleeping wife and infant goodby, mounted his horse and leaped over the palace wall. In a symbolic gesture of renunciation, he cut off his beautiful long hair and embarked on the pursuit of spiritual enlightenment through a life of austerity.

Gautama soon became highly adept at the ascetic and meditative practices of the wandering monk. In essence, this life was the equivalent of the sannyasin in the Vedantic tradition and (as we shall see in chapter nine) of Mahavira, the founder of Jainism. Gautama would deprive himself of all human comforts, sometimes living on only one grain of rice a day or maybe even his own excrement. He would inflict any conceivable torture on himself. A group of five monks became his disciples out of respect for the proficiency they observed in Gautama. Still, enlightenment did not come.

Finally, after seven years of self-mortification, Gautama decided to let his entire pursuit end in success or death. He accepted a meal of rice (according to some versions, the gleam of the golden bowl triggered his thoughts toward the truth) and sat under a fig tree to meditate until he found enlightenment or died of starvation. The gods, knowing that Gautama was close to the critical moment, rejoiced. But Mara, the evil god of desire, started to tempt Gautama in various ways, trying to ruin his concentration. However, Gautama persisted and by morning had attained enlightenment. He had now become a Buddha, literally an "awakened one." This fig tree would forever be known as the "bodhi tree" (or "bo tree").

A question now presented itself: should the Buddha keep what he had just learned to himself or should he embark on a life of teaching? Again Mara tried to distract him, but the god Brahma prevailed on the Buddha to start teaching others the way to enlightenment. Thus he rose, accepted food and started to make disciples. Among the first few converts were Gautama's five previous companions, whom he located in the deer park of nearby Benares. When they saw him coming, they at first despised him because they noticed that he was now fed and clothed. But eventually they listened to Buddha's sermon (his first public preaching) and became his disciples. Much later Buddha went home, where Suddhona, Yasodara, Rahula and Gautama's brother Ananda were all converted to his teaching. His evil stepbrother Devadatta held out for a long time and caused much mischief. The legend holds that the Buddha ascended to heaven, where he taught his mother, Mahamaya, and the gods the way of enlightenment. Even an elephant and a monkey received his teaching gladly.

Gautama Buddha died after eating a spoiled piece of pork that had been presented to him as an offering. His place of departure from the world was a grove of trees in which he reclined in sublime serenity before a crowd of disciples who watched him enter nirvana.

Gautama's Teachings

What Gautama discovered under the bodhi tree was that the secret to enlightenment lay neither in a life of luxury nor in self-deprivation, but in a *middle way* that steers clear of all extremes. The problem with existence, Gautama decided, lies in becoming attached to physical life, which is by nature impermanent. The key to salvation is to let go of everything.

Buddha's view of reality and salvation was analogous to that taught by Vedanta Hinduism, which developed at the same time. Buddha taught that all phenomenal existence is maya, here with the full meaning of illusion. However, instead of positing an ultimate reality (such as the Vedantic Brahman), Buddha declared that behind the illusion is absolutely nothing. Thus life is nothing more than illusory vibrations that detract from the fundamental nothingness: *sunyata,* the void.

The same nothingness applies to the human self. Instead of the Vedantic at-man, Buddha taught the ultimate non-self, *anatman*.[2] Metaphysically speaking, the moment of salvation occurs when the person comes to realize his place of non-self in the void. This is enlightenment. All attachments have been overcome, and now the person can enter the non-

Depiction at Wat Dhammaram of Prince Siddhartha cutting his hair as he begins his renunciation.

state of nirvana, which means literally "blown out." It is sometimes said that self-extinction is the goal of Buddha's philosophy; it would be better to put it as realizing one's self-extinctedness. Nonexistence is the reality; one simply has to become of aware of it. Until a person attains that realization, he or she continues through the cycle of samsara, prodded on by karma.

Gautama distilled these ideas into the "four noble truths." First, *to live is to suffer* (*dukha*). This idea is not unique to Buddhism. It is at the heart of almost all Indian philosophy. The various schools distinguish themselves from each other by the reasons they advance to explain the suffering and the remedies they suggest. Second, *suffering is caused by desire (tanha)*. Humans suffer because we allow ourselves to get attached to the illusory world. Desire needs to be understood as grasping or attachment. Simply wanting something is not desire in that sense. Thus Buddha does not say that we need to desire enlightenment. Third, *one can eliminate suffering by eliminating desire*. Obviously, if suffering is caused by being attached to life, the solution to suffering is to get rid of the attachment. Simply put, we suffer due to poverty, poor health or the death of a loved one only as long as we cling to desiring material goods, good health or the loved one's presence. Fourth, *desire is eliminated by means of the noble eightfold path*.

The goal of ridding oneself of attachment can be attained only through a rigorous life of concentrated effort. This undertaking is summarized as the "noble eightfold path," which consists of (1) the right view—understanding the truths of existence; (2) the right intention—being willing to achieve enlightenment; (3) the right speech—saying all that is, and only what is, required; (4) the right action—doing all that is, and only what is, required; (5) the right livelihood—being a monk; (6) the right effort—directing one's energy properly; (7) the right mindfulness—meditating properly; (8) the right concentration—maintaining continuous focus. Clearly this program requires full-time effort. Thus Gautama's followers formed an order of monks, the *sangha*, which was given over to pursuing the goal of enlightenment. Gautama also ordained women (Yasodara, for example) into an order of nuns.

The relationship of Gautama's teachings to Hinduism needs to be clarified. For one thing, the Hindu gods figure prominently in the story of Buddha's life. When it comes down to the actual teaching, however, the gods have no place other than as beings who themselves do not know the way of enlightenment. Gautama took over from Hinduism the beliefs in samsara, karma and ultimate (non)reality. The denial of Brahman in itself is not cause to exclude Buddhism from Hinduism, since there are other atheistic schools of Hindu philosophy. Gautama's eliminating the caste system for his followers and rejecting the Vedas as authoritative is what made Buddhism a heterodox school of Hinduism.

Theravada Buddhism

Buddha's teachings spread rapidly throughout India, particularly in the southwest and on the island of Sri Lanka. Shortly after his death, a conclave of important followers, the First Council, took place. At this time the early writings, some of which were said to reflect Buddha's own teachings, were collected under the name of Tripitaka, literally, the "three baskets." The Second Council followed about a hundred years later. By this time the seeds of division had begun to sprout. A large group of representatives argued for less strict discipline and more openness toward the laity. Eventually, another two hundred years later (by about 200 B.C.), those who defended stricter discipline split away from those who were less strict. This led to the two main branches of Buddhism, which are now called Theravada and Mahayana.

The name *Theravada* is derived from an expression meaning "tradition of the elders." This school remained relatively true to the teachings of Gautama by maintaining a religion that centers on monks. The other group was called Mahayana ("the big raft") because it accommodated large numbers of people, including the laity. Their term for the Theravadins, Hinayana, means "little raft" and was originally intended as pejorative, but is widely used by Theravadins themselves today.

In India, Buddhism achieved its glory days in the middle of the third century B.C. under King Asoka, who instituted it as the national religion. From that point on, though, it declined rapidly. Today Theravada Buddhism is dominant in Sri Lanka and Southeast Asia. The rest of the Buddhist Far East (China, Japan, Korea) belongs to Mahayana. Buddhism is practically nonexistent in India today.

Theravada Buddhism is a religion of and for monks. The monks, *bikhus,* are the only ones who can attain nirvana; they are the focal point of religious practice. The laity's primary job is to support the monks. They can thereby earn merit that will improve their own future incarnations. Ordination as a bikhu involves having one's head shaved and donning the traditional yellow robe. Monks vow to follow the Ten Precepts: (1) not to take any life (the principle of *ahimsa*), (2) not to steal, (3) not to commit sexual immorality, (4) not to lie, (5) not to take intoxicating drinks, (6) not to eat in excess and not after noon, (7) not to attend any entertainment, such as dancing, singing or drama, (8) not to decorate oneself or use cosmetics, (9) not to sleep in high or wide beds, (10) not to touch any gold or silver.

A bikhu spends most of his day in meditation. Hours not given to spiritual pursuits are spent begging for food (in the morning) and doing household chores around the temple. The object of meditation is to focus on the total impermanence of all existence and thereby to pull oneself away from anything distracting. A bikhu who has attained full realization is an *arhat,* a "holy man." On death he will enter nirvana. The difference between a Buddha and an arhat is that a Buddha must have been perfect in all of his previous incarnations, whereas an arhat will not have been. Thus most Theravada Buddhists today believe that a Buddha comes into the world as a spiritual, special being. A bikhu usually lives in a monastery connected to a particular temple. He may also live as a hermit.

Meanwhile, the laity never become more than secondary participants in the religion. The goal for laypeople in Theravada Buddhism is to lead a good life in order to store up sufficient merit for a better incarnation. It is even possible to earn some time in a heaven between incarnations on earth. Theravada cosmology pictures the universe as consisting of many levels. The higher ones are states of bliss worth pursuing, but they are not as ultimate as nirvana. On all important religious occasions laypeople recite the "creed" of Theravada, known as the Three Refuges: I seek refuge in the Buddha; I seek refuge in the dharma (the way taught by Buddha); I seek refuge in the sangha (the order of bikhus).

Laypeople have three basic obligations. First, they must keep the five precepts. Whereas the bikhus must observe all ten precepts, only the first five (not killing, not stealing, sexual fidelity in marriage, truth telling and abstention from alcohol) are mandated for the laity. Sometimes on special days laypeople take a vow to obey eight precepts by accepting three more (not to eat after noon, not to decorate oneself, not to attend any entertainment). Their exertions may be recognized by the white clothes they wear in the temple.

Burmese monk gilding a statue of Buddha.

Second, laypeople must support the bikhus. They are expected to provide the monks with food, clothing (material for robes) and any other material necessities. Third, laypeople are expected to maintain the temples. A Theravada temple is usually erected by the generosity of a lay founder. Typically a statue of the founder in monk's garb is placed somewhere on the premises and is venerated for his generosity. Laypeople continue his work by increasingly decorating the temple. A traditional form of this work is to apply gold leaf to the roof or to statues of the Buddha. For a sum, people can purchase a small (roughly one square centimeter) patch of gold to be applied on their behalf. It takes years to completely cover a statue in this fashion.

A basic Theravada temple can be relatively plain or highly ornate. On the whole, the pattern of a Theravada temple in Sri Lanka tends to be less encumbered than its counterparts in Southeast Asia. The main hall of the temple contains a statue of Buddha, usually shown in the most basic position—sitting cross-legged with his left hand open on his lap and his right hand directed toward the earth (calling on the earth to witness to his Buddhahood and indicating his steadfastness). Only a Buddha can hold his hands in this position (*mudra*). This characteristic posture helps sort out the multiplicity of representations of spiritual beings in later developments. Other mudras include the teaching position—thumb and forefinger brought together on the right hand—and the protecting position—the right hand held up palm out.

In front of the main statue of the Buddha is usually a counter on which flowers, oil lights and other worship offerings are placed. There may be other icons or Buddha statues. Many temples have a statue of a standing Buddha or a reclining Buddha that represents Buddha entering nirvana in serenity. Thai Buddhist temples tend to be extremely ornate. In addition to statues of the Buddha and of other Buddhist beings, a Thai temple typically has a statue of the Hindu god Brahma (complete with four faces), who is revered for his service to Buddha, as well as statues of other gods or goddesses (such as the earth goddess) that are loosely connected to Buddhist mythology. Many temples proudly display pieces of the original bodhi tree (which supposedly was transplanted to Sri Lanka shortly after Buddha's time) or even an offshoot thereof.

The position of the Buddha in the context of lay Theravada Buddhism is somewhat ambiguous. Theoretically, Gautama has entered nirvana and is now unreachable; in practice, however, Buddha is considered an exalted spiritual being who is worshiped, prayed to and expected to provide blessings. In this respect Theravada Buddhism provides another classic example of the difference between the standard form of a religion and its counterpart in folk religion. Nothing infuriates a knowledgeable Buddhist more than asserting that Buddhists worship the Buddha as god. Yet on the level of the laypeople this is precisely what takes place, and a layperson may not be embarrassed to tell you so. Of course, this development is not surprising; the hope of nirvana in some distant incarnation is not sufficient to help people with the stresses of daily life. When a child becomes ill, when the crops fail and when a loved one dies, the human religious impulse demands some immediate spiritual assistance. Consequently, laypeople either reinterpret Buddhist practices to supply them with the needed spiritual help or incorporate non-Buddhist elements into their religion—or both.

A layperson can add to his storehouse of merit by becoming a bikhu for a short time. In some areas this practice has taken on the character of a puberty rite of passage as a child spends several months (perhaps an extended summer vacation) in the company of monks. It is also common practice for an adult man to commit himself to spending a few years in the temple. This will not permit him to attain nirvana, but he does improve his chances for advancement in the next life.

Given the typical trends of religious development, it is not surprising that the solitary Buddha soon found himself in the company of other Buddhas. Gautama became one of twenty-five Buddhas, all of whom came to teach the same way of enlightenment. Furthermore, and very importantly, the idea developed that there is another Buddha already in the last stages of preparation to come to earth. His name is Maitreya; he is considered a Bodhisattva, a "Buddha-in-the-making." When Maitreya comes, the tradition claims, he will usher in a golden age of enlightenment for all.

Mahayana Schools

It was not long before innovations occurred in Buddhism that accommodated the needs of laypeople as well as monks. The "greater raft" of Mahayana was devised in order to allow people to attain salvation in ways other than becoming monks. Mahayana gave rise to four significant innovations, the first of which is

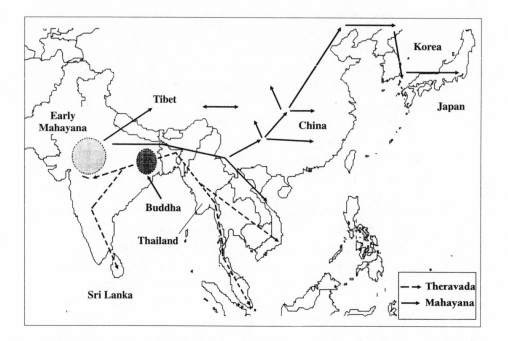

Map 8.1. Expansion of Buddhism

picturing sunyata, formerly the void, as absolute compassion. The theoretical abstraction of losing oneself in complete emptiness was replaced by the idea of finding oneself in the absolute compassion that is sunyata (a notion that has retroactively colored Theravada conceptions of nirvana today). In Mahayana, benevolent compassion becomes the ultimate motivating force for all aspects of the religion.

The second innovation of Mahayana is the multiplication of divine beings. In Mahayana, the number of Buddhas and Bodhisattvas continued to grow. They fall into three categories: Manushi Buddhas, Dhyani Buddhas and Bodhisattvas. Manushi Buddhas are Buddhas who, like Gautama, achieved enlightenment on earth. Because the word *Buddha* can refer to so many individuals, Gautama is frequently identified as Sakyamuni, literally, "the sage of the Sakya clan." For the development of Mahayana

Buddhism, the Manushi Buddhas, including Gautama, tend to be of lesser importance than the other divine beings, partly because they are now unreachable in nirvana.

Dhyani Buddhas are Buddhas who attained enlightenment in heaven. Thus they have not died, and so they are still available to humans. They can answer prayers and provide help with salvation. One example of a Dhyani Buddha is the widely popular Amithaba of the Pure Land school. In fact, pictures or statues from Japan or Korea, generically identified as Buddhas, usually depict Amithaba, not Sakyamuni.

Bodhisattvas typify the essence of Mahayana. It recognizes myriads of Bodhisattvas, "Buddhas-in-the-making," of which Mai-

Worshiper prostrate before Buddha. The seats on the platform in back are for monks during meditation.

treya is the only example in Theravada. Theoretically, any human being can become a Bodhisattva through a commitment to compassion for all human beings in this and in all coming incarnations. In the Mahayana mythology, the Bodhisattvas are divine beings who are now in heaven, having taken a vow to forgo their own entry into nirvana until "the last soul has been redeemed from hell," that is, from the lower levels of incarnation. These spiritual beings are now in heaven, having stored up insurmountable quantities of merit and of spiritual energy. They are available to human beings in whatever needs or crises they may have.

One example of a Bodhisattva is Avalokitesvara (frequently pictured with eleven heads and multiple arms), who came out of Indian Mahayana as the ultimate embodiment of mercy and was adapted into various other schools of Mahayana. In Tibetan Buddhism, under the name Chenresi, he is believed to be incarnated by the Dalai Lama. In China, Avalokitesvara became merged with the folk goddess of mercy, Guanyin, and thus appears in feminine form. Finally, in Japan he/she is revered as the feminine Kannon.

The third innovation of Mahayana is the Lotus Sutra and other scriptures. The writings associated with the Mahayana movement proliferated greatly from the outset, but none attained the stature of the Lotus Sutra. In its final form it consists of several layers, at the core of which is the teaching of Mahayana doctrine attributed to

Sakyamuni (Gautama) himself. Some of its more innovative doctrines include the idea that the human Buddha, Sakyamuni, was a manifestation of the true celestial Buddha; the notion that all human beings are eligible for Buddhahood; explicit references to various Buddhas and Bodhisattvas by name; the assertion that Hinayana teaching is applicable only to selfish, uncaring people.

The fourth innovation of Mahayana was the development of many schools. Once a pattern of adaptation had been set, Mahayana Buddhism began evolving into a large number of schools and subschools, particularly as the religion crossed many geographical and cultural boundaries in the process of expansion. Mentioning some of the bigger schools and ignoring the multitudinous subschools, we get the following general picture (see figure 8.1). From the original Indian form of Mahayana developed

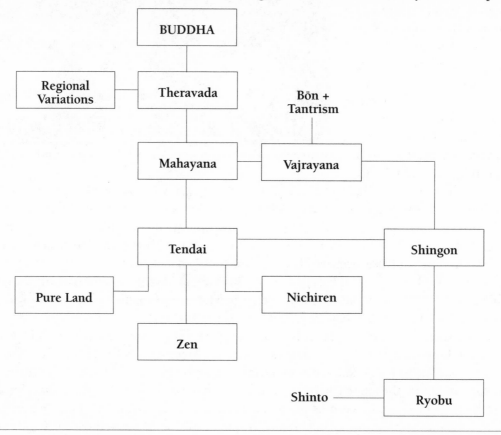

Figure 8.1. Schools of Buddhism

the (rationalist) Tendai school. Out of Tendai arose the (compassionate) Pure Land school as well as, by way of reaction, (intuitive) Zen and (chanting) Nichiren. Meanwhile in Tibet a very different school, Vajrayana (lamaist), developed. Features of Vajrayana were combined with ideas of Tendai to give rise to the magical school, Shingon. In Japan, Shingon existed for a long time as Ryobu, a synthesis of Shingon with the indigenous Shinto religion. We shall now look at each of these schools individually (see table 8.1).

Tendai. Tendai is generally known as the rationalist school of Buddhism. It was an attempt to create a viable compromise among all the various, sometimes contradictory, schools of Mahayana that had found their way into China. It was organized formally by a Chinese monk, Chih-i, in the sixth century A.D. The three major components of Tendai teaching include the superiority of the Lotus Sutra, the unity of reality and universal salvation.

School	Persons	Distribution	Scripture	Distinctives
Tendai (rational)	Chih-i	China, Japan	Lotus Sutra	Unity, universality
Pure Land, Jodo (compassion)	Honen, Shinran	China, Korea, Japan	Sukhavati-Vyuha, Amitabha Sutra	Amida, Nembutsu, western paradise
Zen (intuitive)	Bodhidharma, Soto, Rinzai	China, Japan	Platform Sutra	Satori, nondual, "third eye," koan, mondo
Nichiren Shoshu, Soka Gakkai (chanting)	Nichiren	Japan, worldwide	Lotus Sutra	Daimoku, Gohonzen, *Namu myo-horengekyo*
Vajrayana (Lamaist)	Dalai Lama, Panchen Lama	Tibet, northren India	Book of the Dead	Dalai Lama, *om mani padme hum* meditation, prayer wheel
Shingon, Chenyen (magical)	Mizu, Kobo Daishi	China, Japan		Vairocana, Ryobu fusion with Shinto

Table 8.1. Comparative characteristics of schools of Buddhism

It is no exaggeration to say that for Tendai Buddhism the Lotus Sutra is the inspired scripture. Since this sutra attempts to pull all of Buddhism together under one umbrella, it works as a foundation for showing that all other Buddhist ways were ultimately various inferior paths to Buddhahood. Chih-i taught that all reality is equally a part of Buddha's nature. He claimed, counter to the Theravada doctrine of the void, that reality is both empty (and thereby nonexistent) and caused (and thereby existing in time); thus it is sunyatta and maya at the same time. Since all beings are indiscriminately part of the same Buddha nature, eventually all beings will attain Buddhahood.

The Tendai school emphasized the practice of meditation for achieving insight into true reality. Compared to the many other developments in Mahayana, Tendai represents a middle-of-the-road approach to Buddhism.

Pure Land schools. A number of schools of Mahayana developed under the name Pure Land, including the Japanese school "the true Pure Land," Jodo-Shin-Shu. Already a part of the many meditative practices of Tendai Buddhism in Japan was the repetition of the phrase *namu amida butsu,* "I bow down to (worship) the Buddha Amida." Under the leadership of the monks Honen (generally credited with mobilizing the Pure Land movement as a whole) and Shinran (the founder of the specific school under consideration) this practice of recitation became centrally important.

Amida is the Japanese name for the Dhyani Buddha, Amithaba. According to the mythology associated with him, Amida, while yet proceeding through his human incarnations, was overwhelmed with the misery of human beings and the prospects of so few people ever being able to attain nirvana. He vowed that someday he would provide a means of salvation to all human beings.

Once Amida had become a Buddha, he was able to carry out his intentions. With the pure mental power available to him in his spiritual state, he created a paradise in the western regions of heaven where he resided. This paradise is a "pure land," also known as a "Buddha field" or as the "western paradise." Anyone who sincerely trusts Amida is permitted to enter the paradise at death. Once in the pure land, any soul can attain enlightenment. In practice, the Pure Land and nirvana are treated as equivalent.

Trust in Amida Buddha is expressed through recitation of the phrase namu amida butsu, usually referred to as the nembutsu. Some Pure Land schools maintain that recitation of the nembutsu is required to enter paradise, but the Jodo-shin-shu claims that the nembutsu merely expresses gratitude for something that Amida has already done.

This Pure Land school makes no demands on its followers other than what they want to do to show Amida how thankful they are. Consequently, Jodo-shin-shu has blossomed in Japan as the most widespread form of Buddhism. Anyone who cannot practice the rigor associated with other schools of Buddhism finds a promise of salvation in this school. There are no monks in Jodo-shin-shu (in contrast to other Pure Land schools). Religious services, held on a weekly or a daily basis, are performed by ordained clergy. The services are times of chanting, meditation and adoration of Amida.

Zen. Possibly under the influence of the Chinese philosophy of Daoism,[3] definitely in reaction against the philosophical speculations of Tendai, Zen Buddhism arose in China beginning in the sixth century A.D. Like all Mahayana schools, Zen claims that its origins reach back to Gautama. The legend is that one day the Buddha simply stood before his disciples silently holding a flower. While all the others waited for him to say something in explanation, one disciple, Mahakasyapa, merely looked at the Buddha and smiled. Gautama acknowledged that Mahakasyapa had understood and that this treasure of nirvana was entrusted to him. This story points to the essence of Zen: the realization of enlightenment apart from words and explanations.

Traditionally, the founder of Zen is said to be Bodhidharma, an Indian monk who emigrated to China more than a thousand years after Mahakasyapa. Bodhidharma practiced meditation regularly. In order to keep himself awake, he cut off his eyelids, which gives his representations a rather shocking appearance. According to the legend,

Bodhidharma spent three years meditating in front of a bare wall. When some bystanders gave him a blow on the head just to see how he would react, he finally attained enlightenment. Two major schools of Zen Buddhism developed in Japan, each named after its founding master: Soto, which sees enlightenment as the result of a gradual process of growth, and Rinzai, which holds that enlightenment occurs abruptly after a lengthy period of preparation.

All schools of Zen believe that the most important preparation for enlightenment is to clear one's mind of all the conceptual clutter that impedes true insight. The popular twentieth-century writer D. T. Suzuki has summarized the nature of Zen in four statements: (1) a special transmission outside the scriptures, (2) no dependence on words and letters, (3) direct pointing to the soul of man and (4) seeing into one's nature and the attainment of Buddhahood.[4]

There are Zen scriptures, particularly the Platform Sutra, but they are not considered to be directly authoritative, let alone the source of belief. True Zen knowledge can be transmitted only from a master to his disciple, and the master can only direct the disciple to see what only he can see for himself.

Another popular writer, Alan Watts, has likened the message of Zen to listening to music. "To hear the whole symphony one must concentrate on the flow of notes and harmonies as they come into being and pass away, keeping one's mind continuously in the same rhythm. To think over what has passed, to wonder what is about to come, or to analyse the effect upon oneself is to interrupt the symphony and to lose the reality."[5]

Zen functions something like a joke. You have to "get" it spontaneously without having it explained to you by someone. Once explained, a joke is hardly ever

This small statue of Buddha has been covered with gold by worshipers, one spot at a time.

funny, and it becomes pointless. A joke produces a laugh when it "hits" you. Similarly, Zen wants to get beyond explanations and distinctions. The person who attains that level "gets the joke."[6] In the experience of enlightenment, referred to as satori, the person has a direct, unmediated insight into the self, the world and the truth.

What stands in the way of enlightenment, according to Zen, is our habit of "dualistic thinking." This phrase refers to thinking that seems to consist of making distinctions. Everything is classified according to rational categories and is divided logically into what is real, what is really real and what is not really real. Zen wants to take people beyond the habit of dualistic thinking and get them to accept what is, plain and simple. In Zen, human knowledge is likened to a finger pointing at the moon. Once someone has seen the moon, the finger has served its purpose and can be taken away; only a fool continues to look at the finger. In the same way, Zen maintains, naive people continue to occupy themselves with words and rational categories instead of accepting reality for what it is. Satori is the moment at which one comes to terms with simply taking reality as reality. "When it rains, you get wet," a Zen master told my class. "When I get hungry, I eat." He meant that to explain the phenomena of life is to bury them under a rubble of useless concepts. To receive reality just as it is represents pure, nondual thinking.

Thus Zen also dispenses with traditional Buddhist philosophy. In several traditional stories a Zen master uses his staff as an illustration of the difference between Zen and the other Buddhist schools. Zen master Ummon once held up his staff and pointed out that "the ignorant take this for a real thing, the Hinayanists resolve it into a nonentity, the [low level Buddhas][7] regard it as a hallucination, while the Bodhisattvas admit its apparent reality, which is, however, essentially empty. But . . . monks, you simply call it a staff when you see one."[8] Thus Zen recognizes three levels of understanding: the naive dualistic one that takes particular things for genuine reality, the various philosophical interpretations that deny genuine reality and finally Zen's nondual approach to accepting reality exactly as it is given. Zen talks about developing a "third eye" to see reality in this way.

Zen Buddhism has traditionally made use of four methods that take a person to satori. First there is Zazen meditation. Used particularly in the Soto school of gradual awareness, Zazen meditation constitutes a highly demanding process of physical and mental discipline. In fact, the name Zen is the Japanese version of the Chinese *Chan*, which in turn is derived from the Sanskrit *dhyana*, meaning "meditation." Zazen literally means "sitting," but one must forget all notions of being comfortably seated in a favorite chair. Instead, the adept sits in the cross-legged position with a perfectly straight back for hours on end, focusing on the thought provided by the master. At first, sheer physical agony may hinder the attainment of spiritual insights. Any lapses in bodily posture or wakefulness are rewarded by a slap of the master's stick, not necessarily painful but definitely noticeable. The disciple is supposed to show proper gratitude for this assistance. Because of the discipline involved, Japanese companies frequently send lower-level executives to Zen retreats, where they engage in Zazen meditation.

The second method is *mondos*, stories involving conversations of great Zen masters of the past or accounts of how they received enlightenment. The pupil is supposed to study these narratives as examples to learn from. The third method, the koan, is a Zen riddle. Koans seem to be conundrums—riddles without genuine answers, such as "What is the sound of one hand clapping?" or "Does a dog have Buddha nature?" or "How crooked is straight?" Far from being unanswerable, koans are supposed to carry their answers within their very formulation. But they can be discovered only when a person stops thinking analytically and ceases looking for the "trick." The answer to a koan must be a spontaneous internal realization, not just an intellectual resolution.

The fourth method Zen uses is cultural activities. Various Zen forms of art and culture, particularly as they have become at home in Japan, are used as aids in attaining satori as well as in expressing an enlightened view of reality. Zen has found aesthetic expression in the tea ceremony, calligraphy, martial arts, haiku poetry and rock gardens. As diverse as these activities are, they have one thing in common: they focus on capturing reality in its nondual state. All the details have to be just right, and yet they receive their meaning from the whole. Thus Zen works to see reality just as it is given.

Nichiren Shoshu (Soka Gakkai). Another school that arose as a reaction against Tendai was the school founded by the thirteenth-century Japanese monk Nichiren. Nichiren spent his early life within Tendai but increasingly found it unacceptable. No other school of Buddhism provided what he was looking for either. Eventually he concluded that all hitherto existing schools of Buddhism were false. In a statement that must startle anyone who thinks that all Eastern religions are inclusivist, Nichiren asserted, "The Nembutsu is hell; Zen is a devil; Shingon is the nation's ruin; and Ritsu [Hinayana philosophy] is treason." Nichiren proposed a return to Sakyamuni and what he considered to be true Buddhist teaching.

Avalokitasvara, the Bodhisattva. Bright Hill Temple, Singapore.

Nichiren was subjected to persecution and twice, just as he was about to be executed, a natural disaster intervened. He was released when everyone concluded that these calamities were omens. He gathered a group of disciples, who propagated his teachings and predictably split into numerous subschools. Nichiren Shoshu means "the true Nichiren." Its teachings were revived in the 1930s in Japan under the banner of the Soka Gakkai, the "society for the creation of values," and it became extremely popular in the 1950s. Today it has easily twenty million adherents worldwide. In Japan this form of Buddhism is second in popularity only to Pure Land.

As befits a Mahayana movement, Soka Gakkai holds that enlightenment is available to all human beings, regardless of previous incarnations and current state. There are ten states of life; the key to happiness lies in traversing them from the lowest to the highest. These states are states of consciousness more than metaphysical realities, but people's state at death determines their karma and thereby their next incarnation. Those who attain Buddhahood are finished with any further incarnations.

The ten states are hell, anger, animality, hunger, tranquillity, rapture, learning, realization, Bodhisattva and Buddhahood. This progression begins with the worst forms of human experience and then moves from the physical through the mental, culminating in the pure consciousness of enlightenment. It is claimed that any human being can attain Buddhahood after only few years of effort.

The key to spiritual advancement in Soka Gakkai is chanting. The phrase that is chanted is called the *daimoku*. It is inscribed on a piece of paper called the *gohonzon*, which is considered the object of worship. Its history goes back to Nichiren himself. Faced with the bewildering array of conflicting claims made by the various schools of Buddhism that he rejected, Nichiren advocated a return to the pure teaching of Sakyamuni (Gautama Buddha) as embodied in the Lotus Sutra. In order to capture the spiritual force of this sutra, he wrote its title on a highly decorated piece of paper, the gohonzon. The gohonzon or its replications may never be photographed, so a description must suffice. Picture a slightly oversized piece of rectangular white paper. Written vertically in the center is the actual title, the daimoku, in Sanskrit: *sat dharma pundarika sutram*. Along the sides are the names of various heavenly deities (Buddhas and Bodhisattvas) as well as the names of individuals representing the ten states of life. On the lower right and left corners are drawings of a crane, symbolizing peace and hope.

The gohonzon is freely referred to as the object of worship. The original is kept in Japan. Each temple has a copy that is stored in a cabinet (the *butsudan*—"Buddhist altar") in its main sanctuary, called the "hall of eternal happiness." Early each evening, the butsudan is opened for a two-hour period of chanting by all adherents present. The individual practitioner puts in another hour or so of chanting each morning.

What is chanted is the daimoku in Japanese: *namu myo-horenge-kyo*, "I bow down to (worship) the beautiful teaching of the Lotus Sutra." The chanters assume a straight-backed kneeling position facing the gohonzon and rapidly repeat this mantra over and over. The words are slurred in such a way that an observer cannot make out what is being chanted; the practitioners keep track of their progress by means of a small "rosary."

The practice of chanting is intended to propel the believer to the level of Buddhahood. A person who has attained that state can regress, although the common understanding seems to be that anyone who has attained Buddhahood will die in perfect bliss even if at the moment of death he or she has reverted momentarily to the state of Bodhisattva. Soka Gakkai also promises more immediate benefits to its adherents. Chanting the daimoku establishes a proper relationship to the life force of the universe and thus brings good fortune to the chanter. For example, a person who is in poor physical health may have a disharmonious relationship with the cosmic forces. This breach can be healed by way of constant chanting, and physical healing then ensues. Many adherents are drawn to Soka Gakkai more for its immediate benefits than for philosophical reasons.

Soka Gakkai is a lay movement; its leaders are quick to point out that they are not priests. Wherever it is found in the world, it occupies itself with the promotion of social justice, charities and the arts. In Japan Soka Gakkai sponsors a political party, the Komeito, which represents a moderately socialistic position, as well as Soka University.

Vajrayana: Tibetan Buddhism. Tibetan Mahayana Buddhism assumed a very distinctive form. Its adherents like to think of it as a third major division, *vajrayana,* the "diamond vehicle."[9] Nevertheless, it shares the essential features of Mahayana. Whether it differs from other Mahayana schools more than Pure Land, Zen and Nichiren differ from each other is difficult to say. Tibetan Buddhism is also known as Lamaism, named for the lama, the Tibetan monk.

The essence of Tibetan Buddhism is not easy to pin down. Scholars point to its sublime philosophy and meditative practice, some of which has been likened to modern Western psychoanalysis. Common people emphasize the magical practices that are employed around the

In the picturesque hills of southern Indiana, just outside of Bloomington, there is this *chorten,* a memorial to Tibetan Buddhists who have died under persecution.

clock to control evil spirits. This difference between the religion of the elite and the uneducated is stark, yet the two coexist peacefully in one multilayered culture.

Tibetan Buddhism is the product of three convergent streams of religious influences: Bön, tantrism and Mahayana Buddhism. Bön is the pre-Buddhist animistic religion of

Tibet. Not much is known about this religion, but it can be safely inferred that present Tibetan Buddhism incorporated many magical practices from it. Apparently it was a very demanding religion that was based on the need to appease threatening evil forces. Its practice may have included rites of immolation and human sacrifice.

Tantrism is an Indian philosophy of male-female complementarity. The Shaktite school of Hinduism, which emphasizes the release of spiritual force as the male and female principles are conjoined, gave rise to the philosophy of tantrism. Tantrism also influenced the development of Buddhism, including the emergence of Tibetan Buddhism. It had its most specific application in the idea that the Buddhas, Bodhisattvas and other gods were all endowed with female consorts. Philosophically this move emphasized the idea of unity existing in the complementarity of opposites.

When Buddhism came to Tibet, the main beliefs, including the Buddhas and Bodhisattvas as well as the quest for nirvana, were adapted to the new context. Buddhism had a hard time gaining a solid foothold in Tibet and did not became established until the eighth century A.D. Eventually, however, it became the state religion and spread outward in its Tibetan form to Mongolia and China.

Gautama Buddha (Sakyamuni), along with the other Manushi Buddhas, plays a very minor role in Tibetan Buddhism. Primary attention is focused on the Dhyani Buddhas. One of those, Vairocana, is the manifestation of the primeval Buddha (the Adi-Buddha, known as Varjasattva). Vairocana in turn gave rise to the Buddhas of the four corners of the universe, one of whom is Amithaba, the Buddha of the west—the Buddha of the Pure Land schools.[10] Out of these five Dhyani Buddhas arose the two main Bodhisattvas, Maitreya and Avalokitesvara, the latter of whom is the spiritual father of Sakyamuni.

All of these spiritual beings have female counterparts. Most notable in this group is Avalokitesvara's consort, Tara, who subsequently received recognition as a goddess in her own right outside Tibet. Tara's influence waned when Avalokitesvara changed himself into a female being in China (Guanyin) and Japan (Kannon).

The philosophical, meditative side of Tibetan Buddhism strives to attain nirvana through removing all impurities from the person. It is thought that mastering the spiritual forces within oneself subdues the spiritual forces of the universe, and vice versa. Thus the human being is a microcosm of the entire spiritual universe. Mastering the interconnections between these two realms moves a person toward nirvana. In the Tibetan context meditation has two aspects, the first of which is mastering one's passions through exercising them. The tantric masters hold that one cannot escape from one's passions. Some act out this principle in physical intercourse, but others view it only as a philosophical and psychological scheme. The only way to master passions is to exercise them and so learn to control them. Eventually the passions are mastered and subdued. Then, finally, they no longer stand in the way of spiritual progress.

The second aspect of meditation in the Tibetan tradition is gradual merging with a deity. The meditator concentrates totally on the compassion of the Buddha or Bodhisattva. As he allows the spiritual power of the deity to take over, the meditator slowly experiences the escape of the negative forces (pictured as demons) that have inhabited him. As he is increasingly purified, his identity merges with that of the deity until he finally enters a purely spiritual state. The practitioner attains enlightenment when he recognizes that all realities, including his own life, the deities and the evil spirits, are projections of himself and thus are subject to his own control.[11]

The mantra, the chanting of powerful words, is an aid to this form of meditation. The most famous Tibetan mantra is *om mani padme hum,* literally, "om, the jewel is in the lotus, hum." *Om* is, of course, the ancient Hindu phrase expressing the All; *hum* is a variation thereof. Which jewel is in which lotus is a matter of great scholarly debate.

Various interpretations hold that it refers to (1) Avalokitesvara's supremacy, (2) the perfect positioning of the mind in nirvana, (3) a form of tantric sexual symbolism, (4) the location of Mount Neru (a holy mountain at the center of the universe), (5) all of the above or (6) nothing. In keeping with our understanding that the practice of ritual usually precedes its literal meaning (as stated in chapter one), the correct interpretation is probably 5 or 6.

Tibetan Buddhism developed the idea of written chants. Mantras are written on flags fluttering in the breeze, on water wheels and on the ever-present hand-held prayer wheels. The latter are cylinders that rotate around a handle as axis. A weighted string is attached to the top of the cylinder and propels the cylinder into rotation each time the hand is flicked a little. Inside the cylinder is a paper bearing a written mantra. For each clockwise rotation, the mantra is consid-

Buddha in a Burmese temple. The right hand pointing to the earth carries a dual meaning: calling on the earth to witness to his enlightenment and representing his rootedness and stability.

ered to be recited. It is important not to move the cylinder counterclockwise accidentally, for then the recitations are undone.

A mandala is a cosmic diagram. Most religious cultures in the world incorporate such designs. The word literally means "circle." At a minimum a mandala consists of a circle or a disk with a design on it that indicates the subdivision of the universe, usually into four parts. Examples of mandalas in the technical sense include the yin-yang symbol of Chinese religion (as depicted on the South Korean flag), the Celtic cross, the Buddhist eight-spoked wheel and the Nazi swastika. In Tibet, the mandala became a highly elaborate diagram of the cosmos. It is thought that gaining spiritual control over the mandala helps gain control over the forces of the universe. Conversely, a person progressing toward enlightenment is encouraged to express this experience through the depiction of a mandala.

Mudra refers to hand position. The position of the hands of the Buddha in various representations carries important meaning. Many schools of meditation emphasize mudras as an aspect of successful spiritual attainment. This idea received particularly attention in Tibet.

Tibetan Buddhism has accumulated many writings, but none has become as famous in the West as the so-called Tibetan Book of the Dead.[12] This book consists of a three-part recitation to be made on behalf of someone who has died for up to forty-nine days after the death. The first part, appropriate to the first four days after death, directs the deceased to the bright white light he or she is seeing. The deceased who recognizes the light as the projection of his or her life force attains nirvana. The second part, which is geared to the next two weeks, directs the deceased to work through all of the images accumulated by his or her karma. In a colorful mandala of lights the deceased sees deities in their benign and wrathful attitudes; again the key is for the departed to master these images as projections derived from his or her karmic experiences. Upon this realization, the person can proceed to eternal bliss. The third part, however, prepares the many unenlightened souls for the next rebirth. Even though it is still possible to escape samsara (the cycle of reincarnations) at the last moment, during this stage the soul is prepared for its next round of experiences in the world. After forty-nine days it is believed that the person has assumed his or her identity in a new incarnation. The Tibetan Book of the Dead is a good summary of Tibetan thought. Even though spiritual forces and experiences are real, the key to salvation lies in recognizing them as real projections.

Like Theravada, Tibetan Buddhism focuses on monks, called lamas. The role of the laypeople is to support the monks. Though theoretically the laity can attain enlightenment, the lamas have the greatest chances. The word *lama* itself means "a superior person." Laypeople generally focus on trying to cope with magic ritual properly so that they may have a better incarnation.

It has been estimated that at one time a fifth of the population of Tibet consisted of lamas. There are several orders and numerous suborders. Two of the more prominent ones are the Red Hats and the Yellow Hats, which go back to the original Buddhist incursion into Tibet. The Red Hats tend to take a literal view of tantric symbolism, and they hold to hereditary leadership positions. The most famous Tibetan order, the

Yellow Hats (Gelugpa), is headed by the Dalai Lama. This order believes in purity of practice and celibacy for lamas.

The first official Dalai Lama lived in the fifteenth century A.D. and is supposed to have reincarnated as the next Dalai Lama each time he died. The term *Dalai Lama* was originally bestowed as an honorific on the third one of the line (retroactive to his two predecessors) by a Mongol ruler. Its meaning is "the lama whose wisdom is as great as the ocean." The fifth Dalai Lama discovered by way of some ancient texts that he and his predecessors were the incarnation of Avalokitesvara.

When a Dalai Lama dies, a nationwide search is undertaken to find his reincarnation. The search may take years. In order to be recognized as the new Dalai Lama, a child must have been born exactly forty-nine days after the death of the preceding one, must bear certain physical characteristics and must show an immediate affinity toward objects that belonged to the previous Dalai Lama.

The Dalai Lama as of this writing, Tenzen Gyatso, is the fourteenth officeholder. When the Chinese Communists took over Tibet in 1959, he had to flee to northern India. Since then he has continued guiding the faithful of his religion as well as speaking on behalf of worldwide peace and tolerance.

There were factions in Tibet that opposed the Dalai Lama before the Chinese takeover. One such group in earlier times was headed by the Panchen Lama ("great scholar"), who is considered the incarnation of Amitabha (thus making him spiritually superior to the Dalai Lama). When the Chinese took over Tibet, they installed the Panchen Lama as puppet head of Tibet, but they removed him when the existing officeholder refused to denounce the Dalai Lama. As of this writing, theoretically the practice of Tibetan

The "Thousand Lights" Temple in Singapore boasts of a piece of the tree under which Gautama found enlightenment.

Buddhism has been permitted once again. However, the Communists are maintaining a campaign of suppression through propaganda and economic control. The brother of the Dalai Lama, who for many years was a professor of Tibetan language at Indiana University, was instrumental in erecting a *chorten* (traditionally a funerary monument) in a parklike setting just outside Bloomington, Indiana, in commemoration of the many

Tibetans who have died from persecution over the last fifty years.

Shingon. Tibetan Buddhism spread eastward and made itself particularly at home in Mongolia, thanks to the conversion of Kublai Khan to this form of Buddhism. Removed from its Tibetan soil, it lost some of the most flamboyant aspects of lamaism. Under the influence of some of the same factors that eventually gave rise to Tendai, it was streamlined by the addition of more conventional forms of Buddhism. The person who systematized this philosophy in China was Mizu. He in turn inspired the Japanese Kobo Daishi (Kukai), who is credited with being the founder of the Shingon school. The Japanese word *shingon* is the equivalent of the Sanskrit *mantra*. Thus Shingon is the "school of the powerful word." In the Chinese context it is known as *Chenyen*.

Shingon centers on the worship of the Dhyani Buddha, Vairocana, who is considered to be the cosmic embodiment of Buddha nature. Vairocana is believed to have revealed mystical teachings that are not to be written down; they must be transmitted orally from master to disciple. These techniques come under the general heading of magic practices. Faithfully following these instructions enables one to receive enlightenment. As a fringe benefit, the same magic also helps smooth the way in this life.

Shingon follows its Vajrayana heritage by producing many of the same aids to practice and meditation: the recitation of mantras, the employment of mudras and the representation of the cosmos in mandalas. Shingon has had many followers who were attracted by the mysteriousness of the rituals. In Japan, Shingon combined with the indigenous Shinto (see chapter eleven) to form the Ryobu synthesis, which makes it possible for someone to practice Buddhism and Shinto at the same time. For example, in Ryobu the Japanese sun goddess, Amaterasu, is equated with Vairocana; thus to worship one is to worship the other as well.

General Buddhist Practices

This description of the many schools of Buddhism shows that it is virtually impossible to make generalizations concerning Buddhist beliefs and practices. Food, clothing and rites of passage depend not only on the particular school one adheres to but also on one's geographical location.

For instance, in theory the Theravada Buddhism of Sri Lanka is much like that of Thailand; in practice they are very different. Sri Lankan temples are beautiful, but they are relatively plain. Gentle curves predominate in the structures (such as the roofs) and the images. Individual lay worship consists of making offerings, prostrating oneself before the Buddha and personal meditation.

In contrast, a Thai temple is extremely ornate. Pointed forms such as steep, gabled roofs and the flamelike tip of Buddha's head are everywhere in evidence. There are intricate gold and jade decorations and a proliferation of statues, not only of Buddha but also of some Hindu gods such as Brahma. Individual lay worship includes the usual veneration of Buddha, but it also includes further ritual practices. During open hours at a Thai temple, one of the bikhus functions in a priestlike capacity. As people come to receive blessings, they kneel prostrate before the bikhu, who is enthroned on a high seat and sprinkles the worshiper with holy water while quietly chanting lines from sutras. Thai believers also like to have good-luck ornaments blessed in this way; particularly auspicious is the elephant that graces many a Thai automobile. Let this example suffice for illustrating how different practices become popular, even in the same tradition. Throughout the history of its development, Buddhism has been nothing if not adaptable.

The life cycle. Buddhist rites of passage are well illustrated in Thai practices.[13] Since this religious culture falls into the Theravada rubric, monkhood is central. We already indicated that temporary monkhood is a rite of passage of adolescence. Monks who leave the order after attaining a certain amount of merit continue to hold respected places in the society. They are responsible for the parts of the life cycle that address physical life: pregnancy, birth and marriage. The more critical experiences of ordination and death are handled by the monks.

Pregnancy and birth rituals express local culture and custom. The Buddhist stamp impresses itself on ordination as a rite of passage. At some point in his young life, preferably during the summer, each boy is expected to become a monk. The ceremony reenacts the story of Prince Siddhartha, with the boy initially dressing in a white robe and then reenacting the renunciation of Gautama by shaving his head and donning a yellow robe. In the Thai version of this rite (which is similar throughout Theravada), before the ordination the boy undergoes the ceremony of *sukhwan,* in which he is

Façade of a Burmese temple. The snakelike *naga* decorations are intended to dispel evil spirits.

tied with a string to a pyramid of offerings that harnesses the life forces as a channel to the energy of Buddha. (In fact, another typical feature of a Thai Buddhist temple is the presence of strings establishing a flow of spiritual current between the central Buddha image, other parts of the temple and the worshiper.) At the ordination, which is valid if five bikhus are present, the parents and a girlfriend of the candidate send him off to the temporary life of a monk with the requisite equipment: two yellow robes, an umbrella (against the sun's burning his shaved head), a begging bowl for food, sandals, a lamp, a razor, a spitting bowl and a pillow (from the girl). Young men commit themselves to the permanent monkhood in the same ceremony, but subsequent higher stages of ordination await them.

The marriage ceremony focuses on establishing the couple in the life force. A sukhwan ceremony is carried out once again with offering pyramid and string. The couple transfers the life force (khwan, which seems to be a variation of the mana idea) to each other amid offerings of flowers and admonitions addressed to them. In this particular culture, the marriage pattern begins matrilocally—that is, the groom goes to live in the bride's family's house until several children are born.

Funerals consist of cremations. As is necessary in a Buddhist rite, the ceremony reflects the different options that await the deceased. Preparations are made for the worship of Buddha in heaven as well as for subsequent incarnations. Heaven is considered a favorable intermediate existence prior to the next incarnation; for common laypeople, for whom nirvana is not an option, heaven remains the best immediately attainable goal. Several days after the body has been burned, the remaining bones are buried in a pot.

Holidays and festivals. The Buddhist new year begins in the month of April. New Year's Day is an occasion of rejoicing and rededication. In addition to various temple ceremonies, a distinctive part of this holiday is that in Myanmar and Thailand young people dump water on each other as part of the revelry.

Buddha's birthday is an important occasion; it is a national holiday in some Theravada countries. Monks receive special attention, and temples hold lengthy services in which the story of Gautama Buddha is recounted. In Southeast Asia this day is observed during the last full moon of May; in Japan and China, on April 8.

Most Buddhist cultures observe a day of the dead (which, incidentally, is not confined to Buddhism). This occasion, known in the Chinese context as Hungry Ghost Festival, may last several days. Souls of ancestors that were not properly cared for or souls that are in an uncomfortable state between incarnations are thought to come back to earth to cause mischief. They need to be given food offerings and other forms of attention. Special ceremonies of offerings and of ancestor veneration are held during this period. The day of the dead festival illustrates how traditional patterns that have virtually nothing to do with the idealized form of the religion can retain a central place in common practice.

The rain retreat is an important time for Theravada monks during the monsoon season. Prior to this period, they are sent off by the laypeople and are supposed to spend two months or so in seclusion. The monks are welcomed back with a great ceremony. Laypeople earn merit by presenting the monks with gifts, particularly new robes, from which this celebration has received the name the Robe Ceremony.

■ *So You Meet a Buddhist . . .*

What You Might Expect

Buddhism includes an enormous range of diversity in belief and practice. Learning that someone is Buddhist does not tell you much about that person's beliefs. Knowing his or her geographical origin may or may not be helpful. For example, knowing that a Buddhist is from Sri Lanka, Myanmar or Thailand can be helpful because these countries are dominated by Theravada Buddhism. On the other hand, knowing that a Buddhist is from China or Japan leaves matters completely open. Asking Buddhists from China and Japan what school of Buddhism they adhere to may not be of much help either. Many people think of the Buddhism they practice as Buddhism—plain and simple. They are not necessarily attuned to the Western practice of differentiating one specific group from all others and believing that it is right and all others are false. For them, they are Buddhists, and that's all that they are concerned with. And what they actually practice may have very little to do with any "official" school of Buddhism. An important exception is the highly evangelistic group Soka Gakkai (Nichiren Shoshu). But they also refer to their belief system as Buddhist first and foremost.

An ordinary Buddhist may not know —or care—about the four noble truths or nirvana, let alone anything as esoteric as differentiations among the various schools. In a sense the subject matter of this chapter represents an enormous paradox. On the one hand, understanding the beliefs of a particular Buddhist requires being acquainted with his or her heritage and the tradition of that particular school. On the other hand, that person may not be able to identify the historical source of that material but may simply accept the tradition as "Buddhist" or "common sense."

Maitreya, the Buddha of the coming age, is usually depicted as the epitome of good-naturedness and prosperity.

What unites Buddhists is not specific belief or practice but a twofold orientation toward existence. First, there is a fundamental negative attitude toward life. All the schools (Theravada, Tendai, Pure Land, Zen, Vajrayana, Shingon) begin with a pessimistic approach to ordinary existence. Life, lived on the level of the common, unenlightened individual, is frustrating. But then all religions (in fact, all people who have thought much about life) recognize the frustrations in life and are looking for some way out, whether it be a technique, an attitude or the hope of a better world to come. What distinguishes the Buddhist understanding is that existence itself is the problem with life. As long as there is existence at all, there is suffering (the first noble truth).

The second point of common orientation is that Buddha, no matter how conceived, provides a solution to the frustrations of life. Each school of Buddhism furnishes some guidance on how to overcome the meaninglessness of life (in many cases by escaping from it), and this direction is provided in the name of a Buddha figure. Thus, on a very minimal level, what all Buddhists have in common is a recognition of (the/a) Buddha as the solution to life's dilemma.

Buddhists coming from the more traditional schools may be vegetarian or may limit their animal protein to fish. For laypeople, Buddhism may be the umbrella for a very conservative moral code. The veneration of ancestors is an important aspect of family life. Even though honoring the departed is not a central tenet of any of the major schools of Buddhism, it is part of the instructions to the laity in all of them. The common believer carries out the ancestor practices of his or her culture and believes that they are a very crucial part of Buddhism.

Relating the Gospel
New Testament Christianity provides a clear contrast to Buddhist attitudes. As we have seen, the history of Buddhism is a history of religious and philosophical speculation. The teachings of the historical Gautama (themselves a form of Indian speculative philosophy) became overlaid with increasing levels of divine beings, metaphysics, intuitions, rituals and more speculations. In contrast, Christianity—though enjoying its own history of speculation and complexity—begins with a set of bedrock data that provide the origin of the religion and control what becomes a part of it.

Second Peter 1:16 makes the contrast crystal-clear. In distinction to the philosophical myths of early Gnosticism (itself a movement of speculative philosophy), Christianity is based on some factual events that were witnessed by the disciples. "For we did not follow cleverly devised myths when we made known to you the power and coming of our Lord Jesus Christ, but we were eyewitnesses of his majesty" (RSV). Thus Christianity comes with a set of core events (the historical Christ, his life, death, resurrection and so on) that provide the backbone of its beliefs.

Thus, in response to Buddhism, the Christian can point to the factual grounding of Christianity in the context of first-century history. There is nothing easy about this strategy. For one thing, Buddhists may feel that a religion based on historical facts is inferior to one that originates in pure thought. For another, the exclusive claims of Christ, particularly the self-focused ones that begin with "I am . . . ," may evoke repugnance in someone brought up within the soft logic of many Buddhist traditions. Before Buddhists can accept the truth of Christian history, they may have to be convinced that history matters.

The greatest opportunity for Christians to establish a communication bridge with Buddhists may lie in the ambivalence of Buddhism itself. We have taken a quick look at some of the schools of Buddhism and their ongoing attempts at redefinition. For laypeople most specifically, Buddhism has never provided a clear-cut answer to the questions of life and salvation. To put the matter forcefully: *for the common believer, Buddhism has always had relevance in direct proportion to how well it has accommodated itself to prevailing folk beliefs and practices.*

Whereas Buddhist sages see themselves on the way to the personal extinction of nirvana, laypersons pick up the pieces of their lives in hopes of good fortune and a better incarnation. No wonder that on the lay level, the history of Buddhism is a history of syncretism!

The Christian gospel redefines the issues, which makes for a difficult task of communication. Instead of karma and reincarnation, it speaks of sin and redemption; instead of various Buddhist deities, it focuses on a personal God who has revealed himself in history. However, the Christian message also provides a level of assurance, for both this life and eternity, that Buddhism cannot provide. The focus shifts from denying the meaning of life to finding meaning in a life with Jesus Christ.

Let me mention a few examples of this contrast. Jodo-shin-shu, the Japanese school of Pure Land, seems to have a doctrine of grace. Amida Buddha grants entry into the western paradise to anyone seeking refuge in him. But note how this differs from the Christian understanding

The tall cabinet at the front of a Nichiren Shoshu temple contains the gohonzon on which the daimoku is inscribed.

of God's grace. First of all, although legends have accrued in regard to Amitabha's previous incarnations, the fact remains that he is not a historical person in any meaningful sense of the term. Thus this promise of salvation is based on nothing more than empty speculation. Monks such as Honen and Shinran believe this teaching, but it has no basis in any data that can be investigated. In contrast, the Christian gospel is based on the historical person of Christ. His death on the cross assured our eternal life because he provided proof of it with his physical resurrection from the dead.

The Lotus Sutra contains a story that provides an interesting contrast to the parable of the prodigal son in Christ's teaching (Lk 15:11-32) as well as to Pure Land doctrine. In the sutra, the Buddha tells of a poor and destitute son returning to his wealthy father. Although the father loves his son very much and wants to give him his wealth, he realizes that the son is not yet ready and needs to be prepared for his glorious state. Thus the father first sends the son to work in the stable and has him earn his inheritance. The father disguises himself and works alongside the son, but the son must prove himself worthy.[14] The New Testament parable, on the other hand, has the father coming out and meeting the son to receive him before the son has even set foot in the house. Rather than making the son earn anything, the father provides him with shoes, a ring and a feast. Surely the Lotus Sutra makes an important point insofar as the fallen human condition cannot be ignored, but—in contrast to the whimsy of Pure Land belief—in Christianity human sinfulness is not overlooked. It is expiated through Christ's atoning death.

One final contrast may be brought up with regard to Zen Buddhism. Zen is an entertaining religion to study, full of clever puzzles and startling stories. Further, there seems to be something wholesome about the end goal of Zen—to accept life as it is without overanalyzing it. After all, the apostle Paul himself said, "I have learned, in whatever state I am, to be content" (Phil 4:11 RSV). However, if this acceptance is based on nothing other than an immediate intuition, it is really nothing more than a nihilistic resignation to give up and let life be whatever it wants to be. And life can be very disturbing. At the risk of being overly simplistic, we could say that Zen has a great method of capturing the "is-ness" of life, but it must capitulate before life's "if-ness." The point is that life comes with many problems and demands that cannot be solved simply by an attitude of resignation. Accepting the world and our place in it requires some kind of assurance that the world is meaningful and coherent. Christianity shows us that in the final analysis we are in the competent hands of God, the Creator and Redeemer. Thus we are secure and life continues to be meaningful even when our "third eye" has gone dark.

In summary, Christianity counters Buddhist speculation with a story in which we can find ourselves as redeemed creatures. This story is based on historical reality and provides the same access to salvation for all people.

Mastering the Material
When you have finished studying this chapter, you should be able to
  1. tell the story of the life of Gautama Buddha;
  2. summarize the main teachings of the Buddha, including his view of reality, the

four noble truths, the eightfold path and the ten precepts;

   3. describe the main characteristics of Theravada Buddhism;

   4. point out the important ways in which Theravada and Mahayana are distinct from each other and state the main distinctives of Mahayana;

   5. state the contribution of the Tendai school;

   6. summarize the claims of Jodo-shin-shu and why it appeals to so many people;

   7. explain the essence of Zen (with words!), its teachings and techniques;

   8. outline the contribution of Nichiren Shoshu and the teachings and practice associated with its contemporary version, Soka Gakkai;

   9. recount the distinctives of Vajrayana Tibetan Buddhism, including its constituent parts, nature and aids of meditations, and the role of the Dalai Lama;

   10. point out the origin and subsequent fate of the Shingon school;

   11. recognize the importance of ordination as a rite of passage in Theravada and name three important Buddhist holidays.

Term Paper Ideas

   1. Discover what can be known about the historical Buddha. To what extent do the legends reflect historical facts?

   2. Undertake a philosophical study of some concept of Buddhism, for example, the self, karma, reality, logic and so on.

   3. Trace the artistic depictions of Buddha from earliest times to contemporary cultures.

   4. Show how a Theravada version of Buddhism has become amalgamated with folk religion in one particular culture.

   5. Trace the history of the Pure Land schools in their various versions.

   6. Describe in detail one school, technique or cultural manifestation of Zen Buddhism.

   7. Compile a history of one phase or one order of Tibetan Buddhism.

   8. Inventory the history, beliefs and influence of various major schools of Buddhism at home in Japan today.

   9. Do an in-depth "biography" of one Bodhisattva or Buddha other than Sakyamuni. Include previous incarnations and cultural differentiations.

   10. Interview one Christian worker or study the literature of one Christian organization ministering in a Buddhist setting; compile everything you learn concerning Christian mission strategy to Buddhists.

Core Bibliography

Burtt, E. A., ed. *The Teachings of the Compassionate Buddha*. New York: New American Library, 1955.

Conze, Edward. *Buddhist Scriptures*. New York: Penguin, 1959.

Gard, Richard A., ed. *Buddhism*. New York: Braziller, 1961.

Hopkins, Jeffrey, and Geshe Lhundup Sopa. *Practice and Theory of Tibetan Buddhism*. New York: Grove, 1976.

Lester, Robert C. *Buddhism: The Path to Nirvana*. San Francisco: Harper & Row, 1987.

Robinson, Richard H., and Willard L. Johnson. *The Buddhist Religion*. Belmont, Calif.: Wadsworth, 1982.

Suzuki, D. T. *Zen Buddhism*. Edited by William Barrett. Garden City, N.J.: Doubleday, 1956.

Chapter 9

Three Offshoot Religions
Jainism, Sikhism & Baha'i

The three religions discussed in this chapter—Jainism, Sikhism and Baha'i—have little in common. Although they are brought together for discussion in one chapter, they are considered separately. Although each religion has relatively few adherents, each has made important contributions to the world and will probably continue to do so.

Each of these three religions arose as an offshoot of an established religion. We will consider them in chronological order: Jainism, which arose at the same time as Vedanta and Buddhism; Sikhism, which arose in the sixteenth century as an attempt to blend Hinduism and Islam; and Baha'i, which is a modern offshoot of Shi'ite Islam but has left its roots far behind.

Hinduism and Buddhism spawned many different schools of thought and worship. Two further movements went on to establish themselves as religions in their own right: Jainism and Sikhism. Both maintained much of their Hindu heritage, but like Buddhism, they impugned the Vedas and the caste system and are thus not accepted as "official" Hindu schools. Both of these religions have existed as minorities in India since their inception; however, they took divergent paths in arriving at the positions they finally came to occupy in their respective societies. Jainism became associated with the upper class of Indian society, while Sikhism developed into a powerful military subculture. Today both religions have spread around the world.

Jainism

Estimated Membership
Worldwide: 4,886,000
North America: 4,000

Life of Mahavira. The life of the founder of Jainism, Mahavira,[1] uncannily resembles the early part of Gautama Buddha's life. In fact, some scholars suspect a mutual influence between the two legends.[2] Mahavira was born Nataputta Vardhamana. The appellation *Mahavira* is actually an honorific title meaning "great man," a fairly understated term considering the magnitude of titles usually bestowed on religious founders. Like Gautama, Mahavira grew up in a noble household of the Kshatrya caste. In the course of time he acquired a wife and a daughter. Around thirty years of age, however, he became disillusioned with the life of luxury and wealth. He forsook

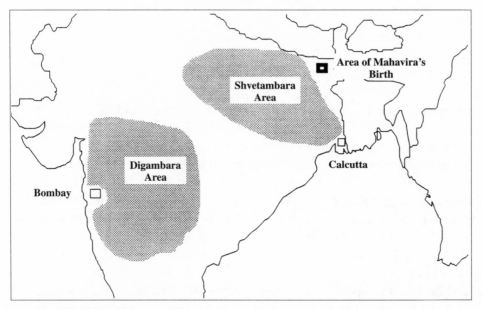

Map 9.1. Jain origins

everything for an existence of ascetic self-abnegation. According to the legend, he waited until his parents died and then set out to seek enlightenment. Whereas Gautama eventually discovered the "middle way" and abandoned his radically austere practices, Mahavira never departed from the extreme asceticism to which he subjected himself.

Mahavira probably wore no clothes (his nakedness is still disputed by Jains). He sought no shelter and exposed himself to all the elements of weather. Many of his practices came out of his commitment to avoid harming any living being, whether animal or plant. He wore a veil over his mouth and nose to avoid accidentally inhaling any insects but allowed them to feast on his body. He always swept the path before him with a soft broom lest he crush any living thing underfoot. Mahavira ate as sparingly as possible and limited himself to vegetarian food that was destined to be thrown out. That way he would not be the direct occasion of taking any living being's life. Mahavira believed that through his practices he was in the process of liberating his soul.

According to the legend, in the thirteenth year of his ascetic practice, Mahavira attained the goal for which he was striving. This state of enlightenment is described as a kind of omniscience called *kaivalya*. He knew and understood the universe and thereby mastered the path of liberation. From this point on he was a *jina*, a "conqueror"; the name Jainism thus literally means "those who follow the conqueror." Mahavira accu-

Colonnade outside of a Jain temple in Nairobi, Kenya.

mulated a large number of followers, possibly due to the fact that his fellow members of the Kshatrya caste appreciated any teaching that would insulate them from the Brahmin sphere of influence. Mahavira's most devoted followers sought to emulate his way of life so that they could also attain spiritual release for their souls. Thus Jainism, like Buddhism, began with people who were able to undertake the necessary renunciation and retreat to the forest as monks.

Mahavira's teaching. At the heart of Mahavira's message is a cosmology that includes many distinct souls. Thus Jainism does not believe in one universal world soul (it is not a monism [belief in only one ultimate reality], as are Vedanta or Buddhism). Jainism recognizes many beings, each with its own eternal identity and each with its distinct experience. All of these individual souls are considered *jiva*, which means literally "life" or "soul."[3] All living entities are included on the list of *jiva* souls, from blades of grass to human beings to the gods. There is also ajiva, "nonlife," such as rocks, dirt and dust.

Left entirely to themselves, all the souls in the universe would float like balloons up to the top of the human-shaped universe (*isatpragbhara*) and exist there forever in pure bliss, which is referred to as nirvana, as in Hinduism and Buddhism. Unfortunately, the souls have become contaminated. Jainism does not have a consistent explanation of how and why this defilement originally occurred; the religion begins with the fact of this contamination. Adhering to all the many jivas are varying amounts of ajiva, holding the "balloons" on lower levels by weighing them down. This ajiva has to be purged in order for the jivas to rise.

Karma is responsible for the accumulation of this dead matter on the living soul. In fact, the little chunks of ajiva are known as karma matter. Thus in Jainism karma has a physical manifestation. Violating the rules of life adds karma matter. Living a pure life with as little direct action as possible removes karma matter. The amount of karma matter accumulated or removed in one lifetime determines the level of rebirth for that particular soul in the next life. One soul may have only a sprinkling of ajiva dust on it, while another may be covered with large clumps of heavy karma matter. The former may return as a holy man on the verge of redemption; the latter may have to endure many more lives as plants or worms before it is sufficiently purified.

Jain monks. Jain monks take many different vows and are subject to a large number of regulations. But five vows in particular—*ahimsa*, truth telling, abstaining from theft, conquering sexual desire and detachment—are essential. The first four are identical to the Buddhist ones, though they are interpreted far more rigorously. The first vow, ahimsa, more than any other aspect of the religion, has become the hallmark of Jainism. Jains believe that killing anything—person, animal or plant—loads up the soul with karma matter. A Jain monk must take every possible precaution to avoid hurting any living being. Ahimsa has influenced other aspects of Indian thought also. For example, it was an integral element in the teaching of Mahatma Gandhi.

In its simplest form, the second vow, truth telling, can be understood as a commandment not to lie. However, in Jain philosophy it became interpreted as a vow never to mislead anyone by speech. Thus it includes a prohibition against loose, frivolous talk or any other unguarded statements.

The commitment to stay as close as possible to the truth led to the development of a unique approach to logic in Jainism. Jain teachers held that what one accepts as true always depends on one's perspective. Seen from one angle something may be true, whereas seen from another viewpoint, it may be false. Hence they suggested that in formal assertions all statements should be modified by the word *syadvada*, which means "maybe" or "somehow." As long as one modifies one's assertions with *syadvada*, the chances of accidentally saying something false are greatly reduced. "Maybe" something exists, but then again "maybe" it does not exist.

It is sometimes argued that in this way Jainism attempts to construct a logic that supersedes the law of contradiction, since "maybe" opposites can both be true. But a little further thought shows that, to the contrary, the practice of qualifying all statements with *syadvada* is necessary precisely to avoid accidentally committing a contradiction. By expressing how limited our viewpoint can be, we do not run the risk of accidentally contradicting reality. The use of *syadvada* does not negate the law of noncontradiction. Instead it presupposes the law.

The obvious meaning of the third vow, abstaining from theft, is that the Jain monk does not steal. But the effect of this vow is much stronger. A Jain monk should never take anything that was not given, and then only insofar as the item is necessary for existence. In short, this vow prevents monks from owning property.

Besides prohibiting sexual intercourse, the fourth vow, conquering sexual desire, came to mean that the monks should suppress all carnal inclinations.

Just to make sure the message is clear, the fifth vow, detachment, is a sweeping prohibition of anything that the monk could allow himself to get attached to, including his family, his body, his personal identity or even his own name. Everything must be renounced for the sake of ultimate enlightenment.

Thus the Jain monk leads a solitary life of self-abnegation. Persistent practice eventually leads to the release of one's soul. The monk who attains this level is called an *arhat*, a "holy man." Those who have reached the highest stages of spirituality are expected to starve themselves to death while meditating under a tree.

There are several divisions within Jainism. The Digambara believe that salvation can only be reached by discarding all physical attachments, including clothes. Thus *Digambara* means "clad in the sky." The Shvetambara are those who are "clad in white"—although what they are clad in is not much more than a loincloth. Somewhat more substantial points of divergence between these two groups include differences in the Mahavira legend; the Digambara insist that

The front of a Jain temple contains a place of general worship, behind which is the sanctum that houses the Thirthankara representations. All worshipers may enter the sanctum, but only with purificatory preparations.

Mahavira went about naked. The Shvetambara accept an order of women as legitimate pursuers of salvation, and Digambara do not.

Provisions for laypeople. The survival of any monastic religion depends on the existence of a laity that has been given sufficient inducements to support the monks in their task. Jainism appealed to people who had no intention of becoming monks by providing a way out of the domination of the Brahmins and the caste system. Laypeople cannot attain liberation, but they can purge sufficient karma from their souls to achieve an incarnation in which the final goal is achieved.

Laypeople must observe softened versions of the five vows. Ahimsa becomes a prohibition against taking life *needlessly*. This rule effectively kept Jains out of agriculture, which implies the killing of life forms. Instead, they pursued commerce and banking with great success. To this day Jains have shown great aptitude for the various levels of trade.

No.	Vow	Laity	Monk
1	Ahimsa	vegetarian	no killing
2	truth-telling	no lying	*syadvada*
3	no theft	respect property	no property
4	continence	marital fidelity	no desires
5	detachment	abstain from greed	self-denial
6		limit travel	
7		limit things	
8		guard against avoidable evils	
9		specific times for meditation	
10		special periods of self-denial	
11		occasional days as monk	
12		alms in support of monks	

Table 9.1. Jain vows

The second vow enjoins simple truth telling, the third vow prohibits simple theft, the fourth commands marital fidelity and the fifth proscribes greed. Furthermore, Jains are exhorted to live simple and benevolent lives and to spend some short period of their lives in acts of austerity. These obligations are classified as seven more vows, making a total of twelve: (6) avoiding temptation by limiting travel, (7) limiting the number of items that are used on a daily basis, (8) guarding against avoidable evils, (9) reserving specific times for meditation, (10) imposing special periods of self-denial, (11) spending occasional days as monks, (12) giving alms in support of the monks. Table 9.1 summarizes Jain vows.

The problem encountered by Theravada Buddhism also rears its head in connection with Jainism. Where does the believer find the spiritual power needed to get through life successfully? Who is there to help in the crises of life? Jainism is not about the gods. Jains believe that the gods exist but play no role in the quest for enlightenment. Nevertheless, in deference to the laity, Jains reincorporated prevailing Hindu deities into their personal piety. This happened early in the development of Jainism. Today's Jains have no problem worshiping Hindu gods and goddesses as needed. Jainism also developed its own collection of spiritual beings.

The Tirthankaras. According to Jain thought, Mahavira was not the only person to attain enlightenment and become a teacher for the world. There were twenty-three similar beings before him who carried out the same task. These persons, all of whom were human beings at one time, are called Tirthankaras, which literally means "ford finders"—that is, they find the way to cross over into enlightenment. In Jainism these twenty-four Tirthankaras perform the role of divinities. They are not gods, but they have superior powers that they make available to their worshipers on a cosmic basis (compare Buddhas and Bodhisattvas). For individual minor petitions, however, the people are directed to deities.

No.	Name	Height	Life span	Skin color	Symbol
1	Rishaba	500 bowshots	8,400,000 purva	golden yellow	bull
2	Ajita	450 bowshots	7,200,000 purva	yellow	elephant
3	Sambhava	400 bowshots	6,000,000 purva	golden yellow	horse
4	Abhinandana	350 bowshots	5,000,000 purva	golden yellow	monkey
5	Sumati	300 bowshots	4,000,000 purva	golden yellow	curlew
6	Padmaprabha	280 bowshots	3,000,000 purva	red	red lotus
7	Suparshva	300 bowshots	2,000,000 purva	green	swastika
8	Chandraprabha	150 bowshots	1,000,000 purva	white	crescent (moon)
9	Subidhi (Shvet) Pushpadanta (Dig)	100 bowshots	200,000 purva	white	crocodile crab
10	Shitala	90 bowshots	100,000 purva	golden yellow	swastika fig tree
11	Shreyamsa	80 bowshots	8,400,000 years	golden yellow	rhinoceros eagle
12	Vasupujya	72 bowshots	7,200,000 years	red	buffalo
13	Vimala	60 bowshots	6,000,000 years	golden yellow	boar
14	Ananta	50 bowshots	3,000,000 years	golden yellow	bear
15	Dharma	45 bowshots	1,000,000 years	golden yellow	thunder bolt
16	Shanti	40 bowshots	100,000 years	golden yellow	deer
17	Kuntha	35 bowshots	95,000 years	golden yellow	goat
18	Ara	30 bowshots	84,000 years	golden yellow	fish
19	Malli (Shvet: female)	25 bowshots	55,000 years	golden blue	water jar
20	Munisuvrata	20 bowshots	30,000 years	dark	tortoise
21	Nami	15 bowshots	10,000 years	golden yellow	blue lotus
22	Nemi/Arishtanemi Krishna's cousin	10 bowshots	1,000 years	dark with red	conch
23	Parshva	9 cubits	100 years	dark blue	serpent
24	Mahavira	7 cubits	72 years	golden yellow	lion

Table 9.2. The twenty-four Tirthankaras

Think of the world as a point on the circumference of a rotating wheel, cycling endlessly between upward and downward motion. According to Jain cosmology, the world oscillates between an ascending time period, in which everything slowly improves, and a descending one, in which life gets increasingly worse. Jainism believes that the world is now in the descending phase. Eventually the cosmos will start improving. The twenty-four Tirthankaras have come during this descending era. All but Mahavira and his predecessor, Parshva, are mythological figures. Parshva lived in the ninth century B.C. and founded an ascetic order, although it is doubtful that his teaching dovetailed in many details with Mahavira's.

Jain worshipers.

According to Jain thought, this period of descent is composed of six ages: (1) Susama Susama, (2) Susama, (3) Susama Dusama, (4) Dusama Susama, (5) Dusama, (6) Dusama Dusama. The first two Tirthankaras came in the third period. The others, except for Mahavira, came in Dusama Susama. Dusama Dusama will be an age of abject ignorance, immorality and lack of spirituality. Table 9.2 lists the twenty-four Thirthankaras along with height, life span, skin color and symbol (a purva is an imaginary time period lasting 70,560,000,000,000 years).[4]

Are Jains expecting a messianic Tirthankara in the future? Once the universe begins cycling upward again, there will be twenty-four new Tirthankaras who will guide the world in its forward progress. These figures, about whom a full mythology exists in Jain lore already, are currently engaged in eliminating their karma so that they will be ready to take charge when the time comes.

Jain temple worship. Jain temples are distinguished by their beauty and intricacy. Whereas Hindu temples love to display many bright colors, Jain temples are usually white. The statues of the Tirthankaras are kept in a segregated area at the front of the temple. Whereas the main Hindu gods are relatively easy to distinguish from each other (for example, Brahma with four heads, Krishna with a flute, and so on), the Tirthankaras are almost identical. Most are carved from white alabaster and include little detail. Only a small symbol, sometimes a sign with the name, reveals which

Tirthankara is represented by the statue.

A Jain temple may contain implements called *aksata puja* for devotional design making. Kernels of rice are left out on low tables. In acts of worship, believers may form designs consisting of swastikas, three dots, a crescent and another dot at the top. The swastika is a common symbol in Eastern religions. In Jainism it represents the energy of the universe, with its four arms standing for the four types of souls: animals, *narks* (low spirits), *devs* (gods) and humans. The three dots stand for three paths toward enlightenment (studying the example of the Tirthankaras, knowledge and character). The crescent represents liberation, and the topmost dot indicates nirvana.

Toward the front of the main room, but separated from the place of the Tirthankaras by some columns, is an area for prayer. Jains carry out their devotions by reciting prayers and using various implements in the process: a duster, a mirror or lights. These actions symbolize purity.

The main act of worship consists of anointing or decorating the statues of the Tirthankaras. In order to enter the most sacred area, the worshiper must be wrapped in a veil that covers the face completely. When the personal service is over, a temple attendant (not a priest) wipes off the decorations.

■ *So You Meet a Jain . . .*

What You Might Expect

The Jains you meet may be hard to recognize, since they may call themselves Hindus. Being called Hindus is not insulting to them. They are accustomed to relating to people in a general way and do not expect people to be able to differentiate one Indian religion from another. Jains share Hindu deities and may even use Brahmin priests in their private (not temple) worship.

Jain laypeople demonstrate no particular interest in practicing the asceticism of the monks. A wide gulf exists between the religion of austerities, as exemplified by Mahavira, and the religion of rituals, as practiced by common people. They follow the prescribed obligations in the temple and at home. Few Jains seem to pursue spiritual quests. This lack of interest further distinguishes them from the monks.

The Jains' principles make themselves felt in general ways. Ahimsa bars the pursuit of agriculture. Laypeople are vegetarians. Their religious commitments clearly direct them toward pacifistic attitudes, although this belief has not spawned a prominent Jain peace movement to date. (Mahatma Gandhi claimed the principle of ahimsa, but not necessarily as stemming from the Jainist system.) Respect for life has, however, led Jains to construct animal hospitals.

The second vow, truth telling, has made the greatest impact on the position of Jains today. Because of their reputation for punctiliousness and honesty, Jains are trusted as bookkeepers and accountants. Although their own religious commitments barred them from working the land, Jains were soon able to establish themselves as successful entrepreneurs in commerce and finance in their own right. Today many Jains are leaders in the business world in India and in countries of Indian immigration, such as Kenya.

Relating the Gospel

At first glance, ahimsa seems to be an attractive concept, similar to the respect for life that is a part of biblical revelation. But there are two clear points of distinction between

Alabaster representations of three Thirthankaras.

Christian principles that manifest themselves in alleviating suffering and preserving life and the Jainist notion of the sacredness of life.

First, in Jainism the worth of life is absolute; in the Bible it is the gift of God and is under God's jurisdiction. Jains believe that there is nothing of higher value than life itself. The biblical belief places all of life in God's hands. God, as the Creator of life, can also direct people to take life. Thus we see God in the Old Testament directing the Hebrews to exterminate the Canaanites and instituting capital punishment as retribution for various crimes. The Old Testament mandates animal sacrifices, and the New Testament authorizes eating meat. Thus an absolute reverence for life that forbids ever taking any life could be seen as practically idolatrous because it usurps the absoluteness that belongs to God alone.

Second, by biblical standards, ahimsa devalues human life. Jainism recognizes an unbroken continuity between all life forms, from the lowest blade of grass to the Tirthankaras. In the final analysis they are all jiva on different levels of attainment. Although the intent of this system is enhanced appreciation of blades of grass, cockroaches and chickens, in the final analysis the effect goes in the opposite direction: a human being is worth no more than a blade of grass, a cockroach or a chicken. But in the biblical view human beings alone are created in the image of God, and they occupy a privileged position in the created order. Human beings are responsible to take care of the rest of creation, and they may not abuse other living beings. However, this mandate comes to humans as beings who are uniquely able to have a personal relationship with the Creator.[5]

A second Christian response to Jainism can focus on the burdensome nature of Jain beliefs. Like all other people, Jains do not necessarily think through the deeper implications of their faith. If they did so, however, they might realize that the outlook for them is pretty bleak. Even the most careful person cannot avoid harming various life forms. Existence as a layperson is likely to accrue more karma than it eliminates. In some ways, Jainism represents the extreme picture of a works-oriented religion with the concomitant lack of hope such a religion can entail. There is no savior, no intermediary and no concept of grace to shortcut the long process of purging one's karma.

Of course, Christianity cannot present itself as an easy way out of the karmic obligation arising from Jain cosmology. Jesus did not die to deliver people from reincarnation. Christians need to show that the problem with human existence is that people are alienated from their proper relationship with God, not that people have accumulated karma as a result of violating of certain principles. Human beings break such principles (for example, hurt other beings gratuitously, lie and so on) only because they have a deeper problem to begin with. Christians also need to show that Christ's death creates the possibility of a restored relationship with God. Alienation (sin, not karma) from God can be overcome by faith in Christ.

Sikhism

Estimated Membership
Worldwide: 19,161,000
North America: 490,000

Settings and precursors. Historically, Sikhism rose out of an attempt to create harmony between Islam and Hinduism by fusing them. However, Sikhs believe their religion is true in its own right, not as an attempt at compromise. Although it makes sense to a non-Sikh to study Sikhism in terms of its historical origins, Sikhs do not see things that way. They believe that they have new and original revelation.

In the sixteenth century A.D. India was ruled by Muslim emperors. The relationship between the Hindu population and the Muslim government was perpetually volatile. Addressing the tension from time to time were isolated voices pleading for mutual understanding. This was a time of great creativity within Hinduism, as various new Bhakti schools were introduced. Islam witnessed a resurgence of Sufi mysticism. Thus people in this era may have been more open than usual to new insights. One person calling for a renewed vital faith was the poet Kabir (1440-1518), whose father was a Muslim and whose mother was a Hindu. Kabir was a teacher in the Sant movement, a school of Vaishnavite Hinduism that preached the equality of all people to the point of disparaging the caste system. Kabir wrote that people of all religions should look beyond their differences to the greater realities of spirituality.

Nanak. Nanak (1469-1538), who is considered to be the founder of Sikhism, was born to a Hindu father and a Muslim mother. Reared as a Sant Hindu, Nanak came to realize that the true God transcends established religious distinctions. Legend tells us that at the age of thirty Nanak experienced a direct call from God that established his identity as a guru. The word *guru* in usual Indian usage simply refers to a spiritual

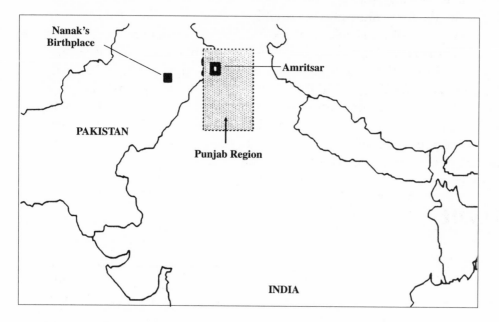

Map 9.2. Sikh origins

in Sikhism the guru is considered the very embodiment of God who teaches with divine infallibility.

"There is no Muslim, and there is no Hindu!" resounded Nanak's slogan. Nanak dressed in a combination of typical Hindu and Muslim garments. He traveled around the Punjab region of northeastern India, gathering disciples (sikhs), preaching and performing the occasional miracle. Nanak's piety was a unique blend of devotion and iconoclasm. He observed some Hindu acts of worship (for examle, bathing) and some Muslim acts (according to legend, visiting Mecca). On the other hand, he recognized and publicly ridiculed hypocrisy whenever he encountered it.

The story is told about Nanak (and Kabir) that at his death his followers argued about whether to dispose of his body according to Hindu custom (cremation) or Muslim custom (burial). His body was left overnight. The next day his followers found that it had miraculously vanished and had been replaced by a large pile of flowers.

Nanak's teaching. Most fundamentally, Nanak taught that there is only one God. He may be called by different names, but his identity is beyond the categorizations imposed on him by either Muslims or Hindus. Nanak referred to God simply as Sat Nam, the "true name," thus avoiding questions of personal identity. He also designated God as Ekankar, which is derived from the syllables *ek*, the one, undivided; *aum* or *om*—the mystical sound expressing God; and *kar*—the lord. Thus God is Ek-aum-kar, the one lord. Later Sikh literature referred to God as Wahi Guru—"hail to the guru!" Today's Sikhs, however, tend to use Ekankar as the most basic term for God.[6] Nanak's God is one. However, Nanak avoided the idea of a personal God, as in Islam or Judaism, as well as Hindu pantheism, which identifies God with all reality.

Nanak retained the Hindu notions of reincarnation and karma. A person undergoes rebirths in the world of maya until the experience of release. In this context, *maya* refers to the lesser, painful reality of mundane existence, not illusion. Devotion to God is essential for escaping the cycle of samsara. Thus Sikhism is sometimes classed among the Hindu Bhakti traditions in addition to its origins in the Sant movement. Devotion to God is not a matter of rituals or legalism. Nanak counseled his disciples to seek a more mystical experience with God, focusing particularly on chanting *nam* and various hymns. A soul that has become joined to God merges its light with the pure light of God at death. Thus the end result of Sikh salvation does not differ categorically from the Atman-Brahman merging in Hindu Vedanta.

The succession of gurus. Table 9.3 lists the ten gurus of Sikhism and highlights their contributions.

No.	Name	Dates	Notes
1	Nanak	1469-1538	founder
2	Angad	1538-1552	began collecting hymns
3	Amar Das	1552-1574	subdivisons; taxes
4	Ram Das	1574-1581	founded Amritsar
5	Arjan	1581-1606	martyred; Amritsar completed; collected Adi Granth
6	Har Gobind	1606-1645	founded Sikh army
7	Har Rai	1645-1661	
8	Har Kishan	1661-1664	
9	Tegh Bahad	1664-1675	martyred
10	Gobind Rai	1675-1708	established Khalsa; declared Granth as Guru

Table 9.3. Succession of gurus

Angad was favored by Nanak to succeed him (over Nanak's own sons), thereby establishing that guruship depended primarily on character and spirituality, not descent. This theme recurs several times in the line of succession. Angad composed hymns and added them to Nanak's hymns to form a collection.

Amar Das formalized the organization of Sikhs by establishing subdivisions and collecting a tax on behalf of the community. He also initiated the practice of pilgrimages to sacred places, particularly in conjunction with sacred wells.

Ram Das established the town that would eventually be known as Amritsar ("pool of nectar," referring to the nectar of immortality) and began digging out a large water basin at the site. The Mogul emperor at the time was Akbar, who was appreciative of Ram Das's spiritual qualifications. When he came to visit the guru, the emperor's entourage was scandalized that Ram Das had the emperor eat side by side with ordinary people in the communal kitchen (*langar*), but the emperor gladly complied. This episode exemplifies Akbar's goodwill and Ram Das's prestige. This incident laid the foundation for the emphasis on communal meals in subsequent Sikhism.

Sikh temple in Johor Baru, Malaysia.

Arjan continued to enjoy great honor and authority. But Akbar's son, Jahangir, objected to what he considered Arjan's blasphemy of Islam and had the guru tortured to death. He boiled Arjan in a large pot of water. At the last moment, he allowed Arjan to go free, and the guru died cooling his wounds in the river. Arjan made several major contributions. He finished the building projects begun by Ram Das at Amritsar. Arjan collected hymns that he had composed as well as those composed by his predecessors and joined them with the hymns and poetry of other holy men such as Kabir in a book called the Adi Granth, which became the holy scripture of Sikhism. Knowing that the pacifistic ways enjoined by the gurus would eventually become impossible to maintain, Arjan instructed Har Gobind, his son and successor, to embrace a more militaristic way of life.

Har Gobind, having replaced the guru's beads with a sword belt, mounted the throne holding two swords that symbolized political and spiritual authority. He established a bodyguard and a small army. Although his military adventures were not very successful (he was captured and then imprisoned for a while), Har Gobind managed to protect the continued physical existence of his community against increasing onslaughts.

Har Rai and Harkishan did not provide great innovations but were important in the process of solidifying the Sikh community as a religious and, more important, an increasingly political entity. Tegh Bahadur was the second guru to be martyred; he resisted the emperor Aurangzeb's demands that he convert to Islam and was decapitated.

Gobind Rai (1666-1708), the tenth guru, has become better known as Gobind Singh, from the military order of singhs that he established. Fed up with the persecution inflicted on his people, Gobind decided that the community could survive only by becoming completely militaristic. He decreed that his followers should become singhs, which means "lions," and he formed a special order, the Khalsa. Even though no one was forced to join the Khalsa, it was highly encouraged and many complied.

The Khalsa of singhs began when Gobind asked the people if anyone was willing to give his life in devotion to him. When someone consented, Gobind took him into his tent. The guru emerged a moment later, alone, carrying a sword dripping with blood. He asked for another volunteer and reenacted the procedure. This scenario was repeated three more times. Then the guru entered his tent and emerged with all five followers, who were alive. The textbook explanation is that the volunteers had been secluded alive in the tent and that Gobind used animal blood on his sword; devout Sikhs, however, insist that the guru killed the five men and then effected their resurrection.[7] He initiated the five followers by sprinkling them with "nectar" (water that had been used to wash the guru's feet) that had been stirred in an iron bowl with a dagger and by having them take a vow before God. Then they in turn initiated him.

The Khalsa was based on the philosophy that Sikh survival required a defiant attitude. Rather than hiding meekly, Sikhs were supposed to call attention to themselves and show their willingness to resist persecution. All male members of the Khalsa took the surname Singh ("lion"), and women were called Kaur ("princess"). The men dressed conspicuously, as prescribed with five *k*'s: *kesh,* long hair; *kangha,* a steel comb in the hair; *kach,* shorts; *kara,* a steel bracelet; and *kirpan,* a sword or a dagger worn on the side. Becoming a singh involved an initiation rite using water stirred with a dagger that was similar to the one undergone by the five original followers.

Gobind Singh decreed that he was the last of the human gurus. After he died, the holy book, the Adi Granth, would be the only guru. Gobind was assassinated by a Muslim henchman.

Subsequent history. By the time of Gobind Singh's death, the British were already in India, beginning the period of colonization that culminated in the raj—British rule over India. The Sikhs made indomitable soldiers, and after an uneasy start the British were able to recruit them as their best local forces in expanding their colonial rule. Thus the history of the Sikhs for three hundred years was the history of Sikh military prowess, though it would be a mistake to look at Sikhism from this political perspective exclusively. The British used the Sikhs not only as part of their military forces in India but also as bodyguards and police forces in other British colonies (for example, Hong Kong). Today they continue to carry out many such functions in India. Sikhs have been involved in violent incidents, both as victims and as perpetrators.

Current political troubles involving Sikhs in India stem from the 1947 partition of the subcontinent into India (Hindu) and Pakistan (Muslim). The boundary line between the two states (three states, since East Pakistan became Bangladesh) cuts through the Punjab region, an area in which Sikhs had relative autonomy until the partition. They lost their political identity and became caught up in the massacres between Hindus and Muslims as victims of both.[8] Since then, radical factions among Sikhs have called for the establishment of an independent Sikh state, Khalistan, and have backed up their demands with terrorist actions. The Indian government granted the Sikhs certain concessions in the Punjab, but it has also attempted to suppress

Depiction of the martyrdom of Guru Arjan Dev. Sikh Temple, Nairobi.

violence. In 1982, when Zail Singh began serving as president of India (a ceremonial office), Indian prime minister Indira Gandhi ordered Indian troops to occupy the temple precincts at Amritsar, where they confiscated large caches of weapons. Indira Gandhi was assassinated by her own Sikh bodyguards, and violence of fluctuating intensity continues in the Punjab.

The overwhelming majority of Sikhs, however, are gentle, peaceful people. Nothing in the life and worship of common Sikh people, other than the remembrance of the tradition, is particularly militaristic in nature. Sikh religious life centers on worshiping of God as represented by the Adi Granth, maintaining high moral standards and practicing solidarity with the Sikh community.

Sikh worship. Someone seeking full membership in the Sikh community undergoes "baptism": drinking a small amount of holy water received in the name of the gurus. From that point on the emphasis is on a life lived in devotion to God, not on ritual. Regular participation in the services held at temples (*gurdwaras*) is part of that life.

The central temple of Sikhism is the Golden Temple at Amritsar. It is situated on an island in a large basin and can be approached only by a bridge. It has four entrances to symbolize that people from all castes can worship together in harmony. The Golden Temple houses the original copy of the Adi Granth. Although Sikhism does not have a formal requirement for pilgrimage (such as the pilgrimage to Mecca in Islam), Sikhs the world over hope to travel to Amritsar at least once in their lives and expect great spiritual benefit from making the pilgrimage.

Sikh temples resemble mosques in that they are basically large empty halls with carpet-covered floors. At the front of the room, usually on a rostrum under a canopy, is a copy of the Adi Granth. Flowers and other decorations, as well as an offering box, complete the scene.

The Adi Granth is also called Guru Granth or Granth Sahib (the "illustrious book"). Just as the human gurus embodied the light of God, so the book is considered the embodiment of God's light and is treated with high veneration. Sikhs resist the charge that they worship the book, yet they do accord it divine honors. During the night, the Adi Granth is kept in its "bed" (the expression used by Sikhs themselves), either a small separate room kept off to the side or a draped compartment with sheets and silk curtains. In the morning the book is brought out and a short chanting service is held. The ritual is repeated in the evening when the book is placed to rest.

Sikh temples are usually open for personal devotions. A midweek service is held for women in addition to a male-dominated service, now usually held on Sundays. Visiting a temple provides an interesting combination of formality and informality. Those entering the temple must wash their hands and feet and cover their heads, but they face few serious restrictions once inside the hall. There is no sacred precinct. Accidentally disrespectful actions like turning one's back on the holy book or sitting with one's feet pointing toward the book are to be avoided.[9]

Sikh worship consists of chanting hymns out of the Adi Granth. Women sit on the left side of the hall; men sit on the right. The singing, which is relatively melodious, is accompanied by various rhythm instruments and possibly a harmonium. The music does not show the stridency characteristic of Hindu temple music. The mood is less than solemn, and people seem to enjoy being with each other and singing together. A few people may come and go during the service. Someone who enters or leaves walks to the book, bows in a prostrate position for a moment, places a few coins into the offering box and retreats, the first few steps backward so as not to show disrespect for the holy book.

During the chanting, an honored member of the community (not necessarily a priest) sits or stands behind the book and from time to time waves a horsetail on a silver handle over the book (which is covered with a decorated sheet). Presumably the practice originated with a concern to keep flies away from the holy book, but now it is simply a part of the ritual. The first time that I visited a Sikh temple, a women's service was in progress. I asked the man sitting in back with me why the lady in front was waving the "tail." He took on a puzzled expression and said, "She has to; the holy book is there." What a lesson in the fact that ritual does not need an explanation!

At the end of the service everyone receives a small lump of a mixture that is mostly brown sugar. Anyone who visits a Sikh temple is given a lump of sugar or some other

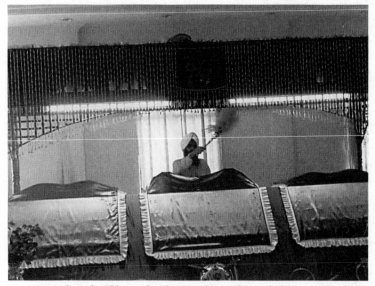

sweet. The sweets are stored at the front near the Adi Granth, but the meaning of this gesture is essentially communal, expressing solidarity with the Sikh community. It is not "transubstantiated" into some spiritual essence.[10]

A communal meal follows the chanting service. Langar, the communal kitchen, is in some ways the most telling part of Sikh community life. Even the Mogul emperor, when he sought an audience with Ram Das, was obliged to partake of the communal

Main altar of a Sikh temple. The Granth is underneath the covering. The attendant is waving impurities away. The writing on the canopy represents Ekankar, the most prevalent word for God.

meal sitting side by side with all other people, which would have included people from Muslim backgrounds as well as Hindus of all four castes. To this day, the meal, to which visitors are always welcomed, celebrates the equality of all Sikh believers. It is notable that although social distinctions are observed, on the whole women occupy a far more equal place in Sikh society than they do in most other Indian religions.

■ *So You Meet a Sikh . . .*

What You Might Expect

The Sikh community has had to fight for its survival ever since its inception. As a consequence, Sikhism has taken on several distinct faces toward the outside world. On the one hand, there is the highly militaristic image, sharpened by centuries of armed conflict and propagated today by the militant Khalsa Dal organization. On the other hand, there is the image of the community peacefully settling around the Adi Granth in the temple. This is the religious side of Sikhism that is most frequently encountered. However, there is a third image as well, of the Sikh losing contact with his religious and cultural roots and embracing the contemporary secular world.

All religions face an ongoing battle with secularism, but the threat is more serious for a religion that is tied to a particular culture or community. This phenomenon also holds for Zoroastrianism and (of necessity) for traditional religions. The religion demands a cultural and communal context, which makes private practice of the religion next to impossible. That condition also applies strongly to Sikhism. At the very heart of the Sikh belief system is the Sikh community. Leaving the community means breaking religious commitments.

This situation is exacerbated by the fact that Sikhism, as it stands today, is a fairly static religion. It does not focus on future goals. There is no expectation of a future messianic figure in formal Sikh teaching. Salvation is a mystical concept that involves being absorbed impersonally into the light of God. Aspirations for Sikhism's future role in the larger society are fairly unrealistic. Sikhism does not provide any great incentive for someone who becomes disconnected from the community to continue to practice it.

Relating the Gospel

Christianity, in contrast to Sikhism, provides hope: the assurance of personal eternal life and the consummation of history at Christ's second coming. This fact does not in itself make Christianity true; rather, because Christianity is true, it can fill a void.

Sikhism is ambivalent toward other religions. It does not deny all truth to non-Sikh beliefs that are expressions of devotion to God, but it maintains that full salvation can only be found through devotion to Sat Nam. The Christian may have a point of entry in showing the Sikh person that God revealed himself a long time before Sikhism, not through a guru but through his own coming into the world. The Christian can also show the Sikh that Christ's finished work on the cross provides a tangible solution to the human problem of sin that goes beyond abstractions and mystical experiences.

Baha'i

Estimated Membership
Worldwide: 6,104,000
United States: 300,000

The youngest world religion, Baha'i, originated in the nineteenth century as an offshoot of Islam.

Precursor: the Babi religion. Each of the various forms of Shi'a had a succession of imams that ended with the last one of the line going into concealment. The imams were thought to have the same supernatural standing that Muhammad had. They were not only political leaders, like the caliphs in Sunni Islam, but they were also endowed with the spiritual knowledge, the nass, that Muhammad had. Some Shi'ite Muslims believed that the last imam, while in concealment, would communicate to each generation through a special person acting as his mouthpiece. This person would be his gate, the Bab, for that particular generation until the imam would return as the Mahdi.

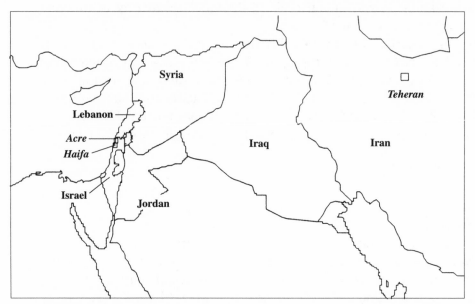

Map 9.3. Baha'i origins

In 1844 a young Persian named Ali Muhammad declared himself to be the next Bab. He journeyed to Mecca and made the declaration at the Grand Mosque. Upon returning to Persia, he attracted a sizable group of supporters to whom it became clear that, in distinction to previous Babs, Ali Muhammad was in fact the Mahdi himself and thus the direct prophet of God. His followers came to be known as the Babis.

The Babi movement was treated with hostility right from the start. The established Islamic order opposed it because it violated the belief in Muhammad's supremacy, not to mention their own leaders' authority. But the government of the shah also rightly feared that the coming of a Mahdi would imply its own demise, since the Mahdi would be political ruler as well as prophet. Thus the forces of the establishment immediately began suppressing the Bab's activities.

The Bab was arrested. In 1848 it came to violence between the Babis and the government. Both sides probably contributed equally to exacerbating the situation—the government by overreacting with force, the Babis by pressing their claim of the Bab's supremacy with force. Predictably, the government won out. Many Babis, including the Bab himself, were executed. In 1850 it looked as though the movement would die out as quickly as it had arisen.

The struggle for succession. Before the Bab died, however, he had predicted that he would be succeeded by another prophet. He left no doubt about the successor's identity because he put the matter in writing.[11] His successor would be Mirza Yahya, a young man of noble family who had shown great devotion to the Bab. Yahya took on the name Subh-i-Azal, which means "dawn of eternity." In the conflicts that would ensue, his followers became known as the Azalis.

Yahya's half-brother, Husayn Ali, was passed over in the succession, even though a good case could have been made that Husayn was the more qualified of the two. Husayn Ali was also a man of great spiritual aptitude, and he had the added capability of leadership, which Yahya apparently lacked. Initially Husayn Ali submitted to Yahya's authority, but he grew increasingly restless in the subordinate position.

In 1863 Husayn Ali declared publicly that he was the intended successor to the Bab. He took on the name Baha'ullah—the "glory of God"—which may actually have been conferred on him by the Bab many years earlier.[12] His followers became known as the Baha'is. From this point on many Babis recognized Husayn Ali's leadership over Yahya's. The subsequent physical violence included the Azalis fighting the Baha'is fighting the government. The Turkish government eventually sent the two leaders into exile: Yahya to Cyprus and Husayn Ali to Acre.

Development and further succession. Severed from his domestic roots, Baha'ullah began to preach a faith for the world. He wrote letters to some of the crowned heads of Europe, exhorting them to work for peace in a united world. Although he was technically imprisoned for most of the rest of his life, Baha'ullah was able to exert much influence through his books, letters and personal interviews. Baha'ullah's writings included *The Most Holy Book* (Kitab-i-Aqdas), *The Book of Certitudes* and *The Hidden Words*. By the time he died in 1892, Baha'ullah was recognized by his followers as the Great Manifestation, namely, the ultimate prophet. The old Babi faith had been left behind as a separate precursor religion.

A new rivalry broke out after Baha'ullah died. Baha'ullah had clearly designated his son Abbas Effendi as his successor. Abbas took on the title Abdul Baha, "servant of the glory," and proclaimed himself the sole authorized interpreter of Baha'ullah's writings, thus placing himself on a virtual par with the Great Manifestation himself. However, Abdul Baha was supposed to share the authority with his brother, Muhammad Ali, who had already been designated by Baha'ullah as successor to Abdul. Nevertheless, Abdul did not permit Muhammad to participate, and once again hostilities ensued.

Abdul Baha persevered and carried the Baha'i movement forward. Under his guidance the religion gained a small worldwide following. In 1912 he personally laid the cornerstone of the Baha'i temple in Wilmette, Illinois. When Abdul Baha died in 1921, his grandson Shoghi Effendi assumed leadership and carried it on until 1957. Shoghi translated most of Baha'ullah's writings into English.

Since then, leadership in Baha'i has been determined on a representative basis. Local groups report to national boards, which in turn are represented on an international governing body. The central shrine of Baha'i, known as the Universal House of Justice, is located in Haifa, Israel. There are other temples around the world, including one in Wilmette, Illinois, just north of Chicago. Although Baha'i is the religion of a relatively small number of people, it ranks right after Christianity as the second most widely distributed religion in the world. Figure 9.1 summarizes its leadership history.

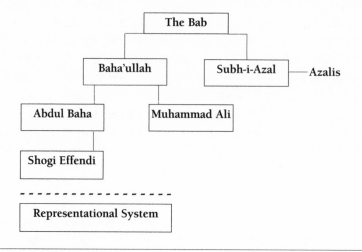

Figure 9.1. History of Baha'i leadership

Baha'i teachings. Arising as it did out of Islam, Baha'i is a monotheistic faith. Baha'ullah taught that there is one God, the eternal Creator, who is essentially unknowable. However, God has manifested himself from time to time through prophets who are also babs. These prophets are direct manifestations of God, not just spokesmen for God. Thus the babs are divine in their persons as well as in their messages.

Baha'ullah recognized nine babs, all of whom were valid manifestations of God, including Abraham, Krishna, Moses, Zoroaster, Buddha, Jesus, Muhammad, the Bab and Baha'ullah. Each prophet provided the divine manifestation for his time and culture, but the babs' messages also supersede each other. Consequently, Baha'ullah's teachings are not the only divine teachings, but at this time they are supposed to be superior to all others. "The prophetic cycle hath, verily, ended. The Eternal Truth is now come."[13] At the same time Baha'i (somewhat paradoxically) reckons with the theoretical possibility that in a later age, there may be a new manifestation to maintain the true teaching of God for that generation.

Baha'i emphasizes personal devotion and social action, but social action has received far more attention. Baha'i followers are supposed to pray daily and observe special days. There is no clergy and virtually no ritual. The overwhelming thrust of the teachings goes toward social and political world reform.

The principles of Baha'i stem from the writings of Baha'ullah and their interpretations by Abdul Baha. One Baha'i publication arranges them in a collection of ten, though other numerical arrangements are also possible.[14] The first principle is *the oneness of mankind*. The essential unity of humanity lies at the very core of Baha'i belief. In a sense all other beliefs flow from this premise. The second principle is *the independent investigation of truth*. Baha'i teaches that all human beings should have equal access to truth. No one should be compelled by some authority to accept a particular viewpoint. The third principle is *the common foundation of all religions*. According to Baha'ullah, all genuine religions have their basis in a manifestation of God that is similar to his own identity. The great prophets listed in figure 9.2 taught their perspective on the same divine reality. Unfortunately, their pure truth became clouded by ritual and superstition. Baha'ullah urged the members of the world's religions to leave their inessential differences behind and to unite on the basis of their essential unity—which, of course, looks like Baha'ullah's teachings.

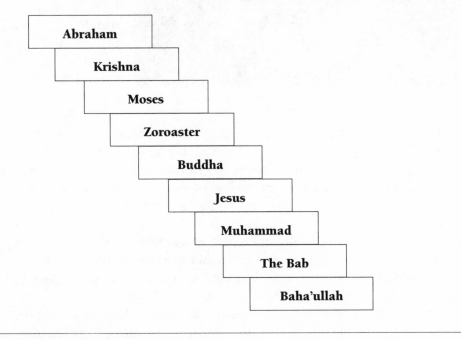

Figure 9.2.   The nine manifestations

The fourth principle is *the essential harmony of science and religion*. Baha'i is committed to the idea that religion and science are not adversaries. Science, when based properly on reason, supports the truth of religion. The fifth principle is *the equality of men and women*. This particular principle goes back to the teachings of the Bab himself. It is one of several doctrines that got him into trouble with the prevailing Islamic establishment. Baha'i holds that equality between the sexes is an essential requirement for the world ever to progress. The sixth principle is *the elimination of prejudice of all kinds.* Given the unity of the human race and the equality of all people, Baha'i contends that there is no room for any prejudice—racial, political or religious.

The Baha'i House of Worship in Wilmette, Illinois.

The seventh principle is *universal compulsory education.* Baha'ullah believed that ignorance is the greatest threat to a unified, peaceful world. Consequently he argued for compulsory education of all children. He believed that fathers were primarily responsible for the education of children. If for some reason a father was unable to perform that duty, then a public school supported by the community should be available. The eighth principle is *a spiritual solution to the economic problem.* The problem referred to is the great disparity between the rich and the poor of this world. As the people of the world attain a higher spiritual state, they will begin to abolish the extremes of wealth and poverty. The poor will benefit materially, and the rich will benefit spiritually by not having their existence encumbered by their wealth. Service in bettering the condition of poor people is considered in itself an act of worship. The ninth principle is *a universal auxiliary language.* Baha'ullah believed that in order for the unity of the human race to become functional, people must communicate through a shared language. Thus he taught that the world should agree on one particular language (living, dead or artificial) as the universal language of humanity. All people should learn two languages: their native tongue and the universal language.

The tenth principle is *universal peace upheld by a world government.* Much of Baha'i's world appeal is attributable to its commitment to the implementation of world peace. Baha'i is pacifistic, considering all armed conflict to be counterproductive (consequently, Baha'i interprets its early struggles as purely one-sided on the part of the enemies of Baha'i). Baha'ullah called for a world tribunal to adjudicate conflicts between nations and a central authority that would oversee the implementation of justice around the world. True peace, permanent and universal, will emerge as people and governments put aside their differences.

Even though this point is downplayed in the popular literature, it is important to keep in mind that Baha'ullah and Abdul Baha were not promoting a secular world confederation. They believed that the problems of humanity are spiritual in nature and can be solved only on a mutual spiritual basis. Thus the ten principles represent a blueprint for a theocracy administered under the guardianship of Baha'i. It would take the spiritual wisdom of Baha'ullah and possibly subsequent manifestations to keep the world on a true course.

Baha'i practice. Baha'i does not emphasize ritual and devotional practice, although they are not absent. Baha'is are enjoined to pray daily (one, three or five times, depending on the personal plan that is chosen).

The number nine—the highest single integer, representing unity in diversity—figures prominently in Baha'i. The local, national and worldwide representative bodies each have nine members. Each temple (of which there are only eight as of this writing) has nine entrances.

In terms of the calendar, the number nineteen takes on great significance. The Baha'i solar calendar has nineteen months of nineteen days (plus the days needed to bring the total to 365), beginning on March 21. The last month, which has nineteen days, is set aside for fasting, similar to the Muslim observance of Ramadan. Baha'is are asked to abstain from food and drink during daylight hours throughout this month. The ensuing New Year's Day constitutes a major celebration. Another important holiday is the feast of Ridvan, which is a nine-day commemoration of Baha'ullah's declaration as manifestation, observed toward the end of April. November 12 is set aside to celebrate Baha'ullah's birthday.

Although there are several large Baha'i temples around the world, a temple is not the normal place of worship. Baha'i congregational meetings usually take place in a member's home. There is no clergy. Believers are elected to leadership, which is exercised in keeping with basic democratic principles. Monthly meetings last about two hours. The first hour or so is given over to worship, consisting mostly of hymn singing. During the second hour concrete plans for ministry as well as administrative details are enacted.

The real impact of Baha'i on modern society occurs on the level of social service. In the United States, active members of Baha'i typically serve within organizations promoting civil rights, economic opportunities for the poor, plans for world peace and various empowerment agendas. Baha'i has also taken a leading role in various ecumenical programs, such as local interfaith councils and the centennial world parliament of religions.

■ *So You Meet a Baha'i . . .*

What You Might Expect

Baha'i is a young religion and has not yet established a permanent social base for itself.

People tend to be Baha'is because they want to be, not because they were channeled into it by upbringing or community (though this phenomenon is disappearing within the current generation). Baha'i has attracted people who are interested in matters of religion and are inclined to work on the task of solving the world's social problems.

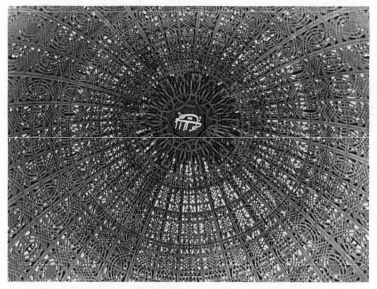

The domed ceiling inside the Baha'i Temple (Wilmette, Illinois) graphically depicts the theme of unity.

Though we should remind ourselves once more that all these descriptions are of necessity somewhat overgeneralized, the Baha'is I have met and talked to in the United States tend to have certain characteristics in common. First, they are professional people who are in the habit of using their minds and contributing to causes that they support. Second, they have thought about their religion and are able to articulate their beliefs. In fact, some of them have told me that they became Baha'i precisely because they thought through spiritual issues and found the most truth within the teachings of Baha'ullah. Although officially Baha'i does not do evangelism, Baha'is encourage the active exploration of religious issues. Third, Baha'is tend to be involved in social and political causes such as civil rights, world peace or abolition of poverty. They involve themselves either through their affiliation with Baha'i or in addition to it.

Baha'i has not existed long enough to give rise to a genuine folk version of the religion. What the textbooks describe is pretty much what's out there. As a matter of fact, there have been times when talking to a Baha'i was like talking to Baha'ullah himself.

Relating the Gospel

A conversation with a Baha'i on religious matters is almost always positive in tone and intellectually stimulating. For a Christian the challenging side of the conversation tends to center around Baha'i inclusivism. Baha'i sees itself as the culmination of many teachings, all of which contain truth. Thus Baha'is do not question the truth of Christian beliefs. They endorse the truth of Christianity as a part of the greater scheme.

I have talked with Baha'i people who assert that they are committed followers of

Jesus Christ, not just in the vague sense of finding some truth in all world religions but specifically as observing precisely what Jesus taught (and presumably what I as a Christian also believe). But they do not accept all of what the New Testament declares as truth. Instead, they embrace only what they consider to be the authentic teachings of Christ according to their own principles. And these so-called authentic teachings, it turns out, are the ones that agree with the teachings of Baha'ullah. Thus, while Baha'is see themselves as open and inclusive, they ironically interpret Christian claims to exclusiveness (for example, Jn 14:6; Acts 4:12) according to the inclusive Baha'i scheme.[15]

How inclusive is Baha'i? When talking to a Baha'i believer, I sometimes find it difficult to sort out where Baha'i teaching leaves off and contemporary relativism takes over. I have talked with Baha'is who say that *all* religions are legitimate ways to God. Others say that only religions that are based on the nine great manifestations (babs) have validity. I believe that the second option is closer to Baha'ullah's intention. Inclusive or not, Baha'ullah did recognize a basic true-false distinction. Not everything can be true.

Clearly, Baha'i's inclusivism is based on an agenda that determines exactly what is and what is not acceptable. In regard to specific issues, Baha'ullah's authority supersedes other considerations. Baha'i's assertion of what all bona fide religions supposedly have in common yields no more and no less than the teachings of Baha'ullah. Anything that contradicts his teaching is relegated to the periphery of superstition that has accrued over the core teaching.

The same heavy hand can be seen in Baha'i's social agenda. In the final analysis tolerance and inclusivism extend only to those aspects of the world that are compatible with Baha'i goals. This circularity does not necessarily invalidate Baha'i intentions, but it reveals the fact that Baha'i is certainly not neutral or all-inclusive.

Baha'i represents the essence of ideological correctness. It seems to promote all the right causes, such as the unity of the human race and universal world peace. Yet the spiritual underpinning of Baha'i's social program seems quite thin. The faith moves rapidly from a relatively vague notion of God and his manifestations to social programs implemented by merely human means. Why should Baha'i have any more success in establishing a human utopia than any other faith or philosophy, particularly as it offers a very generic spiritual dimension? A Christian response to Baha'i begins with the sad recognition of human sinfulness, which does not yield to simple ideological prescriptions and, with all due respect, seems to be evident in the lives of Baha'i's founders as well.

In contrast to Baha'i's ambitious worldwide agenda, evangelical Christianity provides an individual-centered orientation for the present era. Christianity teaches that until God himself re-creates the world as a whole, human sinfulness will block the attainment of a perfect human society. For now, God's focus is on redeeming individuals. God's intervention will bring about a perfect world in the future. Christianity is predicated on the notion that the agency of an infinite God provides the only possible guarantee that a radical change in the world can ever be realized.

Mastering the Material
When you have finished studying this chapter, you should be able to

1. summarize the life and teachings of Mahavira;

2. state the vows of a Jain monk and interpret their meaning;

3. describe the facets of lay Jainism and its place in the history of Jainism;

4. clarify the roles of the Tirthankaras (without being able to name all twenty-four) and the nature of Jain worship;

5. recount the history of Sikhism from Nanak through the present and identify significant changes brought about by some gurus;

6. list the attributes of a Singh;

7. describe Sikh temple and community worship;

8. summarize the history of Baha'i;

9. explain the Baha'i understanding of prophethood;

10. state and interpret the ten Baha'i principles.

Term Paper Ideas
1. Research the details of Mahavira's life in the total context of the sixth century in India.

2. Present a detailed summary of Jain philosophy, including the nature of the universe and the role of karma.

3. Compare and contrast the teachings of Shvetambara and Digambara Jainism.

4. Compile an account of the practical impact of Jainism in India, such as the establishment of animal hospitals.

5. Bring together information on Christian ministry to Jain people. What ideas have served as bridges?

6. Undertake a detailed study of the state of Sikhism in political India today. What are the historical antecedents? What are the prospects for the future?

7. Gather information on the nature of the guru in Sikhism. How does the Adi Granth function as guru today compared to, say, Nanak?

8. Discuss the role of women in Sikhism as compared to the role of women in other Indian religions.

9. Describe missionary and evangelistic approaches that Christians use to approach Sikhs.

10. Compile the teachings of the Bab with an eye to similarities and differences toward Shi'ite Islam as well as Baha'i.

11. Write a biography of either Baha'ullah or Abdul Baha.

12. Describe the relationship of Baha'i to other religions in theory and in practice.

13. Provide a study of one specific social agenda advocated by Baha'i today and what steps have been taken to accomplish it.

14. Interview a member of Baha'i and pursue his or her reaction to Christianity's claim to exclusiveness. Write up your results and reactions.

Core Bibliography

Baha Abdul and Baha'ullah. *Baha'i World Faith: Selected Writings.* Wilmette, Ill.: Baha'i Publishing Trust, 1943.

Cole, W. Owen, and Piara Singh Sambhi. *The Sikhs: Their Religious Beliefs and Practices.* London: Routledge & Kegan Paul, 1978.

Gopalan, S. *Outlines of Jainism.* New York: Halsted, 1973.

Hatcher, William S., and J. Douglas Martin. *The Baha'i Faith: The Emerging Global Religion.* San Francisco: Harper & Row, 1985.

Jain, Jyotiprasad. *Religion and Culture of the Jains.* New Delhi, India: Bharatiya Jnanapith, 1975.

Jaini, Jagmanderlal. *Outlines of Jainism.* Westport, Conn.: Hyperion, 1940.

Miller, William McElwee. *The Bahai Faith: Its History and Teachings.* South Pasadena, Calif.: William Carey Library, 1974.

Sikh Religion. Detroit: Sikh Missionary Center, 1990.

Singh, Kushwant. *A History of the Sikhs.* 2 vols. Princeton, N.J.: Princeton University Press, 1966.

Chapter 10

Chinese Popular Religion

Estimated Practitioners[1]
Worldwide: 230,391,000
North America: 124,000

What is your religion? Many Chinese people might find this question difficult to answer because their religion is a synthesis of separate elements: traditional religion, Buddhism, Confucianism and Daoism (Taoism).[2] What they believe and practice is drawn from various elements of these systems brought together in a more or less coherent fashion. For them it only makes sense to draw from the best of the ancient wisdom. Buddhism exists independently of this syncretism. Daoism could do the same and has done so to some extent. However, in terms of Chinese folk religion, these constituents come together, along with other elements, to make up the complex system that is the faith of millions. I shall refer to this folk religion as Chinese popular religion. It is still practiced widely by Chinese people outside of the People's Republic of China and is making a comeback even there since the political climate has become more favorable.

Chinese popular religion continues to develop. By its very nature it is fluid, adaptable and subject to various influences. For example, the currently popular cult of female deities, particularly Ma-zu and Guan-yin, has come to blossom over the last two hundred years. We can expect the synthesis to continue to evolve into new forms in the future under the impetus of modern communication. In this chapter we shall look at each of the various systems of origin and how they have come to shape Chinese popular religion today.

Traditional Religion
Chinese culture treats old age as a noble attainment and seeks to endow even relatively

late developments with a venerable heritage. Thus it is not easy to separate what is said to be ancient from what actually represents earliest antiquity. For example, the traditional mythic emperors were probably not known until the time of Confucius at the earliest, some of them even later.

Front of an altar in a Chinese temple showing the yin and yang, the Yi-jing hexagram and the forces of the universe.

The earliest reliable reports come from the Shang dynasty, which ruled a part of China from about 1500 B.C. to 1040 B.C. This is the first of the many Chinese dynasties about which we have at least some historical information.[3] Around the time that the Aryans invaded India and Iran and Moses led the Israelites out of Egypt, the people of the Shang tribe in central China were able to establish a relatively stable kingdom. They engaged in agriculture, knew how to work metal and lived in fortified towns. They also developed a form of writing.

The religion of the Shang dynasty was traditional (see discussion of traditional religion in chapter one). The highest spiritual power belonged to a god in heaven, even as ancestors and nature spirits increasingly became the objects of ritual. The god in heaven was called Shang-di.[4] He was seen as the author of a moral law that all people, particularly the rulers, were obligated to observe. He was worshiped with animal sacrifices. The ensuing Zhou dynasty also worshiped Shang-di as the universal god but started to identify Shang-di with heaven itself, his abode, which they revered with the name Tian.

Two distinctive traits characterized early Chinese religion and continue to influence Chinese beliefs and practice to this day. First, there was a close relationship between state and religion. In both the Shang and Zhou dynasties, the welfare of the empire[5] was thought to depend on the piety of the people, particularly the rulers. The Zhou rulers claimed that they had been given the throne because the Shang had become corrupt and had abandoned obedience to God. Conversely, it was believed that if the emperor was a man of virtue and was faithful in exercising his ritual obligations, such as performing the fall and spring sacrifices, all would be well with the empire.

This interconnectedness of political and religious spheres was important for two reasons. For one, it was the eventual political breakdown of ancient China that spawned religious creativity. In China, right into the twentieth century, questions of state government have always been seen as basically religious questions.[6] Second, the Chinese deities, as they were developed much later, were established in an administrative hierarchy in heaven that mirrored the feudal order of the earthly government.

The second distinctive trait of early Chinese religion was an emphasis on divination. Many, if not most, traditional religions include some form of divination in their ritual. In some cases, the practice achieves greater prominence, as it did among the West African Yoruba (chapter five). Another such case, from its very beginnings to the present day, is Chinese religion.

At the heart of Chinese divination practice, as it has come down from the earliest records, is the idea that there is a basic balance of nature. If that balance is disrupted in some way, the resulting disturbance leaves marks on the natural order that can be discerned by the trained eye.

The whole world consists of two opposing yet complementary forces, yin and yang, which are optimally in perfect balance with each other. Table 10.1 displays their characteristics.

Yin	Yang
passive	active
earth-related	sky-related
cold	hot
moist	dry
mysterious	clear
dark	light
feminine	masculine

Table 10.1. Yin and yang

It is important to recognize that neither force in itself is good or evil. Good is the proper balance between the two; evil is an imbalance in either direction. When there is too much yin, there needs to be more yang; if there is an excess of yang, more yin needs to be injected.

The correctly balanced state of yin and yang is expressed by the Dao (Tao). Dao means "the way," the correct flow of things in proper harmony. The philosophy and religion of Daoism exploits this notion much further. However, the basic notion of Dao, consisting of the right balance between yin and yang, is the property of all of Chinese thought in all of its schools.

Early traditional Chinese religion always associated divination with the practice of its rituals. For example, when the emperor performed the great semiannual sacrifices, his priests would also perform auguries on behalf of the person of the emperor and the empire. One favorite method was to heat a tortoise shell in the fire until it cracked. Interpreting the cracks revealed the occult causes of current events or predicted future events.

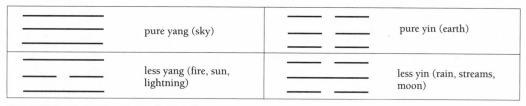

Figure 10.1. Representations of yin and yang

Another method of divination was described in a very early book, the *Yi-jing (I-ching)*, the *Book of Changes*. A series of broken and unbroken sticks were cast, and their arrangement in groups of three (trigrams) or six (hexagrams) revealed whether yin or yang was dominant at the moment. For example, three unbroken sticks represented the sky (total yang), whereas three broken ones stood for the earth (total yin). Two unbroken sticks surrounding a broken one indicated slightly less yang (as in fire, the sun and lightning), and two broken sticks surrounding an unbroken one pointed to slightly moderated yin (as in rain, streams or the moon; see figure 10.1).

There were many possible positions covering many contingencies of life. The information gained from divination practices could be used in making personal decisions. Korea (like Japan) adopted many aspects of Chinese culture. South Korea's flag today bears the symbols for yin and yang surrounded by a stylized arrangement of the Yi-jing formation.

Ancient Chinese religion also emphasized ancestor veneration and the appeasement of nature spirits. The dragon has come to symbolize the positive forces of nature that grant fertility and prosperity. This symbol has been retained throughout the history of Chinese culture.

Daoism

The crisis in politics, religion and language. The Zhou dynasty eventually weakened itself through abuse of power and internal corruption, and the empire entered a long period of disintegration. With the weakening of the central authority, the various smaller states severed themselves from the empire and began a centuries-long struggle for ascendancy. Eventually this fragmentation led to the era known as the "warring states" period (the last two hundred years or so of nominal Zhou rule). But even before that time of virtual anarchy, there was great political and social turmoil.

The stability of the empire was a necessary condition for the equilibrium of Chinese religion. The sacrificial ritual carried out by the emperor validated all the sacrifices performed by others farther down the chain of the feudal hierarchy. The collapse of the social order destroyed the efficacy of ritual practices throughout the empire. Thus the political crisis signaled a religious crisis.

The ancient Chinese sages saw the political crisis as a crisis in communication also. Individual words were accruing different layers of meaning, and the Chinese language was becoming increasingly awkward.[7] Even though this phenomenon may sound improbable to us, it was real enough that Confucius, when asked what he would do first if he were king, replied that he would "rectify names," that is, assign unequivocal meanings to words. Apparently one word amassed so many different meanings that any written code of law would be too ambiguous to be useful. Think of how English words acquire new meanings: the word *dial* is derived from the

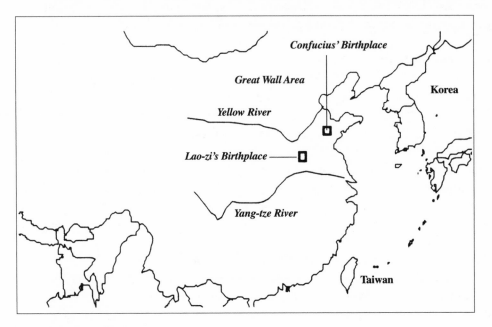

Map 10.1. China

Latin *dies,* meaning "day." It became the word for the face of a sundial and then the face of any clock. Subsequently *dial* was used for any round selecting disk, such as the rotating part of a telephone. Then radios had dials, and then telephones were designed with push-button "dials." This process occurred in the Chinese language in far more crucial areas. Arthur Waley states that

> *hsiang* [Pinyin: *xiang*] meant elephant, and hence ivory. Hence carved ivory tablets representing omen objects, hence anything that "stood for" or represented something else; an image or symbol. Finally, though not, I think till well after

the Christian era, the word came to mean "like," "as," "resembling," as it does in current Chinese today.[8]

Clearly the ancient Chinese themselves felt that the language problem was serious and addressed it through various philosophical remedies.

School	Important person	Action	Language
Mohists	Mo-zi	love and benevolence	personal empathy
Legalists, Fa-jia	Emperor Zheng	law and order	decreed by the state
Daoism	Lao-zi	quietism (*wu-wei*)	nonduality
Confucianism	Confucius, Kong fu-zi	*li* and *ren*	must be corrected

Table 10.2. Four Chinese schools

Mohists and legalists. In the sixth century B.C., a century that saw the beginnings of many religious movements worldwide, a number of schools of thought arose in China that attempted to address the problems of the Chinese empire. Two of them, Daoism and Confucianism, will be discussed at greater length. There were two others that also had some impact on the development of subsequent Chinese thought.

The teaching of Mo-zi (468-376 B.C.) rivaled Confucianism in popularity for a time. The Mohists, named after their teacher, maintained that embracing the principle of all-pervasive and universal love would restore the empire. Tian (heaven) is a god of love and wants all human beings to live on the basis of love. Rules, rituals and wars of aggression that are counterproductive to this divine love must be abandoned in favor of personal relationships. Then material prosperity will result for all.

On the other side of this debate was the legalist school, Fa-jia. This school proposed resolving the problems of the empire through a strong government. A ruler should allocate to himself whatever power it takes to reestablish the proper social order. Language meanings should be legislated; crimes should be punished severely; the emperor should hold absolute power; all rebellions should be suppressed. The legalists assumed political power in the person of the emperor Zheng (who called himself Shi-huang-di, the "first emperor") of the Qin dynasty. Zhen and the rest of this very short-lived dynasty ruled China in totalitarian style, complete with book burnings and the torture of dissidents. Their one lasting contribution was that their country became known as "land of the Quin." In earlier transcriptions this is "land of the Ch'in," or Chin-a.

Lao-zi. According to legend, Lao-zi (Lao-tzu) was born at the age of seventy-two. The justification for this rather surprising notion is that anyone as wise as this man could not possibly have been born as a squalling infant. Instead, he came into the world possessing white hair and the ability to speak. The name Lao-zi means "old sage," although another tradition interprets it in light of the birth story as "old child."

Neither legend nor historical research tells us much about the life of Lao-zi. A traditional date for his birth is 604 B.C., thus making him a rough contemporary of Confucius. Lao-zi lived a quiet life. He was archivist at the court of a nobleman and taught a handful of disciples. Eventually he decided to leave China altogether and travel west.

When Lao-zi reached the western boundary of the Chinese empire, the gatekeeper at the border, Yin-xi, would not let him pass unless he wrote down his wisdom for posterity. The sage complied and in one sitting composed the entire book now known as the Dao-de-jing (Tao-te-ching). When Yin-xi gave him permission to pass, Lao-zi mounted his ox and rode off. A final embellishment of the legend has Lao-zi arriving in India just in time to instruct the Buddha in the way of enlightenment.

Contemporary scholarship doubts this legend. Did Lao-zi actually exist? If so, did he live at this time? Did he write the book? Does the book come from this time? It has become customary to refer to the book itself as the Lao-zi. Beyond dispute is the fact that Daoism as a philosophy has been around for a while, that it received a certain impetus during the sixth century and that its teachings were embodied in the Dao-de-jing no later than the third century B.C., probably a little earlier.

Front of a small temple in Singapore.

The Dao-de-jing. Dao means "way," *de* means "power or virtue" and *jing* means "book." Thus the Dao-de-jing is the "book of the way and its power." The title says that by following the "way," the power for a virtuous life will be realized. The philosophy of the Dao-de-jing can be summarized in the word *quietism.* The solution to the problems of the empire lies in doing as little as possible.

I already mentioned that all Chinese thought shares the notion of a Dao, the "way" of balance, but the different schools are at odds as to how the Dao is found. The point of Daoism is that it cannot be found, neither through words nor through actions. It must reveal itself. Anything that anyone does or says only obscures the Dao.

True Dao lies beyond words. The first chapter of the Dao-de-jing states that "it was from the Nameless that Heaven and Earth sprang."[9] What this means is that the Dao itself lies beyond human categorization in terms of language and rational thought. Trying to put its reality into words produces a mere imitation that does not convey the reality of the Dao. Thus Dao is "nondual" (that term also describes the Zen view of reality as being neither one nor multiple, but being beyond categories). In point of fact, there is a certain amount of scholarly consensus that it was the Daoist idea of the Dao that spurred on the development of Zen in China.

What should be done about language in the empire? The Daoist's answer is obvious: nothing. Since ultimate truth lies beyond words, trying to coerce a firm meaning into language is counterproductive. Thus Daoism took a third path on this issue.

The first chapter of the Dao-de-jing asserts, "Only he that rids himself forever of desire can see the Secret Essences."[10] The parallels to Buddhism in this quotation are too obvious to ignore. It is more likely that Lao-zi (or the anonymous author) converged with Buddha on this point than that there was actual Buddhist influence on Lao-zi (or Daoist influence on Gautama Buddha). We saw a similar notion in the Bhagavad-Gita when Krishna instructed Arjuna to act without desiring the fruits of his actions. The idea is that the person following this advice will do as little as possible and will do it without being attached to the action or its results. For instance, people eat and breathe because they must, not for the sake of any pleasure that results.

Thus one must act without intention. The idea for the Daoist philosopher is to return to the "state of the uncarved block," namely, a condition of letting oneself become at one with nature without trying to manipulate one's condition. This concept is called wu-wei, sometimes translated as "actionless action."

Early Daoism attempted to combine this philosophical conclusion with meditative techniques. Some adherents withdrew from the world and attempted to lead totally passive lives on the basis of these principles. One of their methods of returning to a primordial state was called "embryonic breathing." The adepts would attempt to emulate the condition of an infant in its mother's womb through pure, undivided concentration on breathing exercises.

The Dao-de-jing teaches that value judgments made by human minds are based on arbitrary standards. Chapter two states, "It is because every one under Heaven recognizes beauty as beauty, that the idea of ugliness exists."[11] Since ultimate reality is beyond categories, opposing values are not truly real; they are expressions of human conventions. This chapter asserts that opposing categories such as beauty and ugliness, virtue and wickedness, difficult and easy, long and short, high and low and even the supposedly fundamental categories of being and nonbeing are merely relative. The only valid response is to escape from making judgments altogether.

Chapter fifty-seven of the Dao-de-jing states the following little syllogism: "The more prohibitions there are, the more ritual avoidances, the poorer the people will be." A little later it says, "The more laws are promulgated, the more thieves and bandits there will be." Thus the principle that applies to personal action also applies to the actions of government. The more a government does, the worse the situation becomes. Consequently, the book puts into the mouth of a hypothetical ruler, "So long as I 'do nothing' the people will of themselves be transformed. . . . So long as I have no wants the people will of themselves return to the 'state of the Uncarved Block.'"[12]

To summarize the Dao-de-jing: When people abandon all attempts to force a better life for themselves or for society and when they retreat into wu-wei alone, the Dao will manifest itself, and natural harmony, for people and society, will come about by itself.

Popularization and transformation. Clearly these philosophical speculations are a far cry from an organized religion with temples, priests and rituals. Daoism needed to undergo serious transformation if it was to become a religion of the people. Revisions in Daoism occurred as the philosophy became popularized. First it became the undergirding for endeavors in alchemy and in the search for immortality. Then it eventually evolved personal gods and religious rituals.

A popularizer of Daoism in the fourth century B.C. was Zhuang-zi (Chuang-Tzu). He wrote a series of essays in which he illustrated with anecdotes the philosophy of Daoism. Lao-zi was the protagonist in some of these stories. In one amusing episode, he describes a fictional meeting between Lao-zi and Confucius. After Confucius returned from talking with Lao-zi, his disciples asked him how he had admonished Lao-zi. Zhuang-zi has Confucius reply, "I saw a dragon. . . . My mouth was agape: I could not shut it. How then do you think I was going to admonish Lao Tze?"[13] With stories such as these, Zhuang-zi made the point that Daoist philosophy provided a genuine alternative to Confucian ritualism.

Confucianism became the state-sanctioned philosophy during the Han dynasty. Consequently, dissident political movements frequently allied themselves with non-Confucian schools of thought. Thus the Dao-de-jing became scripture for several popular movements that dissented from the political and religious establishment. A group that came to be known as the Yellow Turbans attempted to establish a utopian state in which everyone lived in happiness and prosperity. They did not practice the quietistic philosophy of the Dao-de-jing, but they revered the book and worshiped Lao-zi as a god. A similar, more successful group was known as the Celestial Masters. For our purposes, the important development is that the outward forms of Daoism were transferred into a religious context. Inevitably, the principles of the book were compromised in the process.

A parallel development at this time occurred when another group of people developed an increasing interest in magic and alchemy. Philosophically inclined scholars in the southern part of China used the precariously balanced forces of nature for their own benefit. They believed that by harnessing the appropriate energy they would be able to increase their own *qi (ch'i)*, their life force. Qi is a manalike force that pervades all things. The greater the amount of qi something has, the longer it will live. For example, a crane has a very large amount of qi and thus can live up to a thousand years or more. These adepts were known as *fang-shi*, "masters of the recipes," because it was believed that they had found the recipe for immortality.

The fang-shi, who came from different ways of life, explored methods of boosting their own qi in order to attain immortality. They pursued philosophy, yogalike exercises, methods of hygiene and alchemy in the pursuit of this goal. Alchemy can be thought of as a kind of spiritualized chemistry. It acts on the belief that it may be possible to duplicate the mechanisms that led to the birth of ancient substances, particularly gold, out of the womb of the earth. Then it applies the same operation to itself.[14]

Legend has it that a number of people achieved immortality in this way. They are known as the "immortals," *xian (hsien)*. The xian live in forests, on mountains and on the isles of immortality. Some of them make their newfound spiritual power available to others. For example, one of the most popular temples in Hong Kong is dedicated

Ancestor altar.

to the immortal being Wang Tai Sin, who achieved immortality about a thousand years ago. Attached to his temple complex is a medical building. The majority of worshipers, however, come to him because he provides favorable energy for betting on horse races.

The xian have become the focus of much attention, and they are favorites in today's Chinese popular religion. The so-called Eight Immortals (ba-xian) have become a ubiquitous presence. They achieved everlasting life in different ways but banded together to carry out important feats that have become the subject of legend. They are frequently pictured in works of art, and they are a staple of folklore and bedtime stories.

Li Tie Guai (Li T'ieh-kuai) is pictured as an old beggar carrying an iron crutch and a gourd of magical medicine.

Zhang Guo Lao (Chang Kuo-lao) was a historical person during the Tang dynasty. According to the legend, he owned a white donkey capable of journeying a thousand miles a day. When Zhang did not need the donkey, he could fold it up like a handkerchief and store it in his pocket. In iconography he is shown as an old man with a magical wooden drum.

Cao Guo Jiu (Ts'ao Kuo-chiu) was a historical person, the brother-in-law of an emperor of the Song dynasty. He lived as a hermit and is usually depicted wearing an embroidered robe and carrying a pair of castanets.

Han Xiang Zi (Han Hsiang-tzu), according to legend, was the nephew of a well-known scholar. He had a fierce temperament and is usually pictured with a peach, a corsage or (most often) a magic flute.

Lu Dong Bin (Lü Tung-pin) was a historical person, a scholar who is said to have received a magic sword from the fire dragon. He could use the sword to hide in heaven and is usually pictured with it.

Name	Role	Features
Li Tie Guai	old beggar	iron crutch, gourd of magic
Zhan Guo Lao	old man	magic wooden drum, magic white donkey
Cao Guo Jiu	hermit, in-law of emperor	embroidered robe, castanets
Han Xiang Zi	nephew of scholar	fierce; peach, corsage or flute
Lu Dong Bin	scholar	magic sword
Xian Gu	unmarried female	able to fly, lotus blossom
Lan Cai He	drunken derelict	rags, one boot, basket of flowers
Zhong Li Quan	military officer	fat man, magic fan

Table 10.3. The Eight Immortals

Xian Gu (Ho Hsien-ku) is the only undisputed female among the Eight Immortals. Legend has it that a spirit commanded her to eat powder ground from a magic stone when she was fourteen years old. Then she was able to fly from mountaintop to mountaintop and gather fruit for her mother. She no longer needed to eat and eventually, unmarried, disappeared into immortality. Neither she nor any later female divinity ever married, because in her single state she accumulated a large amount of excess qi that could be put to some other purpose. She is shown holding a lotus blossom.

Lan Cai He (Lan Ts'ai-ho) is a man who is very occasionally portrayed as a woman. He is usually dressed in rags, wearing a belt of black wood and only one boot. He carries a basket of flowers. Although the people in the legend thought of him as nothing more than a drunken derelict, he surprised everyone one day by mounting a crane and riding off into immortality.

Zhong Li Quan (Chung Li-ch'üan) was a historical person, possibly a military man who retired into the mountains. He is shown as a fat man with a magical fan. Table 10.3 summarizes the Eight Immortals.

An important development in Daoism is that the fang-shi, seekers after immortality, worshiped various deities in the course of their pursuit. A popular movement that was also appropriated by the fang-shi focused on Xi Wang-mu, the "queen mother of the west." The fang-shi also recognized certain star deities, which were gods and goddesses who resided on the stars and granted some of their powers to worshipers. Among these star deities were three figures that developed into the most popular gods of modern Chinese popular religion. They are depicted as three old men. Fu holds a baby in his arms and is also known as the god of posterity. He symbolizes happiness. Lu carries a sack of money and the staff of authority. He represents prosperity. Shou is bald and has a white beard. He holds a peach and leans on a staff. He represents longevity.

Thus during the first millennium A.D., two strands of religion—the popular religions recognizing the Dao-de-jing and Lao-zi as divine and the philosophical pursuit of immortality—moved toward each other. As they came together, Daoism as a religion, Dao-jiao, arose. This process took shape gradually.

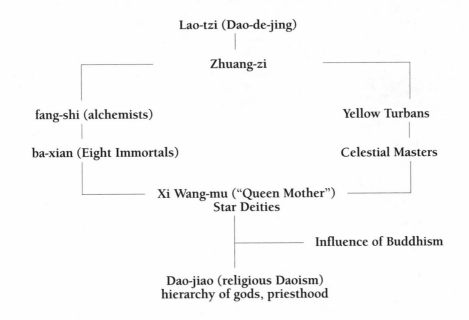

Figure 10.2. Development of Daoism

As Buddhism became popular in China, Daoism needed to define itself more clearly. Buddhism brought with it a large number of divine figures in the persons of the Buddhas and Bodhisattvas. In order to compete, Daoism clarified its own pantheon of personal gods. Around A.D. 1000, a hierarchy of gods was developed. It was arranged in a bureaucracy similar to the bureaucracy of imperial officials. At the lowest level of jurisdiction is the "earth god," *tu-di-gong (t'u-ti-kung)*, who presides over a very small territory such as a field, a street or a neighborhood. If he provides well for his constituents, he may eventually be promoted. If he performs poorly, however, he may be deposed and replaced by another spirit that performs the same function. Local earth gods report to gods in charge of cities and provinces. At the head of the whole pantheon is the jade emperor, Yu-huang (Yü-huang),[15] who is loosely identified with Shang-di and supervises the entire order of the universe. A favorite grouping of deities in contemporary temples consists of the three great emperors—Yu, Yao and Shun. Yu, as the greatest, stands in the middle.

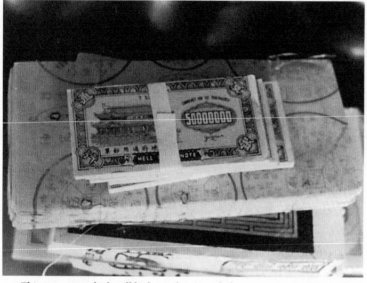

This currency, which will be burned, is intended to maintain the departed in economic prosperity.

One of the most important deities in the Daoist pantheon is the kitchen god, Zao-jun (Tsao-chün). He is said to live in the stove in every house. A tablet is mounted above the stove. The kitchen god receives monthly observances but is especially prominent on New Year's Day, when he reports on the lives of the family members to the jade emperor.

Daoism developed a priesthood that served in temples. The priests took on particular importance in carrying out funeral rituals. Such Daoist-originated practices persist in Chinese popular religion today.

Confucianism

How did an ancient Chinese sage come by a Latin name? His real name was Kong fu-zi (K'ung fu-tzu). *Confucius* was a Latin transcription devised by early Jesuit missionaries.

Confucius (551-479 B.C.) was born into a family of nobility that had fallen on hard times. At age fifteen he entered the civil service, advancing to minister of justice by the time he was fifty. Even as he worked hard at his professional obligations, he continued to study ancient history and philosophy.

Seven years after becoming minister, Confucius fell victim to court intrigues and had to leave, not only the palace but also his home province. He began a long period of itinerant teaching and accumulated a band of disciples who numbered in the thousands by the time of his death. They accompanied him as he tried to convince the people, particularly the rulers, of his ideas. His efforts were ultimately successful. Already during the Han dynasty (which began during the third century B.C.), Confucianism had become the official imperial philosophy.

Confucius has been credited with authoring numerous books. In fact, most ancient Chinese classics (for example, the *Yi-jing*) have been attributed in part to him, though probably without warrant. But the central writing containing his teachings is known in English as the *Analects* or *Conversations,* the *Lun-yu* (*Lun-yü*).

Confucius's solutions to the problems of the empire steered a middle course between the quietism of the Daoists, the authoritarianism of the legalists and the personalism of the Mohists. In simple terms, Confucius wanted all people to return to the basic model of an ideal state as it was supposedly lived out in a golden age a long time ago under the original ideal emperors. If everyone studied exactly how people behaved back then and emulated their ways, then harmony, peace and prosperity would result. Thus, in contrast to Daoism, action is necessary to attain the Dao. Over against legalism, the actions are not arbitrary but based on an ideal model. Unlike Mohism, personal virtue and love are only a part of the total model for society.

Confucius thought that healing the state should begin with the "rectification of names." What he had in mind was a two-edged reform of language. On the one hand, language should be clarified so that people could fulfill their duties exactly and there would be no question about what constitutes a crime and its punishment. On the other hand, Confucius also believed that things ought to be brought in line with their names. Particularly, people should act according to the title they hold. For example, a prince should act like a prince.

One looks in vain for any new religious doctrines in the teachings of Confucius. There are no new gods, acts of worship or revelations in his message. He concentrated entirely on the proper execution of duties. If those duties included ritual obligations toward departed ancestors, then they should be fulfilled punctiliously. But Confucius shied away from any further speculation about the spirit world or life after death. He saw himself as having been called by Tian (heaven) to perform his teaching ministry. He understood that call as a preordained fate allocated to him, not a religious experience.

The core concept in Confucius's teaching is the principle of *ren* (*jen*), which can be roughly translated as "the attitude of seeking the welfare of other people." The meaning of ren stops short of altruistic love—it does not include sacrificing one's own aims completely for other people. Ren provides the inner basis for carrying out what would otherwise be simply mechanical roles in society. People should care for others and respect their humanity, allowing their aims to take precedence if at all possible. Confucius stated what Westerners have patronizingly called his "silver rule": "Do *not* do unto others what you do *not* want others to do unto you."

The second great principle of Confucius's teaching is *li*—the principle of doing the right thing at the right time. It can be translated as "propriety." The principle of li delineates correct manners and conduct for all social situations. It becomes extremely specific in regard to clothing, speech, body postures, even facial expressions. There is a right way for people to carry themselves in every situation, and Confucius wanted all people to master their specific obligations.

Combining ren and li leads to the model of ideal human society. Confucius summarized human interaction as consisting of five basic relationships. Each partner in each relationship is expected to exhibit one particular attitude. If all people did their part in each relationship, society would be healed. Figure 10.3 displays Confucius's five basic relationships.

father: kindness	son: filial piety
eldest brother: gentility	younger brother: humility
husband: righteous behavior	wife: obedience
elder: humane consideration	junior: deference
ruler: benevolence	subject: loyalty

Figure 10.3. The five basic relationships

A modern reader is struck by the fact that women are involved here only in terms of showing obedience to their husbands. They seem to have no further role in Confucius's ideal society. For Confucius, social reform meant moving backward in time, not forward. Traditionally, women had no significant place in society at large, and Confucius meant to keep it that way.

In terms of the character of Chinese culture, there is nothing more important than the notion of filial piety—the obedience that children owe to their parents. Filial piety is an unconditional obligation. It does not depend on the parents' deservingness or rectitude. Even if parents expect something of a son that may strike the son as wrong, he is still obligated to fulfill his parents' wishes. And he must do so without causing his parents to lose face.

A favorite illustration of the force of filial piety is a part of the legend of Lady White Snake. A snake was able to turn itself into a human woman, Bai Su Zhen, through a thousand years of magic. She married and was very happy, but her husband was abducted through the conniving of an evil monk. Lady White Snake rescued her husband but destroyed thousands of innocent lives in the process. For these killings she was justly condemned to be imprisoned in a magical pagoda for all eternity. Her son, Meng Jiao, who had distinguished himself in imperial service, traveled to the pagoda in order to pray for her release. Heaven recognized Meng Jiao's supreme filial piety and, with lightning and thunder, burst open the pagoda to release Lady White Snake.

Filial piety is also invoked as the justification for ancestor veneration. The same veneration that is due to parents in life must be continued after death. Chinese thought also implies that parents need this veneration, and if the proper rites are not fulfilled, the postmortem existence of the parents may be severely hampered.

Later developments. Chinese religion recognizes Confucius as a god, but it is possible to make too much of that fact. First, Confucius would have received his due veneration as esteemed ancestor along with many other people. Second, the ladder of promotion from esteemed ancestor to widely venerated ancestor to eventual godhood is one that has been traversed by numerous other human beings, including the original mythical emperors, the xian (immortals) and even the tu-di-gong (earth gods on the first rung of godhood). The point here is that Confucianism is not an important part of Chinese religion because it introduced the worship of Confucius. The fact that he was eventually worshiped as a god is almost incidental.

It is true that a cult worshiping Confucius as a god developed, which eventually declined. The first Han emperor, who took the throne after the disastrous Qin dynasty with its legalistic philosophy, decreed that Confucianism was the official state philosophy. This decree had the twofold effect of giving Confucius a permanent place among Chinese sages, even when

Roadside fortune teller with his client.

Confucianism was not in the forefront of thought, and also reserving for Confucius a place of highest veneration. Eventually temples were dedicated to his worship, and the emperors of the later Tang dynasty carried out opulent sacrifices in his honor. The Ming dynasty scaled back the public worship of Confucius, but by then his thought had become permanently ingrained in the lives of the Chinese.

Confucius's thought was also the subject of interpretation and elaboration. Three philosophers stand out. Meng-zi (Meng-tzu, 372-289 B.C.), who came to the notice of the West as the Latinized Mencius, stressed the notion that human nature is intrinsically good. Confucian principles can change society because they bring out the inherent goodness of human beings. Xun-zi (Hsün Tzu, 298-238 B.C.) disagreed; he believed that nature consists of an impersonal order and that the Confucian principles were necessary to restrain human nature from evil. In terms of the history of Confucianism, Mencius eventually carried the day.

A third important interpreter of Confucius was Zhu Xi (Chu Hsi, A.D. 1130-1200). Zhu Xi argued that there are two fundamental principles of nature: li (the principle of propriety in Confucius), which he expanded into the principle of all orderliness in the universe, and qi, the life force, which he understood as the basic principle of all vitality. The practice of Confucianism on the personal level thus became a matter of letting one's personal qi be brought into line with the universal li.

The influence of Confucianism on Chinese history and culture was profound. Empirewide, Confucianism provided sanction for a firm bureaucracy of officials trained in classical learning. Preparing to enter civil service and then earn promotion was primarily a matter of studying the Confucian literature. Consequently, Confucianism imbued a rigid conservatism into Chinese society that included social stratification and codes governing dress, ritual and communication. The revolutionary movements of the twentieth century, from which communism emerged supreme, made Confucianism one of its main ideological targets because it represented to them all that was reactionary in Chinese culture.

Confucianism provided an external framework for traditional and Daoist practices. No doubt Chinese people would have venerated ancestors and would have observed a complex code of social obligations even if Confucianism had not come along; after all, many other cultures do so. But Confucianism drew together the many levels of obligation into one philosophical system and, most crucially, cemented it into a permanent framework for people in Chinese culture and for people in Japanese and Korean culture as well. Filial piety is the highest commandment of Confucian virtue. As a result, the system saw to it that those who are the primary transmitters of the culture (the parents) are also the ones gaining the greatest advantage from the system (that is, receiving the obedience of their offspring). It takes a serious wrenching for anyone brought up in this system to step out of it, whether we are talking about the revolution in mainland China or personal conversion to Christianity.

Buddhism

Many Chinese people, if asked about their religion, will say that they are Buddhist, though what they mean by that term has relatively little to do with textbook descriptions of Buddhism. But Buddhism does play a role in Chinese popular religion.

All scholarly protestations notwithstanding, there is no getting around the fact that common people within the various schools of Buddhism do worship the Buddha as god (whether they should or not is a different matter). In fact, it was the advent of Buddhism with its various divinities that spurred on the development of the Daoist pantheon. From there a certain amount of mutual absorption seems to be only a short step. It would be wrong to say that Buddha was adopted as just another deity, but it certainly is true that Buddha did come to be worshiped *along with* the many other gods of Daoism as the synthesis developed.

This is not to say that Buddha lost all meaning as Buddha. It is still recognized that he is the one who overcame death and reincarnation by pointing the way to nirvana. However, in popular religion, Buddha's achievement is no longer the impetus for others to seek the Buddha's way to nirvana. Instead, his spiritual state provides the power for humans to make the transition into death and the afterlife successfully.

It has already been noted that Avalokitasvara, originally the (male) Bodhisattva of mercy, was merged with the figure of Guan-yin, the Chinese goddess of mercy. Similarly, other spiritual beings of Buddhism have taken on new personalities as spirits, gods or goddesses in Chinese popular religion.

The Popular Synthesis

Basic beliefs. The whole character of Chinese popular religion flows in the direction of a plethora of rituals and obligations without much discernible doctrinal underpinning. The philosophy of the Dao-de-jing, the learned ruminations of Confucius and the abstract speculation of Buddhism have all receded from sight. Nevertheless, it is possible to discern a metaphysical underpinning that motivates the religion.

Chinese popular thought tends to be materialistic in orientation. The goal of the religion, broadly speaking, is this-worldly. In a sense the popular religious infrastructure exists to support the human being's pursuit of prosperity, health and overall success in life. Even funerals are no exception. In popular religion they aim at providing a materially prosperous existence for the deceased while at the same time possibly improving the life of surviving relatives.

A second important aspect of the popular Chinese philosophy of life is an emphasis on luck. Speculatively inclined people may explain the vicissitudes of fortune in terms of the balance of natural forces, but for the common person it simply comes down to luck. All of life is something of a gamble: with luck, things go well; without luck, there may be trouble. Divination provides some insight into a situation and allows for planning. Nevertheless, no one can escape the complexities of good or bad fortune.

The home. Much of what is central to Chinese popular religion takes place at home. Traditionally, each home contains a small shrine, usually not much more than a little shelf mounted in a red frame on the wall. On the shelf are implements for the daily veneration of family ancestors: a container that holds a few incense sticks, possibly a bowl with token food offerings and decorations such as a peacock feather. Behind the shelf are small tablets that bear the names of the departed and, possibly, their pictures. Nowadays many Chinese home altars include a perpetually glowing red bulb. Every morning the head of the household lights some incense in remembrance of the departed family members.

A Chinese home may also include small figurines of the gods (for example, the kitchen god or the three gods of happiness, prosperity and longevity). Such figures are sold in stores. People take them to the temple for a consecration ceremony called "opening the eyes." From this point on, the figure itself is imbued with spiritual force. Hindus believe that a god lives inside a figure as long as he is treated properly. In contrast, in Chinese religion, the actual physical statue has become divinized. The very material is considered to be charged with spiritual power. Figures that have been kept in temples for some time are considered particularly effective. Thus temples stock up on small home deities and auction them off at the Hungry Ghost Festival.

In order to ensure good fortune, a Chinese home ought to be built and kept according to the principles of *feng-shui* (geomancy). Feng-shui is the attempt to situate

oneself in the optimal current (feng-shui literally means "wind and water") of spiritual forces, avoiding the evil ones and harnessing the good ones. If a household seems to be subjected to an unusual amount of bad luck, the search is on for geomantic flaws that can be corrected to improve the situation. For example, the door to a house should never open directly onto the road. The walkway to the door should neither lead straight to the door nor bend at a sharp right angle. A house should not be too close to running water, and it should not be hidden completely by trees.

A house that is cluttered and messy inside is a spiritual disaster waiting to happen. Fire (yang) and water (yin) should not be too close to each other. Mirrors should be covered when not in use. Beds and desks should not be placed straight out from the wall or flat against

Roadside shrine to Guanin, the goddess of mercy.

a wall; instead, they should be set at an angle, cutting off the corner of a room. A modicum of plants and flowers, both outside and inside, enhance spiritual qualities.

There are many further regulations. It takes an expert to know all of them, to appraise each individual location for maximum spiritual benefit and to discover geomantic blunders that have brought misfortune on a family. Diseases or business failures are traced to an environment that ignores the principles of feng-shui. Many modern Chinese people, even ones who are not particularly religious in other respects, are willing to pay a lot of money for help from a feng-shui expert.

The temple. The temples of popular Chinese religion are places of communication and transaction. Although worship is a part of the regular activities within a temple, it would be misleading to think of these buildings as "houses of worship." Worship is only a means to an end. It is part of the obligatory pattern of dealing with the gods—gods that exist primarily to serve human beings.

Ideally, according to feng-shui principles, a temple should face south (yang) with a body of water behind it to the north (yin). Local conditions, of course, may dictate a different arrangement. Chinese temples are easily recognized by the curved, highly decorated roof. The entrance to the temple is guarded by several representations of guardian spirits. Sometimes there is a tiger (yang) on one side and a dragon (yin) on the other. Chinese temples usually have a high threshold because it is thought that evil spirits tend to walk with a shuffling gait and they will trip over the threshold if they try to enter.

Standing outside the entrance is what may be the most important object in the temple: a large pot to hold incense sticks (joss sticks). A worshiper lights several incense sticks, grasps them between the hands (brought together in prayer), faces heaven (Tian) for a few moments and then deposits the sticks in the pot. The person hopes to have established a connection with the spirit world so that the divine beings will pay attention to everything the worshiper does.

There are several incense pots in the temple. At the front of the temple are the figures of the gods, and to one side or in a different room are the ancestor tablets of local families. There are also implements for fortunetelling (divination), a counter where joss sticks and possibly a few additional items are sold. Visitors to a Chinese temple may be struck by the predominance of the color red. If the temple is old and established, the visitor will also notice the untidiness of the place; layers of black smoke from the incense have settled over everything, including the gods and decorations. Temples are left in this condition to demonstrate that the temple is used very frequently. Surely its gods must be highly efficacious.

In a popular temple, the deities are usually a mixture of Buddhist divinities and Daoist gods. Sometimes the two traditions are separated by a partition, but even then there is no further concern to maintain the distinctions. Temples contain images of deities that are of purely local interest, such as the tu-di-gong or other notables of the vicinity, as well as popular figures with broader reputations. There will be images of Lao-zi, Confucius, the Buddha and the jade emperor.

Particular attention is paid nowadays to a number of female deities. A favorite goddess is Ma-zu. According to legend, she was the daughter of a fisherman. She once rescued her father and brothers by leaving her physical body and transporting herself across the water to bring them aid. Because she died young and unmarried, her qi is available to people in distress. Ma-zu first became popular among sailors, but she is now widely worshiped as Tian-hau, the queen of heaven. Similarly, Guan-yin (the original Bodhisattva Avalokitas-vara) has been endowed with a legend that places her among the poor folk in the mountains. Worshipers appeal to her as the goddess of mercy.

The main gods of the temple are usually flanked by further guardian spirits, some of whom are said to have extraordinary powers in their own right. In front of the display of gods is a counterlike altar on which are piled the offerings brought by worshipers. A familiar item is a small pyramid of four oranges (three on the bottom, one on top). Sometimes worshipers insert joss sticks into them. People approach the gods, install their offerings and bow prostrate before the deities.

The atmosphere in the temple is completely informal. Popular temples have no priests, in contrast to traditional Daoism. Temple attendants are laypeople who maintain the premises and sell joss sticks. When they are not assisting worshipers, they may chat with people or go about the normal activities of their lives on the premises (for example, eating or watching television). Standing outside the main room is usually a large oven in which special paper offerings are burned for ancestors. A worshiper who performs this duty usually beats a large drum in order to alert the spirits that it is being done. On the whole, there is nothing serene or worshipful about the bustling atmosphere in a Chinese temple.

Divination. Having performed acts of obeisance to the gods, a worshiper in a Chinese temple then frequently settles down to the all-important business of fortunetelling. There are several methods of divination, but the one most commonly used involves several items: a tumbler of sticks, two crescent-shaped hollow blocks and printed slips of paper. The underlying theory is that, given a method that tries to be as random as possible, the spiritual forces of nature will manifest themselves and indicate the configuration a person is in at the time.

Divination can be performed by men or women. Typically a woman seeking to uncover her fortune kneels on the floor, possibly with some incense propped up in front of her. She holds a tumbler containing the sticks. Since different sources give different figures for the number of sticks in the tumbler, I have counted them in several temples and have found that they actually number between sixty and one hundred. The sticks are about one foot long. Each one bears a different symbol, which the inquirer herself most likely cannot interpret. The woman holds the tumbler at about a forty-five degree angle chest high and starts shaking it continuously. Slowly some of the sticks start to move up in the tumbler until eventually one slides all the way out and falls down in front of the woman.

Now the inquirer needs to find out whether that stick is the right one for her at this moment. She grasps the two blocks between her hands, shakes them a few times and lets them fall to the ground in front of her. It they land in such a way that one block lies hollow side up and the other one lies hollow side down (resembling yin and yang, of course), then the answer is yes, and she has the right stick. If they both land facing down (yang-yang), the answer is no, and the stick is placed aside. If they land both sides up, the answer is indeterminate, and the stick is put back in the tumbler. In either of the last two cases, the process of shaking the tumbler is repeated.

If the stick is approved, the inquirer takes it to a fortuneteller. There is never a shortage of fortunetellers around Chinese temples. Usually some are right on the premises. The fortuneteller matches the stick with the appropriate slip of paper bearing a cryptic message. This message needs to be interpreted, and then the inquirer must make her decisions on the basis of the interpretation.

The results of the fortunetelling procedure may not be irrevocable. For example, a temple in Singapore that is primarily used for divination is presided over by the goddess of mercy, Guan-yin. Worshipers come prepared to make a present to the goddess. If their fortune comes out as favorable, they present their gifts in gratitude; if it is unfavorable, they make their offerings to Guan-yin in the hope of getting her to avert the coming calamity.

Divination guides the lives of many Chinese people today. Its application ranges all the way from trivial matters to serious decisions such as marriage or career choices. If bad fortune has beset a person or a family, divination is used to find the cause so that it can be rectified. Frequently the disturbance is seen to stem from an ancestor's needing to be mollified in some way.

Guardian spirit in the Ten Hock Temple, Singapore.

Funerals and ancestors. A funeral is the process by which a person makes the transition from living human being to ancestor status. In traditional Daoism, funeral rituals are performed by professional priests. An extremely elaborate funeral ceremony may take several days. In popular Chinese religion, Buddhist monks have the responsibility for funerals.

Traditionally, the corpse was dressed in auspicious clothes and laid out in the deceased's home. Nowadays, the central place of mourning is often a tent erected by the side of the street. In front of the tent is an altar containing an effigy of the deceased with a photograph where the head would be. This altar may include space for offerings of food and incense. The rest of the tent contains chairs from which the mourners can observe the proceedings. Further ceremonies will be carried out in the temple at the time of interment or cremation.

Buddhist monks serve by reciting the proper chants on behalf of the family members for the welfare of the deceased. At the temple ceremony, the monks may sit at a table and perform these chants to the occasional accompaniment of a rhythm instrument such as a gong. The family is present but is not involved in the ceremony at all. In fact, since this is a moment of auspicious contact with the spirit world, they may conclude certain economic decisions for the coming years on the spot. This is a clear instance in which people have consigned their ritual obligations to those having professional expertise.

The deceased is prepared to live in the underworld in material comfort. He or she is supplied with a beautifully made paper house complete with paper furniture, as well as possibly a paper car, clothes and boxes on boxes of paper money. This religious currency may be marked in Mandarin on one side and in English on the other side: "Bank of Hell: Pay to the Underworld 10,000." All of these items are piled together in one large stack of luggage that is burned at the appropriate moment.

Traditional practice is to bury the deceased, but cremation is frequently practiced in popular religion, under the influence of Buddhism. At this point, the spirit of the deceased, or at least a representative part of it,[16] is conveyed into the spirit tablet. Together with a picture of the deceased, this little plaque will eventually be placed on the little shrine in the home. But first it may be maintained in the temple for a while. For the first thirty days and then at decreasing intervals thereafter, regular food offerings will be made to the deceased, assisted by the Buddhist monks as necessary. If there is an eldest son, it is his particular responsibility to make sure all the needed rituals are carried out punctiliously.

Food offerings for the dead again require the crescent-shaped blocks to determine whether or not the departed has accepted the offering. The person stands in front of the tablet and throws the blocks, looking for one to land up and the other one to land down. If numerous tries produce a negative answer, the person may have to undertake further spiritual remedies, possibly a seance.

Séances. A black flag hanging outside a Chinese popular temple indicates that it is used for séances. Having a séance requires a sizable fee. The medium is usually an older man. He goes into a trance and then reveals the will of the spirits to the person making the inquiry. In the process, the medium frequently pierces himself with sharp weaponry, and the client may be required to sample a token of his blood or saliva. The medium's commands are considered absolute.

The life cycle. Chinese society emphasizes rites of passage less than other cultures. Part of the reason for that phenomenon may be the emphasis on the community of which each person is an integral part. Since the traditional, nearly universal rites of passage (birth, puberty, marriage and death) focus on the individual's journey through life, it is quite natural that the Chinese deemphasize them (except, of course, for funerals).

Birth, though obviously a joyous event, is not considered a religious occasion in the sense that it calls for great temple celebrations. The communal orientation of Chinese culture is such that traditionally all people are reckoned to have become a year older on New Year's Day, not on the anniversary of their birth. Regardless of the exact date on which each individual was born, all people have their birthday on New Year's Day. The Chinese zodiac is also calculated on the basis of the year of one's birth, not the specific day.

Except for some minor local customs, Chinese culture does not recognize a rite of passage associated with puberty. Apparently there was such a ritual at one time, but it became absorbed into the marriage ceremony.[17]

Marriage in Chinese culture is best understood as the extension of the existing family, not as the establishment of a new family unit. The ceremony is primarily an event between the two families, not between the couple and a god. Gods and spirits are acknowledged, but the highlight of the ceremony comes when the bride and groom present cups of tea to their respective in-laws. The groom takes a cup of tea, presents it to each of the bride's parents and kneels prostrate before them. The bride does the same for the groom's parents. Thus they acknowledge their new filial obligations and, at least implicitly, commit themselves to support the care of their in-laws when they become ancestor spirits.

Lu Dong Bin, one of the nine immortals, depicted at Haw Par Villa, Singapore. He is dressed in the garb of a scholar and carrying his magic sword.

Festivals. In addition to various local festivals and observances, three main holidays are celebrated in Chinese religion. The Chinese New Year, reckoned according to a lunar calendar, occurs in January or February of our Gregorian calendar. In a twelve-year cycle, successive years are named according to animals. Thus 1998 is the year of the boar, followed by the tiger rabbit, dragon, snake, horse, sheep, monkey, cock, dog, rat and ox. As the new year approaches, houses are cleaned and decorated. This is a time of commercial importance as people buy new clothes and presents for each other. The animal of the upcoming year is featured prominently in decorations.

On New Year's Eve people prepare themselves physically (with baths and new clothes) as well as spiritually. The head of the household makes his formal report to the kitchen god, whose lips have been smeared with honey in the hope that his report to the jade emperor will be sweet and favorable. The Chinese New Year is observed for at least two days. People exchange presents, particularly oranges (because of their gold color). Unmarried young people receive "lucky money" (hong-bao) in little red envelopes. People go from house to house visiting each other. There may be parades, fireworks and other public celebrations. Religious observances focus particularly on Fu, Lu and Shou, the gods of happiness, prosperity and longevity. Traditionally, everyone is considered to be a year older on New Year's Day, regardless of the actual birth date.

Qing-ming is a joyful spring festival, the highlight of which is a trip to the cemetery. Families take the day to visit the graves of their departed. They spruce up the grave sites and make offerings of food, firecrackers and the usual joss sticks. Then the family gathers together for a picnic on the grounds. It is very important that each family member partakes of the food just offered to the ancestor.

For the sake of any spirit among the departed that has not received proper care, there is the Hungry Ghost Festival. The idea behind this season, which usually falls in the month of August, is that dissatisfied spirits leave their underworld abode and roam the earth, possibly causing havoc. At this time special observances for the deceased are performed. People erect special roadside shrines and burn paper money in the streets. Older sons may hire Buddhist monks to say special prayers on their behalf.

Other special practices are connected to the Hungry Ghost Festival. Theatrical companies construct outdoor stages and perform musical plays for the public (as well as for any roving spirit) free of charge. The content of the plays themselves is not religious, but a religious dedication ceremony precedes the performance. It is during Hungry Ghost that temples auction off figures of deities that have been kept on the premises to become imbued with spiritual power.

■ So You Meet a Chinese with Ties to Popular Religion . . .

What You Might Expect

Clearly there is no way to discuss all of the many important distinctions that come into play in the interface between American culture and Chinese culture.[18] There are, after all, more than a billion Chinese. For purposes of our brief discussion here, we need to restrict the meaning as much as possible to encountering someone who practices popular Chinese religion. Of course, cultural distinctions are an important aspect of such an encounter. Anyone intending to have meaningful relationships with Chinese people would do well to prepare by learning what to do and what to avoid.

American culture tends to be individualistic; Chinese culture is communally oriented. On numerous occasions, when I asked a Chinese person, "What do *you* like?" the answer came back, "Oh, *we* like . . ."

American culture tends to be direct and confrontational; Chinese culture prefers less direct interaction. The worst fate that can befall a Chinese person (as well as other Asians) is to "lose face," that is, to be put on the spot with embarrassment. Thus it is crucial never to put someone on the spot by directly exposing a mistake or arguing that person into a corner.

American culture tends to allow more public expression of emotion than Chinese culture does. American culture is not excessively emotional, yet it may encourage people to show how they feel. Thus Americans are touched by occasional public tears. If they think that a person has been wronged sufficiently, they may allow him to lose his temper. In Chinese culture, public display of emotion is considered a loss of face. Rather than raising one's voice in an argument, the general rule of thumb is that the quieter a conversation gets, the more serious the conflict.

Relating the Gospel

These matters become significant when we consider the nature of American Christian evangelism: it is individualistic, confrontational and often emotional. Consequently, once again, the universal question of cultural contextualization—how to present the gospel within a specific culture without violating either the integrity of the culture or the gospel message—becomes paramount.

Consider what the Chinese person brings to the religious conversation. First, the Chinese worldview is explicitly supernatural. People from traditional Chinese homes do not need to be persuaded of the reality of a spiritual world. If anything, their world is overpopulated with spiritual reality. This is not to say that Chinese people cannot be atheists. Nevertheless, even the vehemence of communists' and freethinkers' reactions against the supernatural indicates what an important part of the Chinese psyche religion continues to be.

Second, Chinese persons typically display the loyalty to community and family that is so firmly rooted in Confucian principles. From the vantage point of Christian contact, this heritage carries both positives and negatives. An advantage lies in the fact that the Chinese person is used to thinking in terms of objective obligations; the notion of divine commandments is not foreign to him or her. The disadvantage in terms of inviting a person to become a Christian lies in the absolute loyalty to parents and ancestors that Chinese culture demands. The greatest obstacle by far to a Chinese young person's becoming a Christian lies in the fact that this decision would offend his parents. From the parent's perspective, if the oldest son (or daughter) does not perform the proper rites, the parent can anticipate an afterlife as a hungry ghost in hell. People involved in Chinese evangelism often hear the statement "I would become a Christian, but my parents have forbidden it."

Third, the person coming out of Chinese religion is likely to carry a sense of inadequacy. The Chinese person often lives in a universe consisting of forces beyond human control. People are expected to control those forces through ritual, and yet the same forces can double back again and again and shatter their existence. Like a character in a Franz Kafka novel, the person is required to win in a game that is stacked against her right from the beginning. Consequently, a sense of "sin," loosely defined, a sense of not having measured up to some absolute requirements, is never far from the Chinese experience.

For a small annual fee one can rent one of these small compartments so that one's light will burn before the gods.

The question then becomes whether the person can understand the nature of sin as offense against God and is willing to accept Jesus Christ as Savior. As mentioned before, the obligation of filial piety stands in the way more often than any other barrier. Many Chinese find it impossible to give up their most important obligation.

Some Christians have made certain allowances for allegiance to ancestors. The earliest Catholic missionaries did not object to ancestor worship, since Catholic Christianity has maintained a fairly robust cult for the dead in its own right. Protestants have generally objected to the practice as non-Christian spirit worship. Of late, some missionaries have attempted to pursue a mediating position. They advocate putting a representation of Jesus and the cross in the place formerly occupied by the shrine. Perhaps a pictorial history of the family could be displayed as well.[19] This practice, however, seems naive about the degree to which human nature is inclined toward animistic ritual. The danger is that such substitution could wind up undermining the very faith it is supposed to facilitate.

The family ties that can keep a person from becoming a Christian are real and powerful. Accepting Christ as Savior can be seen as a total abnegation of a Chinese young person's identity. The conflict is internal as well as external. The cost of becoming a Christian can be very great. In view of this fact, it would be very easy to downplay the confrontation by reasoning that as long as a person would be willing under more favorable circumstances to become a Christian, the good intention must be sufficient. But Christ himself made it clear that loyalty to him may demand sacrificing family allegiance for the sake of salvation. He said, "He who loves father or mother more than me is not worthy of me; and he who loves son or daughter more than me is not worthy of me; and he who does not take his cross and follow me is not worthy of me" (Mt 10:37-38 RSV). And Christ also stated, "Every one who acknowledges me before men, the Son of man also will acknowledge before the angels of God; but he who denies me before men will be denied before the angels of God" (Lk 12:8-9 RSV).

These harsh demands are easy to contemplate in the lax, pseudoreligious environment of American culture. They are not easy to live out in a setting that is hostile to Christianity. Perhaps we need to think of the American culture—where for the most part becoming a Christian, at least a nominal Christian, carries virtually no price tag—as the exception, and the many other parts of the world—where far more sacrifice may be required—as the rule. The fact of the matter is that American culture has produced a type of Christianity that is so intermingled with the culture itself that it can hardly be distinguished from the culture. Where would one stand up for Christ and be counted in America? Without wanting to diminish the cost involved, traditional Chinese society provides more concrete opportunity for a person to give personal testimony of having received Christ and having broken with the past.

Of course, despite these very real obstacles, millions of Chinese people have responded to the gospel with faith in Christ. Not only are there many thriving churches in Hong Kong, Taiwan and Singapore, but even within the People's Republic of China, where Confucian-style authoritarianism has been used to promote atheism, Christianity has persisted and grown. Indeed, for many American Christians, Watchman Nee (1903-1972), a first-generation Christian convert who founded the Little Flock movement, has become a favorite author and teacher.

Watchman Nee in his own testimony, without meaning to do so, illustrates how Confucian attitudes have lived on as part of Christian family life in China.[20] When Nee was about to finish college, he intended to pursue Christian missionary work on a particular island. He raised his support through donations and recruited numerous Christians to pray for him. But shortly before he was to set out, for no apparent reason his parents forbade him to go. Watchman Nee did not defy his parents and go anyway. Neither did he tell his supporters that his parents would not let him go, for that would have disgraced them. Instead, he shouldered all the blame himself and simply told all of his supporters that he had changed his mind, even though they thought less of him as a consequence. Being a Christian did not nullify filial piety for him, just as it does not for numerous authentic Chinese Christians today.

Mastering the Material

When you have finished studying this chapter, you should be able to

1. summarize the main elements and the distinctives of traditional Chinese religion and practice;

2. describe the breakdown of the Chinese empire in the late Zhou period and how it led to the formation of various schools;

3. indicate the main teachings of the Mohists and legalists;

4. summarize the life of Lao-zi and the teaching of the Dao-de-jing;

5. trace the history of Daoism from its philosophical phase through its becoming a religion with many deities;

6. describe Confucianism in terms of the person of Confucius, his teaching and the later implementation thereof;

7. point out the contribution Buddhism has made to popular Chinese religion;

8. summarize the basic elements of Chinese popular religion including home observance, feng-shui, temples, gods, funerals, seances, ancestor relationships and festivals;

9. outline some of the basic considerations in an American Christian's contact with an adherent of Chinese popular religion for the sake of evangelism.

Term Paper Ideas

1. Explore the specific beliefs and rituals of early traditional religion in China.

2. Describe in detail the beliefs of one of the schools rivaling Confucianism or Daoism in the warring states period, for example, Mohism or legalism.

3. Compile what can be known about some of the earliest Daoist practices.

4. Write out the full story of the Yellow Turbans, the Celestial Master (School of Five Rice Kernels), one of the fang-shi or one of the xian.

5. Do an analysis of some Chinese myths and show how they exemplify phases of Chinese religion.

6. Do a philosophical analysis of one of the interpretations of Confucianism.

7. Trace the development and impact of the notion of filial piety in Chinese thought.

8. Report on life in a traditional Chinese home; describe the various roles and how they fit into the religious commitments.

9. Write out the story of a modern Chinese deity (for example, the jade emperor or Ma-zu) and see if you can find variations on the same story.

10. Describe in depth the observance of a Chinese festival, marriage or funeral.

11. Trace the fate of religion in China from the beginning of the twentieth century to its current situation under Communist rule.

12. On the basis of research or interviews, identify strategies used by Christian missionaries to Chinese people.

Core Bibliography

Confucius. *The Analects*. Translated by D. C. Lau. New York: Penguin, 1979.

Fung Yu-lan. *A Short History of Chinese Philosophy*. New York: Macmillan, 1962.

Overmyer, Daniel L. *Religions of China: The World as Living System*. San Francisco: HarperSanFrancisco, 1986.

Thompson, Laurence G. *Chinese Religion*. Belmont, Calif.: Wadsworth, 1989.

Waley, Arthur. *The Way and Its Power: A Study of the Tao Te Ching and Its Place in Chinese Thought*. New York: Grove, 1958.

Chapter 11

Shinto & the Japanese Synthesis

Estimated Practitioners of Shinto
Worldwide: 2,844,000
North America: 1,000

The religion of Japan, Shinto, represents a synthesis of religious traditions. In China, traditional religion, Daoism, Buddhism and Confucianism fused to form a popular religion. Similarly, Japan saw a fusion of traditional religion, Shinto, Confucianism and Buddhism. But Japanese religion never came together in quite the same way that Chinese religion did. There is a form of Japanese folk religion, but it has not attained the same institutional character that Chinese popular religion has achieved. If Chinese religion is like a mighty river formed from the confluence of lesser streams, then Japanese religion is like numerous rivers constantly crossing each other, sometimes flowing together, sometimes going their own ways only to come together again in another place. The Japanese experience has resulted in numerous ongoing experiments in bringing different systems together. Of course, this image is meant to depict a general pattern of trends and is not an absolute characterization.

Buddhism, for example, fused with Shinto to form the Ryobu synthesis. But Buddhism also popularized itself in its own right by adapting Buddhist schools to common people, as in the Pure Land schools, to a much greater extent than it did in China. Japan is home to a virtually uncountable number of subschools of Buddhist belief and practice. (A popular saying puts the number at eighty-four thousand.) To this day, one fascinating aspect of Japanese religion is the ongoing synthesizing of new religions, which for the most part bring together old ideas in novel and creative ways. This Japanese synthesis combines various elements, but they do not completely discard their original identity. A leading scholar of Japanese religion puts it this way: "A person might be married in a Shinto shrine, live his life according to Confucian social teachings, hold some Taoistic beliefs about 'lucky' and 'unlucky,' participate in folk festivals, and have his funeral conducted by a Buddhist temple."[1]

Shinto

Shinto is rightfully identified as the Japanese national religion for two reasons. For one thing, it is the religion based on Japan's own indigenous mythology. For another, it was incorporated into the Japanese nation-state as headed up by the emperor. Nevertheless, it has existed as a separate religion for only short periods of time. For most of Japan's history, Shinto has existed in conjunction with other religions, particularly Buddhism.

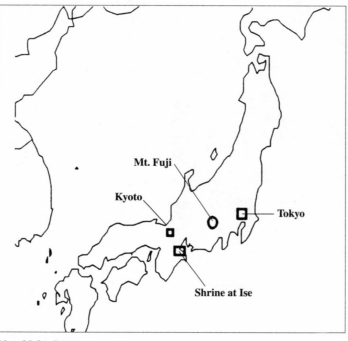

Map 11.1. Japan

The word *shinto* is a Japanese adaptation of the Chinese term *shen-dao,* which means "the way of the gods." The Japanese expression for Shinto is *kami-no-michi,* which has the same meaning. The gods are known as the *kami.* Shinto defines itself as a way of relating to the spirit world. It is not a set of clearly defined doctrines or a speculative philosophy. For that reason the term *Shintoism* is to be avoided. In a sense, Shinto simply means "religion." It came to stand for Japan's ancient religious heritage in contrast to imported religions.

The kami. The term *kami* resists definition because it refers to a broad range of divine powers. In the most general sense it simply means "divine" or "sacred." In the most specific sense it can refer to personal deities. The term *kami* can also refer to an impersonal spiritual force (similar to the notion of mana), loosely identified personal spirits dwelling in natural phenomena and more specifically identified personal spirits. Thus kami are spiritual realities that pervade all levels of being.

Kami are particularly associated with distinctive natural phenomena. An unusual

rock, a tree, a brook or a mountain can be seen as a manifestation of kami. Kami are particularly associated with evergreen trees and, for obvious economic reasons, with rice fields. Special places of kami manifestations are frequently marked. For example, a pointed rock may be encircled with a straw rope or a two-rock formation, considered "married," may be indicated with a straw rope and a pole identifying the male rock.

All agricultural economies, Japan's included, are at the mercy of the forces of nature, especially the weather. Calamity is never more than a drought away. Agricultural economies are almost invariably preoccupied with fertility, and the people's religion manifests this concern with a proliferation of symbols and rituals that have significant sexual meaning. Shinto follows this pattern, and Shinto symbolism can frequently be construed along the lines of sexuality or fertility.[2]

Kamakura Daibutsu, bronze figure of Amida at Kotokuin Temple in Kamakura (approximately 40 feet high). Photograph: Michael Harbin.

Ancient historical origins. We have little firm knowledge about Japan in ancient times. Apparently the islands were populated by various tribes that attempted to gain ascendancy over each other. At least some of the islands may have been governed by matriarchies. These female rulers may have been shamans who maintained their position by allowing spirits to speak and work through them. What can be pieced together about early Japanese traditional religion includes the usual strong cult of spirits, fertility deities and ancestors. The absence of written sources makes reconstruction of this prehistory precarious.

Sometime around the fourth century A.D., Japan became unified under one emperor of the Yamato clan. It is a safe assumption that he also centralized religious practices to the extent that he set up his own religion as supreme and made others subservient to it. This clan may have worshiped the sun goddess, Amaterasu, for quite a while.

Apparently the emperor legitimated his claim to the throne by asserting that he descended from this goddess.

The Japanese islands underwent a cultural revolution beginning around the sixth century A.D. People came to Japan from Korea and China, bringing a new and more advanced culture. Most importantly, the Chinese brought their system of writing. The Japanese adopted the Chinese system almost immediately and modified it to suit their needs. The Chinese also brought innovations in architecture, clothing and implements for daily living.

Another crucial Chinese contribution to Japanese culture was philosophy and religion. The Confucian system, which emphasized filial piety and chains of authority, appealed to the Japanese because it undergirded already existing practices. Daoism brought a few philosophical concepts such as yin and yang but did not make great inroads with its religious practices. However, Buddhism strongly influenced the ongoing development of Japanese culture. What Buddhism provided was something that had been lacking in Japanese culture up to that point, namely, a comprehensive worldview and a system of clearly ordered celestial beings (the Buddhas and Bodhisattvas). Consequently, Buddhism flourished on Japanese soil in unprecedented ways.

The Kojiki. In response to the coming of Buddhism, possibly even in reaction against it, Shinto needed to define itself more clearly. Thus early in the eighth century A.D. the emperor ordered a minor official named Yasumaro to collect all available information concerning the kami and the ancient origins of Japan. Undoubtedly the emperor wanted to shore up his claims to authority by demonstrating his divine descent. Yasumaro traveled all over Japan and in A.D. 712 produced a coherent narrative called the *Kojiki* ("record of ancient matters"). Exhorted by the emperor to record all variations of the same story, in A.D. 720 Yasumaro also wrote the *Nihon Shoki* (also known as the *Nihongi,* the "chronicles of Japan"). These writings represent a mythological history of Japan from the creation of the world to the seventh century A.D. The *Nihongi* apparently includes a writing that predates the *Kojiki,* the *Kiujiki,* of which we have no extant ancient manuscripts (modern versions of the *Kiujiki* are reconstructions).

It would be wrong to understand the *Kojiki* and the *Nihongi* as the Bible of Shinto, for they are not considered divine, authoritative revelation. The *Kojiki* is not a book of instruction in morality or ritual. It is a narrative that endorses political and religious practices by deriving them from the times of the gods. The role of a manual of ritual and prayer is fulfilled by a tenth-century collection of prayers, the Amatsu Norito.

The myth. The central myth of Shinto is depicted in the *Kojiki* and is repeated with many variations in the *Nihongi.* The myth begins with the time of primordial chaos, when yin and yang were intermixed in a kind of egg-shaped formation. Out of this original ooze emerged a number of kami in pairs, some of which were male and female pairs.

The recorded myth contains only obscure references to an original creator god. This is not surprising because, first, the authentic Japanese elements in the myth are the products of an ancient (possibly matriarchal) fertility-oriented religion. Such cultures were shown by Wilhelm Schmidt's Vienna school to have had some of the longest development away from an original monotheism. Second, the Chinese influences on the myth were themselves the result of more than a thousand years of development from the ancient recognition of Shang-di. Consequently, the very hypothesis that religions develop away from monotheism demands that any trace of original monotheism be at best vestigial. This is precisely the case.

In the *Nihongi* the first kami emerging from the chaos arises out of a reed shoot. He is called Kuni-toko-tachi-no-Mikoto ("land eternal-stand-august thing"). He does not fulfill a particular creator role. In the *Kojiki* he arises after other kami. However, the interesting thing about this deity is that in the *Nihongi,* as the first kami, he is invested with special dignity. An early commentary (possibly contemporary with the composition) states with regard to the special script that is used to write his name,

Torri gate at Hachiman Shrine, Kamakura. Photograph: Michael Harbin.

"The character . . . is used owing to the extreme dignity of this Deity. For the others [a different character of writing] is used. Both are read Mikoto."[3] This statement does not prove anything (it does not even say much, especially since the text later on does not observe the distinction). However, if the theory of original monotheism is accepted, then this kind of differentiation of the first kami is just the kind of vestige that would be expected at this point.

The seventh generation of emerging kami was Izanagi ("man-who-invites") and Izanami ("woman-who-invites"). At the behest of the earlier kami, these two proceeded to create the Japanese islands. Izanagi stirred the egg-shaped mass with his spear. When he lifted it out, some coagulated brine dropped off and formed the first island. Izanagi and Izanami descended to this newly formed soil in order to get married.

The couple erected a stone pillar on the island and began walking around it, apparently in typical enactment of an ancient wedding ceremony. As they performed this ritual, Izanami addressed her husband first, a violation of protocol (possibly harking back to early matriarchal custom). As a result of her misbehavior, she gave birth to a monster. When they repeated the ceremony, Izanagi spoke first and all went well. A time of bliss ensued, and Izanagi continued to create islands, plants, animals and human beings. Izanami gave birth to many more kami.

When Izanami gave birth to the kami of fire, she was burned severely and died. At death Izanami went to the land of Yomi, the abode of the dead, which was already populated by sinister spirits. The grief-stricken Izanagi descended into the nether-world to reclaim his beloved. When he arrived in the darkness of this deep cave, Izanami warned him not to look at her because she was already in the advanced stages of decomposition. But Izanagi nevertheless lighted the end of his comb as a torch. One glimpse of Izanami's maggot-ridden remains filled him with horror and revulsion, and he fled in terror. Izanami was livid and sent several evil spirits after him, but he escaped through clever tactics. Once Izanagi had escaped, Izanami came to the entrance of the cave and cursed him and all of his offspring. He then replied in kind. The mutual maledictions ended with Izanami saying that she would kill a thousand persons a year and Izanagi replying that he would cause one and a half as many people to be born each year. Thus originated the burden of death along with the promise of new life.

Izanagi proceeded to the ocean in order to purify himself with water. As he washed different parts of his body, further kami emerged. From his left eye came Amaterasu, the sun goddess; from his right eye appeared Tsukiyomi, the moon god.[4] Finally out of his nostril there emerged Susa-no-wo, the storm god. These three kami became some of the highest Shinto deities. Izanagi presented Amaterasu with a beautiful pearl necklace.

On the face of it, the sun goddess and the storm god might have a compatibility problem, and that is how the mythology continues. Susa-no-wo was wreaking havoc and disturbing the other kami. Eventually his sister, Amaterasu, retreated into a cave, vowing never to come out again. Unabated darkness covered the universe. The other kami missed the sun goddess, so they devised a plan to lure her out. On a tree facing the cave entrance they hung a mirror and her pearl necklace. Then a female kami performed a passionate dance to the accompaniment of a drum as the other kami laughed and clapped along. Overcome with curiosity, Amaterasu stepped out of the cave to see what was going on. As soon as she emerged, she beheld her dazzling countenance in the mirror and was overcome by her own splendor. Just then a strong kami closed off the cave with a rock so that she would not be able to return. Mollified, she remained in the company of the other kami.

Now Amaterasu ruled in the plain of heaven while a descendant of Susa-no-wo, the storm kami, governed on earth. This ruler did a very poor job, so Amaterasu sent her grandson Ni-ni-gi to take charge. Thus for a time earth was governed by a kami descended from Amaterasu. Ni-ni-gi's great-grandson Jimmu Tenno was considered human, though he was a lineal descendant of Amaterasu. According to the legend, he was the first human emperor of Japan. This tradition dates his accession at 660 B.C., although studies in Japanese history indicate that this date is highly unlikely. All subsequent Japanese emperors, including the current occupant of the throne, are supposed to be directly descended from Jimmu Tenno and thus from Amaterasu, the sun goddess.

Mount Fuji from Fuji Peace Park. Photograph: Michael Harbin.

The history of Shinto. Since Shinto started its self-reflective existence in response to Buddhism, it is not surprising that much of its continuing history is also the story of the interaction between Shinto and Buddhism. The first part of this story is about the slow absorption of Shinto into Buddhism and vice versa. Early on, there was lively debate between adherents of Shinto and Buddhists as to whose deities were superior, with each side claiming its own as primary and the other's as secondary. However, the more Buddhism adapted itself to Japanese culture, the less hostile the relationship became. Pure Land and Zen produced increasingly Japanese versions of Buddhist teachings, and the Shingon school turned into an indigenous form of Buddhism. Thus it became possible to undertake a grand synthesis, and this is exactly what happened. The new form of Shinto-Buddhism was called Ryobu ("two-sided Shinto").

Even as part of Ryobu, however, Shinto was losing ground to Buddhism. Reversing this trend took as long as the original amalgamation. During the Tokugawa period (1603-1867), the emperors were not much more than titular figureheads. Japan was actually ruled by military leaders called shoguns. Buddhism was ascendant, and Zen, combined with a large dose of Confucianism, became the philosophy of the samurai warriors, with their strict feudal code of honor known as Bushido. Shinto provided the element of patriotism that fueled their devotion, but Buddhism supplied the religious elements. Paradoxically, the ascendancy of Buddhism allowed Shinto to disengage itself, and thus the Ryobu synthesis began slowly to unravel. Once again Shinto began to sell itself as a separate religion and provided a clear alternative to Buddhism. The animistic rituals of Shinto appealed to common people, and a Shinto revival occurred. During this period Japan isolated itself from all foreign influences, particularly the countries of Europe and the United States. Christianity, which had gained significant minority status (its adherents constituting about 10 percent of the total population) on the basis of earlier Catholic missionary efforts, was forcefully eradicated.

Shinto had its moment of glory in 1868 with the so-called Meiji restoration. This period lasted until the end of World War II in 1945. During this era, a new mindset developed, which combined, somewhat paradoxically, strong nationalistic sentiments with a new openness toward foreign contacts.[5] Tragically, nationalism bred imperialism (as it did in many other countries) and eventually led to World War II.

A rehabilitation of Shinto played an important role in the Meiji restoration. Not since the early days of the Buddhist intrusion had Shinto enjoyed such prominence. By political decree, the Meiji regime created state Shinto, which now existed side by side with shrine Shinto and domestic Shinto, and spawned sectarian Shinto.[6]

State Shinto. Not all Shinto priests supported the developments of the Meiji era. Some of them saw unwarranted usurpation of the religion by the government. Nonetheless, a constitution issued in 1889 placed Shinto entirely in the hands of the Japanese state. The establishment of state Shinto included three major decrees. First, Shinto is not a religion. It is an expression of patriotism that supersedes all religious loyalties. All Japanese people are expected to honor this tradition.

Second, all Shinto shrines are in the custody of the state. Suddenly every Shinto priest was a government employee, a status that functioned as something of a double-edged sword. On the one hand, government ownership guaranteed a secure future for the shrines and their attendants. Shinto establishments did not need to worry about raising funds to keep up the premises and pay the priests. On the other hand, the government was in a position to decree the practices of Shinto. As one example, Shinto priests were forbidden to perform funerals, because such acts were purely religious in character and not something the government had an interest in.

Third, the head of the Japanese government is the divine emperor. As we have seen, the Shinto myth includes the legitimation of the emperor as the direct descendant of the sun goddess. The Meiji constitution reasserted this belief, implementing it by recognizing the emperor as both the ruler of Japan and the head of the "nonreligion" Shinto. He was thereby in a position to demand unquestioned allegiance on all levels. Part of the political realization of this dogma was that the military reported directly to the emperor, not the parliament.

The Meiji establishment of state Shinto bore the seeds of its own destruction (as do all forms of authoritarianism). For one thing, the total usurpation of Shinto by the government was never fully actualized, partially because it is just not possible to establish religious allegiance on political grounds.[7] For another, the absolutized nationalism fed on its own appetite for ever-increasing world dominion until Japan found itself on the losing end of World War II. The kamikazi (the winds of the kami) pilots, who carried out suicide missions in the closing years of the war, symbolize well what happened to this system. They destroyed themselves on behalf of an unwinnable cause in total nationalistic and religious fervor for the emperor. In 1946 the victorious Allies abolished state Shinto and coerced the emperor into declaring that he was not divine.

Shrine Shinto. The abolition of state Shinto left the shrines of Japan in a precarious economic situation. The loss of government funding was a serious setback, but in essence it simply meant a reversion to the situation prior to the Meiji regime. Many shrines had to lay off priests, and many priests had to find supplementary employment.

Shinto shrines follow a basic pattern that is adapted to specific local conditions. The entrance to the grounds of a shrine is marked by the traditional gate, the torii. A torii always consists of two vertical posts covered by two parallel horizontal beams.[8] Beyond that basic design, torii can be made of different materials, although wood is the most common. They can be plain or extremely ornate. There may be a single gate or a series of gates leading to the shrine. In addition to marking the entrance to a shrine area, torii are placed in other locations where a strong presence of kami is affirmed, such as on a large rock.

Dragon and washbasin, small Shinto shrine, Kamakura. Photograph: Michael Harbin.

Where possible, shrines are located in a parklike setting that includes natural water and evergreen trees. The path leading to the actual shrine should curve to the left so that people do not walk into the presence of the kami directly. Along the path there may be figures of certain animals that represent spiritual power.

In approaching a shrine, worshipers must purify themselves with water. In terms of the Shinto myth, they are emulating Izanagi's purification at the ocean. The basic ritual consists of some perfunctory washing actions and a sip of water.

A Shinto shrine is divided into two main segments, the first one of which may be subdivided as well. The outer part of the shrine is called the *haiden,* or "hall of worship." It can be in a building or in an open area under a canopy. If it is outside, it will have several more evergreen trees. There is a bell on a rope and an offering box as well as a facility that receives food offerings. As the worshipers approach the site, they solicit the attention of the kami by ringing the bell and clapping their hands. Now that the kami have been alerted, the worshipers can present their offerings, either some money or a gift of food. Almost any food or drink, other than red meat, is an appropriate gift.

The inner area of the shrine is called the *honden*. Worshipers do not usually enter it. The honden is the repository of the most sacred objects associated with the shrine. These items are known as the *shintai*. There may be anything from a mirror to a paper with special writing on it. The shintai are in some way attached to the kami of that shrine. Even though statues of kami are not unknown in Shinto, they are not objects of worship in a typical Shinto shrine.

The highest Shinto shrine in Japan is the grand shrine at Ise, which is dedicated to Amaterasu and serves as the emperor's official shrine. According to the Nihon Shoki, the emperor used to keep the shintai of Amaterasu close to his person at all times. He would even sleep with these objects—an iron sword, a pearl necklace (Izanagi's gift to Amaterasu) and a mirror (the one used to lure the goddess out of the cave). Keeping these spiritually charged items near him caused the emperor great anxiety, which was not allayed by carrying replicas. Consequently he looked for a way to deposit them in a shrine, and eventually Amaterasu herself showed a princess where her shintai should be kept. She designated Ise, located about two hundred miles from Tokyo, and the princess built the central shrine there.

The shrine at Ise is situated on extremely spacious grounds. The precinct also houses the shrine of Toyo-Uke-Hime, the female kami of food. Both shrines conform to the same ancient architectural pattern. They are made of bare logs constructed into steeply gabled buildings that are erected on stiltlike poles. The main buildings are razed every twenty years and rebuilt with fresh wood. The emperor is expected to appear at the grand shrine to announce any major policy decisions. After all, he rules the country at the behest of the goddess.

A major shrine complex may include other structures, such as a Buddhist temple. Chances are there will be a fortunetelling booth and a place that sells amulets, such as the sacred pieces of paper called *gohei*.

In addition to providing facilities for personal worship, Shinto shrines carry out other functions in the community. For one thing, they are the centers for various festivals. In general, Shinto is not tied to its shrines for religious observances. Most rituals are carried out in the home. Nevertheless, special festivals are celebrated in the shrine area because they involve the whole community. One such special day is the annual occasion when a shrine parades its shintai around the town. With music and lay participation, the priests place the wrapped shintai in a special covering and carry them throughout the community. Other special occasions observed at a shrine may be seasonal festivals and religious drama.

Japanese couples may be married at a Shinto shrine. Funerals are overseen by the Buddhists, who are supposed to have solved the riddle of death, but beginning a new family falls under the sponsorship of Shinto. Traditionally Shinto priests keep family records for the local community. They also carry out little ceremonies for blessing new objects acquired by individuals (such as a new car) or by corporations (such as a new piece of factory machinery).

Domestic Shinto. Shinto is mainly practiced in the home. Each traditional home contains a *kamidana,* a shrine designated for the veneration of the kami. It is actually a little shelf that is mounted fairly high in the home. On it are placed little items of offerings, for example, food (rice or fruit) and water. The kamidana is also the place where various amulets are kept in order to ensure good fortune for the family. A central place is often occupied by an inscribed wooden tablet. If so, chances are it was brought back by someone who made a pilgrimage to Ise.

Even modern homes that do not have a kamidana will often have its Buddhist counterpart, the Butsudan. Devout traditional families will have both. The Butsudan is a small cabinet with doors

Inari foxes guarding Sasuke no Inari Shinto Shrine, Kamakura. Photograph: Michael Harbin.

made of black wood. It usually contains a figure of a Buddhist deity (frequently Amida) and the tablets of the family ancestors. Ancestor veneration is thus maintained under the umbrella of Buddhism rather than Shinto. In addition to recognizing the family kami every day, the family performs daily obligations to the ancestors.

The same twofold allegiance holds in the broader context as well. A family is typically affiliated with both a Buddhist temple and the shrine of a local kami. In English these kami are referred to as tutelary kami, which means that they are the guardian spirits of a particular location. The kami oversee a village or a neighborhood. This shrine is the center of ceremonies involving all parts of the life cycle, except funerals, which, as already noted, are observed in the Buddhist temple.

A typical village Buddhist temple may be aligned with either the Shingon or the Pure Land tradition. Again, Amida is the deity most frequently represented. The temple also houses the ancestor tablets of prominent people and serves as the funeral center for the entire community. In some highly traditional areas, where there is a clear distinction in rank between different families and their branches, the home of the foremost family may also serve as a central Buddhist temple. In that case, the Butsudan is a full-fledged Buddhist altar.

Sectarian Shinto and the new religions. Among the religions of the world it is not unusual for a new branch to arise from an established religion. The new religion may begin with a charismatic personality who accumulates a number of followers who eventually set themselves apart as a new group. Typical examples that come to mind are Jewish Hasidism, led by the Baal Shem Tov, Sikhism, originating with Nanak, and the Sai Baba movement of Hinduism. Because of unique historical and cultural factors, Japan has seen a proliferation of such movements. They are usually classified together as the "new religions."

As we have already mentioned, the nineteenth century was an uneasy time for religion in Japan. The chaotic last years of the shogunate gave way to the Meiji restoration, and both regimes co-opted religion for their purposes. Simultaneously, repressive social and economic conditions predictably spawned innovations in religious thought. They began with an individual (man or woman) initiating a new doctrine or practice, more often than not associated with faith healing or material blessings and the growth of a sizable following. During the Meiji period (and even before), such activities were frequently considered treasonous, and the leaders were often persecuted. A new group could avoid such trouble by identifying itself as just another part of Shinto. As we shall see, this identification was rather contrived in many instances, but thirteen groups did receive official approval as "denominations" of Shinto. They were then classified as belonging to "sectarian Shinto."

Other groups did not receive approval and persisted as underground movements. The defeat of Japan in World War II and the subsequent Allied occupation provided further impetus for the birth of new religious groups. Since the old order had closely tied itself to established religion, its demise stimulated many people to look in new and different directions for religious answers. Groups with Shinto, Buddhist and even nominally Christian semblances established themselves. The Christian influence manifested itself primarily in terms of the messianic claims made by various founders and in the congregational structure adopted by some of the groups. In Japan, where religious organizations must report themselves to a government office, they are officially categorized as "new religions."

Despite their many differences, the new religions seem to follow a discernible pattern that includes six elements.[9] First, the new religions usually begin with one person, either a man or a woman. The founder tends to come out of an established setting. He or she usually has had the experience of being possessed by a divine being who authorizes him or her to spread the new teaching. The founder's self-descriptions are likely to be of the very highest order, even on a par with descriptions of Jesus or Buddha. His or her writings become the authoritative scriptures for the movement.

Second, the doctrinal teachings of the movements tend to be highly simplistic and superficial. More often than not, they do not go much further than identifying one divine being or one insight into life as ultimate and claiming the method revealed to the founder as the optimal appropriation of this truth. The teaching can be syncretistic (bringing together elements from different religions) or relativistic (recognizing all religions as true), in which case the new revelation is seen as the supreme formulation of universal truth. More than anything else, the founder as the source of truth and bliss is the content of the belief (which is to say that the messenger is the message and vice versa).

Third, the goals offered by the religion are this-worldly, in the words of a constantly recurring phrase: "happiness, health and prosperity." Anyone who follows the teachings of the founder is assured of these results. Anyone who doesn't has only himself to blame for his misery. Even though the new religions are not silent on the more remote

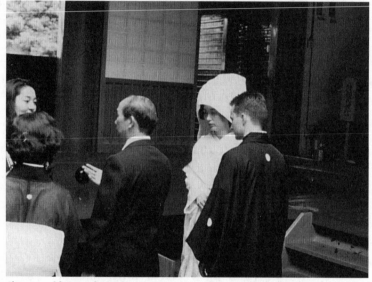

Shinto wedding performed at Tsurugaoka Hachiman Shrine, Kamakura. Photograph: Michael Harbin.

future—in fact, some of them carry broad apocalyptic predictions—their marketing appeal lies in their promises for immediate success in life. Many of the new religions began as faith healing cults and continue those practices. Again, the formula for success is fairly simple: healing demonstrates the power of the teaching; lack of healing indicates a failure in faith or devotion on the part of the follower.

Fourth, new religions tend to promote social egalitarianism. Many of the founders are women, and women play an equal role. In many cases female officials and heads continue in the generations succeeding the founder. Furthermore, other social distinctions involving rank and economic standing tend to be diffused. Each follower has equal standing. There is usually no official priesthood.

Fifth, organizational structure is usually tight. Even though there may not be any clergy and all followers are considered equal as followers, many new religions are governed very strictly by an official body. In many cases the founder's word is absolute, and the founder's successors exercise the same kind of authority. Often the leadership is hereditary. Many groups have an official headquarters that functions as the source of absolute revelation and as a center for regular pilgrimages.

Sixth, new religions provide optimistic responses to negative situations. To a large extent they are successful because they offer a way to achieve a happy life despite all odds to the contrary. In some ways they are not so much religions as they are religious recipes for a shortcut to better fortune.

In a country that has traveled a long way down the road to secularism, the numbers of adherents of the new religions seem astonishing. The reported figures for 1958 included 171 religions totaling 18 million adherents. One-third of those claim affinity with Shinto, one-third see themselves as primarily Buddhist, thirty register under the word *miscellaneous,* and two or three say they are Christians.[10]

Tenri-kyo is in some ways the prototype of the new religions. It began as a faith healing cult in the nineteenth century, survived by becoming one of the thirteen permitted Shinto sects and continues to flourish as an independent movement today, with no pretense of being a part of Shinto. The founder of Tenri-kyo was Nakayama Miki (1798-1887). She was brought up in the Pure Land Buddhist tradition. At a time of personal tragedies, Miki went into a trance and was possessed by the kami Tenri-O-no-Mikoto, who endowed her with the power of spiritual healing. She usually referred to this kami as Oyagami, "god the parent," and considered him creator and sustainer of the world. She worshiped him with a symbolic dance. Miki taught her followers that obedience to Oyagami brings bliss, whereas disobedience causes spiritual dust that must be swept away before it accumulates on human souls. Her writings are considered authoritative scripture.

The headquarters of Tenri-kyo are at Nara. Faithful followers believe that Miki has not died but continues to live in seclusion. She is brought three meals a day. In a symbolic act of faith, Tenri-kyo followers sweep the large hallway at the headquarters many times a day.

Konko-kyo is another of the original thirteen authorized Shinto sects. It emphasizes the need for mediation between humans and the spirit world. The founder, Kawate Bunjiro (1814-1883), saw himself as the chosen instrument of such mediation. Kawate, who eventually changed his name to Konko Daijin, received his calling when he was first possessed by the kami Konjin. Konjin is traditionally considered to be a malevolent spirit, but under Kawate's teaching he received a new, benevolent identity and a new name: Tenchi-Kane-no-Kami.

Kawate taught that Tenchi and human beings are mutually dependent on each other. Tenchi is the parent god of the universe, and human beings need him for fulfillment. Conversely, Tenchi needs human beings for his fulfillment. Thus both can receive what they need if they are brought together properly, and that task is left to Kawate and his successors. Kawate's writings appear together as the Kongo-kyo scriptures. The group's headquarters is in the town now known as Konko, formerly Otani. The religion performs a ministry of benevolent outreach.

Omoto was founded by Deguchi Nao (1836-1918), who was originally a member of Konko-kyo. She was a peasant girl who made a reputation for herself as a seer,

 claiming to be possessed by the same kami Konjin, but without his transformation into Tenchi. Eventually she provided revelations through automatic writing. These have become the scriptures of the movement.

Deguchi Nao taught spiritual and political world unity. All religions are one, and eventually a world government will come that rules in peace and universal brotherhood. She also predicted the coming of a savior, whom she then recognized in her adopted son, Deguchi Onisaburo. The religion focuses on worship of the founder and on activities geared to bringing about the ideal world. It is headquartered in the Kyoto area.

Seicho No Ie promotes teaching that is very similar to Christian Science. Because Tenri-kyo began as a faith healing cult founded by a woman, it has at times been called the "Christian Science of

Sasuke no Inari, Shinto shrine, Kamakura. Photograph: Michael Harbin.

Japan." But the resemblance does not extend to the teaching. By contrast, the teaching of Seicho No Ie is considered allied with this Western movement. This religion began with Taniguchi Masaharu (b. 1893) and his quest for religious insight. Taniguchi, who was a member of Omoto, became exposed to Western philosophy, New Thought and psychic explorations. The conviction that eventually emerged from this amalgamation, along with a visit by an angel, was that the material world is simply the shadow of the human mind and that suffering is unreal.

More specifically, Taniguchi taught that all human beings are children of God, whom he called Buddha. In their natural state, humans are happy and healthy. But they let negative thinking influence them into beliefs of sin and guilt that produce the illusion of suffering. When people come to realize their identity as children of God and come to understand the unreality of all suffering, then health, happiness and prosperity result. This salvation comes through a meditation technique into which people must be initiated by the movement.

During World War II Seicho No Ie affiliated itself with Japan's imperial aims. Consequently, the Allied occupation attempted to suppress its activities. After the occupation the movement once again flourished in association with strong nationalistic leanings. Its headquarters is in Tokyo.

Sekai Kyusei-kyo also originated in Omoto; it prefers to be known as Sekai Meshia-kyo, the "church of world messianity." The founder is Okada Mokichi (1882-1955). He claimed that in 1926 he was entered by Kannon[11] (the Japanese version of Guan-yin, the female Avalokitasvara) and received the divine light. From this point on his mission was to spread the divine light and thereby create an ideal world.

Okada's followers attempt to contribute to this cause by natural farming, the creation and appreciation of beauty (art) and *jorei,* a manual technique of channeling the divine light from person to person. The divine light provides healing and removes spiritual pollution, thereby engendering health, prosperity and harmony. They pray the Amatsu Norito (a collection of prayers stemming from the tenth century) as their main act of worship. The organization has several centers, including two resorts that are intended to provide a foretaste of the paradise to come.

P L Kyodon received its real start after World War II, although its antecedents go back much further. The two initial letters stand for the English words *perfect liberty.* Among this organization's precursors are Kanada Tokumitsu (1863-1919), a notable faith healer, and his disciple Miki Tokuharu, who died in 1938. Tokuharu's son Miki Tokuchika became the real founder of the present organization.

P L Kyodon proclaims that "life is art." This statement is the first of twenty-one precepts, and it summarizes the entire teaching of the religion. All people are responsible for treating their lives as works of art in progress and so must choose and implement all options carefully. When they do this properly, health, happiness and prosperity result. Suffering and misfortune ought to be regarded as a message from God to change one's life. The spiritual masters of the religion provide guidance, as well as vicarious suffering, in the process of discerning the correct plan.

Soka Gakkai is the contemporary form of Nichiren Shoshu (see discussion in chapter eight). In the twentieth century this movement began to look more like a new religion than a historical version of Buddhism. The initial founder was Tsunesaburo Makiguchi (1871-1944), an elementary school principal who was concerned about the erosion of values in modern Japan. He began his group, Soka Kyoiku Gakkai, the "society for the education in the creation of values," in order to promote the three fundamental values of the good, the beautiful and the beneficent. It was not until after the organization had already become established that Tsunebaro began to undergird his teachings with the religious doctrines of Nichiren Buddhism. He died in prison in 1944, convicted of the crime of not paying homage to Amaterasu in state Shinto.

The organization was revived under the leadership of Toda Josei, an early associate of Tasiburo. Toda shortened the name to Soka Gakkai, completed the process of aligning the fundamental teaching of the group with Nichiren Shoshu and propagated it with techniques bordering on brainwashing. Daisaku Ikeda, Toda's successor, redirected Soka Gakkai once again. He softened the evangelistic approach of the organization and made it a worldwide movement. Nowadays, wherever there is a Soka Gakkai association, it gets involved in community projects that promote social welfare and the arts, particularly. Although the basic teaching of Soka Gakkai has changed drastically from the original premises of Tsunesaburo, the basic aim, education in fundamental values, has continued. Soka Gakkai's headquarters are situated picturesquely at the foot of Mount Fuji on a site that goes back to the original Nichiren school.

The very nature of the new religious movements implies that many of them will have a short life span. Their uncomplicated origins, as the authoritative teaching of someone who is divinely possessed, makes it fairly easy for new movements to come into existence. There is never a shortage of frustrated people who are looking for a new way to achieve success, particularly if that method comes as a straightforward technique with few doctrinal adumbrations.[12] The other 164 or so new religions follow similar patterns.

Religion	Founder	Deity	Teaching
Tenri-kyo	Nakayama Miki	Tenri (Oyagami)	Obedience = bliss; disobedience causes dust
Konko-kyo	Konko Daijin	Tenchi (Konjin)	Mutual need of Tenchi and humans
Omoto	Deguchi Nao	Konjin	Coming spiritual and world unity
Seicho No Ie	Tanaguchi Masaharu	Buddha	Children of God; unreality of pain
Sekai Kyuseikyo	Okada Mokichi	Kannon	Channeling the Divine Light
P L Kyodon	Miki Tokuchika	God	"Life is art"
Soka Gakkai	Tsunesaburo Makiguchi	Buddha	Nichiren Shoshu
Aum Shinri Kyo	Chizuo Mazumoto	Aum	Monistic mysticism; antigovernment

Table 11.1. Some new religions

Sadly, a new religion can serve as a cover for criminal activities. In March 1995 a deadly nerve gas was released into the Tokyo subway, killing twelve people and injuring more than five thousand. The police soon suspected that the crime had been carried out by the group Aum Shinri Kyo, which was registered as one of the new religions.

Aum Shinri Kyo (roughly, "supreme truth") was founded by Chizuo Matsumoto, a legally blind purveyor of miracle medicines and yoga instructions. Matsumoto bore a grudge against the Japanese government for being denied admittance to Tokyo University when he was in his twenties. He found escape from his frustrations in the mysticism business. As his movement gained followers, he changed his name to Shoko Asahara and the name of his cult from Aum Association of Mountain Wizards to Aum Shinri Kyo. In the early 1990s many of Asahara's followers became disenchanted with him. His attitude toward his remaining followers grew oppressive as his rhetoric expressed increasing paranoia and hostility toward the government. Now in his forties, he is the head not so much of a religious group but of a tiny band of armed guerillas. Even if the link to the subway massacre is not established definitively in

the courts, Aum Shinri Kyo illustrates all that can go wrong as religious sects proliferate under authoritarian figures.

Folk Religion

In addition to the Shinto, Buddhist, Confucian and "new religion" elements that define Japanese religion, folk religion continues to exist. I mentioned at the outset of this chapter that Japanese folk religion differs from Chinese popular religion. Whereas Chinese folk re-

Oracles written on rice paper attached to bush as petition for fulfillment at Tsurugaoka Hachiman Shrine, Kamakura. Photograph: Michael Harbin.

ligion has become an institution in its own right, complete with its own temples and practices, Japanese folk religion represents an undercurrent of beliefs and practices that have attached themselves to the prevailing Shinto and Buddhist forms.

Undoubtedly much of Japanese folk religion goes back to the early traditional religion before it was codified as Shinto under Buddhist pressure.[13] Since that early period was dominated by rivalry between the different tribes and their specific cultures on the various islands, no unified religious system developed. Nevertheless, some common religious traits from this period left their mark on subsequent development.

Clearly there was an emphasis on fertility. Rice fields need the protection of the spirits in order to survive and yield a bountiful harvest, and consequently the rice transplanting festival remains an important part of Japanese folk religion to this day. Farmers celebrate this festival in early summer, when seedlings grown in nurseries are big enough to be transplanted to the fields. Rice planters, along with ceremonial dancers, first present some representative rice shoots to the kami at the local Shinto shrine. Then, under the auspices of priests, the dancers holding the shoots are carried to the rice field. The shoots are inserted into the ground to the accompaniment of music. The dancers perform for the benefit of the kami. In this way the success of the year's rice crop is put into the hands of the spirits.

Small Shinto shrine in hills of Kamakura. Photograph: Michael Harbin.

There is evidence that ancient Japanese religion included a strong emphasis on shamanism. Shamans are mediators between spirits and humans who allow themselves to be possessed by the spirits. Thus they speak to people in the voice of the spirits themselves. Apparently most of the ancient Japanese shamans were women. Some of them may have been queens of their respective islands.

The practice of shamanism continues as an important part of Japanese religious life. There are several different strands of shamanism. Some shamans inherit the office, while others must train for it through an apprenticeship with an established shaman. Shamans who inherit the shamanic role may be identified through the onset of a serious physical or mental disorder that persists until the subject has committed herself to the life of a shaman. Most of the new religions began when their founders had a shamanistic experience. Today shamans function as diviners, faith healers and (rarely) mediums for contact with ancestors.

Ancient Japanese religion emphasized nature spirits. The very concept of kami includes the notion that kami frequently manifest themselves in remarkable objects of nature, such as rocks, trees and mountains. The veneration of mountains has become a particularly important aspect of Japanese folk religion. In its contemporary form, it has made itself at home in conjunction with both a form of Buddhism practiced by mountain-dwelling ascetics and a magical practice called Shugen-do.

Shugen-do is the heritage of Daoism in Japanese culture. Although the original influx of Chinese culture included Daoism as well as Buddhism, Daoism lost out to Buddhism, probably because it had to compete on the turf that Shinto already inhabited. Thus

Daoism's influence was limited to two more minor roles. One was the realm of philosophical speculations, such as the yin-yang concepts with which the Nihongi (though not the Kojiki) opens. The other was a practice of exorcism and magic that laid the foundation for Shugen-do. The Shugen-do priest, frequently accompanied by a female shaman, would move from mountain to mountain ridding the countryside of evil spirits.

The contemporary significance of mountain spirituality seems to be threefold.[14] First, conical, volcanic mountains (like Mount Fuji) embody the creative power of the kami. Second, mountains as sources of water are seen as sources of fertility. In fact, to this day, the names of rice kami and mountain kami are interchangeable. Some mountains are also believed to be the home of a "divine mother." Third, mountains are recognized as the abode of or connecting point with ancestor spirits. Thus mountain pilgrimages form an important part of popular piety. In addition to individuals' trips to mountains, many of the larger mountains of Japan have regular spring or autumn festivals, during which groups of consecrated individuals make the strenuous ascent and perform ancient rituals.[15]

Ancient Japanese religion undoubtedly stressed magic, since the development of magic tends to be an ongoing process in all religious traditions (see chapter one). Japanese folk religion has adopted practices derived from major religious traditions and has adapted them into magic techniques. An interesting example of this transformation is the use of the nembutsu as an incantation formula.

The nembutsu is the central formula of Pure Land Buddhism. *Namu Amida Butsu* means "I bow down to (worship) the Buddha Amida." In this original context, it is the expression of faith in Amida, who will admit anyone who asserts this formula into the western paradise. People began to reason that if this phrase is so effective, it must also contain a spiritual charge that is powerful enough to drive away hostile spirits. For a time, the nembutsu became the central focus of ritualistic practices. Today that formal use has pretty much died out, but individuals continue to invoke the nembutsu as an expression to ward off bad spirits or to reconcile good ones.

The Life Cycle

The rites of passage associated with Japanese religion are an amalgam of different traditions that come together in a somewhat unsteady balance. Since Japan as a whole has followed the West into secularism, this description is about what a religious Japanese person might experience, not about average life in Japan today.[16]

Birth and childhood. In Japanese religion, birth is considered the gift of the family tutelary kami. There seems to have been ambivalence in the traditional understanding of whether this gift implies simply that the kami has created the new life or that an actual part of the kami has incarnated itself in the life of the infant. Regardless of these nuances, the kami is the giver of the life. Consequently, when the baby in the traditional setting takes its first trip at the age of one month, the destination is the shrine of the tutelary kami, to which the infant will be presented in gratitude. The birth taboos on the mother end at this time. The ancient religious proscriptions completely isolated the mother for a month (or even longer) because her blood was considered to be extremely unclean. Although it would not have been understood in this fashion, this practice probably prevented countless new mothers from contracting postpartum infections.

A childhood rite of passage is the "seven-five-three" festival, which recognizes girls aged three and seven and boys aged five. The children are dressed up and presented in a special way to the tutelary kami at his shrine. Children receive a lot of overt attention in Japanese religious culture, in contrast to cultures that fear calling attention to children lest the spirits snatch them away. In Japan the attitude toward children is one of positive celebration.

Pond and garden at Hasa-dera, Buddhist temple in Kamakura. Photograph: Michael Harbin.

Puberty. Japanese rites of passage into adulthood declined as the culture moved away from a warrior mentality. At one time in the distant past there was a ritual in which young men received the official warrior loincloth and joined the "young men's society." Young girls received an underskirt in a ritual immediately after their first menses. Even in religious settings, these practices have been replaced by more functional recognitions, such as the first time a boy carries the shintai container in a shrine procession, finds a job or establishes his majority (twenty years of age) on January 15 of that year.

Marriage. Japanese weddings have undergone changes in the last one hundred years or so. It used to be that a wedding was considered a legal transaction between two families and was carried out at home. However, since Meiji times the ceremony has been largely carried out in a Shinto shrine. Bride and groom once wore traditional outfits—a kimono for the man and several layers of robes for the woman. With modernization, men started to wear formal Western tails as women retained the traditional dress. Recently women have become attached to Western bridal outfits, whereas some men have gone back to the kimono. The ceremonies are often conducted in rented wedding halls. The high point of the ceremony occurs when bride and groom exchange glasses of saki (Japanese rice wine).

Death. As in China, the convergence of many religious beliefs has given rise to various ideas concerning the afterlife, not all of which can be reconciled with each other. There appear to be three strands of thought. First, there is the notion that the deceased becomes an ancestor that lives in proximity to the family. Second, the Buddhist idea of reincarnation and karma is included in the mix. Third, there is the belief that the soul of the deceased reverts to the kami who gave it life to begin with. It may eventually be reborn into the family as a new child. This last belief would constitute a non-Buddhist understanding of reincarnation without karma.

Funerals may include burial or cremation. The corpse is processed into ancestor-hood through ritual washing. Traditionally a bowl of rice for nourishment and a small weapon to ward off evil spirits are sent along. Since Buddhism is the custodian of the ancestors, the necessary ceremonies are carried out under Buddhist auspices.

There is a mourning period of exactly forty-nine days (the number of days allotted to the soul's reassignment in Buddhism). During this time there is a temporary ancestor tablet on the family's Butsudan, and the family lives in virtual isolation. At the end of this period, a permanent tablet is installed. The deceased has joined the ranks of the ancestors and will be remembered as such in regular ceremonies. The family may also entertain one or more of the following ideas: the deceased has been reunited with the tutelary kami, has become a kami or has been reborn as a new human being.

Holidays and Festivals

The Japanese calendar of special days by and large follows the Gregorian calendar. Almost every month has a festival arranged so that the special day falls on the day that bears the number of the month, such as the third of March, the fifth of May, and so on.

New Year's Day. Originally observed as the beginning of a lunar calendar, New Year's Day has been changed to coincide with January 1. The Japanese celebration of New Year's Day emphasizes purification. Homes are purified and decorated with straw ropes and evergreen branches in preparation for the holiday, and a third altar is erected in the house for the ancestors. Families visit the Shinto shrine, where the priests sound a gong 108 times, representing 108 different purifications. Individuals make special offerings and consult their fortunes on small pieces of paper.

Spring festivals and the soybean festival. In Japan spring begins on February 3. Soybeans are thrown for children to catch for good luck. Many localities also hold locally oriented celebrations, perhaps in conjunction with the climbing of mountains. There is also be a spring rite for the tutelary kami and for ancestors that is observed in close conjunction with the vernal equinox.

Doll festival. This festival now centers around girls' receiving and displaying their doll collections. It may originally have been a rite of imitative magic in which paper dolls were floated down rivers in order to remove impurities. Those associations are no longer remembered today.

Flower festival. April 8 is observed as the birthday of the Buddha in Japan. It is also the day when the rice kami descend from the mountains, providing yet another spring festival. Flowers and sweet tea are poured on statues of the Buddha.

Boys' day. On May 5 families celebrate their male children. Boys make arrangements of warrior dolls, and the family hangs out carp-shaped windsocks for every boy in the family.

Great purification. Halfway through the year, the time has come to renew the purification made on New Year's Day. On June 30, a similar form of purificatory rites is undertaken in home and shrine.

Star festival. Interestingly, this festival has its origin in a Chinese myth. A cowherd and a weaver girl fell in love. In the course of events both were transformed into stars of the Milky Way. This day, in the Chinese legend as well as in the Japanese version, is the only time of the year when they meet. Consequently, this is a day for the celebration of love and romance (perhaps the Japanese version of Valentine's Day). It is marked by elaborate decorations.

Festival of the dead. The Buddhist Day of the Dead (which has its counterpart in the Chinese Hungry Ghost Festival) is also observed in Japan, where it falls in the middle of

Mount Fuji and pagoda from Fuji Peace Park. Photograph: Michael Harbin.

July. It is a period marked by intense provision for the ancestor spirits.

Fall festivals. Several observations are connected with the coming of fall. Once again, there is a special ceremony for the tutelary kami; there may be mountain pilgrimages and harvest festivals. The celebration period falls around the autumnal equinox. As fall progresses and as the rice harvest proceeds, there are special celebrations for the rice/mountain kami as they return to their abodes in the mountains.

■ *So You Meet a Japanese Who Practices an Indigenous Religion . . .*
What You Might Expect
Our focus is on meeting someone who is an adherent of a Japanese religion. The many

cultural differences between American culture, broadly speaking, and Japanese culture deserve book-length treatment.[17] These differences have a profound impact on the way religions are understood and discussed as well.

A major difference, speaking very generally, lies in American individualism versus the Japanese communal orientation. American culture prizes being different, sticking out from the crowd and asserting personal independence, whereas Japanese culture values loyalty to family and society. A similar observation has already been made in regard to Chinese culture.

Japanese thinking seems to be less oriented than American thinking toward finding causes for problems.[18] In American culture, the first question on encountering a problem seems to be, What caused it? In Japanese thinking the first question tends to be, How can we avoid the same problem in the future? Thus Japanese thinking tends to be oriented toward modifying the process in which the problem came up. For our purposes, a good example of this mode of thought appears in the proliferation of new religions. These many movements are very short on doctrine, but they present their adherents with a simple methodology for finding all they expect in life. Soka Gakkai is a consummate example. Adherents practice their chanting for years without even being able to recount something as elementary as the ten stages of existence, let alone any classical Buddhist doctrines. As long as the outcomes are favorable, there is no need to worry about the theory behind the technique.

Thus an encounter with a person who practices a Japanese religion presents an interesting paradox to the Westerner. On the one hand, there is the communal aspect, defined by the value placed on being a loyal member of a group. On the other hand, there is the second, process-oriented aspect that leads the Japanese person to make deliberate individual choices, namely, which group to become a part of. The person may pursue the path of family and community or may decide to join a new religion if the promise of success is convincing enough.

Relating the Gospel

Allegiance to the community (beginning with the family) may keep a Japanese person from making a decision for Christ. Missionaries who have had experience in Japan report that it can be hard even to get a hearing for the gospel, because the Japanese communal orientation is offended by the individualistic way in which the gospel is often presented. If a Christian begins a presentation of the gospel with an emphasis on making a decision that will tear the person out of the community, the Japanese person's initial response will be negative.

Further, Westerners tend to emphasize the root causes of the human predicament, namely, the Fall and original sin. Then they present the atonement as a direct solution to these fundamental problems. The Japanese person's orientation toward processes may make the Westerner's emphasis on root causes difficult to follow at first. The

Japanese person looks for plans of action and wants to know first of all what to do. Learning to understand the total theological scheme of things can come later. Once again, contextualization of the gospel without compromising it is needed for evangelism to make any sense.

However, these differences can be addressed successfully. Even if the gospel is contextualized, it may present a stumbling block. But the problem may not reside in the gospel message itself but in the methods Westerners use to present it. Perhaps they have not thought through the cultural implications sufficiently. Today missionaries and local workers have learned to make the necessary adaptations.

In order to build a bridge to the communal orientation, evangelists emphasize the idea of the family of God, which is, of course, very much a part of the New Testament. In numerous places (Rom 12; 1 Cor 12; Eph 4), the church is presented as the body of Christ. The emphasis is not on individuals' finding their unique roles but on the church as an organism that represents Christ on earth by being loyal in mutual edification. God calls us out of certain associations, but he also calls us into new ones.

Clearly, Christianity has much to say about the causes of the world's condition, and a full presentation of the gospel cannot afford to leave out those concerns. But in thinking about the choices that every Christian worker needs to make on how to present the gospel initially, it may be wise to address the nature of faith in Christ first and discuss the origins of sin as an elaboration.

Religion in Japan has been a highly variable set of innovations and compromises. Christianity's place in this mix has been very limited, largely due to governmental restrictions. The Jesuits enjoyed considerable success under Francis Xavier in the sixteenth century, but soon the Tokugawa regime suppressed Christianity as a foreign religion (while giving first place to Buddhism, which, of course, was also originally imported). A minuscule, severely persecuted church remained.

Widespread regular missionary activity began after World War II. Christianity's association with Western culture gave it ambivalent standing. On the one hand, Christianity was the religion of the victorious Allies, who had crushed Japan, and of the United States, Japan's most powerful economic rival. By the 1950s and 1960s Christianity was stimulating a lot of resentment. It was associated with the new world of industrialized democracy and thus created a lot of interest, but perhaps for the wrong reasons, namely, that Christianity was seen as a tool for economic success.

Christians in Japan today make up about 2 percent of the population. To be authentic, Christians must not present the gospel as one alternative among many, and definitely not as the religion of Western prosperity, but as the unique word of salvation from God.

A Final Word

Thus I come to some concluding comments that go beyond Japan. In my travels, as well as in stateside encounters, I have come to realize that the Christian church frequently falls into a self-defeating trap: the Christian group competes with indigenous religions for adherents. But isn't this exactly what Christians are supposed to do? Are we not supposed to work at increasing the number of people who identify with Christianity? No. Creating numbers of official converts has never been the church's mission from God. The task of the church is to present the gospel in a properly contextualized way, to make it possible for people to make a decision for Christ and to nurture the new converts. God will provide the numbers (Acts 2:47).

Thus the church's mission is defined by the tasks given by God: evangelism and nurture. Its mission is *not* defined by numerical objectives or successes the church may have in these tasks. I am emphasizing this fact because to violate it will almost invariably violate the nature of Christianity as well. Christians may erect buildings that compete favorably with local temples; they may link Christian worship to various practices that are associated with pagan worship in the minds of local people; they may soft-pedal the gospel in order to gain a hearing. And they might just raise the numbers of nominal Christians in the process. But if the gospel is no longer the true message of redemption from God, nothing of genuine consequence has been gained.

As a Christian, I see the gospel of Jesus Christ as the only way of salvation. Consequently, sharing the gospel is the highest good I can do for another person. Clearly, I need to abide by New Testament exhortations regarding my conduct in doing so. For instance, I may never force the gospel on another person. However, I also need to remember that by compromising the gospel in order not to cause offense, I may actually deprive someone of the good news that has been entrusted to me. In the end, everyone needs to know the authentic gospel: that Jesus Christ is Savior and Lord.

Mastering the Material

When you have finished studying this chapter, you should be able to

1. sketch the early history of religion in Japan;

2. state the religious highlights of the Shinto myth;

3. outline the history of Shinto in Japan from its beginnings to the Meiji era of state Shinto;

4. summarize the practices of Shinto and their Buddhist complements in a traditional Japanese home;

5. describe the essential parts of a Shinto shrine and the practices associated with them;

6. draw together the basic nature of the new religions and illustrate it with some examples (not necessarily memorizing all the information given);

7. list the distinctives of Japanese rites of passage and of traditional Japanese holidays.

Term Paper Ideas

1. Research the history of the emperors in Japanese mythology and correlate the information with what is now considered to be historically accurate.

2. Trace the influx of Daoism into Japanese thought.

3. Describe the many facets of samurai warriors' beliefs and practices.

4. Do a detailed study of the history of Christianity in Japan from Xavier to 1945.

5. With pictures and sketches, provide a detailed description of a Shinto shrine, for example, at Ise.

6. Research how the Japanese emperor is viewed today, officially and in popular thought.

7. Analyze how the distinctive forms of Buddhism in Japan have been influenced by Shinto.

8. Make a detailed exploration of a new religion in Japan, either one mentioned in this text or one of the many others.

9. Using interviews or research, write up a report on the strategies used by evangelists in Japan today.

Core Bibliography

Aston, W. G. *Nihongi: Chronicles of Japan from the Earliest Times to* A.D. *697.* Fair Lawn, N.J.: Essential Books, 1956.

Chamberlain, Basil Hall, trans. *The Kojiki: Records of Ancient Matters.* Rutland, Vt.: Tuttle, 1981.

Earhart, H. Byron. *Japanese Religion: Unity and Diversity.* Belmont, Calif.: Wadsworth, 1982.

————. *Religions of Japan: Many Traditions Within One Sacred Way.* San Francisco: Harper & Row, 1984.

Hori, Ichiro. *Folk Religion in Japan: Continuity and Change.* Chicago: University of Chicago Press, 1968.

Thomsen, Harry. *The New Religions of Japan.* Rutland, Vt.: Tuttle, 1963.

Notes

Introduction

[1]Terry C. Muck, *Those Other Religions in Your Neighborhood: Loving Your Neighbor When You Don't Know How* (Grand Rapids, Mich.: Zondervan, 1992).

[2]In order to satisfy any curiosity as to my allegiance on this issue, my view, at least in its conclusions, coincides with that of Ronald H. Nash, *Is Jesus the Only Savior?* (Grand Rapids, Mich.: Zondervan, 1994). Nash argues that conscious faith in Christ is necessary for a person's salvation. For more inclusive views, see Clark H. Pinnock, *A Wideness in God's Mercy* (Grand Rapids, Mich.: Zondervan, 1992); John Hick, *God Has Many Names* (London: Macmillan, 1980); John Sanders, *No Other Name* (Grand Rapids, Mich.: Eerdmans, 1992).

[3]I want to mention the esteem I have for my colleague Michael Harbin. He wrote the manuscript for his book *To Serve Other Gods: An Evangelical History of Religion* (New York: University Press of America, 1994) before coming to Taylor University. Approaching the topic of world religions from the perspective of an Old Testament scholar, Harbin has drawn many conclusions that are the same as the ones I maintain in this book.

Chapter 1: Religion

[1]The figures for population data used throughout this book come from *The World Almanac and Book of Facts 1997*, ed. Robert Famighetti (Mahwah, N.J.: K-III Reference, 1996), pp. 644, 646.

[2]I arrived at this number by subtracting the *World Almanac's* figures for "atheists" and "nonreligious" from the stated number of non-Christians. I suspect that the actual number is far higher, since there are probably many people (for example, in the People's Republic of China) who would not necessarily report any religious affiliation, although they do practice a religion, possibly surreptitiously.

[3]Friedrich Schleiermacher, *On Religion: Speeches to Its Cultured Despisers* (New York: Harper & Row, 1958); Friedrich Schleiermacher, *The Christian Faith* (Philadelphia: Fortress, 1976).

[4]Ludwig Feuerbach, *The Essence of Christianity* (London: John Chapman, 1854).

[5]Sigmund Freud, *The Future of an Illusion* (New York: Liveright, 1928); Sigmund Freud, *Moses and Monotheism* (New York: Alfred A. Knopf, 1939).

[6]Rudolf Otto, *The Idea of the Holy* (New York: Oxford University Press, 1950).

[7]Mircea Eliade, *The Sacred and the Profane* (New York: Harcourt, Brace and World, 1959); Mircea Eliade, *Patterns in Comparative Religion* (Cleveland, Ohio: World, 1958).

[8]Carl Gustav Jung, *Man and His Symbols* (New York: Doubleday, 1964).

[9]Joseph Campbell, *The Power of Myth* (New York: Doubleday, 1988).

[10]Needless to say, no two scholars agree completely on the details. What I am presenting here is a generalized version of a hundred schemes, all of which differ in regard to specific points.

[11]Sir J. George Frazer, *The Golden Bough* (New York: Macmillan, 1960). This version was abridged by Frazer himself. He expanded the original two-volume work to twelve volumes. The original work was also abridged by Theodor Gaster as *The New Golden Bough* (New York: Phillips, 1959). Gaster eliminated all of Frazer's references to the evolution of religion, thereby defeating Frazer's own purpose.

[12]John Dewey, *A Common Faith* (New Haven, Conn.: Yale University Press, 1934).

[13]R. M. Meyer, *Altgermanische Religionsgeschichte* (Stuttgart: Magnus-Verlag, 1909), pp. 67-68.

[14]Robert Brow, *Religion: Origins and Ideas* (Chicago: InterVarsity Press, 1966), p. 13.

[15]Wilhelm Schmidt, *Der Ursprung der Gottesidee,* 12 vols. (Münster: Albrecht, 1926-1955). Schmidt mercifully provided a shorter one-volume work, translated into English by H. J. Rose, *The Origin and Growth of Religion: Facts and Theories* (London: Methuen, 1931). Schmidt was not the first scholar to defend original monotheism on anthropological grounds. Schmidt himself gives the credit to Andrew Lang, *The Making of Religion* (London: Longmans, Green, 1898).

[16]A thorough discussion of this phenomenon, complete with an abundance of specific examples, is provided by Eliade in *Patterns,* pp. 38-123. Excerpts from the reports by anthropologists on the subject are collected by Eliade in *From Primitives to Zen: A Thematic Sourcebook of the History of Religions* (New York: Harper & Row, 1967), pp. 3-51.

[17]Michael Harbin, *To Serve Other Gods: An Evangelical History of Religion* (New York: University Press of America, 1994), is an in-depth description of this worldwide decay in most of the major world religions. Harbin allows for the thesis that in some cases the worship of actually existing fallen angels may have been substituted for the worship of God.

[18]Sociologist Max Weber made similar observations, although he construed them in essentially social and economic terms, a thesis that I do not support. Max Weber, "The Social Psychology of the World Religions," in *From Max Weber: Essays in Sociology,* trans. and ed. H. H. Gerth and C. Wright Mills (New York: Oxford University Press, 1946), pp. 267-301.

[19]Every once in a while adherents of non-Christian religions have seen fit to "correct" my understanding of Christianity, explaining, for example, that Jesus did not really die on the cross, did not really claim to be God or did not really mean that he was the only way to God in John 14:6. Members of (in alphabetical order) Baha'i, Buddhism, Hinduism (in both Hare Krishna and more traditional forms), Islam, Judaism, and Sikhism have told me that Christ did not really teach what I think he taught and that he actually taught their particular version of religious truth. In other words, Jesus really taught Baha'i, Buddhism, Hinduism, Islam and so on. Needless to say, these conversations have left me a little breathless, but they have taught me not to impose my preconceptions on a religion not my own.

[20]Hemingway's Catherine and Frederick notwithstanding. See *Farewell to Arms* (New York: Scribner's, 1929), pp. 112-15.

[21]Two classic books that have yet to be improved on are Paul Little, *How to Give Away Your Faith* (Downers Grove, Ill.: InterVarsity Press, 1966), and J. I. Packer, *Evangelism and the Sovereignty of God* (Downers Grove, Ill.: InterVarsity Press, 1961).

Chapter 2: Judaism

[1]Even where it is allowed, conversion to Judaism can be a controversial matter. Judaism is solidly identified with an ethnic heritage that includes a history of suffering, and many Jews resist the notion of allowing Judaism to be included in the cafeteria of modern Western religions for people to try out. Yet so many Jews are marrying non-Jews that the conversion of Gentile marital partners is seen by some as necessary to keeping the religious tradition of Judaism alive.

[2]Of course, these dates are highly disputed. Biblical scholarship is marked by broadly differing theories of composition (authorship, occasions for writing and so on) and dates of composition. In keeping with the evangelical presuppositions of this work, I am assuming the conservative theories, as advocated, for example, by Gleason L. Archer, *A Survey of Old Testament Introduction* (Chicago: Moody Press, 1966).

[3]Yigael Yadin, *The Temple Scroll* (New York: Random House, 1985), understands Essenes and Herodians as constituting the same group.

[4]Precisely as predicted by Jesus in Mark 13:2.

[5]*The Mishnah,* trans. Herbert Danby (Oxford, U.K.: Oxford University Press, 1933), pp. 136-40.

[6]The rabbinic method of balancing out opposing viewpoints had probably been practiced orally for a long time before the Mishnah and may explain the crowd's reaction to the teaching of Christ: they were amazed at his teaching "for he taught them as one having authority, and not as their scribes" (Mt 7:29 NRSV).

[7]*The Babylonian Talmud,* ed. I. Epstein (London: Soncino, 1935).

[8]By medieval standards—which is not saying much—Aquinas was remarkably tolerant of Jews. Although he advocated burning heretics, he thought the Jews should be left alone. Since they did not claim to be Christians, they could not adulterate Christian beliefs.

[9]This century's most authoritative study of Jewish mysticism is Gershom G. Scholem, *Major Trends in Jewish Mysticism* (New York: Schocken, 1946).

[10]Compare my *Mysticism: An Evangelical Option?* (Grand Rapids, Mich.: Zondervan, 1991), pp. 21-39.

[11]Peter Schäfer, "New Testament and Hekhalot Literature: The Journey into Heaven in Paul and in Merkavah Mysticism," *Journal of Jewish Studies* 35 (1984): 19-35.

[12]Actually, that is the literal name of another medieval kabalistic work.

[13]Chaim Potok, *The Chosen* (New York: Fawcett Crest, 1967), p. 127.

[14]Scholem, *Major Trends,* p. 246.

[15]As a native-speaking German, I can follow the gist of a Yiddish conversation.

[16]Scholem, *Major Trends,* pp. 299-304.

[17]This temple claims to be the oldest *continually operating* synagogue in the United States. Charleston also contains

many fine old churches that are also maintained in the old style of architecture and furnishings.

[18]*The World Almanac*, p. 644.

[19]As described vividly by Leon Uris in *Exodus* (New York: Bantam, 1958), pp. 557-71.

[20]They are Exodus 13:1-10, Exodus 13:11-16, Deuteronomy 6:4-9, Deuteronomy 11:13-21.

[21]An English version of a Passover Seder geared specifically to Hebrew Christians is Harold A. Sevener, ed., *Passover Haggadah for Biblical Jews and Christians* (Orangeburg, N.Y.: Beth Sar Shalom, n.d.).

[22]A valuable chronicle of events from the vote in the United Nations to the partitioning of Palestine into Jewish and Palestinian homelands to the end of the ensuing war is provided by Larry Collins and Dominique Lapierre in *O Jerusalem!* (New York: Pocket Books, 1972). This book is sympathetic toward and critical of both sides of the conflict. The apparent objectivity of this account is vouchsafed to me by the fact that both Zionist Israeli Jews and radical Palestinian activists have told me, "If you want to know what really happened, read *O Jerusalem!*"

[23]The so-called secular theology of the 1960s is less a counterexample to this claim and more an instance of the illogicality of the point. Saying there are square circles does not mean that there can be square circles.

[24]This issue has been a Catch-22 in the history of Judaism. A Jew who segregated himself from society at large was accused of being arrogant, even as a Jew who attempted to blend into society was suspected of being a subversive. Thus persecution was inevitable.

[25]Bernard B. Gair, "Fulfillment in the Messiah," in *The Messiahship of Jesus: What Jews and Jewish Christians Say*, ed. Arthur W. Kac (Chicago: Moody Press, 1980), p. 267.

Chapter 3: Islam

[1]The caveat mentioned here can be seen as part of the larger complaint against understanding the development of religions as the juggling of so many "influences." I shall make that case again very explicitly in the context of the so-called Zoroastrian influence on Judaism. The problem with influence chasing, which was so much a cornerstone of nineteenth-century scholarship in the "history of religions" school, is that it never explains anything. If Muhammad was influenced by Jewish monotheism, why not by the Christian doctrine of the Trinity? If he was influenced by the Torah, why not by the belief in an atonement? The point is, influences were there, but they were only as effective as Muhammad would let them be.

[2]The Arabic word combines the meanings of "Read!" and "Proclaim!" The text Muhammad was commanded to recite is supposed to have been recorded as Sura 96 of the Qur'an. This sura is commonly called "the clot." The version of the Qur'an used throughout this chapter is *The Holy Qur'an: Text, Translation and Commentary*, ed. A. Yusuf Ali (Brentwood, Md.: Amana, 1983). Originally published in 1934, this volume includes Arabic and English text, notes, commentary and a concordance.

[3]This point is brought out beautifully in Salman Rushdie's controversial novel *Satanic Verses*. If the Islamic establishment had read the book instead of condemning it on the basis of hearsay, they would have realized that Rushdie actually portrayed Muhammad in an admirable light as a prophet who was tempted by Satan and the religious establishment to compromise his faith but in the end refused to give in. Rushdie lampooned the religious establishment for putting wealth and power ahead of truth, which was his real offense. How ironic that one of the characters in the book says, " 'But would it not seem blasphemous, a crime against.' . . . 'Certainly not,' Billy Battuta insisted. 'Fiction is fiction; facts are facts.' " Salman Rushdie, *Satanic Verses* (New York: Viking, 1988), p. 272.

[4]It does not take higher math to figure out that if the hijra occurred in A.D. 622, then there are only 1,376 years until 1998. Where do the extra years come from? The explanation lies in the fact that the Muslim year consists of thirteen lunar months (about twenty-eight days rather than thirty or thirty-one). Thus the year is shorter than the Western solar year, and an extra forty-four years A.H. have occurred up to A.D. 1998.

[5]When the French departed Lebanon in 1941, they left behind a constitution directing that public officeholders reflect the demographic distribution at the time: the president was to be a Christian (the majority religion), the prime minister a Sunni Muslim, and the speaker of the parliament, a Shi'ite. But the population pattern has changed since then. Muslims now outnumber Christians, and among the Muslims, a much larger number are Shi'ite. This fact has contributed greatly to recent instability in that country.

[6]A comparison that breaks down fairly quickly (but is not totally without value) is that Shi'ite Muslims are in some ways similar to Roman Catholic Christians. There is a hierarchy of clergy, at the top of which is one man who speaks infallibly.

[7]Relying on the chart by John B. Noss and David S. Noss, *A History of the World's Religions* (New York: Macmillan, 1994), p. 624.

[8]For instance, Nestorianism, which virtually splits Christ into a divine person and a human person, and monophysi-

tism, which thinks in terms of Christ's having only one nature, composed of a mixture of divine and human elements.

[9]Gordon received his nickname for his campaign in China. He was known for his undaunted biblical faith combined with unorthodox, no-holds-barred military tactics. In Jerusalem, "Gordon's Calvary," the Protestant counterpart to the Church of the Holy Sepulchre, was Gordon's well-intentioned but inauthentic innovation.

[10]Suzanne Haneef, *What Everyone Should Know About Islam and Muslims* (Chicago: Kazi, 1979), p. 37.

[11]It would be wrong for an outsider to judge what Muslims should believe on this ticklish point when Islam itself is divided. As a Christian, I can do no more than report what seems to be a paradox, which the Islamic world has not resolved. Since I am in no position to judge, I must accept the ambivalence or resolution as presented to me in any given conversation. What I would like to ask in return, however, is that the Muslims who have told me countless times what I should believe concerning the Trinity or the deity of Christ would accord me the same privilege. In fact, it was a memorable moment for me when a Muslim chided Christianity for the doctrine of predestination.

[12]Isma'il Ragi al Faruqi, "Islam," in *The Great Asian Religions: An Anthology,* ed. W. Chan, I. Ragi al Faruqi, J. M. Kitagawa and P. T. Raju (New York: Macmillan, 1969). This article provides a good overview of some of the basic principles of shari'a. Jihad is treated on pages 374-75.

[13]See my discussion in *Handmaid to Theology* (Grand Rapids, Mich.: Baker Book House, 1981), pp. 149-66.

[14]For further exposition of these revealed realities, see a good book on doctrines, for example, Millard J. Erickson, *Introducing Christian Doctrine* (Grand Rapids, Mich.: Baker Book House, 1992). As to why one should believe these things, consult a book on Christian apologetics, for example, my *Reasonable Faith: A Textbook in Christian Apologetics* (Nashville, Tenn.: Broadman & Holman, 1993).

[15]Once more, I need to defer to Christian apologetics texts at this point.

[16]For more information on how the process of textual criticism works and how it supports the integrity of the New Testament, see F. F. Bruce, *The New Testament Documents: Are They Reliable?* (Downers Grove, Ill.: InterVarsity Press, 1960); F. W. Hall, *A Companion to Classical Texts* (Oxford, U.K.: Clarendon, 1913); Bruce M. Metzger, *The Text of the New Testament* (New York: Oxford University Press, 1964).

[17]See, for example, Gleason L. Archer, *Encyclopedia of Bible Difficulties* (Grand Rapids, Mich.: Zondervan, 1982).

[18]Phil Parshall, *New Paths in Muslim Evangelism: Evangelical Approaches to Contextualization* (Grand Rapids, Mich.: Baker Book House, 1980).

Chapter 4: Zoroastrianism

[1]The *World Almanac* does not give figures for participation in the United States for some religions. In those cases I am using the number for North America, which is always given. Furthermore, this number strikes me as extremely low. Other works give figures up to eight times greater than this one. I decided to post the number from the *World Almanac* here because I do not think that it is wise to pick and choose among reference works depending on whether I like the number or not. We may be looking here at the difference between the numbers claimed by a religious group and the actual number that is established in a census.

[2]R. C. Zaehner, *The Dawn and Twilight of Zoroastrianism* (London: Weidenfeld & Nicolson, 1961).

[3]To this extent, Hitler's calling Germans *Aryans* was based ever so loosely on historical facts. His lunacies about the "Aryan master race" are, of course, without foundation.

[4]Wilhelm Schmidt, *The Origin and Growth of Religion: Facts and Theories* (London: Methuen, 1931), p. 43.

[5]People are forever inventing new names for their gods, without actually changing their identities. Just think how many titles Christians apply to Jesus—Lord, Savior, the Nazarene, the Good Shepherd and so on. Thus there is nothing unusual about Ahura Mazda becoming the replacement name for the original god. In Hinduism, as we shall see later, the shifts in names create virtually impenetrable confusion. For example, Rudra, the fearsome mountain god, became known as Shiva, "the auspicious one."

[6]Robert Brow says, "In the sixth century B.C. there was a tidal wave of revolt against the priestcraft of the ancient world. This wave shattered the power of the old religions, though their cults continued to exist as backwaters for centuries. Seven world religions appeared within fifty years of each other and all continue to this day." Robert Brow, *Religion: Origins and Ideas* (Chicago: InterVarsity Press, 1966), p. 27.

[7]Nowadays the name Zarathustra has become associated with the figure in Friedrich Nietzsche's writings. Clearly Nietzsche deliberately chose Zarathustra, the prophet who taught the absolute opposition of good and evil, to represent his own prophet of decadence who taught the abolition of the distinction between good and evil. Friedrich Nietzsche, *Thus Spoke Zarathustra,* in *The Portable Nietzsche,* ed. and trans. Walter Kaufmann (New York: Viking, 1954), pp. 103-439.

[8]Mary Boyce, *Zoroastrians: Their Religious Beliefs and Practices* (London: Routledge & Kegan Paul, 1979), p. 2.

[9]Zaehner, *Dawn and Twilight,* p. 33.

[10]Few textbooks on world religions are able to refrain from commenting on how significant the age of thirty seems to be in the lives of religious founders. Though any generalization (based on Jesus, Zoroaster or Gautama Buddha) can be disproven (for example, by Muhammad), the fourth decade in these men's lives seems to be highly crucial.

[11]This "king," probably a courtesy title for a tribal chieftain, has not been identified with certainty. Some scholars see him as related to Cyrus, who eventually took over the Babylonian kingdom for the Persians; others see him as a rival to Cyrus. The father of Darius I is called Hystaspes. If he is identical with the Hystaspes in question, our "king" is the father of the first Zoroastrian king of Persia—a neat hypothesis, but far from certain. See S. A. Nigosian, *The Zoroastrian Faith: Tradition and Modern Research* (Montreal, Quebec: McGill-Queen's University Press, 1993), pp. 25-30.

[12]That kind of statement always puts one out on a limb, given the controversy raging in historical scholarship. My justification for the claim is this: it is not the case that there are many conflicting Zoroastrian sources which must be balanced against each other. The ones named are the greatest bulk of them. The only choice is between relying on the few there are or doing without sources at all and relying on one's creative imagination, which I, for one, consider inferior methodology.

[13]Irach J. S. Taraporewala, "Zoroastrianism," in *Living Schools of Religion,* ed. Vergilius Ferm (Paterson, N.J.: Littlefield, Adams, 1965), p. 23.

[14]Niels C. Nielsen Jr., ed., *Religions of the World,* (New York: St. Martin's, 1983), p. 375.

[15]Nigosian, *Zoroastrian Faith,* p. 25.

[16]One scholar believes that the magi in question thought Jesus might have been their messiah figure, Saoshyant. That idea still does not explain why they would look to a Jewish infant, born in Palestine, for this person. Those circumstances, after all, do not seem to fit into the rest of the Zoroastrian Saoshyant myth. James H. Moulton, *Early Zoroastrianism* (London: Williams & Norgate, 1913).

[17]Here is the real answer to the question you may have been searching for all your life: Why do we have to dress up for church?

[18]R. C. Zaehner, *Zurvan: A Zoroastrian Dilemma* (New York: Biblo & Tannen, 1972).

[19]Hans Jonas, *The Gnostic Religion,* 2nd ed. (New York: Beacon, 1963), pp. 206-36.

[20]David S. Noss and John B. Noss, *A History of the World's Religions* (New York: Macmillan, 1994), p. 403.

[21]A good summary of contemporary observances is found in Nigosian, *Zoroastrian Faith,* pp. 98-118.

[22]In distinction to the five prayer times of Islam (sunrise, noon, afternoon, sunset, one hour after sunset), the Zoroastrian times are divided more evenly around the clock: morning, noon, afternoon, evening to midnight, midnight to dawn. It is hypothesized that these times may originally have corresponded to the watches of ancient palace guards.

[23]For example, Lewis M. Hopfe, *Religions of the World,* 6th ed. (New York: Macmillan, 1994), p. 259.

[24]*Talmud Yerushalmi* (Jerusalem Talmud), Tractate "Rosh Hashanah," trans. Edward A. Goldman (Chicago: University of Chicago Press, 1988), chap. 1 sec. 2 (cited in many works, including Moulton, *Early Zoroastrianism,* p. 323). However, the reference is only to the names of the angels; the names are not Persian, let alone Zoroastrian. Finally, if the reference is to the exile, then the Jews were out of Babylonia before Zoroastrianism took hold anyway.

[25]Moulton, *Early Zoroastrianism,* p. 317.

[26]I wish to thank Mr. John Makujino, a Christian convert who grew up in a Parsi family, who helped me with this section.

[27]Nigosian, *Zoroastrian Faith,* pp. 116-18.

Chapter 5: Traditional Religions

[1]See also the discussion of this point in Edward G. Newing, "Religions of Pre-literary Societies," in *The World's Religions,* ed. Sir Norman Anderson (Grand Rapids, Mich.: Eerdmans, 1975), pp. 11-48.

[2]Wilhelm Schmidt, *The Origin and Growth of Religion: Facts and Theories,* trans. H. J. Rose (London: Methuen, 1931), p. 162.

[3]*The Way of the Ancestors,* in *The Long Search,* video series produced by BBC (New York: Ambrose Video Publishing, 1978).

[4]In the history of Christian missions, the actions of missionaries in violating taboos without incurring dire consequence have led to large-scale conversions. For a long time the Christian monk Winfried Boniface preached among the pagan Germans without great results. Finally he decided to chop down a massive oak dedicated to the god Wodan. When Boniface was not immediately struck by lightning, the spectators realized that their religion was not true and became Christians. Remember also the treatment of a fetish object by St. Olaf mentioned in the first chapter.

[5]Nevertheless, the Tlingit Indians of Alaska are totemic and matrilineal.

[6]For example, Lewis M. Hopfe, *Religions of the World*, 6th ed. (New York: Macmillan, 1994), p. 28.

[7]Schmidt, *Origin and Growth of Religion*, p. 114.

[8]Sigmund Freud, *Totem and Taboo* (New York: Random House/Vintage, 1948).

[9]Jomo Kenyatta, *Facing Mt. Kenya: The Tribal Life of the Gikuyu* (New York: Random House, 1965). Kenyatta wrote this book when he was studying anthropology in London in the 1930s, long before he returned to Kenya and became that country's first president. Although the true spelling for this tribe is *Gikuyu*, *Kikuyu* reflects common usage in this century. The Kikuyu left their mark on the history of the twentieth century with the Mau Mau uprising of the 1950s.

[10]Tepilit Ole Saitoti, *Maasai* (New York: Abrams, 1980). Again different spellings abound, for example, *Massai* and *Masai*.

[11]Henry John Drewal and John Pemberton III, *Yoruba: Nine Centuries of African Art and Thought* (New York: Abrams, 1989).

[12]E. Thomas Lawson, *Religions of Africa* (San Francisco: Harper & Row, 1985). Lawson undertakes a comparative analysis of the Zulu and the Yoruba.

[13]Two good studies that provide further guidance to ATR are John S. Mbiti, *African Religions and Philosophy* (Nairobi, Kenya: East African Educational Publishers, 1969), and Richard J. Gehman, *African Traditional Religion in Biblical Perspective* (Kijabe, Kenya: Kesho, 1989). Both books include extensive bibliographies.

[14]Mbiti, *African Religions and Philosophy*, pp. 108-9.

[15]Lawson, *Religions of Africa*, p. 26.

[16]Irving Hexham, "Lord of the Sky—King of the Earth: Zulu Traditional Religion and Belief in the Sky God," *Studies in Religion* 10, no. 3: 273-85. Hexham argues against the use of Unkulunkulu as the traditional name but points out the difficulty in making authoritative pronouncements on the subject.

[17]Mbiti, *African Religions and Philosophy*, p. 50.

[18]Saitoti, *Maasai*, p. 26.

[19]For example, Lawson does so throughout *Religions of Africa*.

[20]For example, Mbiti, *African Religion and Philosophy*, pp. 75-77.

[21]Ibid., p. 83.

[22]Ibid., p. 162.

[23]On my own short research trip to Africa, the word *fear* crept into all of the interviews I was able to carry out. Every conversation included some reference to fear of the ancestors. Gehman, after many years of work in Africa, impressed this point on me as well. He also writes, "Fear is a dominant feature" (*African Traditional Religion*, p. 136). I want to thank Samson Agenga for spending almost an entire day with me sharing his experiences.

[24]Mbiti, *African Religions and Philosophy*, p. 58. Emphasis mine.

[25]Gehman, *African Traditional Religion*, p. 142.

[26]Lawson, *Religions of Africa*, pp. 71-76.

[27]Saitoti, *Maasai*. The entire book is organized according to the various stages in a Maasai's life.

[28]Kenyatta, *Facing Mount Kenya*, pp. 125-221.

[29]Lawson, *Religions of Africa*, pp. 33-40.

[30]Kenyatta, *Facing Mount Kenya*, pp. 38-41.

[31]Just to keep the record straight: as of this writing there is a lot of bad blood between Kikuyu and Maasai over the same issue. The Maasai claim that the Kikuyu are violating their land rights by moving into their traditional territory to set up farms at the expense of Maasai grazing country. History moves in circles.

[32]Kenyatta, *Facing Mount Kenya*, pp. 280-85.

[33]Lawson, *Religions of Africa*, p. 23. Such evil magic is also at times called sorcery. Again, there are no absolute linguistic distinctions.

[34]Kenyatta, *Facing Mount Kenya*, p. 294.

[35]Gehman, *African Traditional Religion*, pp. 15-22.

[36]I am indebted to Professor Julius Murikwa for sharing the fruits of his research with me in a long conversation.

[37]Some writers have seen what I am calling syncretism as the only legitimate expression of faith by Africans. Apparently some of them, in the name of "liberation," are forcing a virtual straitjacket of mandatory African forms on Christianity in Africa. See, for example, Kofi Appiah-Kubi, "Indigenous African Christian Churches: Signs of Authenticity," in *Third World Liberation Theologies: A Reader*, ed. Deane William Ferm (Maryknoll, N.Y.: Orbis, 1986), pp. 222-30.

[38]Edward C. Stewart and Milton J. Bennett, *American Cultural Patterns: A Cross-Cultural Perspective* (Yarmouth, Maine: Intercultural, 1991), p. 156.

[39]And I need to once more express my gratitude to Dr. Gehman for his long-suffering patience in bringing me to see this point.

Chapter 6: Native American Religion

[1]This conception was popularized by the works of James Fenimore Cooper with his chief Chingachcook, as well as in the works of Karl May, the inventor of the noble chief Winnetou, in German.

[2]As a Christian, once again, I expect human culture to reflect the best that human beings are capable of as well as human fallenness. All human cultures have some positive traits. But because all of them have been devised by sinful human beings, they fall far short of divine standards. Cultures are not intrinsically neutral; all cultures are a mix of good and bad, whether we are talking about African, Asian, European or Native American cultures.

[3]This discussion follows closely Robert F. Spencer et al., *The Native Americans: Ethnology and Backgrounds of the North American Indians* (New York: Harper & Row, 1977).

[4]The discussion and this chart continue to follow Spencer, *Native Americans*. To keep this discussion from becoming too confusing, I had to settle on the past tense in the course of compiling this survey. Of course, many of these people and their practices are now extinct or have shifted drastically. On the other hand, some of them continue to this day.

[5]Ruth M. Underhill, *Red Man's Religion: Beliefs and Practices of the Indians North of Mexico* (Chicago: University of Chicago Press, 1965).

[6]Remember the point made in chapter one. Some groups living on the lowest levels of human culture, such as stone-tool-using hunter-gatherers, show some of the clearest commitment to a belief in a sky god.

[7]Extensive studies in this area were undertaken by A. L. Kroeber, who summarized them in various monographs. Ultimately all of this material was pulled together as *Handbook of the Indians of California* (Washington, D.C.: Government Printing Office, 1925).

[8]Wilhelm Schmidt, *The Origin and Growth of Religion: Facts and Theories* (London: Methuen, 1931). This combination of a primitive existence and a strong belief in God with little magic, here and among the Pygmies of Africa, the Pygmoid peoples of Asia and the Australian aborigines, led Schmidt to his theory of original monotheism.

[9]J. R. Walker, *The Sun Dance and Other Ceremonies of the Oglala Division of the Teton Dakota*, p. 125, cited in Mircea Eliade, *From Primitives to Zen* (New York: Harper & Row, 1967), p. 12.

[10]For example, Underhill, *Red Man's Religion*, p. 21.

[11]Paul Radin, "Religion of the North American Indians," *Journal of American Folk-Lore* 27 (1914): 335-73.

[12]Eliade, *Primitives to Zen*, p. 12.

[13]John M. Cooper, *The Northern Algonquian Supreme Being* (Washington, D.C.: Catholic University Press, 1934).

[14]Spencer, *Native Americans*, p. 356.

[15]In the 1980s the Hopi tribe brought suit against developers in New Mexico who were expanding ski resorts on the mountains overlooking the Hopi reservation on which the Kachinas are supposed to dwell. However, a federal court ruled in *Block v. Wilson*, 1983, that maintaining the pristine setting of the mountains, which are not located on the reservation itself, is not indispensable to the Hopi religion, and the development was permitted. For a study of contemporary Hopi life, see John D. Loftin, *Religion and Hopi Life in the Twentieth Century* (Bloomington: Indiana University Press, 1991).

[16]Spencer, *Native Americans*, p. 442.

[17]Ibid., pp. 423-24.

[18]John G. Neihardt, *Black Elk Speaks: Being the Life Story of a Holy Man of the Oglala Sioux* (New York: Pocket Books, 1932). Interestingly, a fact left out by Neihardt's romanticized portrayal is that Black Elk eventually converted to Roman Catholicism. The attentive reader wishing to pursue the story of Black Elk needs to be forewarned that there are *two* shamans by that name who have received extensive attention in print. Wallace Howard Black Elk lived later than the subject of our discussion and remained a shaman. His contributions are recorded in Joseph Epes Brown, *The Sacred Pipe: Black Elk's Account of the Seven Rites of the Oglala Sioux* (Norman: University of Oklahoma Press, 1953). Older readers may remember Benjamin Black Elk, who greeted visitors to Mount Rushmore for many years. He was the son of our Black Elk.

[19]John A. Grim, *The Shaman: Patterns of Religious Healing Among the Ojibway Indians* (Norman: University of Oklahoma, 1983). This highly detailed study is marred somewhat by Grim's attempt to cram his indisputable observations into the questionable categories of naturalistic psychophilosophy.

[20]Livingston F. Jones, *A Study of the Thlingets of Alaska* (New York: Revell, 1914), pp. 154-67, and O. M. Salisbury, *The Customs and Legends of the Thlinget Indians of Alaska* (New York: Bonanza, 1962), pp. 231-36.

[21]Underhill, *Red Man's Religion*, pp. 82-85.

[22]Spencer, *Native Americans,* pp. 306-10.

[23]Jones, *Study of the Thlingets,* p. 171.

[24]Salisbury, *Customs and Legends,* p. 198.

[25]Robert H. Lowie, *The Religion of the Crow Indians* (New York: American Museum of Natural History, 1922).

[26]Jones, *Thlingets of Alaska,* p. 45.

[27]Spencer, *Native Americans,* p. 142.

[28]Ibid., pp. 351, 354.

[29]Loftin, *Religion and Hopi Life,* p. 55.

[30]Spencer, *Native Americans,* pp. 197-98.

[31]Jones, *Study of the Thlingets,* p. 126.

[32]Underhill, *Red Man's Religion,* p. 176.

[33]Ibid., p. 142.

[34]Underhill, ibid., pp. 142-53, gives a description of a Cheyenne version along with a very helpful chart to demonstrate the variety from tribe to tribe. Spencer, *Native Americans,* pp. 357-60, provides detailed information on the Oglala sun dance.

[35]Spencer, *Native Americans,* p. 305.

[36]Jones, *Study of the Thlingets,* pp. 147-53.

[37]Ibid., p. 149.

[38]Spencer, *Native Americans,* p. 417.

[39]This attempt to emulate Christian teaching was a core concept in the movement. See Neihardt, *Black Elk Speaks,* pp. 195-223, and Dee Brown, *Bury My Heart at Wounded Knee: An Indian History of the American West* (New York: Bantam, 1970), pp. 406-18. From the standpoint of evaluating scholarship, it is fascinating that an important reference source virtually ignores the Christian-syncretistic character of the movement (Hirschfelder and Molin, *Encyclopedia of Native American Religions,* pp. 98-99.) But it was precisely this part of the movement, the idea that the red people were now going to be revived with the white man's own religion, that contributed to its appeal.

[40]Here is another example of how quickly a specific ritual can be devised, distributed and modified. If the movement had persisted, an anthropologist stumbling on it without prior knowledge in, say, 1892, could easily be led to believe that this dance was an ancient custom, preserved with little change through the centuries.

[41]Ibid., pp. 193-94, 213-15. Also Alice Marriott and Carol K. Rachlin, *Peyote* (New York: New American Library, 1971).

[42]Hirschfelder and Molin, *Encyclopedia of Native American Religions,* p. 193.

Chapter 7: Hinduism

[1]For example, adherents of the so-called Hare Krishna school of Hinduism (ISKCON) consider the Bhagavad-Gita to be "Vedic."

[2]As we shall see later in this book, the idea can also be extended downward to include plants (as in Jainism) or upward to include spiritual beings, even gods (as in Buddhism).

[3]According to traditional Hindu reincarnation, even high-caste women are automatically at a lower state of incarnation. Carrying out their duties may bring them back as men in their next lives.

[4]J. N. Hattiangadi, "Why Is Indian Religion Mystical?" *Journal of Indian Philosophy* 3 (1975): 253-58.

[5]The term *nirvana* has come to be much more popular in the context of Buddhism, where it refers to the very opposite, the extinction of all being. A critical question arises as to how, if Atman and Brahman are identical, there should be any need for realization. Can the infinite lose its identity or forget who it is? The idea that someone who is Atman-Brahman should be subject to maya and *advaita* (ignorance) represents a mystery that is every bit as unfathomable as the supposed identity of God and Self. Christian thinkers would maintain that this is an irreconcilable contradiction. See my critique of pantheism in *Reasonable Faith: Basic Christian Apologetics* (Nashville, Tenn.: Broadman & Holman, 1993), pp. 92-95.

[6]Vedanta is considered one of the six "orthodox" schools of Hindu philosophy. Keep in mind that these schools are philosophical orientations. They are not actually subsections of Hinduism, let alone "denominations," though they clearly affect larger matters of worship and practice. There are other five schools. *Samkhya*—an atheistic system of forces in the universe; the goal is for the spiritual to overcome the physical. *Yoga*—the addition to the Samkhya system of a god, Ishvara (the creative force of Brahman), and exercises centering on breathing and bodily postures. Physical Yoga (Hatha Yoga) is also a part of many other versions of Hinduism, including the devotion to Krishna or Shiva, discussed below. *Mimansa*—a ritualistic philosophy that propagates the notion that reincarnation can be avoided through strict obedience to the Vedas. *Vaisheshika*—an originally atheistic system that sees the universe as

composed of nine elements. *Nyaya*—a system of thought that focuses on the study of knowledge and logic in the context of Vaisheshika metaphysics.

It is telling for the diversity within Hinduism that three of these six philosophies are essentially atheistic. However, the adherents of these systems of thought consider the Vedas sacred (in some way), maintain the caste system and do not abuse cows. Thus they are included as "orthodox" Hindu thought.

[7]For the longer discussion on which I am basing these three points, see Rudolf Otto, *India's Religion of Grace and Christianity Compared and Contrasted*, trans. Frank Hugh Foster (New York: Macmillan, 1930).

[8]Some contemporary Hindus would also like to see Jesus incorporated into the list of avatars. After all, Jesus Christ is an incarnation of God. If Jesus were absorbed into the pantheon, his unique claims could be neutralized.

[9]I have avoided giving alternative names for the other gods, because many of them have dozens of names and the text would get far too cluttered. However, it is essential for anyone wanting to do a more practical study of Hinduism, particularly by visiting temples, to memorize a long list of names or to carry a reference work. For example, Shiva is known, among other names, as Bhava, Hara, Ishana, Mahadeva, Maheshvara, Nataraja, Pasupati, Sambhu and Shankara. David Knipe, *Hinduism: Experiments in the Sacred* (San Francisco: HarperSanFrancisco, 1991), p. 165.

[10]A fictitious—and highly embellished—version of this cult was the focus of the movie *Indiana Jones and the Temple of Doom*, Paramount Pictures, 1984.

[11]These are only partly the nine planets known to modern astronomy. They are the sun (Surya), the moon (Chandra), Mars (Mangala or Chevvaai), Mercury (Budha), Jupiter (Guru), Venus (Shukra), Saturn (Sani), the moon in its ascending node (Rahu) and the Dragon in its descending node (Ketu).

[12]Also written *AUM*. Sanskrit does not have a separate vowel for *o*.

[13]John Henry Barrows, ed., *The World's Parliament of Religions*, 2 vols. (Chicago: Parliament Publications, 1893). References to and transcripts of Vivekananda's addresses are in 1:65, 101-2, 128, 170, 242; 2:968-78.

[14]Knipe, *Hinduism*, p. 8.

[15]India, like all increasingly industrialized countries, has moved closer to gender egalitarianism. A woman, Indira Gandhi, was prime minister of India for many years, suggesting more that the rules can be broken in any society than that a large-scale leveling of gender distinctions is taking place in India. A similar violation of traditional practice in an Islamic setting is represented by the election of Benazir Bhutto as president of Pakistan.

[16]At least in theory; in practice Hinduism has been involved in as many violent conflicts over matters of faith as any other religion, both as victim and as oppressor.

[17]Satsvarupa Dasa Goswami, *Prabhupada: He Built a House in Which the Whole World Can Live* (Los Angeles: Bhaktivedanta Book Trust, 1983), p. 368.

Chapter 8: Buddhism

[1]A fairly complete version is given in P. Thomas, *Epics, Myths and Legends of India* (Bombay, India: Traporevala, n.d.), pp. 109-19. In some details I am diverging from this version, based on the story of Buddha's life as I have seen it displayed in many Buddhist temples. For purposes of this book, it is best to stick with the version that is in circulation now rather than a historical one.

[2]Sometimes written as *anatta*, which is the transcription of the Pali dialect, the original language of Gautama's Buddhism. For simplicity's sake, I am sticking with the Sanskrit equivalents rather than writing *kamma* for karma, *dhamma* for dharma, *nibhanna* for nirvana, and so on.

[3]This is the religion Westerners are familiar with as *Taoism*. The new rules of transcription of Chinese into the Western alphabet *(pinyin)* require the spelling *Daoism*, which in this case, at least, seems more intuitive. More on Daoism in chapter ten. See also the lengthier note 2 on transcription in that chapter.

[4]D. T. Suzuki, *Zen Buddhism*, ed. William Barrett (Garden City, N.Y.: Doubleday, 1956), p. 9.

[5]Alan W. Watts, *The Spirit of Zen* (New York: Grove, 1958), p. 49.

[6]In fact, Watts quotes a Zen master who says of the Zen experience itself: "Nothing is left to you at this moment . . . but to burst out into a loud laugh." Ibid., p. 67.

[7]The exact quotation refers to the *Pratyekabuddhas*, beings that have attained Buddhahood without perfection. They are enlightened and exist at a higher state than arhats but do not have the perfect standing and power of the true Buddhas.

[8]Suzuki, *Zen Buddhism*, p. 23.

[9]Also sometimes translated as "thunderbolt vehicle." The inference based on this translation is that the adept receives enlightenment as through a thunderbolt. However, some scholars maintain that this is a mistranslation based on an unwarranted interpretation of the Sanskrit *vajra*, which is never used in this way in the Tibetan context. Franz-Karl Ehrrhard, "Vajra," in *Lexikon der östlichen Weisheitslehren*, ed. Stephan Schumacher and Gert Woerner (Munich: Otto

Wilhelm Barth, 1986), p. 422.

[10]The other three are Akshobhya (east), Amoghasiddhi (north), and Rtnasambhava (south). David S. Noss and John B. Noss, *A History of the World's Religions* (New York: Macmillan, 1994), p. 221.

[11]Tibetan scholars claim that this method places them in the position of having discovered Sigmund Freud's psychoanalytic methods many centuries prior to Freud's own work. The obvious parallels are in the recognition and appropriation of physical passions (particularly sex) and the gradual removal of unhealthy internal complexes. See Jeffrey Hopkins and Geshe Lhundup Sopa, *Practice and Theory of Tibetan Buddhism* (New York: Grove, 1976).

[12]*The Tibetan Book of the Dead, or, The After-Death Experiences on the Bardo Plane,* trans. Lama Kazi Dawa Samdup (New York: Oxford University Press, 1960).

[13]As described by Robert C. Lester, *Buddhism: The Path to Nirvana* (San Francisco: Harper & Row, 1987), pp. 109-16.

[14]Ibid., pp. 71-72.

Chapter 9: Three Offshoot Religions

[1]P. Thomas, *Epics, Myths and Legends of India* (Bombay, India: Traporevala, n.d.), pp. 126-30, contains a good summary of Mahavira's life story. It is helpful because it separates the core legend from the added mythology.

[2]According to traditional dates, Mahavira (599-527 B.C.) represents one generation ahead of Gautama (560-480 B.C.). However, later dates (for example, 549-477 B.C.) for Mahavira are accepted by some both inside and outside of Jainism, in which case the two founders were contemporary. This complicated discussion is important to Jains because if Mahavira died before Gautama, he attained nirvana earlier, thus giving him superiority. Muni Shri Nagrajji, *The Contemporaneity and the Chronology of Mahavira and Buddha* (New Delhi, India: Today and Tomorrow's Book Agency, 1970).

[3]In Vedantic Hinduism *jiva* is the word for physical and psychological life; the soul as *jiva* is distinguished from *atman,* the deepest level of one's self, which, as we have seen, is identical to *Brahman.* In Jainism, *jiva* and *atman* can be used interchangeably. There is no universal *Brahman.*

[4]Thomas, *Epics, Myths and Legends,* pp. 131-34; Jagmanderlal Jaini, *Outlines of Jainism* (Westport, Conn.: Hyperion, 1940), pp. 6-7.

[5]Francis Schaeffer made this point clearly over against Albert Schweitzer's "reverence for life." *The God Who Is There* (Downers Grove, Ill.: InterVarsity Press, 1967), pp. 94-95.

[6]In the 1960s and 1970s a relatively minor cult in the United States designated itself as Eckankar. It turns out that the cult's founder, Paul Twitchell, had studied under some Sikh sages and derived the name from that experience.

[7]*Sikh Religion* (Detroit, Mich.: Sikh Missionary Center, 1990), p. 198.

[8]For an accurate and exciting account of the events surrounding the independence and partition of India, see Larry Collins and Dominique Lapierre, *Freedom at Midnight* (New York: Simon & Schuster, 1957).

[9]This rule of behavior seems to embody an interesting paradox. The story is told that Guru Nanak visited Mecca. There he accidentally sat down in such a way that his feet pointed at the ka'ba. When the authorities chastised him for showing disrespect for God, Nanak is supposed to have replied, "Show me a direction where God is not, and I will be glad to point my toes in that direction." A further embellishment, mounting the questionable upon the improbable, states that Nanak went on to rotate his body in a circle, and the ka'ba moved wherever his toes pointed. Thereupon the Muslim leader became a devotee of the guru. Nevertheless, don't point your feet at the holy book in a Sikh temple!

[10]A constant question for a Christian in contact with members of other religions is what to do with food given one in a temple. In 1 Corinthians 8 the apostle Paul seems to make two important points in regard to the matter of food sacrificed to idols: (1) food is food; eating it or not eating it does not affect one's spiritual state and (2) we must be careful in the exercise of this liberty not to provide a stumbling block to people who are still wrestling with truth. In 1 Corinthians 10, Paul adds an important third principle: we must not participate in any ritual, eating or otherwise, that could be construed as the worship of demons.

This issue is a very live one in Christian communities living alongside pagan religions. For example, Chinese Christians are constantly confronted by the question whether to eat a meal that has first been offered to departed family members; not to do so causes severe family strain. Most of the Chinese Christians I know do not partake of such meals. In fact, this refusal creates an opportunity for them to take an open stand for Christ.

As a visitor to temples, I have been offered items such as oranges right off the altar in Hindu and Chinese "Buddhist" temples as well as the mandatory lump of sugar in Sikh temples. I am quite sure that I would not defile myself spiritually by eating them (1 Cor 8:8), but since I want to relate with a clear conscience to my Christian brothers and sisters for whom the battle line is drawn at exactly this point, I have made it my policy to gratefully receive the item (always being careful not to accept it with my left hand!) and to pitch it later when I am outside of the temple. On the other hand, if it is a matter of eating a normal meal in the vicinity of a temple, I do not engage in detective work to find out whether or not the preparers invoked their deities in the process of cooking it. In that case, I consume the food as the gift from the Creator that it is.

[11]The existence of this document, which casts a negative light on subsequent developments, is acknowledged by contemporary Baha'i scholars; they simply deny that it means what it states. William S. Hatcher and J. Douglas Martin, *The Bahai Faith: The Emerging Global Religion* (San Francisco: Harper & Row, 1985), p. 35.

[12]A pointer for anyone wishing to pursue Baha'ullah's books in the library. For reasons known only to itself, the Library of Congress lists Baha'ullah as Baha Allah, under which his books are listed.

[13]Statement made by Baha'ullah, used as the inscription on the title page of the anthology *Bahai World Faith: Selected Writings by Baha'ullah and Abdul Baha* (Wilmette, Ill.: Bahai Publishing Trust, 1943).

[14]*Bahai Teachings for a World Faith* (Wilmette, Ill.: Bahai Publishing Trust, 1972), pp. 3-9.

[15]See, for example, Seena Fazel and Khazeh Fananapazir, "A Bahai Approach to the Claim of Exclusivity and Uniqueness in Christianity," *Journal of Bahai Studies* 3 (1990): 15-24.

Chapter 10: Chinese Popular Religion

[1]The *World Almanac* has separate entries for Chinese folk religionists and Confucians, but none for Daoists. I have added these two figures in the hope that the sum comes close to an estimate of those Chinese practicing "popular religion." Nevertheless, the number is probably far too low. There are many more Chinese practicing some aspect of popular religion in the People's Republic of China who are not on any official record. Though as of this writing the People's Republic tolerates religion, it still actively and publicly discourages it.

[2]The transcription of foreign words into English presents a challenge for most religions, as anyone consulting reference works will soon discover. Depending on time and place written (as well as on the preferences of the translator), for many religions there are several variant transcriptions.

For Chinese religion, the issue becomes even more acute because Chinese linguistics has gone through several official reforms of transcription. Until early in the twentieth century, a system was used in the West that can be recognized by the frequent use of the letter *K*. The spelling of many traditional geographic locations, for example, the cities of "Peking" or "Nanking," retained that particular spelling long after the system went out of style in scholarly circles. This form of transcription is still reflected in the names of Chinese families who came to the United States through the turn into the twentieth century. In the first half of the twentieth century, the Wade-Giles system of Romanization began to dominate. Most books on Chinese religion retain that system as their standard.

However, Chairman Mao of the People's Republic of China declared that there should be one universal standard of Romanization and made a third system, the *Pinyin* system, mandatory. In the People's Republic, all transcriptions are now done according to this system, and thus "Peking" has become "Beijing" and Mao Tse-tung is now Mao Zedong. However, outside of China (for example, Singapore or Hong Kong) names still follow the Wade-Giles system or one of several other systems. There is a trend among scholarly books to use the Pinyin system, but many standard texts continue to use Wade-Giles as well.

Consequently, there is no way around confusion at this point. I follow current practice and use the Pinyin system. For more important terms, which a reader is likely to encounter in even general reading, I add the Wade-Giles Romanization in parentheses the first time the term appears.

Here is one example of the three forms of Romanization: the name of the central Daoist book is Tao-te-King (older system), Tao-te-ching (Wade-Giles), or Dao-de-jing (Pinyin). The Pinyin system has the advantage that it is easy to pronounce. Even when Daoism was spelled as Taoism, it was still pronounced with a *D* sound. Two points to look out for in Pinyin pronunciation: *ong* is pronounced *oong,* and *Q* carries something close to the *ch* sound as in *child*.

Even in Pinyin Romanization there are variations from reference work to reference work! See Yin Binyong and Mary Felley, *Chinese Romanization: Pronunciation and Orthography* (Beijing: Sinolingua, 1990).

[3]Table 10.4 displays the main Chinese dynasties with their dates of accession.

[4]*Shang* as in *Shang-di,* though transcribed the same way in English, is not the same as the Chinese word *Shang,* the name for the dynasty. The name means "the ruler on high." Daniel L. Overmyer, *Religions of China: The World as a Living System* (San Francisco: HarperSanFrancisco, 1986), p. 25. Shang-di is to this day the term of preference for God in Protestant Christianity; however, the word for *god* in the more generic sense of deity is *shen.*

[5]Strictly speaking, the kingdom at the time was hardly an empire. Nevertheless, in retrospect it has become customary to refer to the states of early China as "empires" ruled by emperors, and I shall observe that convention.

[6]Even the atheistic communist system had a kind of religious status by Chinese standards, for it occupied itself with this crucial question of finding an overarching framework for government.

Dynasty	Year of accession
Shang	c. 1500 B.C.
Zhou	1040
Warring States period	
Qin	221
Han (Liu)	202
Assorted rulers, some non-Chinese	
Sui	A.D. 581
Tang (Li)	618
Song	960
Yuan (Mongols)	1127
Ming	1368
Quing (Manchu)	1644
First Republic	1911

Table 10.4. Major Chinese dynasties

[7]Arthur Waley, *The Way and Its Power: A Study of the Tao Te Ching and Its Place in Chinese Thought* (New York: Grove, 1958), pp. 59-68. This book combines an introduction, the text of the Dao-de-jing and commentary from the vantage point of contemporary scholarship.

[8]Ibid., p. 61.

[9]Ibid., p. 141.

[10]Ibid.

[11]Ibid., p. 143.

[12]Ibid., p. 211.

[13]*The Portable World Bible,* ed. Robert O. Ballou (New York: Penguin, 1944), p. 562.

[14]Mircea Eliade, *The Forge and the Crucible: The Origins and Structures of Alchemy* (Chicago: Chicago University Press, 1978). Alchemy was integrated into Christian theology right through the Reformation. See John Warwick Montgomery, *In Defense of Martin Luther* (Milwaukee: Northwestern, 1970), pp. 87-113.

[15]Emperor Yu-huang should not be confused with another mythological hero, Yu the Great, who has been called "the Chinese Noah." Yu the Great is credited with showing the people who were stranded on mountaintops during the cosmic flood how to construct irrigation canals and run off the water. He is frequently worshiped as an agricultural deity.

[16]Chinese popular religion, being the admixture that it is, actually accommodates several apparently conflicting beliefs concerning the afterlife, all at the same time. Thus the practice combines belief in a netherworld existence, the existence of the ancestor in the tablet and a cycle of reincarnation.

[17]Overmyer, *Religions of China,* p. 63.

[18]See the section on Chinese culture in JoAnn Craig, *Culture Shock* (Singapore: Times Books International, 1979), pp. 27-80.

[19]Morris A. Inch, *Doing Theology Across Cultures* (Grand Rapids, Mich.: Baker Book House, 1982), pp. 81-89.

[20]Watchman Nee, *What Shall This Man Do?* (Wheaton, Ill.: Tyndale House, 1978), pp. 39-40.

Chapter 11: Shinto & the Japanese Synthesis

[1]H. Byron Earhart, "Japanese Religion," in *The Perennial Dictionary of World Religions,* ed. Keith Crim (San Francisco: Harper & Row, 1981), p. 374.

[2]In addition to highly explicit sexual references, the Kojiki and Nihongi are filled with numerous scatological anecdotes which, to contemporary ears at least, create a dubious picture of the kami. Consequently a venerable translation of the Kojiki into English wound up rendering all "indecent" passages in Latin. *The Kojiki: Records of Ancient Matters,* trans. Basil Hall Chamberlain (1882; Rutland, Vt.: Tuttle, 1981). However, protecting oneself against

what was obviously an important aspect of the total culture is going to hinder an accurate understanding of the religion.

[3]*Nihongi: Chronicles of Japan from the Earliest Times,* trans. W. G. Aston (1896; London: Allen & Unwin, 1956), p. 3.

[4]Frederic Spiegelberg comments, "That the Japanese should have a male god of the Moon and a female deity of the Sun is not what we have been led to expect, but the explanation may again lie in the aboriginal changeover from a matriarchy to a patriarchy." *Living Religions of the World* (Englewood Cliffs, N.J.: Prentice-Hall, 1956), p. 358.

[5]Some of that "openness" was in fact forced on Japan by an American, Commodore Matthew Perry, who cruised to Japan twice with a powerful fleet of gunboats and wrested trade concessions from the Japanese.

[6]The attempt to present a more or less systematic description of Shinto already becomes complicated at this point. Different works draw different distinctions, all of which are slightly arbitrary because they are in reality commingled with each other. Some classifications leave out home (or domestic) Shinto but add imperial Shinto, which they distinguish from state Shinto. Further, it is possible to add folk Shinto as a separate category of Shinto, though I will follow the prevalent custom of referring to it as folk religion.

[7]Hitler and the German Nazis attempted the same thing. They tried to devise a truly Germanic theology, which they then imposed on the Christian churches. Although this maneuver gave them control of the ecclesiastical structures of Germany, it did not place them in dominion over the hearts of many German Christians. Similarly, with all of its attempts to control the churches, the communist government of East Germany eventually succumbed to a revolt that originated in the churches of Leipzig.

[8]The gates to popular Chinese temples are frequently marked by a similar gate design, except the lower bar is broken in the middle. Another way of putting this would be to say that the Chinese gate consists of two vertical poles, each of which is crossed by one small beam, and the two poles are connected by one long beam over them.

Figure 11.1. Torii and Chinese gate

[9]Harry Thomsen, *The New Religions of Japan* (Rutland, Vt.: Tuttle, 1963), pp. 20-31; Ichiro Hori, *Folk Religion in Japan: Continuity and Change* (Chicago: University of Chicago Press, 1968), pp. 220-27; Clark B. Offner and Henry van Straelen, *Modern Japanese Religions* (Leiden: Brill, 1963).

[10]Thomsen, *New Religions,* p. 17. Thomsen adds: "However, . . . the figures have been reported by the new religions themselves and cannot be heavily relied upon. The only thing that can be said with certainty is that the actual number of believers is not above the figures quoted."

[11]This deity goes by several spellings of her name. Another common spelling is *Kwannon. Canon* is also appropriate. I am using the spelling that is most commonly used in scholarly books at this time.

[12]This phenomenon can be compared to the self-help books and meditational techniques that flourish in the United States from time to time. Who would turn down a chance for lower blood pressure, better finances, promotions and popularity—all without effort—with cosmic bliss thrown in at no extra charge? Even if life is not particularly desperate (though for many people it is), only a fool would turn down such an offer. The only condition is a lack of concern with questions of objective truth.

[13]It might not be too far-fetched here to compare the way midwinter solstice practices and spring fertility practices have remained a part of Christmas and Easter respectively. However, whereas for these superficially Christian holidays the original pagan beliefs behind the practices have disappeared, in Japanese folk religion the beliefs in the spiritual forces that necessitate the practices are also still present.

[14]This analysis stems from Hori, *Folk Religion in Japan,* pp. 149-60.

[15]H. Byron Earhart describes his participation as observer in *Religions of Japan: Many Traditions Within One Sacred Way* (San Francisco: Harper & Row, 1984), pp. 101-14.

[16]Ibid., pp. 92-100.

[17]Though also including examples from many different cultures, the contrast between American culture and Japanese culture is the primary example for Edward C. Stewart and Milton J. Bennett, *American Cultural Patterns* (Yarmouth, Maine: Intercultural, 1991).

[18]Ibid., pp. 36-44.

Index